Alfred Davenport

Camp and Field Life of the Fifth New York Volunteer Infantry

Alfred Davenport

Camp and Field Life of the Fifth New York Volunteer Infantry

ISBN/EAN: 9783337056063

Printed in Europe, USA, Canada, Australia, Japan

Cover: Foto ©ninafisch / pixelio.de

More available books at **www.hansebooks.com**

CAMP AND FIELD LIFE

OF THE

FIFTH NEW YORK

VOLUNTEER INFANTRY.

(DURYEE ZOUAVES.)

BY

ALFRED DAVENPORT.

NEW YORK:
DICK AND FITZGERALD,
18 ANN STREET.
1879.

Copyright, 1879,
BY ALFRED DAVENPORT.

CONTENTS.

LETTERS 9
PREFACE 13

CHAPTER I.
THE DRUM-BEAT.

Fort Sumter—The Attack—The Evacuation—The President's Proclamation—Letter by the Secretary of War—Governor Morgan's Proclamation—Call of the Adjutant-General, State of New York.. 17

CHAPTER II.
FROM NEW YORK TO VIRGINIA.

Organization—Fort Schuyler—First Experiences—Our Quarters—The Men of the Regiment—Sunday at the Fort -The First Gun from Fort Schuyler—A Police Deserter—The Ranks Filled—Taking the Oath—Flag Presentation—Color Sergeant—Striking our Tents—Reception in New York—Moonlight Departure—Arrival at Fortress Monroe—Deserted Village—Our First Bivouac—Hampton Bridge Burned 22

CHAPTER III.
OUR FIRST CAMP IN VIRGINIA.

Kilpatrick's First Raid—An Alarm at Midnight—A Photograph of Camp Life—Battalion Drill—Kilpatrick's First Adventure—Captain Hiram Duryea—Lieutenant Jacob Duryée—Several Expeditions—Sunday Service—Our Chaplain—Lieutenant-Colonel Warren—Adjutant Hamblin—The Location—A Storm—Off Duty—Fox Hill Expedition — Lieutenant-Colonel Warren's Report — Correspondence of the New York *Times* 34

CHAPTER IV.
BIG BETHEL.

Sunday Evening Orders—Our Comrades—A Loyal Negro—Captain Kilpatrick's Advance—A Virginia Prisoner—A Fatal Mistake—

Big Bethel—A Wounded Comrade—A Soldier's Tribute—Death of Lieutenant Greble—Honorable Mention—A Naval Commander —Correspondence of the New York *Tribune*—Flag of Truce 49

CHAPTER V.
LIFE AT CAMP HAMILTON.

Fortress Monroe—Incidents of Camp Life—Drummed Out—Any Port in a Storm—Serious Accident—How to Find a Horse—Contraband Wit—A Graceful Digger—Mrs. Kilpatrick—Notes from the Journal—On Guard by Moonlight—Huts in the Woods—A "Fez" Stolen by Mosquitoes—A Comet—How we Spent Independence Day—Our Postponed Celebration—A Fairy Scene—Donations—Discharges and Recruits—A New Flag—Beautifying the Camp—Losing Blood—A Lost Sentinel—Reports of the Battle of Bull Run—Embarking for Baltimore 74

CHAPTER VI.
LIFE AT BALTIMORE.

Arrival at Baltimore—Camp at Federal Hill—Zouaves at Large— Penalties for Pastimes—Making a Camp—Visitors—A Baltimore Journal Speaks—Running Guard—"Joe" Knott—Changes in the Regiment—A Revolt Subdued—The Guard-house and its Adventures—An Illumination—A Charge—Fort-building—Rebel Recruits Disappointed—Our Bathing Ground—The Battle at the Pump— Camp Ballads of the Fifth—Colonel Duryée Promoted—An Unsuccessful Trip—Changes in the Regiment—Progress of the Fort —How the Days were Spent—Captain Hamblin's Departure— Regimental Dogs—A Loyal Newfoundland—Zouave Song by a Drummer Boy—Maggie Mitchell—Blowing Out the Lights—A Drum Major's Joke—An Expedition—Building the Barracks— Thanksgiving Day—An Elopement............................ 91

CHAPTER VII.
THE EASTERN SHORE—LIFE AT BALTIMORE.

The Eastern Shore—Objects of the Expedition—A Proclamation by General Dix—"Marching Along!"—A Surprised Zouave—Rebel Spirit and Rebel Spirits—A Soldiers' Reunion—Rebel Visitors Singing the Star Spangled Banner—Return of the Expedition— Results—A Sociable Parade—Rebel Flag Reversed—Recruiting— Opening the Barracks—"Fort Federal Hill"—Second Year of the War—Our Surgeon—A Surgical Duelist—Running the Guard— "The Zouave House"—A Musical Masked Battery—Flag Presentation by the Ladies of South Baltimore—Address by John Willis, Esq.—Colonel Warren's Reply—A Grand Ball at Headquarters—Fort Marshall—Washington's Birthday—An Indignant Zouave—Grand City Ball—A Military Execution—Attack Threatened—The Merrimac—Change of Base—Ho for Fortress Monroe!—Farewell to Baltimore—Our Farewell Entertainment—Relieved by the Third New York—Falling into Line—March through Baltimore—Exciting Scenes—Farewell Song...................................... 125

CHAPTER VIII.

THE PENINSULAR CAMPAIGN.

The Trip to Virginia—Scene at Hampton Roads—Changes—Camp Misery—Peep at Big Bethel—Prime Rations for Six—New York *Times* Correspondent—General McClellan's Report—Camp Scott—Corduroy and Ditch—Headquarters—California Jack—The Fourth Michigan—First Death by Sickness—General McClellan's Headquarters—An Officer's Letter—Letter from a Private—Fire and Fun in the Dark—A Strategic Pig—Siege Preparations—Battery No. 1—General Barry's Letter—Camp Warren—After the Battle—Camp Buchanan—A Promise of Battle—March in the Shadows—Magnificent Spectacle—A Night View of the Camp at Pamunkey River—Drooping Skies and a Dripping Army—Review by Hon. Wm. H. Seward—Deserted Territory—Nearing the White House—Stragglers—"Dr." Warren and his "Pills"—The Sick List—The Colonel's Order and a Donkey's Reply...................... 154

CHAPTER IX.

THE PENINSULAR CAMPAIGN—(*Continued*).

Pamunkey Bridge—Crossing the Bridge—Killed at his Birthplace—The Rebels Retire—Rebel Communication Broken—An Astonished Negro—A Descendant of Patrick Henry—Return to Camp—Hanover Court-house—Captain Griffin's Brazen Pet—After the Battle—Burying the Dead—Result—A Raid and a Capture—A Reconnoissance—Back to Old Church—What we Fought for at Hanover—The Chickahominy—New Bridge—A Donation of Flour—A Speculation in Doughnuts—Sal Eratus and what She Did—A Pair of Shoes—Sleeping under Arms—General McClellan's Address to the Army—General Sykes' Speech—Picket at New Bridge—Review by General Prim—Masking a Battery at Night—Stuart's Cavalry on a Raid 180

CHAPTER X.

THE SEVEN DAYS' RETREAT.

Battle of Gaines' Mill—Anniversary of the Battle of Bunker Hill—Then and Now—Freedom against Slavery—Sanitary Condition of the Regiment—Picket Duty—A Sabbath Journal—Death of Sergeant Reynolds—Seven Days' Retreat—Fifth Corps Engaged—Battle of Gaines' Mill—Death of Captain Partridge—Color Sergeant Berrian—A Charge in the Woods—A Rebel Trick—The Field at Night—Losses—Testimony of the Officers—Official Reports—Confederate Reports—Incidents—William McDowell—" Dave " Burns—Walter S. Colby—Francis Spellman—Sad Separations—Colonel Warren's Report—General Sykes' Report................... 198

CHAPTER XI.

MALVERN HILL—HARRISON'S LANDING.

White Oak Swamp—Charles City Cross-roads—General Kearney—Malvern Hill—A Desperate Struggle—Rebel Repulse—Retreat from Malvern Hill—The Rain and the Roads—An Incident—A Life Saved by a Stratagem—Report of Lieutenant-Colonel H. Duryea—Letter from Surgeon Joseph S. Smith—Harrison's Landing—The Camping-Ground—Want of Water—A Review by President Lincoln—Moving our Camp—Reviewed by General McClellan—Resignation of Captain Cambrelling—Changes—Health of the Army—Hospital Grounds—A Death by Poison—Improved Diet—A Rebel Salute—Death in a Tent—Pine Woods Experience—Knapsacks Forwarded—A Night March—Crossing the Chickahominy—Negro Messenger Shot—Soldier Hospitality Refused—Newport News—The March to Manassas Junction—On the Battle-field 240

CHAPTER XII.

SECOND BATTLE OF BULL RUN.

The Field—Distribution of Forces—The Henry House—Position of the Fifth—Generals Jackson and Longstreet—The Fifth Engaged—Fearful Slaughter—Allison, the Color-Bearer, Killed—Annihilation of our Color Company—Bald Ridge—The Texans—" Don't let them take my Flag!"—Overpowering numbers—" Let there be no Faltering in this Line!"—A Zouave Targeted—A Rout—A Terrible Scene—The Remnant of our Regiment—After the Battle—Colonel Warren's Report—General Pope's Report—Personal Sketches and Incidents—Spellman—Chambers—McDowell—Wilson—Hager—Sapher—Humanity—Stonewall Jackson—James

Cathey, a Strange Coincidence—A Rifle Shot—James Patterson—Pollard's Testimony — Bullwinkle—Sturgess—Tyndall—Strachan—Huntsman—A Walk among the Graves—Faulk's Letter—Confederate Testimony—March to Fairfax—McDowell's Brother—General McClellan's Return to the Command—Near Frederick City.. 269

CHAPTER XIII.
BATTLE OF ANTIETAM.

The Confederate Successes—Virginia *versus* The Cotton States—The Battle of Antietam—The Enemy Retires—General McClellan's Report—Crossing the Potomac—Battle of Shepardstown—Tenth New York Regiment Transferred—Scarcity of Supplies—A Mixed Uniform—Penalties of Old Clothes—A Bread Speculation—A Whisky Smuggle—A Drill Challenge Accepted—Crossing at Harper's Ferry—Colonel O'Rourke, of the 140th New York—Snicker's Gap—Warrenton—A Secessionist Town—Farewell Review by General McClellan—General Burnside in Command—The 146th New York—Warrenton Junction—Spotted Tavern—The Henry House—Resignation of Colonel Hiram Duryea—Changes in the Regiment—Before the Battle 310

CHAPTER XIV.
BATTLE OF FREDERICKSBURG.

In Sight of Fredericksburg—The Pontoon—The Burning City—The Position—Across the River—Marye's Hill—A Description by the Philadelphia *Times*—The Attack—The Enemy's Batteries—The Slaughter Path—French's Division—Hooker's Charge—Howard at the Front—Humphreys' Division—Sykes' Division—The Dead and Wounded—Warren's Brigade—The Brigade of Death—The Compte de Paris—The Fifth in a Garden—Our Regulars Severely Placed—The Gloom Pall—Forlorn Hope—Strategy—Intrenchments at Night—Covering the Retreat—The Last Man Crossed—The Pontoon Lifted—Incidents—Henry House—General Sykes' Order 338

CHAPTER XV.
BATTLE OF CHANCELLORSVILLE—OUR LAST STRUGGLE.

The New Year—The Situation—Death of Captain Cartwright—Mortality—Desertions—The Disloyal Press of the North—The Soldiers' Sentiment—An Army of Water-Carriers—The Mud March—Resignation of General Burnside—General Hooker in Command—Picketed in Ice—A Death in Hospital—A Suicide—General Warren Promoted—A Deserted Mansion—Provost Guard—Death of Nicholas Hoyt—Better Supplies—A Square Meal—Cavalry Skirmish—St. Patrick's Day in the Ninth Massachusetts—Cavalry Fight—A Spy—A Smoky Chimney—A Crippled Shoemaker on "Jeff" Davis—Annihilating the Men of the South—A Review—Hybernating under Ground—Easter—Review by President Lincoln—The Two Years' Men—Growling—Review by Generals Togliardi and Meade—An Exploded Shell—The Time Fixed—Kelly's Ford—Ely's Ford—Approaching Fredericksburg—Battle of Chancellorsville—Eighth Pennsylvania Cavalry—The Enemy Repulsed—Jackson's Attack on Howard—Sickles—Slocum—French—Chancellor House Burnt—Woods on Fire—The Two Years' Men Relieved—Parting with Old Comrades—Aquia Creek—Hospitality of the 21st New York—Washington—Baltimore—Philadelphia—Jersey City—New York—Our Reception—New York *Times*—The Fourth Regiment—Mustered Out—In the Battle of Life 361

APPENDIX.

Casualties 399
Statistics 418
Biographies of Officers 423
Names of Officers 475
Colonel Robert C. Buchanan, U. S. A. 485
Lieutenant-Colonel William Chapman, U. S. A. 485

LETTERS.

ORANGE, *Dec.* 5, 1877.

ALFRED DAVENPORT, ESQ., NEW YORK:

MY DEAR SIR:—Yours of the 4th is received. I am very glad to learn that you are engaged upon the history of the 5th New York. The gallant services of that admirable regiment on so many fields certainly merit being handed down, and form no unimportant portion of the history of the war. The pride and interest I have always felt in the regiment, since it first came under my command, will make your work dearly gratifying to me.

In haste, very truly yours,

GEO. B. MCCLELLAN.

NEW YORK, *January* 26, 1878.

ALFRED DAVENPORT, ESQ.:

DEAR SIR:—I have received your note of the 14th inst. informing me that you have undertaken the work of preserving the record of the 5th New York Infantry, and am greatly pleased to learn of your undertaking. Though my connection with the regiment was brief, extending only from April to July, 1861, I have always preserved the kindest memories of my friends and comrades of the Fifth, and felt pride in knowing that I had been a member of so gallant and distinguished an organization.

I know of no regiment that had a better record for courage, gallantry, discipline, and faithful service throughout the war, and the men and officers well deserve to have a complete and correct record of their deeds preserved to their country.

I shall await the publication of the work with great interest, and will much enjoy its perusal.

Remain, etc.,

H. E. DAVIES, JR.,
Late Maj.-Gen. U. S. Vols.

FORT BROWN, TEXAS, *April* 15, 1878.

MR. A. DAVENPORT, NEW YORK:

DEAR SIR:—An absence of more than two months from this Post must be my excuse for not having sooner answered your letter. I am very sorry that I can not send you the "order" you wish. It should be among the records of the 2d Division, 5th Army Corps, but they, as you are aware, did not go with me when I succeeded General Meade in command of the corps. It is barely possible that General Warren, U. S. Engineer, now at Newport, Rhode Island, might furnish you with it.

My opinion of the 5th New York Volunteers never changed. I doubt whether it had an equal, certainly no superior among all the regiments of the Army of the Potomac. Its death-roll and list of casualties will tell how and where it stood better than any words of its commanders. *I have always maintained it to be the best volunteer organization I ever knew.*

Yours very respectfully,

GEORGE SYKES.

In reply to a letter from the author to General Hooker, he speaks as follows:

GARDEN CITY, L. I., N. Y., *June* 2, 1878.

MR. A. DAVENPORT:

. . . . May each and all long live to enjoy the fruit of their noble works. You tell me that General Sykes once had your regiment in his command, and that you have the testimony of that gifted soldier as to your discipline and conduct. This is proof, of the most satisfactory character, of the high claims of your regiment to its soldiership and noble bearing. You could furnish me with no higher authority in our army, and this opinion is cherished, of that officer, by all his associates in arms, not only in our last war, but also that of the war in Mexico.

Let me say, then, through you, to your regiment, that it is almost their duty to themselves and to their old commander to cherish and preserve every syllable he ever uttered in their commendation.

General Sykes never was much of a *blower* for himself, but whenever heavy work had to be done he was a perfect *wheel-horse* in battle or out of it.

Sincerely yours,

J. HOOKER, *Maj.-Gen.*

The following communication, by George L. Catlin, Esq., United States Consul, La Rochelle, France, was addressed to the COMPTE DE PARIS:

CONSULAT GÉNÉRAL DES ETATS UNIS
D'AMERIQUE, 3 RUE SCRIBE, PARIS,
le 30 *Mai*, 1878

MONSEIGNEUR LE COMPTE DE PARIS:

I have the honor to address you in compliance with the request of Mr. Davenport, of New York, who is engaged in the preparation of a history of the volunteer regiment from that city, known as the 5th New York Volunteers (Duryée Zouaves). Both he and I served in that command, which, you may remember, was brigaded with the regular troops under General Sykes; and Mr. Davenport writes me that he is desirous of incorporating in his work a complimentary mention of that regiment which he understands you have been somewhere kind enough to make in your written reminiscences of the Peninsular Campaign in Virginia. In case you recall any such mention, I shall esteem it a great favor if you will direct me to where a copy of it can be found.

Should you, on the other hand, not recall it, I am requested by Mr. Davenport, the author, to say that a brief note from yourself, expressive of your favorable recollection of the 5th New York Zouaves would be received and published as a valuable addition to the interest of his book.

Feeling in common with every Union soldier a gratitude for the service so honorably rendered us by your sympathy and your sword during the trying days of the Rebellion,

I am, sir, with great respect, very truly yours,

GEORGE L. CATLIN.

The Compte de Paris replied to the above note as follows:

CHATEAU D'EU, SEINE INFÉRIEURE,
June 13, 1878.

SIR :—I do not think that I mentioned in any special manner the 5th New York Zouaves in my History of the Civil War in America ; but this is only because, having so many events to recount, I had not space enough to mention singly any organization under that of the brigade. I remember very well the 5th New York in the Peninsula just after the battle of Williamsburg, and the soldier-like appearance of this fine body of men. This appearance struck the best judges, for else the Zouaves would not have been brigaded under General Sykes with the regulars, who were justly considered as a model for the other troops.

This favorable opinion was fully justified when the regiment had to go through the ordeal of the battles on the Chickahominy, and I well remember, on the evening of the bloody day of Gaines' Mill, how few, but how proud, were the remnant of the 5th New York after holding so long their ground, on our right, against Jackson's attacks.

Believe me, sir, yours truly,

L. P. D'ORLEANS,
Compte de Paris.

TO GEO. L. CATLIN, ESQ., *Paris.*

PREFACE.

THE period of American History commencing with the choice of electors for President and Vice-President of the United States, on the first Tuesday of November, 1860, and the immediate adoption by the South Carolina Convention of a resolution repealing the act of admission to the American Union, and ending with the assassination of ABRAHAM LINCOLN, President of the United States, must ever possess a remarkable interest to the student of history; and as the events of that period must necessarily leave influences and conditions, political and social, of an extraordinary character, they must have a greater or less interest to every citizen. The sword is sheathed, and the dilapidated fortresses and crumbling earthworks are deserted and losing their outlines, and peace has for many years blessed the nation that was rocked to its foundations by the upheaval of a civil war unparalleled in history. It may be expedient to "let the dead past bury its dead." But the past is *not* dead; it lives in the hearts, the thoughts, the affections, the hopes, the jealousies, the taxations, and the sufferings of millions. It lives in the memory of the bereaved at the hearthstones of the people—it lives in the remembrance of the active men of the time who still animate, influence, or lead public policy—and it lives in the purposes of whole communities who, moreover, are resolved that the past shall *not* die. To the loyal heart which throbbed with devotion to the country in its peril—to the memories of the men who laid down their lives in its defense—to the survivors of the heroic dead—to the young men of the present, the voices of freedom and humanity utter the injunction, LET THE PAST LIVE IN THE LOYAL HEART FOREVER!

This is the argument of the present volume. The Fifth New York Infantry, known as the Duryée Zouaves, heard the drum-beat, they responded to the appeal to arms, and in a few days were assigned to their post at the front, and held it for two years, during the whole time for which its members were enlisted. It has been deemed only an act of justice to place its record at the side of other similar contributions to the history of the war, and the effort has been made by the author to embody the events in which it took a part, in so complete a form that nothing material to its chronicles should be omitted. Many of the lesser incidents of camp and field life are incorporated, as a faithful picturing of the varied phases of a soldier's life during the war.

It was hoped by the author, as well as by others, that the work would be undertaken by some one or more of the able officers of the regiment, but the active duties of civil life have prevented them from making even the attempt to collect the materials. Under these circumstances the author, albeit with great distrust of his ability to execute the work in a manner worthy of his subject, felt constrained to let no further time be lost in its preparation. He has availed himself of all the aids he could command, but is aware that many interesting incidents and facts are in the possession of officers and members of the regiment whom he has not been able to consult. The record, however, is so full as it is now presented, that no essential link in the narrative has been omitted.

It is proper to make acknowledgments to Lieutenants Samuel Tiebout, R. M. Gedney, and William H. Uckele; Captains William H. Chambers, James McConnell, and Thomas R. Martin; Adjutant A. S. Marvin, Jr.; Sergeants C. V. G.

Forbes, Robert Strachan, E. M. Law, and George A. Mitchell; Corporals James H. Franklin, James R. Murray, and Miron Winslow; Benjamin F. Finley, Joseph Stilwell, Daniel J. Meagher, James W. Webb, Mrs. H. C. Vail and family, Mrs. James H. Lounsberry, Alonzo Ameli; and especially to Hons. S. S. Cox, Fernando Wood, and Lucius N. Robinson, Mrs. Gordon Winslow, and others, for interesting information.

In the preparation of the work the writer has consulted and is indebted to L. P. D'Orleans, *Compte de Paris*, "History of the Civil War in America," "Swinton's Army of the Potomac," A. H. Guernsey, LL.D., "Lossing's History," Rev. J. S. C. Abbott, "Pollard's Southern History of the War," Prince de Joinville, Hon. John T. Headley, Colonel B. Estvan (Confederate Army), "General McClellan's Reports and Campaigns," "Pope's Reports," "The Rebellion Record," "Reports of the Committee on the Conduct of the War," "General W. F. Barry's Report," "Joel Cook's Siege of Richmond," the files of the *Soldier's Friend*, conducted by William Oland Bourne, and the War Correspondence of the various journals of the time.

The work is committed to the press in the somewhat confident hope that whatever may be its imperfections, the officers and members of the regiment, as well as the public who may be interested in its narrative, will accept it with the indulgence which they may kindly accord to the tribute offered by an ex-private to the honor of the regiment in which he served. A. D.

CHAPTER I.

THE DRUM-BEAT.

FORT SUMTER—THE ATTACK—THE EVACUATION—THE PRESIDENT'S PROCLAMATION—LETTER BY THE SECRETARY OF WAR—GOV. MORGAN'S PROCLAMATION—CALL OF THE ADJUTANT-GENERAL, STATE OF NEW YORK.

FRIDAY, the twelfth day of April, 1861, must forever remain memorable in the history of the American Union. On that day a force of ten thousand men, after long preparation, and with well-built and well-appointed batteries, under the command of Gen. Beauregard, opened their fire upon Fort Sumter, in the harbor of Charleston, and continued the bombardment of that fort, defended by a heroic band of seventy men under Major Robert Anderson, until, after thirty-six hours of almost uninterrupted attack, the commander deemed it no longer prudent to maintain the unequal contest, and was permitted to retire his force without the loss of a single man, and bearing with him the flag of honor and renown.

The event had been for some time expected, and the delay of the Government at Washington to take the initiative in offensive measures was regarded by many as evidence of a hesitating and vacillating policy. But the result proved the contrary. The responsibility of a deliberate, long-meditated, and treasonable attack upon the property, the peace, and the existence of the Republic, by the act of the twelfth of April, fell, in all the weight of its momentous consequences, upon those who assumed it. The eyes of the whole nation were turned to this point.

Before the people of the Union there stood a boasting and excited army, exasperated at the cool and defiant heroism of the little band of loyal men who refused to lower their flag or shrink from their post of duty, ambitious of the distinction so long coveted of destroying the Union. Only a few events in the military history of the world present such a contrast. Every hour the interest of the nation was intensified.

The suspense as to the decision of Major Anderson became painfully deep as the hours flew by, and when at last the enemy became convinced that they had no other alternative, the hand of EDMUND RUFFIN, of Virginia, who begged the privilege and the honor, fired the first gun in the actual inauguration of a bloody war. That gun boomed with accumulating thunder over the nation. The flash of its fire blazed through the electric wires, and the hearts of millions bounded with an awakened spirit of loyalty as each successive bomb and shell beat against the slowly crumbling walls of Sumter. The die was cast. The deep, devoted loyalty of the people was with the Government and the flag, and when on the second day the heroic band left the shattered ruin, it was only as the advance guard of the millions who rallied to the honor and the glory of the Republic.

Two days afterward the President of the United States issued the following proclamation:

BY THE PRESIDENT OF THE UNITED STATES OF AMERICA.

A PROCLAMATION.

Whereas, the laws of the United States have been for some time past, and now are, opposed, and the execution thereof obstructed, in the States of South Carolina, Georgia, Alabama, Florida, Mississippi, Louisiana, and Texas, by combinations too powerful to be suppressed by the ordinary course of judicial proceeding, or by the powers vested in the marshals by law;

Now, therefore, I, Abraham Lincoln, President of the United States, in virtue of the power in me vested by the Constitution and the Laws, have thought fit to call forth, and hereby do call forth, the militia of the several States of the Union, to the aggregate number of seventy-five thousand, in order to suppress said combinations, and to cause the Laws to be duly executed.

The details for this object will be immediately communicated to the State authorities through the War Department.

I appeal to all loyal citizens to favor, facilitate, and aid this effort to maintain the honor, the integrity, and the existence of our National Union, and the perpetuity of popular government, and to redress wrongs already long enough endured.

I deem it proper to say that the first service assigned to the forces hereby called forth will probably be to repossess the forts, places, and property which have been seized from the Union; and in every event the utmost care will be observed consistently with the objects aforesaid, to avoid any devastation, any destruction of or interference with property, or any disturbance of peaceful citizens in any part of the country.

And I hereby command the persons composing the combinations aforesaid to disperse, and retire peaceably to their respective abodes, within twenty days from this date.

Deeming that the present condition of public affairs presents an extraordinary occasion, I do hereby, in virtue of the power in me vested by the Constitution, convene both Houses of Congress. Senators and Representatives are, therefore, summoned to assemble at their respective chambers, at twelve o'clock, noon, on Thursday, the fourth day of July next, then and there to consider and determine such measures as, in their wisdom, the public safety and interest may seem to demand.

In witness whereof, I have hereunto set my hand, and caused the seal of the United States to be affixed.

Done at the city of Washington, this fifteenth day of April, in the year of our Lord one thousand eight hundred and sixty-one, and the Independence of the United States the eighty-fifth.

ABRAHAM LINCOLN.

By the President:

WILLIAM H. SEWARD, *Secretary of State.*

At the same time the calls were made upon the several States, and the Governor of New York, Hon. EDWIN D. MORGAN, received the following communication from the War Department:

WAR DEPARTMENT, WASHINGTON,
April 15, 1861.

SIR:—Under the Act of Congress "for calling forth the militia to execute the laws of the Union, suppress insurrections, repel invasions," etc., approved February 28, 1795, I have the honor to request your Excellency to cause to be immediately detached from the militia of your State the quota designated in the table below, to serve as infantry or riflemen for the period of three months, unless sooner discharged.

Your Excellency will please communicate to me the time at or about which your quota will be expected at its rendezvous, as it will be met as soon as practicable by an officer or officers to muster it into the service and pay of the United States. At the same time the oath of fidelity to the United States will be administered to every officer and man.

The mustering officer will be instructed to receive no man under the rank of commissioned officer who is in years apparently over forty-five or under eighteen, or who is not in physical strength and vigor.

The rendezvous for your State will be at New York, Albany, and Elmira.

I have the honor to be, very respectfully,
Your obedient servant,

SIMON CAMERON, *Secretary of War.*

To his Excellency, EDWIN D. MORGAN,
Governor of New York.

The quota for New York State was seventeen regiments, with an aggregate total of, officers and men, 13,280.

April 16, 1861, the Senate and Assembly of the State being then in session passed an Act, "To authorize the embodying and equipment of a volunteer militia, and to provide for the public defense," and the following proclamation, by Governor Morgan, was issued:

PROCLAMATION BY EDWIN D. MORGAN,
Governor of the State of New York.

The President of the United States, by proclamation, and through the Secretary of War, by formal requisition, has called upon this State for a quota of seventeen regiments of seven hundred and eighty men each, to be immediately detached from the militia of this State, to serve as infantry or riflemen, for a period of three months, unless sooner discharged. Now, in conformity with the aforesaid demand, and by virtue of the Act of the Legislature of this State, passed on the 16th day of April, instant, entitled "An Act to authorize the embodying and equipment of a volunteer militia, and to provide for the public defense," and the power vested in me by the Constitution and Laws, I do call for the aforesaid quota, consisting of six hundred and forty-nine officers and twelve thousand six hundred and thirty-one men, forming an aggregate of thirteen thousand two hundred and eighty.

The organization of this force to be in conformity with article eleven, section two, of the Constitution of this State, and with the rules and regulations embraced in general orders, number thirteen, promulgated this day. The rendezvous for this State will be at New York, Albany, and Elmira, headquarters at Albany.

In witness whereof, I have hereunto set my hand and affixed the privy seal of the State, at the city of Albany, this [L.S.] eighteenth day of April, in the year of our Lord one thousand eight hundred and sixty-one.

EDWIN D. MORGAN.

By the Governor:
LOCKWOOD L. DOTY, *Private Secretary.*

The Adjutant-General of the State, J. MEREDITH READ, Jr., issued a General Order, No. 13, under date of the 18th day of April, specifying the number of regiments to be raised, directions for the election of officers, etc., and declaring that the force volunteering under the provisions of the Act, would be enrolled *for the term of two years*, unless sooner discharged.

CHAPTER II.

FROM NEW YORK TO VIRGINIA.

ORGANIZATION — FORT SCHUYLER — FIRST EXPERIENCES — OUR QUARTERS — THE MEN OF THE REGIMENT—SUNDAY AT THE FORT—THE FIRST GUN FROM FORT SCHUYLER—A POLICE DESERTER—THE RANKS FILLED—TAKING THE OATH— FLAG PRESENTATION—COLOR SERGEANT—STRIKING OUR TENTS—RECEPTION IN NEW YORK—MOONLIGHT DEPARTURE—ARRIVAL AT FORTRESS MONROE— DESERTED VILLAGE—OUR FIRST BIVOUAC—HAMPTON BRIDGE BURNED.

THIS regiment was organized under the Proclamation of the President of the United States, issued April 15, 1861, calling upon the several Governors of the loyal States for seventy-five thousand men.

On Thursday, the 18th day of April, 1861, J. M. Read, Jr., Adjutant-General of the State of New York, issued a general order for the organization of seventeen regiments of volunteers, the quota called for from this State; and on the following day, the 19th, some of the best material in the city and its suburbs began to enlist under the banner of Colonel ABRAM DURYÉE. This officer was well known to the citizens of New York, and had a wide reputation beyond its limits, having been in command of the Seventh Regiment, N. G. S. N. Y., with which he had been connected for a period of twenty-one years, and which was universally acknowledged to be the best drilled and most efficient militia organization in the United States. "The Seventh Regiment is to the National Guard what West Point is to the Regular Army." On Tuesday, the 23d, four days after the recruiting commenced, so great was the zeal and ambition to serve under this popular leader, that enough picked men were enrolled to make up eight companies of about fifty men each; and accordingly, on the evening of this day,

A, B, C, D, E, F, G, and K, were inspected and mustered into the State service, at their rooms in Canal Street, a little east of Broadway. Companies I and H subsequently joined at Fort Schuyler. A guard was stationed at the doors to prevent the men from leaving at night, notwithstanding which many of them found opportunity to make their parting visits to the city, from which they were so soon to be exiled. The organization was called, at this time, "The First Regiment, Advance Guard."

The next day each man was given a blanket, and marched by fours front, down to the foot of Canal Street, North River; embarked on a steam-tug, and after a pleasant sail around the Battery and up the East River, arrived at Fort Schuyler about 6 P.M., nothing of importance having occurred on the trip. Immediately on arriving, they commenced their active duties by carrying lumber, barrels of provisions, etc., to their respective places of storage at the fort. At about 10 P.M. supper was served, and the regiment made their first acquaintance with the biscuit which afterward became so proverbially known as "hard-tack."

Thursday, April 25.—The men, in good spirits and humor, were turned out at 5 A.M. A wash at the pump was the first preparation for a drill, which lasted until breakfast, at 7.30. We were then at liberty until 10.30 A.M., when we were again assembled for drill, which lasted until noon. Dinner was served at 1 P.M., after which we were off duty until 4.30, when we were again drilled until 6 P.M., the hour for supper, after which we were again at liberty. At 10 P.M. all lights were extinguished, and silence deep and profound fell upon us, until roused by the reveille.

Friday, April 26.—Colonel Duryée, in full dress, inspected the regiment in the evening, and their movements pleased him so highly that he complimented them on their rapid progress, and, accompanied by ladies, inspected the quarters.

The barracks were very comfortable, about forty-five men

being assigned to each of the compartments, which are a part of the fort. The structure is of stone, with large, roomy fire-places, in which bright wood-fires were kept burning at night. Around these fires the men congregated to smoke their pipes and hold their councils. Outside of the fort were tents, which were a part of those used by the French army in the Crimea. The cook of General Canrobert, the French General, was catering for the regiment. The men quartered in these tents christened them by such names as the "Bower of Beauty," "Schuyler Cottage," and others equally suggestive of sentiment or war, as their fancy dictated. There was one mess at least who lived on the fat of the land and water. They had built a small brick furnace, but where they obtained the material was a mystery. They always had something extra, fried clams, fish, beefsteak, etc., which was equally a mystery. There was evidently a latent talent for foraging, which became subsequently more generally developed under very different circumstances.

The location of the fort is a very healthy one. The constant breeze from the Sound gave to its inmates a supply of fresh air, and there was no impediment to the use of the salt water in which to bathe. The surgeons had nothing to do except in the case of one of the men who had broken an ankle wrestling with a comrade. The steamboat from the city touched every afternoon at the Government wharf and unloaded the stores, which were carried up to the fort by details of men from the different companies. In the afternoon the men mounted the ramparts and saluted the Sound steamers, and were saluted in turn by them. A short time after the regiment arrived at the fort a large flag-staff was erected above the ramparts, which was climbed by one of the men for the purpose of adjusting the halyards. The "Star Spangled Banner" was hoisted for the first time, and there being no ordnance to salute the colors, three hearty cheers were given from several hundred patriotic throats.

There were men among us who could respond to any duty—representatives from all the trades, with a sprinkling of lawyers, book-keepers, sailors, and members of the Volunteer Fire Department, many of the latter belonging to Company G. There were also veteran soldiers who had served in the British army of the Crimea, and elsewhere; Italians who had fought under Garibaldi; Frenchmen who had served in the armies of *la belle France;* Teutons from the Prussian army; and some of the fighting sons of Ireland, ever ready for the fray; others who had fought in the Mexican war, and ex-regulars of the United States. Notwithstanding which, about eighty per cent. of the regiment were natives of the soil, among whom was Havens, a nephew of " Benny Havens, oh !" of West Point memory; the Van Warts from Tarrytown, descendants of " the Van Wart " of Revolutionary memory, and many others of grand old lineage. Although this was a volunteer citizen regiment, there were many veteran warriors who composed, with the educated officers, accomplished in military affairs, a nucleus around which to form one of the best disciplined and most reliable bodies of men that ever left the city of New York, or rallied under any other name, for the seat of war.

On Sunday a service was regularly held in the forenoon, to which all were invited, but the attendance was not compulsory. In addition to the service the " Articles of War " were read. It was the great day for visitors from the city, who came by boat and private conveyance, bringing the newspapers to their friends, and sometimes the remembrances from home which are not found in a soldier's bill of fare. A party made a visit to the fort from a private yacht, one of their friends being enlisted in the regiment. They desired permission from the Colonel to give their friend a sail, but the indulgence was not to be thought of. They were so wroth at the refusal, that upon setting sail for their departure, they showed their defiance by bombarding the fort with a revolver.

On Tuesday, April 30th, our first gun was fired, and it was also the first gun that ever had sent its thunders over the waters from the ramparts of Fort Schuyler. It was a brass piece hoisted into its place by the men.

On the following day, May 1st, we had a different entertainment. Two men, one of them a Metropolitan Police officer, who had come up and enlisted in his uniform, ran the guard. They were overtaken by Capt. Dumont, and put under arrest in the guard-house, and at evening parade were drummed out. Tuesday, May 7th, the men being nearly all supplied with their uniforms, made a fine appearance on drill or dress parade, especially as they were becoming very proficient. They had been kept hard at work drilling by companies, and exercising in the simple battalion movements on the glacis outside the fort. The rapid increase in our numbers made strict government imperative, and the discipline was more severe and exacting after Lieut.-Col. Warren entered upon his duties.

There had been some severe storms of wind and rain, which those on guard were obliged to endure, besides some work with the spade draining the parade-ground under the direction of the Lieut.-Colonel, which began to impress upon the minds of the thoughtless that the life of a soldier was not that of a sinecurist. In addition to this there was some grumbling because rifles were not substituted for Springfield muskets, as was promised on enlisting.

On Thursday, the 9th of May, the men were examined by Dr. ALEXANDER B. MOTT, and a few were rejected; the ranks were full, and he said that a finer body of men could not be found in Christendom.

We were sworn into the United States service by Capt. T. Seymour, 1st U. S. Artillery, who was in Fort Sumter at the time of the bombardment by the rebels. We took the oath to serve for two years, unless sooner discharged, and the men now realized that they were in fact soldiers of the United States.

At evening parade, on Saturday, May 11th, a handsome stand of colors were presented to the regiment, the gift of GEORGE KEMP, Esq., of the firm of Lanman & Kemp. Adjutant Hamblin read the following letter of presentation:

EVERETT HOUSE, *May 7*, 1861.
COLONEL A. DURYÉE,
 Advance Guard, N. Y. Vols., Ft. Schuyler:

SIR :—Having been a member of the 7th M. for many years, during the greater part of which time the corps was under your command, I have noticed with the utmost interest your gallant and successful efforts to raise a regiment of volunteers in aid of our beloved country in her present unhappy difficulties. No one who is acquainted with your patriotism can be surprised at this manifestation of your active and most honorable zeal.

ALL who know your military ability must rejoice that you are in the field in defense of the National Banner. It is, indeed, a consolation, at this period of trouble, to feel that if the noble heritage, bequeathed to us by our fathers, is menaced by treachery and rebellion, Providence has blessed the land with true hearts and strong arms ready for the emergency, and has caused to rise up among us noble and worthy leaders, among whom few are to be named before our old commander of the National Guard, Colonel Duryée.

I now take leave, sir, to present to you, for the Advance Guard of New York Volunteers, a flag of the United States, emblem of our dear country's prosperity, might, and happiness—not less, I sincerely believe, in the future than in the past. This color will be presented to you, on my behalf, by Mr. Thomas W. Cartwright, Jr., and Mr. John Gillen, both young men of irreproachable character and steady habits, who, for the purpose of enlisting in your regiment, have just suspended their labor of several years in my employment—to return to it (I trust with honor and in health) after the triumph of law, order, public faith, and of the Constitutional Government of our country shall have enabled you to release them from the service which they are now entering with the most unbounded confidence in their gallant leader.

May God preserve you, sir, and be favorable to the righteous cause to which, like a true soldier, you have devoted yourself.

Pray accept this flag which I now offer. I know you too well to doubt that the men who are so fortunate as to serve under you will bring it back again to this city with honor and in glory.

> I have the honor to be, sir,
> Very respectfully,
> Your obedient servant,
>
> GEORGE KEMP.

The colors were handed to Color-Sergeant Charles E. Mather, of the Broadway Squad of Police. He was one of the tallest men in the regiment, being 6 feet 4 inches, and handsomely proportioned.

The routine of our camp was enlivened a few days afterward by the arrival of our band of musicians, which added a new interest to our dress parades. A Maine regiment, brought by a steamer, disembarked on Willett's Point, opposite Fort Schuyler, where they went into camp. Some of the men paid the Fifth a visit.

Rumors were current in regard to an early departure of the regiment, and the men were anxious to get into active service. Every day added to their impatience, as they were willing to go anywhere to meet the enemy.

On the morning of Wednesday, the 22d, the regiment was fully armed and equipped, the tents had been struck, and we were under marching orders. Knapsacks were packed, and officers and men ready to move when called.

One of the daily journals of New York gave the following narrative of our movements to its readers :

"The orders to leave the fort reached the regiment on Wednesday last, and the prospect of active employment being so near at hand, delighted the men greatly.

"The greatest activity at once became visible throughout the entire encampment, the tents were struck and everything put in order for immediate evacuation, when, to the chagrin and disappointment of all hands, orders arrived countermanding those previously given, and the regiment was doomed to a new and, what at first appeared, a more acute disappointment. Fortunately the obstacle (whatever it might have been) to their immediate movement was of but brief duration, as the orders postponed their march for only one day. Short as it was, however, there was no disguising the fact that both officers and men were considerably put out of temper by what seemed to be a most extraordinary course of proceeding. The tents having been struck, and the regiment placed in readiness to march, all the materials of comfort and convenience were out of immediate reach, so that when sleeping-time came on Wednesday evening the men were left to select the softest grass on which to make their beds. Still there was no complaint of any kind; everything was taken as it turned up, and both officers and men endeavored to accommodate themselves to circumstances with the best grace. In this they altogether succeeded.

"The bivouac of Wednesday night was one of the most picturesque and delightful that can possibly be imagined. Out in that lone fort, on the soft, green sward, over eight hundred men lay down to repose. There was no covering at all above them save the cerulean sky, but there, wrapped in their blankets, they all lay down, and perhaps slept sweeter and sounder for their devotion to their country and to their duty, than many who are enabled to stretch themselves on beds of down. Some of the officers' tents had not yet been struck, and these were certainly centers of attraction during the night. Camp fires were lighted at short distances from each other all along the encampment, and the watchful sentinel having been placed on his nightly guard, the whole garrison went safely and quietly to rest. The scene at the midnight hour, when so many stalwart men were sleeping as calmly as children, was far different from that of the same afternoon when the roll was called for the last drill within the fortification prior to the departure of the regiment. Over a thousand citizens from New York, Brooklyn, and adjacent places were present to witness what was really a sight worth seeing. The whole regiment was uniformed in the full Zouave costume, and armed and accoutred in splendid style, they presented a gallant and unbroken front. The drill of the past month was certainly not lost upon the men, for their evolutions were as regular and as perfect as if they had always made the science of arms their profession. The spectators were delighted with them, and expressed their pleasure by frequently applauding.

"The final preparations for departure were made early in the morning. The few tents which had remained standing were struck, and the baggage of the regiment packed for transmission to the city. The steamboats chartered to remove the troops were at the dock at an early hour of the morning, and everybody was prepared to start."

Thursday, May 23.—We left Fort Schuyler at one o'clock in the afternoon, and embarked on three tugs—the *Satellite, Only Son,* and *C. P. Smith*—the baggage and tents occupying a fourth.

We were indeed on our way at last. It was an exciting and exhilarating scene. As the tugs moved off, the fort saluted each respectively with one gun, and the men on board gave three hearty cheers for Fort Schuyler, in response to the salute. The officers and men were all in the highest spirits, and as we passed the revenue cutter *Vixen,* near Throg's Neck, each of the steamers were again saluted.

At Riker's Island, where the Hawkins Zouaves were encamped, as the steamboats approached, the men were drawn up in line on the brow of a hill overlooking the river, in honor of the Zouaves. Three guns were then fired from the fort, and the men gave three cheers for Hawkins' Zouaves. The enthusiasm was very great, and cheer after cheer rent the air.

Along the piers as we approached the city, there were crowds of people who saluted us with cheers and waving of handkerchiefs.

The boats landed at the foot of East Fifteenth Street about four P.M., and upon disembarking, the regiment proceeded to Fourteenth Street, and after forming in order, marched through that street to Broadway. The sidewalks and windows of the houses were thronged with people, and from every building floated the national flag.

It was a splendid sight, and one that will not soon be forgotten by those who witnessed it. The regiment, eight hundred and forty-eight strong, fully drilled and disciplined, marched with their long, steady stride in solid ranks, and eyes to the front, amid the cheers and plaudits of thousands of spectators.

It was a proud day for the Fifth. Their faces were bronzed by exposure, and every man of them felt and looked like a soldier; but on the other hand, how many a silent tear was dropped, or a murmured prayer offered by a mother, sister, or wife for the safe return of the well-beloved one who was so proudly marching to do battle to preserve a nation, and die, if need be, under the flag that was waving above him with its stars and stripes, the emblem of the States, one and inseparable. The regiment marched to City Hall Park, which it reached about half-past five o'clock, where they were reviewed by Mayor Wood, Judge Edmonds, Judge Davies, Aldermen Brady and Henry, and others of the Common Council. Superintendent Kennedy and Inspector Carpenter, with a squad of twenty-six of the Eleventh Precinct Police, were in attendance. A large number of ladies and gentlemen occupied the balcony of the Hall, among whom were General Nye, Dr. A. B. Mott, Controller Haws, and a number of the officers of Colonel Blenker's regiment. After going through a parade drill, the Zouaves marched up Broadway through White and North Moore Streets to the pier, receiving an ovation at every step. Finally, a little before sundown, they were all embarked on the good steamship *Alabama*, Captain Schenck, and bound for Fortress Monroe. Kind friends and well-wishers had not forsaken them yet, and as long as the steamer could be reached, they were showered with fruits. In the meantime the rigging and sides of the vessel were swarming with Zouaves, some of them climbing even to the trucks, and waving their fez caps in the air. As the steamer drew off into the stream, the air was rent with cheers.

The vessel made a short stop in the bay, and then departed on her seaward path. It was a beautiful moonlight night, the reflection of the moon's rays on the water making it look like molten silver. The ship was too much crowded for comfort, but as it was not a pleasure excursion, the men did not murmur, but made themselves as comfortable as their new circumstances would permit. Some, unused to the sea, soon became unpleasantly conscious of the change; the ship rolled when it reached the swell of the Atlantic; but the majority of the men enjoyed the novelty of the situation. About seventy-five miles out, the steamer was saluted with a prize in tow, which was shortly afterward followed by another. On Friday, the 24th, as we were steaming along, the cry suddenly resounded through the ship, "Man overboard!" The ship was quickly hove to, and the officers and guard kept the men in their places. In a few moments some of the sailors were seen carrying one of their shipmates below, wet and dripping. The result showed that he was severely injured.

On Saturday, the 25th, we were in sight of Fortress Monroe and the men-of-war in the offing, the crews of which manned the rigging, and loudly cheered us—a compliment which we returned with loyal vigor. We were landed at the Government wharf by the steam-tug *Yankee*, near the Hygeia Hotel, and were surrounded by swarms of soldiers, who asked all manner of questions, and said that they had but just cleared out the little village, the Newport of Virginia.

It was not many minutes before every cottage was looked through, and all sorts of odd traps were found, but of little value. One of the boys appeared dressed in a complete militia uniform of the ancient style. This amusement did not last long, a vigilant guard under orders having brought the men to a halt. It was saddening to see a deserted village; one old negro and a few stray dogs and cats were its only remaining inhabitants.

The regiment was soon formed and marched about two miles, and encamped, or rather bivouacked, the main body being located in a wheat-field, the outward post.

The Colonel took possession of the Segar mansion, which was delightfully situated near the waters of the bay, and Company G, Captain Denike, was encamped in a beautiful orchard near by, as his guard of honor.

This was a splendid location for a camp, with good water and plenty of oysters, fish, etc., close at hand. A short distance from this place the largest female seminary in Virginia was located, but now, of course, deserted, except by the family in charge, with a few slaves. The town of Hampton is about one and a half miles distant, on the other side of Hampton Creek. The bridge connecting with the town was burned the day of the landing of the Zouaves, by the Confederate, Major Carey, and some of our men, skirmishing on their own account, crept near enough to see the rebels in the act. The Zouaves were complimented by the Confederates, at this time, with the name of "Red Devils," which they retained during the war.

2*

CHAPTER III.

OUR FIRST CAMP IN VIRGINIA.

Kilpatrick's First Raid—An Alarm at Midnight—A Photograph of Camp Life—Battalion Drill—Kilpatrick's First Adventure—Captain Hiram Duryea—Lieutenant Jacob Duryée—Several Expeditions—Sunday Service—Our Chaplain—Lieutenant-Colonel Warren—Adjutant Hamblin—The Location—A Storm—Off Duty—Fox Hill Expedition—Lieutenant-Colonel Warren's Report—Correspondence of the New York *Times*.

Colonel Segar, on whose farm the camp was situated, was a Union man, and owner of all the surrounding estate, as well as of the Hygeia Hotel, and had for many years represented his district in the Virginia Legislature. The family had removed, and some of the negroes were leaving with the last load of furniture. The men made themselves at home in the garden, and the demands of so large a number of guests in a few hours left the homestead stripped of everything they could appropriate for their supplies.

Just at this time there was a great commotion on the road. Down the highway there came rushing along, at a two-forty pace, a little mule, harnessed to a small cart, with three or four "Red Devils" in it, and at a little distance in the rear another turnout of a like pattern, with Captains Kilpatrick and Hull trying to overtake them; the former calling emphatically, "Halt! halt!" The chagrin of the future great cavalry General was great, at being beaten in a race, especially by privates, who had no business outside of their quarters. But the boys had no idea of being captured without being run down, and they only went the faster, and were soon out of sight, leaving pursuit and the guard-house behind.

Our First Camp in Virginia. 35

The regiment bivouacked for the night, having as yet no tents. Guards were established on the outskirts of the camp, and soon all were slumbering, except those on post.

About midnight two shots were heard, and instantly there was a tremendous sensation. The drums sounded the long roll; it was taken up in the other camps, and excited men were rushing to arms. Some who were not yet supplied with muskets formed in line with the rest, with dirk-knives and revolvers in hand, ready to fight for their lives. But it was soon learned that one of the sentries had mistaken a sentry of another regiment for a Confederate, and blazed away, and was fired at in turn by him. Happily no blood was shed, and we passed the night without being scalped, after having one other false alarm. These incidents served at least the purpose of good exercise in an important part of a soldier's life.

The events occurring in the regiment were described by a correspondent of the New York *Times* (Friday, May 31), in the following letter:

"CAMP BUTLER, NEAR HAMPTON, VA.,
Tuesday, May 28, 1861.

"The New York Fifth, Colonel Duryée, and Second, Colonel Carr's, regiment, are still encamped between Fortress Monroe and the old village of Hampton, one of the first settled in Virginia. The advent of the Zouaves seems to have produced a panic throughout the surrounding country. The inhabitants have all fled, with the exception of a few who adhere to the cause of the Union. 'Red Devils' is the complimentary appellation which the Secessionists have bestowed upon the followers of Colonel Duryée.

"On Sunday night, Captain Waugh, with his entire company, occupied the Female Seminary, a large building, on an elevated site near the camp, which had given shelter to the enemy. The American flag now waves over it, and can be seen for miles around. The same day Captain Kilpatrick made a reconnoissance, bringing back valuable information concerning the forces of the foe. Major-General Butler, on Monday, reviewed the Zouaves, and expressed to Colonel Duryée and his officers his delight with the excellent discipline of the corps, and his appreciation of the abilities of the commandant."

A Confederate of the enemy had been using the cupola on the top of the Seminary, as a lookout, and from his lofty position, from which the country could be seen for miles around, had been in the habit of signaling information of anything occurring in the neighborhood of the fortress. Colonel Duryée therefore took possession of the building, and, placing the band on the roof, they played the "Star Spangled Banner," while he raised the stars and stripes to the flag-staff, amid the cheers of his men.

General Butler issued the following proclamation, appointing Colonel Duryée to the command of all the forces at Old Point Comfort:

> FORTRESS MONROE, VA.,
> *May* 27, 1861.
>
> SPECIAL ORDERS, NO. 5.
>
> Colonel A. Duryée, Fifth Regiment New York Volunteers, will at once assume command of the camp of the two New York regiments, Segar's farm, and issue such orders and make such regulations, consistent with the Articles of War, as will insure good order and a thorough system of instruction and discipline; he will see that a proper guard is posted each night over the well, and on and near the bridge leading toward the fort, in such manner that there can be no danger of harm to them. Any depredations committed on the property of citizens, or any unnecessary inconvenience imposed upon them by any member of the command, must be promptly noticed, and reported in writing to the Major-General commanding the Department.
>
> By command of
> Major-General BUTLER.
> GRIER TALMADGE,
> *Acting Assistant Adjutant-General.*

Our First Camp in Virginia.

PROCLAMATION BY COLONEL DURYÉE.

To the Inhabitants of Hampton and vicinity:

Having been placed, by order of Major-General BUTLER, in command of the troops in this vicinity, outside of the walls of Fortress Monroe, I hereby notify all, that their rights of person and property will be entirely respected ; that their co-operation in maintaining law and order is expected, both by reporting every violation of them when committed by any one attached to the camp, and by preserving local order and restraining such of their fellow-citizens as may entertain perverted intentions.

You can rely that all offenses against you will be severely punished ; that no effort will be spared to detect the guilty ; and that you, as a community, will also be held responsible for every act committed by any one of your number where the particular offender is not surrendered. Be assured that we are here in no war against you, your liberty, your property, or even your local customs ; but to keep on high that flag of which your own great son was the bearer ; to sustain those institutions and those laws made by our ancestors and defended by their common blood.

Remember all these things, and if there be those among you who, maddened by party feeling, misled by willful falsehoods or a mistaken sense of duty, have thought to obliterate the national existence, let them at least pause till they learn the true value of what they have imperilled, and the nature of that into which they are asked to plunge. We have all confidence that in Virginians in arms against us we have honorable foes, whom we hope yet to make our friends.

COLONEL A. DURYÉE,
Acting Brigadier-General.

The *Times* correspondent, a few days later, photographed the Fifth as follows :

CAMP BUTLER, NEAR HAMPTON, VA.,
Sunday, June 2, 1861.

The friends of Colonel Duryée's Zouaves, who greeted with so much enthusiasm their first public parade in New York, would have been gratified beyond measure had they been here yesterday to witness the battalion-drill in the morning, conducted by Lieutenant-Colonel Warren, and the brigade evolutions, under the direction of Acting Brigadier-General Duryée, in the afternoon. A command composed as this is, constantly under military discipline, in camp,. makes wonderful progress in the course of a single week. They are something more than holiday soldiers, who know how to make a brilliant dress parade, on State occasions, over Russ pavement. If you could see them maneuvering on rough, plowed ground, covered with dust, forming in line of battle, springing into column, compressed into close column by division, deploying into hollow square, charging bayonet as one man, firing by file, by company, and by wing—performing with precision all the evolutions which make war wonderful and soldiering a science—you would imagine that they were veterans of very long standing, rather than hewers of wood, and drawers of drafts, and drivers of quills, who have left their trades, their banking-houses, or their professions, to fight for the old flag that traitors have dared to dishonor.

We have, as yet, had no collision with the enemy, but it has not been because no opportunity has been afforded the secessionists for coming in daily contact with the things they loathe.

On Tuesday, May 28th, Captain Judson Kilpatrick, an officer educated at West Point, in command of Company H, who knows no fear—except the fear that he shall not speedily have an opportunity of paying his compliments to the foe—left camp with forty men, and proceeded to the bridge at Hampton, which had been burned by the enemy, designing to repair it. He found it so much injured that with the implements at hand he could not reconstruct it. He built two docks, took possession of about thirty boats, opened a safe and easy communication with the village, crossed, took possession, and after posting a strong guard at the bridge-head, scoured the country for miles. After leaving the village, he received information that about one thousand secessionists were at hand. Nothing daunted, the intrepid Captain, throwing out scouts in advance, rapidly passed up the road toward Yorktown, and arrived at Newmarket Bridge just in time to see a small force of the enemy pass over, taking up the planks as they left. On his return he dispersed a body of twenty-five men, who had fired on Mr. Isaac Case, agent of Messrs. Wheeler & Wilson, of sewing-machine celebrity, who accompanied the regiment to take care of a charger, worth $600, presented to Major J. Mansfield Davies by that firm. He captured one horse, three mules, four drums, harness, several hundred bushels of grain, arms and military stores. Leaving these in charge of a small guard, commanded by Lieutenant Carlisle Boyd*—one of those quiet, gentlemanly men, who at the post of danger generally give a better account of themselves than the blusterers—he returned to Hampton, where he caused to be published to the assembled citizens the proclamation of General Duryée. Again crossing the stream, he raised the Stars and Stripes on the building but recently occupied by Colonel Mallory, of the Confederate army. His men stood around him while the ceremony was performing and greeted the flag with rousing cheers. The Captain made them a stirring little speech, to which they responded heartily. And then, after a day well spent, marched back to camp, bearing many trophies with him.

The next day, May 29th, Capt. Hiram Duryea, of E Company, marched far back into the country, meeting armed men who fled like deer at his approach. His men were "sp'ilin' for a fight," and bitterly denounced "the chivalry" for the retiring manners for which they are becoming noted in these parts. He brought back large quantities of provisions and tools.

The same day Lieut. Jacob Duryée, of Company G, son of the Colonel, raised the flag of our Union over ex-President Tyler's summer residence, "Marguerite Villa," at Hampton. It was an offset to the performance of Mr. Tyler's daughter, who a short time since, it will be remembered, hoisted a secession flag at a village somewhere at the South. On Thursday, May 30th, Capt. Robert S. Dumont, of Company B, went on a scouting expedition, in the course of which he met many armed men in uniform, who uniformly carried themselves back into the interior of old Virginia at a quadruple quickstep. Lieut. Dumont, with a few men, drove a superior force into the woods, and returned with a very large feather in his cap. Capt. Dumont brought back information of so much importance concerning the position of the op-

---

* Captain U. S. A. (1878).

posing forces, that it was communicated to Gen. Butler in a written report. Capt. Denike, of Company G, and Capt. Swartwout, of Company F, have made similar armed excursions with equally important results. Col. Duryée himself, with a small force, a few days ago returned into camp from Hampton, bearing with him the first secession flag that has been captured,* and a quantity of arms, odd portions of uniforms, etc., which had belonged to the secessionists. This morning the men attended divine service on the lawn in front of the Colonel's quarters. Rev. Dr. Winslow, the Chaplain, conducted the exercises and preached a very eloquent sermon. Dr. Winslow is a parson of the old Revolutionary school, and, on the Colonel's staff, will be as serviceable in the field as he is in the pulpit. Yesterday, under his direction, a bridge was built over a little stream which divides one of the outposts from the camp.

Thus the week has passed, not without its excitements. Rumors were constantly brought into camp that the enemy was advancing in force, and the men have slept on their arms nightly. They evince an excellent military spirit.

The appointment of Col. Duryée to the post of Acting Brigadier-General leaves Lieut.-Col. Warren in command of the Zouaves. Col. Warren has been many years in the regular service, is an accomplished officer, and an excellent disciplinarian. A few nights ago, when scouts rushed in out of breath, reporting that the enemy was advancing in a large body to cut off the picket guard at Hampton Bridge, Col. Warren, without alarming the camp, proceeded with only three men to take command of the guard, and remained all night with it. It was not rashness on his part, by any means, for he knew well how to post his little force so that the enemy could not get the best of him.

The Adjutant of the regiment, Joseph E. Hamblin, has been offered the position of Adjutant-General, but has declined it. He fully deserved the compliment, and the whole regiment was

---

*This flag, which still had a threaded needle sticking in it, was presented by Col. Duryée to the New York Historical Society. The first Confederate flag taken in the field was captured in Alexandria, Va., on May 23d, by two Union men named William McSpedon, of New York City, and Samuel Smith, of Queens County, N. Y. On May 24th Col. Ellsworth captured the Confederate flag, and lost his life, at Alexandria, Va.

pleased with it. But the whole regiment would have united in a protest against his leaving the command; and his reason for declining the promotion was that he was so much attached to the regiment that he could not endure to be detached. No man in the regiment has performed multifarious and arduous duties better, and is more respected by his brother officers and beloved by the men than Adjutant Hamblin.

There are now four regiments encamped here—Col. Allen's, Col. Carr's, Col. Bartlett's, and the Zouaves. The laws protecting the property of private citizens are strictly enforced by the Brigadier, and those of the people that remain are on excellent terms with the soldiers, while families that at first fled are beginning to return. As soon as it becomes generally known that they will nowhere be safer from insult, violence, and lawlessness than within our lines, the deserted villages in this delightful neighborhood will again be populated.

We have experienced as yet but few comparatively of the hardships of a soldier's life. We are particularly fortunate in being sent to this delightful Old Point Comfort. It is one of the healthiest places in the world, and no point could have been selected at which an army may be concentrated, provisioned, and kept in good sanitary condition, that is superior to this. And nature's great bath-tub lies at our feet. We may go further and fare worse.

G. C.

On Tuesday, the 4th, only two companies were left in camp; the rest were sent on a scout to Fox Hill, about five miles distant. They were accompanied by the Troy regiment and others, and expected to have a fight. The night before had been a trying one; the regiment was out on parade, when a storm, which had been threatening to break at any moment, burst upon them in all its fury. The men were dismissed to their tents, but before reaching them were completely drenched. The tents were small, and not being water-proof, the rain soaked through so much that the inmates and the contents were thoroughly wet. The earth floors caught the drippings, and were soon turned into muddy beds. The men passed a sleepless and disagreeable night; the whole camp was flooded, and the next day blankets, overcoats, Bibles, and Prayer-books were spread out to dry, and the men waited patiently for their clothing to dry on their backs.

The provisions were scant at times, and the officers were disposed to be cross—a feature which did not make matters any more cheerful.

Much of the spare time of the men when off duty was occupied in cleaning their arms and accoutrements, and it was required of them that they be kept in prime order, or the guard-house or extra duty awaited the delinquent; and as nothing was allowed to rub them with, the men were compelled to use earth and old pieces of rags, if they could be procured. But all, both officers and privates, were held to a strict account in their various spheres of duty, and the discipline was very severe. It may have been rigorous, but it was the only way to make good soldiers of such a diversified body of men as composed this regiment.

On Wednesday, June 5th, Sergeant D——, of Company G, resigned as a non-commissioned officer, on account of being reproved by Captain D——, of Co. B, the officer of the day, for not compelling six men who had been with others on a scout of fifteen miles that day, to leave their supper immediately, and take some prisoners down to Fortress Monroe. The Captain himself had been lying in camp all day. Exposure and hard service were beginning to show their effect on the men, and there were a number on the sick-list, several being sent to the hospital. In the morning the sound of heavy cannonading was heard in the distance. It was probably some of the men-of-war bombarding Confederate batteries near Norfolk.

Captain Winslow, Lieutenant Hoyt, and Lieutenant Ferguson, with Company K, and a company of the Second Troy Regiment, made a nocturnal expedition into the interior,

Our First Camp in Virginia. 43

capturing two men, a secession flag, uniforms, and other trophies.

According to the following extract from the New York *Daily Times*, the flag was presented to the Union Defense Committee of New York :

"Quartermaster Bailey Myers arrived yesterday from Fortress Monroe, bringing the secession flag which was captured by Colonel Duryée's "Red Devils," the Zouaves, at Hampton. The trophy was sent by Major-General Butler through Quartermaster Myers to the Union Defense Committee, with a letter highly complimenting Colonel Duryée and his command. The flag is made of a coarse red and white flannel, with a blue field of the same material, the stars, eight in number, being made of white cloth ; the ends are somewhat whipped out by the wind. It is at the rooms of the Committee."

The Fox Hill expedition having returned, I can not do better than give the full report of Lieutenant-Colonel Warren, who was in command :

CAMP BUTLER, *June* 4, 1861.

SIR: I have the honor to submit the following report of an expedition in front of our lines, on the 3d and 4th instants. About 4 P.M. on the 3d instant I was handed a communication from Colonel Allen, addressed to Colonel Duryée, commanding the brigade, which was as follows :

CAMP DIX, *June* 3, 1861.
COLONEL DURYÉE :

SIR :—I am directed by General Butler to call upon you for a detachment of men to accompany three companies of my regiment to ascertain the correctness of the reported capture of 126 officers and men of the regiment, this morning, at Fox Hill, and, if so, to recapture them, or if not, to conduct them in.

In haste, yours,
W. H. ALLEN,
Colonel First Regiment.

And, at the same time, I was directed to have ready a detachment for the purpose. Orders were right away given by me to Captain Hull, Captain Kilpatrick, Captain Winslow, and Captain Bartlett, to have their companies in readiness, with canteens, haversacks containing one day's rations, and fifteen rounds of ammunition in their cartridge-boxes. This was promptly complied with, and at 5 P.M. we received the order to march, cross the river at Hampton, and interrupt any parties returning toward Yorktown or Williamsburgh from the neighborhood of Fox Hill. Owing to sickness and the number of men detailed for guard, the aggregate force of the four companies was only eight officers and 200 men. As Captain Kilpatrick's company were drilled in the duty of skirmishers, it was thrown in advance after crossing over to Hampton, and seized the cross-road about a mile beyond, at which point any land expedition returning from Fox Hill would be compelled to pass. The main body passed through Hampton, but being overtaken by a violent rain-storm, took shelter in an abandoned house, and waited there till dawn of day. Numbers of colored persons were examined, and all agreed that no force had passed in the direction of Fox Hill, nor could any rumor of the capture of Colonel Allen's men be discovered.

I determined, however, to advance in the direction of Yorktown sufficiently far to show forces at that place that they could not conduct small expeditions with impunity so near to us, and besides to assure the citizens that all our authorized expeditions would respect peaceable persons and property. With these objects I concluded to go to a place called the County Bridge, about nine miles from Hampton, where there was said to be a battery of several cannon, and capture it if practicable. About two and a half miles beyond Hampton we came to Newmarket Bridge, which spans a branch of Bark River. This was partially destroyed by fire, but not so much so that we did not succeed in making it passable in a few minutes.

About two miles further on the scouts in advance met a wagon containing two or three men, who at once turned around and fled. Several shots were fired over them to induce them to stop, but without effect. From that time on we frequently saw men on our flanks in the woods, and heard shots, giving warning of our advance. At one house, where there were several women, our passing by caused great terror, and their lamentations were piteous. Their cries, "Oh, my dear father; oh, my dear brother," and entreated us to go back and spare the shedding of blood, fell painfully on our ears. The presence of Rev. Dr. Winslow and Dr. Gilbert, however, soon quieted them. Some of my men filled their canteens at the well as we passed on. We reached the County Bridge at 9 A.M. The stream is a branch of the Bark River, and is easily forded, and the bridge is uninjured. There is a frame building church on the other side, in rather a dilapidated condition. No human being was in the vicinity, nor did it give evidence of having been occupied, except by a few persons, since the rain.* Trees cut down near the bridge indicated that arrangements had been made to dispute its passage. There were no breastworks other than an old pit, which had probably been a cellar, which would have effectually sheltered about fifty men. The floor of the church was strewn with corn-cobs, and had been, probably, occupied as a stable.

We were told that horsemen, to the number of forty, came here every night, and that the guns were removed last Saturday, the 1st inst. Some letters, all of a private nature, picked up in the vicinity, indicated a speedy abandonment of the place. We regretted very much to find no enemy there, as the vicinity is very favorable to infantry operations. We returned by a road about one mile to the east of the one by which we advanced, and which crosses the stream, the bridge of which we had repaired in the morning, about one and a half miles lower down. The heat of the sun, on our return, was intense, but on reaching this stream again about 3 P.M., a violent shower came on us, and soon all were wet to the skin. The bridge at this point was entirely destroyed, so we concluded to ford it. Finding the water over the men's heads, the passage was accomplished by swimming. A few who could not swim were passed over on a little scow which was there. This filled once with water, with three men in it who could not swim, but these were all rescued at once by those who could. It continued to rain, with slight

---

* (Big Bethel), "Report of Committee on the Conduct of the War," (Vol. I, p 783.) General Warren says: "I had been on the ground six days previously, and had reconnoitered it, though nobody then present knew that I had done so."

intermission, till our return to our camp, about 5½ P.M. The expedition was out about twenty-four hours. The sleep the men got was while under arms in the house at Hampton, lying on the floor. Owing to inexperience and eagerness to set out, my directions for supplying themselves with rations were imperfectly complied with, and they suffered severely for want of something to eat. Nothing, however, was taken from the people along the road but a little corn-bread and milk, which was paid for at more than twice its value.

The cheerful manner in which most of the command bore their hard march under a broiling sun, and crossed a deep stream by swimming, and finished the last four miles of their march in their jaded condition, with wet clothes, over a muddy road, all show what they may accomplish in the future. And the respect paid to persons and property was, in my opinion, as great a triumph for our cause as would have been a victory over armed men.

After describing the immense resources of the country, in wheat and corn, fowls and cattle, and that if he had been directed to do so he could have brought in large numbers of the latter, the report continues :

The only thing taken was a horse, which was given to the Rev. Dr. Winslow to ride. It was in the possession of a negro boy, who said it belonged to a man (not his master) who had joined the secessionists. A fine Pointer dog followed us in from one of the deserted houses. The negroes we met were seemingly glad to see us. The poor whites seem to desire neutrality, though many of them are with the secessionists. On our return we met a young gentleman with two beautiful, well-dressed ladies—one of them very young—going in a buggy toward Yorktown. I begged them to stay at home and aid us in restoring peace to their country, and told them that I would insure them protection, and also requested the gentleman to inform others he met in the place to which he was repairing to the same effect. He said he would do so, but it would do no good ; they would not believe us. He said frankly that the proclamation of General

Butler had proved but a snare to those who trusted in it; that his uncle, Mr. Sinclair, had seen all his chickens killed before his eyes, not even the mother of a little brood was spared; houses, too, had been plundered of their furniture, and people would never return again while a Northern man remained on the soil of Virginia. To one of the ladies, at her request, I gave the letters we picked up at the County Bridge, the only proof I could give of my sincerity. It is in vain to attempt to pacify or render these people friendly, unless the greatest rigor is used, not merely toward those who are caught committing depredations, which is difficult to do, but toward every one found beyond some established line without authority. I would respectfully suggest that no more seizures of cattle or provisions shall be made, even when left behind by avowed secessionists. They will otherwise carry it off or destroy it. But if it remain unmolested by us, we will find abundance of means at hand to sustain us whenever we choose to advance in force. Small scouting parties in front of our lines keep up a needless alarm, and must fail in capturing detachments of the enemy, who, being well mounted and acquainted with the country, flee at our approach. Besides, these scouting parties tend to demoralize the regiment, and prevent that attention to drill and discipline so essential to the real operations of war. Let us remain quietly within our lines, preparing for the greater struggle; let our foes even think we fear them, if thereby their temerity may place them more within our grasp; and when we do move, let it be like the bound of the lion from his covert.

Then after describing the character of the country for military operations, the report closed by saying:

Feeling that any compliment paid by me to the men under my command might be construed as an indirect one to myself, I respectfully submit this report of their march without further comment.
    Very respectfully, your obedient,
        G. K. WARREN,
       Lieut.-Col. Com. Expedition.
TO COLONEL A. DURYÉE, *Com. 5th Regiment, N. Y. S. V.*

The following narrative is by the correspondent of the New York *Times:*

On the morning of the 4th, at about 1 o'clock, Captain H. Duryea took a detachment of three companies and started for Fox Hill to rescue the men of Colonel Allen's regiment, who were reported to have been captured by the rebels. After a forced march of nine miles they arrived at a farm-house at Fox Hill, where it was reported that there was an intrenched enemy, but there was none to be found.

They halted there a short time, and procuring a guide, started for Back River, a distance of five miles further on; but on arriving there they were again doomed to disappointment—the enemy had gone.

Lieutenant George Duryea took twenty men, and started up the river to secure boats. While on this duty he stopped at a farm-house owned by a Union man, who offered him and his men a bountiful breakfast, which was declined, though milk and corn-bread were furnished to the men. He secured a few boats, but soon after an aide from headquarters reported that Colonel Allen's regiment was safe, so the boats were not needed, and a return to camp was ordered, by a different route, however, the command passing through Hampton. While passing through the village, Lieutenant Burnett, with a flanking party in advance, was struck on the right breast by a spent ball, inflicting but a slight wound, the ball falling from his shirt to the ground. It did not keep him from pursuing the march. With this single exception, everybody arrived safely in camp after a march of ten hours. On Saturday afternoon we had another general call to arms, by a report that two companies of the Troy regiment were being attacked at Hampton. The men sprang into the ranks; some of the Troy regiment rushed down to Hampton, without waiting for the command; aides were galloping along the road at full speed; and the Zouaves, with fifteen rounds of ammunition, left their camping-ground and halted at the main road. There were a few minutes of suspense, and then word came that it was a false alarm. The news was received with great disappointment, and the men marched downcast back to camp.

CHAPTER IV.

BIG BETHEL.

SUNDAY EVENING ORDERS—OUR COMRADES—A LOYAL NEGRO—CAPTAIN KIL- PATRICK'S ADVANCE—A VIRGINIA PRISONER—A FATAL MISTAKE—BIG BETHEL —A WOUNDED COMRADE—A SOLDIER'S TRIBUTE—DEATH OF LIEUTENANT GREBLE—HONORABLE MENTION—A NAVAL COMMANDER—CORRESPONDENCE OF THE NEW YORK *Tribune*—FLAG OF TRUCE.

SUNDAY, the 9th of June, was spent in the usual duties assigned to the day. The regiment was out on parade as usual. After it was dismissed, the men were again assembled, and each man supplied with twenty rounds of cartridges in addition to what he had in his cartridge-box. All was bustle and activity. The men felt confident they were going out on an expedition somewhere, but in what direction was entirely unknown.

Taps were sounded at the usual hour, and all not on special duty were ordered to their tents. A few minutes later the orderlies of the companies went to each tent, and in an undertone notified the occupants that at half-past ten o'clock every man would be called to immediately equip without noise or light, and fall in line in front of the tents; each man was to be supplied with one day's rations and a canteen of water.

They were to tie the white turban twice around the left arm, as a distinguishing mark, and the watchword "Boston" was given. Several able-bodied men were detailed to report to the surgeons, from which it was inferred that something in earnest was to be done. About 9.30 P.M. a body of men marched away from the regiment; they made so little noise that it seemed a mystery where they came from.

They were Companies H and I, under the command of Captains Kilpatrick and Bartlett respectively, and were to proceed in advance of the regiment as scouts and skirmishers, and also to stop all persons that might be going from Hampton toward the enemy. It was now understood that the regiment was to act in concert with Colonel Bendix's 7th New York (Steuben Rifles) from Newport News, for the purpose of surprising and capturing at the point of the bayonet, if possible, a Confederate camp, at a place about eleven miles from Hampton, and known as BIG BETHEL.

Two other regiments were to follow as supports in case they were required—Col. Carr's 2d New York (Troy regiment), and Colonel Townsend's 3d New York (Albany regiment). Lieutenant Greble, of the 2d Artillery, with eleven regulars and one rifled six-pounder from the fortress, accompanied the expedition. A negro named George Scott, who had been working on the Confederate earthworks, had run away, and given such information to General Butler, that he determined to send a force against them, and hence the present movement.

The negro accompanied the forces as a guide, being supplied at his request with a rifle and ammunition. At midnight, the regiment being in line, 740 strong, and fully prepared to move, the order was given to march. They accordingly filed off on the road, and soon reached Hampton River, which was crossed in boats under the charge of the naval brigade. This occasioned some delay, but the march was soon resumed, the men stepping off briskly at route step and arms at will. The men were all in good spirits and sanguine of success. After covering about six miles of ground, a halt was ordered.

Those on the right of the regiment, at head of column, saw a bright light pointing toward the enemy's position. It was a Confederate signal. Further on another was seen, and again we came to a slight halt. For the purpose of understanding our position at this time, we will follow Captain Kilpatrick's movements.

As already stated, he and Captain Bartlett, with their companies, left camp two hours before the departure of the main body of the regiment. He advanced cautiously after getting beyond Hampton, and established pickets one and a quarter and two and a half miles beyond that village, with the necessary reserves.

The pickets fell in with the regiment as it came up to where they were posted. After reaching Newmarket Bridge, Captain Kilpatrick took twenty men with him, after the regiment came up to a supporting distance, and advanced again, posting now and then a picket at important points. After approaching to within a short march of New County Bridge, he saw through the trees what was supposed to be a camp fire. He halted his men and held a short consultation with his non-commissioned officers, among whom there was a diversity of opinion, some thinking that it was a Confederate camp, and others that it was only a picket outpost.

He determined to reconnoiter and ascertain to a certainty if possible, and accordingly selected a squad of eight men for the purpose: Sergeant Benjamin F. Onderdonk, Corporal Andrew B. Allison, Samuel Wilson, Andrew Whitehead, John Rock, James S. Boyd, Fred. Bollet, and Edward Engel.* They crept carefully through the woods, when suddenly they were brought to a halt by a challenge: "Who goes there?" They did not answer. The challenge was repeated a second and third time, when Kilpatrick immediately answered: "Who stands there?" A prompt reply came: "A Virginian." And at the same time they heard steps pattering on the road in retreat, and also saw a horseman, who was not yet mounted,

---

* Sergeant Onderdonk subsequently was Colonel of the 1st Mounted Rifles, and acting Brigadier-General; Allison was killed at second Bull Run, as color-bearer of the Fifth; Boyd lost his arm; Bollet received four wounds; and Engel was severely wounded in the same engagement.

making preparations to leave. Corporal Allison sprang in advance, ordering him to halt, and supposing the enemy in force, the Captain gave his squad the order, "Fire and charge;" which was instantly obeyed, the rest of his company following them. The whole affair was over in a moment. Sam Wilson, putting his hand on the horseman's shoulder, who had not time to mount, ordered him to surrender, at the same time disarming him of one of his revolvers, while another took the remaining one from his belt. On the prisoner instinctively feeling for them, he found they were gone, upon which he delivered his sword. It was an unusually long and sharp one. The prisoner proved to be a Captain Whiting, and the officer of the guard. He was a splendid-looking specimen of a Southerner, standing more than six feet in height, and a perfect gentleman. He was taken with an escort to the rear.

The main body of the regiment had now come up on a double-quick on hearing the reports of the pieces. Soon after this occurred heavy firing was heard in the rear, in which the report of cannon could be distinguished, and supposing that the enemy had in some way come in contact with the Newport News regiment, the Fifth was right-abouted and marched double-quick about two miles back on the road by which it had just approached. Company K, Capt. Winslow, being thrown out on the right as skirmishers, advanced through thick woods and wet wheat-fields. It being now about daylight, upon coming up to where the firing had been heard, it was discovered that a most lamentable mistake had occurred. Col. Bendix, with his command, the 7th New York, who marched from Newport News in company with detachments of the 5th Massachusetts and of Col. Phelps' Vermont regiment, who were to meet and act in conjunction with the Zouaves, according to the plan devised to surprise and capture the Confederate camp at Big Bethel, discovered Col. Townsend's 3d New York, who were marching with two twelve-pound howitzers, on the main road from Hampton, following the Fifth at a proper supporting distance as a reserve; and in the uncertain light of the morning, supposing that they were an enemy, opened fire upon them, and before the mistake was discovered had killed and wounded eleven of Col. Townsend's men. It was saddening to see them lying at the little house just off the road, the victims of carelessness or want of discretion, although prompted by patriotic zeal and courage. Half an hour after, the Zouaves, under orders, singing the "Star Spangled Banner" and other patriotic songs, went hurrying back to the attack.*

Before marching, however, a detail of five men was made from Company G—Benj. F. Finley, John Gillen, Ed. Hoffman, James Martin, and E. M. Law—to burn down a handsome residence from which a shot had been fired at Surgeon Howe, of the 1st New York, who took charge of the detail personally.† It was ascertained to a certainty that the shot was fired by the owner of this elegant place, a Mr. Whiting, who was also an officer of the Confederate army. He was seen escaping to the woods from the rear of the premises, and the negroes also confirmed the intelligence. It was handsomely furnished with all that a refined taste could suggest; but before applying the torch, the former slaves of the owner were allowed to appropriate clothing and whatever

---

* Gen. Warren, "Report of Committee on the Conduct of the War," Vol. I., p. 383: "It was planned for a night attack with very new troops; some of them had never been taught to even load and fire. It was planned to proceed from two different points distant from each other six or seven miles. The ground between was unknown, and then the map which Gen. Butler furnished was a wrong map, made in 1819, and the roads were all laid down wrong. The specific points of instruction were that the troops at Newport News being some three miles nearer, should start about an hour after the others. The true state of the case was that they were about four miles nearer, and that brought on the collision which took place, and that was inevitable. I think the two regiments, when they arrived on the ground in the early morning, finding things not at all as they had been instructed, were justified in firing on each other. I am satisfied of that."

† Gillen was subsequently wounded and crippled, and Hoffman killed at second Bull Run.

their fancy dictated, while Hoffman played the "Star Spangled Banner" and other airs on the elegant piano; after which, Col. Duryée having arrived at the scene, the torch was applied, and on the return march back to camp, there was nothing left of house or contents but the brick chimney and a heap of smouldering ruins.

A consultation of officers was now held as to future movements. Col. Duryée was of the opinion that the object of the whole movement—a surprise of the Confederate camps —having been defeated, it was not good judgment to advance any further, but he would advance if it was the wish of the majority. The latter course was soon decided upon, and Capt. Kilpatrick, with his Company H, and Capt. Bartlett, of Company I, again took the advance as scouts and skirmishers, ahead and on the flanks of the regiment. We soon reached Little Bethel, which the Colonel had particular instructions to destroy. It was a low wooden structure, and was a noted place of meeting for the secessionists of that part of the country, where they planned and matured their schemes of treason. In a few moments it was a mass of burning ruins. Further on, when a short halt was made, some of the Zouaves went into a house on the roadside, and soon appeared with a large earthen pot of honey. But they were not left to enjoy it alone, as they were surrounded in a moment and a score of hands were fighting to get a dip at that unheard-of luxury in camp life. Soon everybody had a fistful, and were licking their dripping fingers with keen relish, when suddenly we heard the command, "Fall in! Shoulder arms! March!" Here was a dilemma not anticipated, but it was the work of a moment to stoop down and grasp a handful of earth to remove the honey from the hand. After marching some distance we came to a halt near a country school-house. In a twinkling it was full of loyal visitors, of whom one played master mounted on the platform, and was trying to preserve order by pounding the desk with a heavy stick, when he was assailed by such a cloud of books and slates that he was glad to vacate. Some were at the blackboard hanging Jeff Davis with a piece of chalk; others writing not very complimentary messages to "the secesh" in general, which must have provoked their ire if they were read after our departure. But this amusement was suddenly cut short by the appearance of an officer, who ordered them to immediately rejoin the command.

At 8 A.M. Captain Kilpatrick met and drove in the enemy's picket guard. He then detached twenty men from his company, made a reconnoissance, and found the enemy about two or three thousand strong, who, as was afterward ascertained, were under the command of Colonel Magruder. They were posted on the opposite side of a stream, which was the north-west branch of the Back River, on ground slightly elevated. The road passed down a hollow as it neared the approach to the bridge over the stream in front of their works, which widened out on each flank into a morass. They were behind two strong earthworks each side of the road, which commanded the bridge, and were intrenched along the bank of a wooded swamp on their right, and had masked their battery, which, as was afterward ascertained during the course of the battle, mounted at least ten guns, some of them rifled. These completely raked the only road, in front, which was the path by which our regiment was approaching. Directly in front of the enemy's right was the morass, impassable for man or beast, without artificial help, and in front of their left was the stream of water, running from the morass or pond. Between their left and the Union troops was comparatively open ground, partly planted with corn, which bordered on a piece of woods, adjoining which was an open plowed field. About half a mile to the rear of this field was a farm-house, being on the right of the road as facing the enemy; on the left of the road was the morass before mentioned, directly in front of the enemy; then a small space of ground, with a rail fence, and some old sheds; a young peach orchard, soil very soft; then a little narrow lane, that ran to the left at right angles with the road, bordered with stone-walls and a barn, next to which was a corn-field. About this time Lieutenant-Colonel Warren came up, and taking command of two companies, went forward as skirmishers.* They advanced on the left and right of the road rapidly, supported by the rest of the regiment. Lieutenant Greble advanced along the road with the three guns. The long roll and the cries of the enemy to "turn out" could now be plainly heard. The regiment formed in line of battle in the corn-field on the left of the road, and soon after advanced in fours by right flank up the road, and turned into the open, plowed field on its right, facing the woods, and formed in line of battle. Colonel Townsend (3d New York) had now come up, and formed on the left of the road. Most of us experienced a strange sensation, as we were standing there, expecting every moment to receive a volley from the woods into our closed ranks. It was our first formal battle. Every man looked a shade paler, but it was the effect of stern determination and suppressed excitement.

Colonel Duryée said the cavalry were coming out, but the result showed that he was mistaken. The Confederates had not the slightest intention of leaving their well-protected and intrenched position, unless it should be to the rear. At twenty minutes of ten o'clock the loud boom of a cannon was heard, and Captain Denike, of Company G., took out his watch, and said, "Men, the ball has opened." This first shot was fired by the brave Lieutenant Greble, a regular officer, who, with eleven regulars from the fort, aided by a few of the Massachusetts men, had charge of one rifled piece and two twelve-pound howitzers, and had placed them

---

* "Report of Committee on the Conduct of the War" (p. 383). General Warren: "I pushed up with two companies ahead of the regiment, within two or three hundred yards of the enemy, and discovered that they had cannon, etc."

in the road side of the woods, within five hundred yards of the enemy's works, supported somewhat by three companies under Lieutenant-Colonel Warren.

Almost instantaneously the first report was followed by another, and a shell came whizzing through the air, with its disagreeable shriek. Now they come thick and fast, and the regiment was ordered to charge through the wood. At the word of command, on they rushed, with a Zouave cheer, through the thick brush of the wood, which was raked by grape and canister, shell and solid shot. Soon the companies became mixed, and separated into detached squads, on account of the thick undergrowth of the woods. It was impossible to preserve the line in breaking through the brush and dodging trees, or even to keep in view of one another. The wood resounded with cries of "This way, Company A," "This way, Company G," mingled with various emphatic injunctions not necessary to be repeated. The firing now became very heavy, but on account of our being so near the rebel works, and their fire directed by inexperienced artillerists, their shots were aimed too high, and cut off the tree tops and boughs, which was more agreeable to the Zouaves than the loss of their own heads and limbs. The men were now ordered to lie down and keep covered as much as possible, and await future developments. In the meantime some of the boys, on their own responsibility, had crept to the outer edge of the woods nearest the enemy, the timber being bounded by a rail fence, and thence kept up a fire on any Confederate that exposed himself above their works. It was a little to the right of this position that Major Winthrop was killed. Part of the Steuben Rifles had also crept up on the right, and kept up a galling fire, while some of the Zouaves charged up the road. Captain Kilpatrick and five or six others were standing well to the front in the woods, with Colonel Duryée, who was about ten feet to the right, trying to get a view of the Confederate position, when a grape-shot cut through the Captain's thigh and scraped the other leg, and went through the thigh of Tom Cartwright, of Company G, who was standing near him; another shot, at the same moment, tore off a portion of the rectangle on the left shoulder of Colonel A. Duryée. Captain Kilpatrick's inquiry on receiving the wound, "Are we going to stay here and be shot down, and do nothing?" was answered by the order to fall back toward the edge of the woods, and to re-form, the Captains and officers using the most strenuous exertions to get their companies together, with only partial success on account of the undergrowth which separated them. There being no order for any general movement to outflank the enemy, or change position, from the Brigadier-General (Pierce) commanding, and the officers and men being eager to get at the enemy in some way, in the absence of direct orders, they were not acting in concert, but more or less on their own responsibility. Colonel Duryée and officers were exerting themselves to get the men again into a battalion front and calm their excitement, and Lieutenant-Colonel Warren called out that they would flank them on the left.

The morass in front, which was impassable, prevented the Zouaves from forcing the batteries at the point of the bayonet, without orders, in which undertaking some of the officers would have gladly led. They were in earnest, and ready for any deed of daring. Captain Kilpatrick, in his written report of his part in the movement, says: "The whole command, officers and men, did themselves the greatest credit, and, I am satisfied, can conquer anything except impossibilities."

At this stage of the contest, some of the men charged up the road; one of them lost a leg, which was cut off close to his body, by a solid shot; another an arm, and one was killed, and the undertaking was found impossible without support. Lieutenant Jacob Duryée, of Company G, called out, "Who will follow me? I will charge the batteries," when he was immediately surrounded by all within the sound

Big Bethel.

of his voice—about forty or fifty—among whom were most of the firemen of his own company, comprising members of Engine Company 12, Engine Company 7, Truck Company 9, and of old Engine Company 46, which had been disbanded on account of the fighting proclivities of its members. Away they rushed, followed by Captain Denike, Captain Winslow, and Lieutenant York, and about 200 of the Zouaves, out of the woods across the road, joined by Kilpatrick, who went limping along with them, notwithstanding his wounds, and it is unnecessary to say that the giant form of William McDowell,* of Truck Company 9, was among them. They dashed toward the peach orchard, on the left of the road, falling flat at each flash of the rebel cannon, then up again and on, as fast as they could move, over the soft and yielding soil, the solid shot and canister shrieking over their heads. About the middle of the field, Kilpatrick's wounded leg gave out, and some of the men halted to assist him to the rear, but he requested them to advance. A number of the men went no further. Robert Strachan, of Company I, who was in the charge, seeing that he was much exhausted, assisted him to the rear. Finally the little storming party, now numbering only about fifty, reached the shelter of the old sheds, already mentioned, and just beyond was that impassable morass that prevented them from achieving a victory. Among that little band were men who had fought fire and flame, and knew no fear, and whom nothing in the shape of man could terrify. This testimonial is to be found on the muster rolls of their company, where the names of the most of those who were in this the first real charge of the war, are to be found as killed or wounded, at Gaines' Mill or on Manassas Plains.†

---

* Killed at second Bull Run.

† The number of members of Company G that belonged to the Volunteer Fire Department of New York City was twenty-two, of whom five were killed, eight wounded and injured (five of whom were discharged therefor), and three returned

They approached within three hundred feet of the enemy's works, and kept up a vigorous fire from the cover of the sheds. Colonel Townsend, with the 3d New York, also came up with his regiment further to the left, in good order, the Colonel leading, and sitting erect on a white horse, the impersonation of a valiant soldier. It seemed a miracle that he was not killed, but such are the chances of war. Frequently the men who seem, by their actions, to almost court death are spared, while the fatal bullet strikes the skulking victim, far away to the rear. Private William H. Burnham, of Company H, formerly in the regular army, had the credit of saving the life of Colonel Townsend by shooting a rebel lodged in a tree, who had drawn his rifle on him. Burnham was presented with a gold medal by the Colonel. The Confederates now abandoned the works on their right, but still the troops could not follow up the advantage on account of the nature of the obstructions described. Colonel Townsend, seeing two companies of his regiment who had become detached from his left in coming through the bushes to the open field, on his left flank, fell back, supposing them to be the enemy, as their uniform was very similar in color, and after holding the sheds for some time, the Zouaves also fell back slowly, for there was no possible use of staying where they were, the troops being on the retreat, having been ordered to do so by General Pierce.

Swinton, in his "History of the Army of the Potomac" (pp. 32–33), says: "But it happened that there was one man there who saw the course of action suited to the case. Lieutenant-Colonel Warren suggested that a regiment should be sent round on each side to take the position in flank, and

---

to duty after recovering. Two were discharged on account of disease, one taken prisoner, August 30, 1862, and paroled, and the others were mustered out with the company, May 14, 1863. Of the whole number (22), one was an officer, two were 1st Sergeants, two Sergeants, and six were Corporals; one, at the time of this writing, is in the regular army.

when these became engaged, those in front, lying in shelter in a wood, should attack. This operation, if carried out, would probably have been successful. But the regiment* that was to make the movement on the enemy's right, instead of being directed by a detour through the woods, was advanced right across an open field, in front of the position, whereby it became exposed to an artillery fire. It happened, too, that the left company became separated from the rest of the regiment by a thicket; and Col. Townsend, not being aware of this, and seeing the glistening of bayonets in the woods, concluded the enemy was outflanking him, and so fell back to his first position. The regiment† that had gone round on the other flank found itself in a difficult situation, where, being exposed to pretty severe fire, it was found hard to bring the men up. Major Winthrop, aide to Gen. Butler, was killed while rallying the troops to the assault. Gen. Pierce ordered a retreat, and the regiments marched off as on parade."‡

About midway of the orchard one of the Zouaves was lying, shot through the chest; Wm. McDowell, Davenport, and one other went to his assistance; Lieut. York took his rifle, and the others carried him about thirty paces, but he begged so hard to be put down again, and knowing that he had a mortal wound, they placed him with his back against a tree, supplied him with water, and left him to die in peace.

---

* Colonel Townsend's 3d New York.

† 7th New York, Col. Bendix.

‡ "Report of the Committee on the Conduct of the War" (Vol. I., p. 383), Gen. Warren says: "Gen. Pierce called a meeting of the Colonels about what should be done, and news of some sort came from Gen. Butler by his aide. I am sorry to say they all determined that we had better retire. I opposed it myself."

Swinton (p. 33). "Col. Warren, who alone protested against the retreat, voluntarily remained on the ground, and together with Rev. Dr. Winslow, of his regiment, brought off the wounded. While he yet remained on the ground, the Confederates abandoned the position; and the reason assigned for this step by Col. D. H. Hill, who was in command of the 1st North Carolina Regiment, is, that he feared reinforcements would be sent up from Fortress Monroe."

Lieut. John T. Greble, with the regulars and a few of the Massachusetts men, as before stated, held the most dangerous post, on the road, with the three guns. The solid shot from the Confederate batteries plowed their way straight up the road, from which there was no cover, except that occasionally some of the men took shelter in the edge of the wood on the right of the road. Lieut. Greble would not deign to leave his post for an instant, but coolly sighted the guns himself and watched the effect of every shot. Capt. Bartlett,* of the Zouaves, stood by his side for some time. When the troops left, he saw that he could not hold the position any longer, and was in the act of sighting or spiking his gun when a cannon ball struck him on the temple, carrying away half of his head. The ball passed through the body of a man standing near and took the leg off of a third. He had only five men left with him at this time. His Sergeant then spiked the gun. Four of the regulars were killed or wounded out of the eleven that came with him from the fort.

Greble's body was laid over a caisson, and was dragged off under the superintendence of Lieut.-Colonel Warren. Lieutenant Greble was the first regular officer who fell in the war. By his bravery in standing by his guns, and keeping up a steady fire on the enemy's works, he prevented them from using their cannon as effectually as they could have done, in which case there would have been a very heavy loss of life on our side. The enemy's guns were under the personal command of Major George W. Randolph, later the Confederate Secretary of War.

A small number remained behind after the regiment moved, among whom were Philip L. Wilson and George L. Guthrie, to rescue the wounded, but the special mission of the former was to bring off Thomas Cartwright, already mentioned as having been shot through the thigh, and who was one of his messmates.

---

* Major 11th U. S. Infantry (1878).

He asked the men guarding Greble's body to assist him, but they refused. He went into the woods and there met Guthrie, who was alone, and shouting for Tom, they were finally overjoyed to hear him answer their call. They carried him with much exertion to the edge of the wood by the road, and leaving Guthrie as companion, Phil went to find a conveyance. He succeeded in obtaining a hand cart, and went back with it to the place where Guthrie and Cartwright were waiting, having first handed the Lieut.-Colonel his rifle, who told him to make haste or he would be taken prisoner. In this way Cartwright's life was probably saved on this occasion. They stopped a few moments at a farm-house on the road, where they found other wounded men, among whom was James L. Taylor, of Company B, who was conveyed there by his friend Corporal, afterward Colonel, Wm. Gilder, and who died there the same night. Chaplain Winslow, of the Zouaves, was waiting on them.

They were obliged to hurry away, as they were closely followed by some of the enemy, who were mounted. This party, which was a mere squad, and was the rear guard, was composed of a few of the Troy regiment, some of the 7th Steuben, some of Townsend's regiment, a few of the Zouaves, and many of the wounded, all under the command of Lieut.-Col. Warren.

At a cross-road they met two of the Troy regiment who were driving a wagon they had seized. They got out and Cartwright was put in. A skirmish soon after ensued with the enemy, who were following, and was kept up all the way to Newmarket Bridge, Tom Cartwright also taking a hand in from the wagon. At the bridge they met Lieut.-Col. Warren, who had left them a little while before, and gone forward to hurry up the detail of the naval brigade, whom he had sent forward when he left camp with two guns.*

---

* Lieut.-Col. Warren did not leave camp with the expedition, but a report having reached Camp Hamilton, occasioned by the unfortunate night encounter of the

The old sea-dogs came pushing up the road, armed with clubs, dragging the cannon after them, crying out every now and then, "Heave hearty! Heave hearty, my lads!" All who were at Camp Hamilton will never forget the "sea-pirates." They were the wildest and most reckless set of men ever got together.

The rear guard, after crossing the bridge, pulled up the planks, and the enemy seeing the cannon, abandoned further pursuit. One of the latter was shot here by one of our men. The regiment, in the meantime, kept on their weary march back to camp, tired and footsore. Their giant Adjutant, Hamblin,* at every short halt to rest, threw himself on the ground with the exclamation, "How I like the mud!" and when the men got up to resume the march, it was with considerable effort they could get their stiffened joints to obey their will. Finally they reached Hampton, and were rowed across the river by the naval brigade in flat-bottomed scows, in one of which lay the body of the lamented George H. Tiebout, of Company A, who was shot through the heart by a canister ball, and was the first martyr of the 5th Regiment, in the first battle of the war. Having arrived on the other side of the river, the march was resumed, and we arrived in camp about 8 P.M., all completely exhausted, after a march of thirty miles since leaving camp, besides standing the brunt of the battle, which lasted two hours and forty minutes. The first gun was fired at twenty minutes before 10 o'clock, and the last at twenty minutes past 12 o'clock.

The men had been without sleep for thirty-six hours, with only slight halts to rest—such as are usual on a long march.

---

two regiments, that an engagement was going on, he procured two guns from the fort and went forward with some of the naval brigade, who were dragging the guns. After seeing them well on their way, he put spurs to his mule and came up just before the engagement.

* Subsequently Brevet Major-General.

Captain Kilpatrick was placed on a white mule after the troops had commenced to retreat, by Captain Winslow, his wound beginning to be painful; and inflammation having set in, he was unable to walk. He thus rode with the regiment back to camp. He mentions in his report the bravery of Captain Winslow, Lieutenants Hoyt and Ferguson, Sergeants Onderdonk, Agnus, and Chambers, Corporals Seymour and Allison, and Private Boyd and others. He further states that private John Dunn, whose arm was shattered by a cannon ball, bore himself with the greatest bravery, and said to Surgeon Gilbert, before amputating his arm, that he could not have lost it in a nobler cause. Private John H. Conway, Company K, is reported to have said, when shot in the leg, "I have yet one leg left, and will follow my Captain to the end of the charge." Private Joseph Knowles, of Company E, said, "Avenge the loss of my arm." But one of the most affecting incidents was that of James L. Taylor, of Company B. When he heard it remarked that he had received a mortal wound, he said to his true friend, Corporal W. H. Gilder, "That's all right, 'Gilly'—don't bother about me; I can't live—take some one off the ground who can live, and fight again." It was terrible, said his devoted comrade, who had succeeded, after great efforts, in securing for a second time transportation for his dying friend, to be compelled to remove him from the wagon to make room for another who could live, and be obliged to desert him at that moment forever. But orders had to be obeyed.

While the regiment was in the woods under a heavy fire, the Color Sergeant, who was a man of extraordinary size, was overcome with exhaustion from the long march, the heat, or some other cause, and fell down with them in his hand. Corporal Joseph A. Vail, of Company A, sprang over and took them from him, and bore them aloft, until ordered to give them up against his will to Sergeant Brouner.

Charles Metcalf was taken prisoner, and never again returned, but preferred to cast his lot with the traitors, and went to work in an iron foundry in Richmond.

Captains Kilpatrick and Bartlett, of Companies H and I, respectively, and their commands, won great credit for the extra duties they performed, having covered at least five miles more of ground than the rest of the companies, on account of their skirmishing duties on the front and flanks of the regiment. Captain Denike also stood bravely to his post, and being the oldest officer in the regiment, deserved equal honor for his courage during the long and tedious march, and facing unflinchingly the fire of the enemy.

It is to be regretted that Colonel Duryée or Lieutenant-Colonel Warren had not been intrusted with the command of the expedition, instead of General Pierce, who, as it appeared, had never been mustered into the United States service, and had at the time no claim to any command. Although General Pierce was much censured on account of the failure of the attack, he proved himself in after years of the war to be a brave and capable officer on many fields in Maryland, Virginia, Tennessee, and Kentucky. He enlisted as a private for three years, and by his bravery soon rose to be Colonel of a regiment, and finally was disabled by having his arm torn off by a 32-pound ball in battle.

The result showed that there was a series of mistakes from the start. And the primary cause of the failure of the expedition should rest where it belongs—on the shoulders of General Butler.* Colonel Duryée, in his official report,

---

* " Report of the Committee on the Conduct of the War" (Vol. I., p. 383), General Warren says: "I suggested to General Pierce to send a regiment on each flan ' — " he gave orders to that effect"—" to the left about half a mile could have crossed the swamp, and been masked in the woods and got behind the battery—am certain of it." "If Colonel Townsend had gone into the woods, the enemy would have been compelled, judging of what I have since learned, to have left the ground at once, or run the risk of having everything captured. He would have been masked, and they would not know where he was until he had taken the battery in the rear."
" General Pierce, as I have learned since from proceedings of court-martial, was never mustered into the service of the United States, and really had no right to com-

Big Bethel. 67

named the following officers as worthy of honorable mention:

Lieutenant-Colonel WARREN, for his aid in forming a plan of attack and remaining among the last to bring away the body of a brother officer (Lieutenant Greble), and the wounded.

Chaplain WINSLOW, for his kind attentions to the wounded.*

Captains BARTLETT, KILPATRICK, and WINSLOW, for the effective manner in which they skirmished before the enemy's fire.

Lieutenant JACOB DURYEE, who led the charge with a handful of men to within three hundred feet of the enemy's works.

Lieutenants YORK and CAMBRELLING, for their brave conduct.

Surgeon GILBERT for performing upon the field of battle successful amputations, and his unremitting care of the wounded.

Colonel Duryée also mentions Lieutenant GOUV. CARR, in command of Company B; Lieutenant GEORGE DURYEA, of Company C; Sergeants AGNUS and ONDERDONK, and Corporals ALLISON and BROUNER.

---

mand the Colonels there, and I think he felt it, though they did not know it." "I think the plan of the fight, which was got up beforehand, from the very beginning involved a failure, so much so, that I was ready to state that it was planned for a failure, and must have been one except by great good luck."

* " Report of the Committee on the Conduct of the War " (Vol. I, p. 383). General Warren says: " Greble's gun was spiked by his men, as they could not draw it off. Ten men of the 1st New York brought away the limber and his body after all that." " Rev. Dr. Winslow and myself remained on the ground, I think an hour and a half, and brought off the wounded we thought could live, every one of them ; we had to draw them off in hand-carts." " I think they left their works while we were on the ground." " We saw no one." " We went up all through the wood and were not fired at. I was dressed in this red Zouave uniform. I went down with six or seven men, about 1 P.M., and put Lieutenant Greble on the limber and went right down the road in plain sight. There was no General then at the fight at all." " The troops marched off as on parade ; the regiment left to cover the retreat went with them." " The 2d New York regiment brought off a gun."

The report says: "There was no flinching on the part of any officer or private, and I might mention many more with honor;" and concludes as follows: "In closing, I can not but speak of Colonel Townsend, of the 3d New York, who, with his whole command, stood up nobly in my support until compelled to retreat by the terrible fire.—Per order Colonel A. DURYEE; Lieutenant MALLORY, A. D. C."

An incident of an amusing character, that occurred while crossing Hampton Creek, is deemed worthy of mention. One of the Captains, with part of his command, had embarked on one of the scows at Hampton, and seeing more men crowding in than he desired, turned to the old salt who appeared to have charge of it, and who was a member of the much-abused "naval brigade," and ordered him rather peremptorily to shove off. It was as good as a play to see the indignant air of insulted authority with which the son of Neptune turned and surveyed the officer.

He straightened himself, as if he was a Commodore on his quarter-deck, and looking at the Captain from head to feet, and from feet to head, burst out with a round sailor's oath, and said: "You! Sergeant, or Corporal, or whatever you are! If you don't like the management of this 'ere craft, just heave yourself ashore—quick! I want you to understand that I am in command of this 'ere vessel!"

On Tuesday, June 11th, the men had passed through so much labor and excitement, that they were thoroughly exhausted, and were allowed to rest at will, and were excused from drill the following day. General Butler paid a compliment to Colonel Duryée and his Zouaves for the conspicuous part they took in the encounter.

The special correspondent of the New York *Tribune* furnished that journal with the following narrative of the sending in of a flag of truce:

Big Bethel.

OLD POINT COMFORT, *June* 13, 1861.

Yesterday Captain H. E. Davies, Jr.,[*] of Company C, in Colonel Duryée's regiment, made a visit with a flag of truce to Yorktown. Tuesday evening he received orders from General Butler to proceed with a flag of truce to the scene of the recent conflict, to look after the dead, wounded, and missing. Lieutenant C. H. Seaman, of Company C, and Assistant-Surgeon Martin, were detailed to accompany him. Starting early Wednesday morning, they proceeded as far as Newmarket Bridge, which they found partially destroyed, and which they repaired so as to pass over. On arriving within a mile of Big Bethel, they were stopped by a guard commanded by Captain Early,[†] of the Virginia forces. On learning the object of the visit, Captain Davies was informed that Colonel Magruder,[‡] commander of the Virginia forces, had left and gone back to Yorktown, and that it would be necessary to see him there. Although he was informed that a number of our men were in that vicinity wounded, Captain D. was not permitted to see them, but was required to proceed at once to Yorktown, twenty miles further on. An escort of four men and a Sergeant was furnished, and the party immediately set out.

They were not permitted to take the usual route; but after proceeding along the Yorktown road for a mile they struck off into the woods by a by-path, which, at frequent intervals, was defended by barricades of fallen trees and other contrivances. Pursuing this path three or four miles, they took the main road again and proceeded to Yorktown.

About half a mile outside of the fortifications at Yorktown, they were halted at a cavalry camp, where they remained till word was sent to Colonel Magruder of their arrival.

This officer soon came to where they were, and received Captain Davies and his party with politeness and consideration. Colonel Magruder, on hearing that Captain D. purposed an exchange of prisoners, and that he desired an opportunity to see the wounded, said that he would reply by letter to General Butler, but refused to allow Captain D. to visit either the wounded or prisoners, saying that as they were within his lines

---

[*] Subsequently Major-General of Cavalry.   [†] Subsequently General Early.
[‡] Subsequently General Magruder.

information might be obtained prejudicial to his intended operations.

Captain Davies remained nearly four hours at the quarters of Colonel Hill's* regiment, where he and his party were hospitably entertained.

Leaving the camp at 4 P.M., under an escort of Captain Phillips and two men, they were conducted by a different route through the woods to the vicinity of Big Bethel, and from thence by the regular route to Newmarket Bridge, which was the limit of the enemy's outposts. Captain Davies and his party then proceeded to Hampton alone, and arrived in camp near midnight.

The opinion of Captain Davies, in which those who accompanied him coincide, is that the force of the enemy on the day of the battle at Big Bethel was at least three regiments; that they were reinforced during the day; that their battery was constructed with skill and deliberation; and that the number of guns in position was at least ten, and that probably it was greater. All information concerning the killed and wounded on their side was studiously withheld from Captain Davies.†

Capt. D. was informed that those of our men who had fallen into the hands of the enemy, wounded and dead, had been properly cared for; that the wounded, two of the Fifth, as he understood, were receiving proper attention, and that the dead, of whom there were two, had been properly buried. Among these was Major Winthrop, who fell gallantly charging on the enemy. Capt. D. was given the spurs, cap, and note-book of the deceased, which, with the watch of the deceased, will be forwarded by Gen. Butler to his friends.

Capt. Davies very properly abstains from giving any opinion of the strength of the enemy at Yorktown, based on what he saw and heard, as that might be deemed an abuse of the flag of truce.

To-day a flag of truce came in from Col. Magruder, in response to the one sent out yesterday. The bearer was halted at the

---

* Subsequently General D. H. Hill; he commanded the 1st North Carolina Regiment at Big Bethel.

† In a cemetery in the city of Richmond, Va., on a little mound, may be seen a plain tablet of wood, on which is inscribed: "Here lies the body of young Wyatt, the first martyr of the war. Killed at Big Bethel, June 10, 1861."

outer pickets at Hampton, and communicated with Gen. Butler by letter, who replied in the same way.

On Wednesday, the 12th of June, at sunset, our comrade, George H. Tiebout, of Company A, was buried. His body was laid in a cemetery near Hampton. Nearly the whole regiment, with the officers, followed his remains to the grave, and paid the last tribute of respect to their departed companion in arms. All were silent and mournful, and impressed with the services in which they were engaged.

The following extract is from the last letter of the deceased to his friends, which was written on the eve of the battle in which he laid down his young life. Long before it was received by those to whom it was addressed, his brave career was ended, for he had been honorably "mustered out of the service" in dying for his country. It is as follows:

CAMP BUTLER, FORTRESS MONROE,
June, 9, 1861.

KIND FRIENDS:—I hope you will excuse my tardiness in not writing before, as I have had but very little time to spare. Between drilling and scouting, our time is pretty much taken up. I have been quite well so far. Soon after we landed, I had a bilious attack, which lasted about forty-eight hours. I have been on two scouting expeditions, but saw very little of the enemy, and none under arms. . . . . This morning Col. Duryée went through the entire regiment to find all the sailors, or those who could pull an oar. It is reported that we are to move soon—we think on Yorktown. Part go by water and part by land, so as to form a junction and surround the "bridge-burners," and take them by surprise. I see by the papers that there are a number of false reports about the food. So far, we have had plenty to eat; our food consisting of pilot bread, salt beef, pork, beans, rice, potatoes, fresh beef, bakers' bread (fresh three times a week), and coffee, with sugar in it. We have two teams to carry our supplies, and, in short, I think we are well provided for. There is one thing: we have good officers, and they look out for their men, to see that they are as comfortable as circumstances will permit. We had divine services to-day—preaching this morning and prayer-meeting this afternoon. They were very well attended.

Our regiment is called "the red-legged devils," and "the terror of evil-doers." I think I have written quite a long letter for me, and no doubt you are getting tired of this scrawl. Remember me to all the kind friends and tell them to write. Write soon, and believe me to be, as ever, your most obedient,

G. H. TIEBOUT,
Company A, 5th Regiment.

The following letter was written by a companion of the deceased:

CAMP HAMILTON, *June* 10, 1861.

FRIEND SIDNEY:—I would sooner drag a ball and chain for a month than to send this bad news to you. Before this will have reached you, you will read the account of our attacking a battery, and the pluck our boys showed in the fight. Our regiment got their orders about seven o'clock last evening to attack a battery about fifteen miles from our camp. As bad luck would have it, there was about seventy of us left behind to guard the camp while the rest of the regiment were away.

But now comes the painful part of my story. As our regiment was advancing to charge on the battery, they opened their fire on us and killed some of our boys. Among the killed was poor George Tiebout. He was shot through the heart by a canister ball as he was advancing on to the charge. The man that stood next to him, and heard his death-cry, said that he died like a man and a soldier, as he was. He was a favorite with his Captain. .... After the engagement the killed and wounded were brought back to camp in boats, landing opposite the Colonel's house. I was detailed, together with some of the guard, to carry the wounded and dead to the hospital. We had to pass through the Colonel's house to get there. As we were carrying the body of poor George through, the Colonel happened to see him, and at the sight he shed tears.

You must excuse my writing, as I am writing on a shoe-box,

by the light of a lantern. I have been on guard forty-eight hours, and I am staying on twenty-four hours longer, as our boys are all fagged out. If it be necessary we will remain on guard twenty-four hours after that. Poor George was the first martyr of our regiment, but he shall and will be avenged. Accept this from one who will fight for the Union.

ROBERT B. TALFOR,
Fortress Monroe, Co. F, 5th Regiment, N. Y. Vols.

On the 13th the Adjutant reported the strength of the regiment as follows: Present, 792; absent, officers and men, 11; sick, including the wounded, 43. Total, 846.

The regiment's loss was seven killed and sixteen wounded.

CHAPTER V.

LIFE AT CAMP HAMILTON.

FORTRESS MONROE—INCIDENTS OF CAMP LIFE—DRUMMED OUT—ANY PORT IN A STORM—SERIOUS ACCIDENT—HOW TO FIND A HORSE—CONTRABAND WIT—A GRACEFUL DIGGER—MRS. KILPATRICK—NOTES FROM THE JOURNAL—ON GUARD BY MOONLIGHT—HUTS IN THE WOODS—A FEZ STOLEN BY MOSQUITOES—A COMET—HOW WE SPENT INDEPENDENCE DAY—OUR POSTPONED CELEBRATION—A FAIRY SCENE—DONATIONS—DISCHARGES AND RECRUITS—A NEW FLAG—BEAUTIFYING THE CAMP—LOSING BLOOD—A LOST SENTINEL—REPORTS OF THE BATTLE OF BULL RUN—EMBARKING FOR BALTIMORE.

THE eventful months were rapidly moving on, while the active forces of the two great sections of the country were, with equal rapidity, determining the moral as well as the political attitude of the people, and their decision on the question of the fearful conflict that must follow, when the actual encounter of arms should take place. It became very evident that there was a division of sentiment in both sections; many of the people of the South were unalterably devoted to the Union, while a large proportion of the people of the North, governed by family relations, commercial interests, or subserviency to their party leaders, were either hostile to the Union, or desired to see the overthrow of the constitutionally elected administration, and the substitution of a partisan and revolutionary administration in its place. Whatever were the motives that animated men, it was clearly evident that the time for reason, compromise, and peace was past, and that preparations were making for a collision whose duration could not be foreseen, whose cost could not be computed, and whose consequences could only be unfolded by the actual results of the future. Various opinions were entertained by men of the highest responsibility in the Government. So astute and experienced a statesman as Senator WM. H. SEWARD, in December, 1860, in a spirit of hope and patriotic faith in the loyalty of the people of both sections, had predicted that "it would be a ninety days' wonder." Gen. WINFIELD SCOTT, a Virginian, well acquainted with the animus and the plans of the Southern leaders, quietly, but mournfully said, "It will be a five years' war." The judgment of the latter was the prediction of many of the political leaders of the North who sympathized with the movement; for it was the purpose of the Southern leaders either to effect a revolution by the aid of Northern allies, and obtain control of the Government by a short and successful war, or to prolong it through the whole four years of the administration which had been placed in power.

The days and nights were now rapidly massing up the combatants, who were putting on their armor, and from the busy walks of commerce and industry, from the field and mountain sides of every State in the Union, already three-quarters of a million of men had responded to the call to arms, and stood ready on either side of the great issue to decide the "irrepressible conflict" on the field of blood. The country was waiting for the first momentous trial on the battle-field.

We were lying near the shore of Hampton Roads, about one mile and a quarter from Fortress Monroe. It is a notable structure, and covers about seventy acres of ground. As one enters the gates the impression is that he is in a large park. You see trees and brick houses at a distance. As you advance you find large dwelling-houses for the residences of the officers, with gardens laid out, a post-office, Adams Express office, etc. Mounting the parapets, the visitor had a commanding view of Hampton Roads, with its numerous merchantmen and men-of-war lying at anchor. The Rip-Raps lie in range of the guns, where another fort was in course of erection by the Government. On the land side the white tents of the various regiments lying at Camp Hamilton were spread out, looking like toys in the distance, additions to which were constantly made. The guns were placed so as to command the points in all directions, and were numbered in large figures by their side on the wall. The fortress was surrounded by a moat about eighty feet wide, crossed by a draw-bridge, and by pulling down a wooden bridge a short distance from the main entrance, could be approached only by a narrow, low, sandy neck, about sixty feet wide, which was commanded by guns at every angle.

Camp life has its incidents as well as the march and the battle-field, and some of those which broke up the monotony of guard duty, drills, and parades were noted at the time of their occurrence. Among them is an instance of the rigor with which the determination to respect the rights of property, and the homes of the people of Virginia, was enforced. The Government and the officers of the army were equally animated with a desire to demonstrate to the people in rebellion that there was no design to do them wrong, either to their property or to their slaves, and thus exert the moral influence of law and order as a pacificator, and thereby secure their return to their allegiance. How vainly this attempt was made, the subsequent events clearly proved. In this spirit, however, on the 13th of June, the extreme penalty of disgrace was inflicted on two men belonging to a regiment from the northern part of the State, who were drummed out of camp, before the entire brigade, for committing depredations in houses in the vicinity. They each had ropes about their necks, and large boards on their backs with the word "Thief" written upon them. It was a humiliating sight.

In contrast with the severity of this occurrence there was more or less of the humorous and the comic to be enjoyed at times.

One evening after supper a drum and fife were heard playing the "Rogue's March." All hands turned out to see what was the matter, when it was discovered that some of the boys had caught one of the colored servants, tied a rope around his neck, on which was a placard, and with charged bayonets, were drumming him about camp. The men might also be heard at almost any hour of the day, singing doggerel verses of their own composition, describing their mode of life, such as, "Oh! here comes the cook along with his cracker scouse, etc., on old Virginia shore."

The men soon recovered from the fatigue of the march to Big Bethel, but naturally felt disappointed at the result, and wanted to try their fortunes over again. So far from being afraid of the enemy, they had several skirmishes, in some cases almost single-handed, while out foraging beyond Hampton, on their own responsibility. The Fifth was rapidly growing in favor with the rest of the army collected around this point. The regulars at the fortress, since the affair at Big Bethel, seemed to think there was nothing too good for our boys whenever any of them visited the fort.

Wednesday, June 19.—The experience of one of the men on guard at night may not be out of place, and as he was one of the whole military family, the reader may sympathize with him and the others of the detail, although the rest of the regiment did not fare much better on that occasion. About the time of guard mount, a tempestuous rain-storm burst upon us. The men not sent immediately on post hurried to the guard-tent, which could hold only about one-half of them, let them squeeze how they might. Our hero being left on the outside, bethought himself of the prisoners' tent, and plunged through the rain to reach it, "any port in a storm" being as good a motto for a soldier as for a sailor. Sometimes, when the prisoners are amiable, they will allow an outsider shelter in an emergency; but on this particular night they were *not* amiable, and he had no sooner entered than he was saluted with a shower of tin cups, plates, hardtack, pieces of pork, and kicks, amid cries of "Bounce him!" "Take his life!" and similar cheerful greetings. Another old proverb—" of two evils choose the least"—was forced upon him. He was not long in coming to a decision, and escaping from his assailants, there was no alternative but to stand up and endure the storm. After being nearly washed away, it stopped raining, and soon after he was sent on post, came off in due time, and partially dried himself at a fire that had been built, and was fortunate enough to find a small space unoccupied in the guard-tent, where he spread his blanket and composed himself for a comfortable rest. He was just congratulating himself on his good fortune when it again commenced to rain in torrents; the cap of the tent having blown off, the water began to come into the opening and fell on his head. Soon some of the guard began to get uneasy and to twist and turn, while some stood up. It was as dark as Egypt, but when the lightning flashed he could see them occasionally, and congratulated himself on his comparative comfort. At last his feet began to feel very cold, then his legs, and then his back. He thought it was time to see what was the matter. Reaching out his hands, he found that a small river was running under him, when he got up on his feet, and in a little time the water ran over the top of his shoes. In all these difficulties a song was started, and they relieved their discomforts by a spirited chorus, in which could be distinguished something about "hanging Jeff Davis on a sour apple tree." Such was one of the episodes in soldier life on "the sacred soil" of the Old Dominion.

The following day, Thursday, June 20th, the weather was delightful, with a fresh breeze blowing, and it was cool and comfortable. One could look over Hampton Roads, as far as Sewall's Point to the south; north were the woods; and the fortress, with its great guns, was in plain view about a mile distant. Most of the men were in good health and spirits, but grumbling somewhat about their rations—a natural thing for a soldier or sailor to do.

A serious accident happened previous to the evening parade. A member of Company G was entering his tent with his musket, which was loaded with one of the new cartridges. This cartridge consisted of three large buckshot in addition to the ball. The hammer, which was down on the cap, caught on the side of the tent, and the charge immediately went off, passing between two men who were in the tent into the next company street, one of the buck passing through the head of Orderly-Sergeant Dunham, of Company B. He was taken up insensible, and was considered to be mortally wounded, but recovered sufficiently to return to duty as Second Lieutenant some months afterward, but was ultimately obliged to resign, and received an honorable discharge. A stack of muskets were standing in front of the Orderly's tent; the buck cut through two straps, and one of them passed obliquely through the stock of one of the muskets.

One of the Captains being ambitious of having a horse to ride, sent for J. G., one of the enlisted men of his company, and told him to take his servant Tommy, an intelligent contraband, and go out into the country and find one for him. The Captain gave him particular instructions not to steal by any means, but to find one. Thus commissioned, John, in company with the faithful Tommy, being furnished with a pass, wended his way toward Hampton. On arriving there Tommy saw a group of colored gentlemen gathered together, and thought it was a very good opportunity to enlighten his down-trodden brethren as to the course they should pursue, and accordingly opened his battery on them forthwith. In the course of his speech he told them that if they wished to better their condition in life, they must make the first effort, and not leave it to others. One of them remarked, "that they put their trust in the Lord, and He would help them." "Yes," said Tommy, "but it is written in Shakespeare, that 'the Lord helps them that help themselves.'" This answer appeared to make a great impression upon the dusky audience, and they seemed to be overcome with his superior learning. Being put in mind of his errand by John, he wound up his discourse amid much applause, and they went to find *that* horse.

After traveling about the country four or five miles, they spied a fine-looking animal grazing in a field. They had provided themselves with a halter, so that all that remained to be done was to catch him, which was done in fine style by Tommy—as John was given strict instructions not to steal one, which he obeyed.

They arrived with him safely at Hampton, and across the creek, when John mounted him, having been lucky enough to "find" an old saddle also, and made very fair time back to camp. He immediately reported to his Captain, who, when he saw the animal, was very much pleased at obtaining such a prize, and at such a low price. "But where is Tommy?" asked the Captain. "Oh! he will be here in a few minutes; he preferred to walk, and so I left him on the road." "Well, take the horse down to the Quartermaster's," said the Captain, "and tell him it belongs to me." "Yes, sir," said John, which he did, and went to his quarters. Soon afterward a message was brought that the Captain wanted him. On reaching the Captain's quarters, the first thing he saw was Tommy in a sad plight, covered with mud, having from his appearance evidently been in the hands of the Philistines. He said that as he was passing by the camp of the 1st New York, some unruly members of that organization had fallen upon him, and given him a severe thumping for their own amusement, and as Tommy was a particular favorite of the Captain, John received a severe reprimand for deserting his colored comrade. The next morning the Captain went to take another look at his stallion, and examine his fine points more closely, but great was his astonishment and chagrin to find that he had disappeared, and no one could tell how he got away, or where he had gone to; but it was suspected that our great practical joker, the Adjutant, had specific information of the merits of the case.

Tommy, who was an unusually sharp specimen of his class, kindly offered to take care of the Captain's watch, which he had always greatly admired. Just before the Big Bethel fight, perhaps—we will not say for certain—it entered into his head that possibly he might fall heir to it. One day the Captain threatened to strike him for some misdemeanor, when he looked at him very innocently, and said, "Massa, you told me the other day that all men were brudders." "Yes," replied the Captain, "but what if I did?" "Nuffin," replied Tommy, "only you wouldn't strike your brudder, would yer?" His wit saved him on that occasion at least.

The weather was now very hot. Guard duty was assigned about twice every week to each man, and the regiments took their turn on picket duty, which the men enjoyed. The outpost was about six miles from camp.

On the 22d of June, a part of the regiment were occupied in commencing the building of batteries near Hampton, which did not indicate an early advance against the enemy. This earthwork was the first one thrown up in the war, in the path to Richmond on the Peninsula. It was the initiation to the months of labor subsequently expended during McClellan's and Grant's campaigns. The following extract in reference to it, from the Brooklyn *Daily Times*, is of interest:

HAMPTON, VA., *June* 23, 1861.

After the plans were laid out, a squad of Duryée's Zouaves came from camp to help dig the trenches. The Zouaves were placed in proper order, viz.: Four men with shovels, forming a square, and a man in the center with a pick. The first shovelful of earth was dug by the wife of Captain Kilpatrick, of Duryée's Zouaves, who distinguished himself at the battle of Big

Bethel; after which the squad gave three hearty cheers by order of their Colonel, and went to work like good fellows. Colonel Duryée's regiment are, without exception, the best set of fighting men stationed hereabouts.

The notes made in the author's journal, for a short period, will give the reader a pretty accurate view of our experiences and expectation while at Camp Hamilton. They are as follows:

Sunday, June 23.—There is a rumor that the regiment will be ordered to Washington, but little faith is placed in it. Several men were sworn into the service yesterday, but there were eight who refused, having had enough of soldiering during the few days they were here. Such fellows are not wanted in the Fifth, and the sooner all that kind forsake us, the better will it be for us and them.

The Home Defense Committee have sent two hundred rifles, and it is said all the regiment are to be supplied with them.

At a meeting of officers, the Fifth was assigned to the right of the brigade, Colonel Townsend's 3d New York next in line.

Last night was magnificent—just such as a soldier loves. The moon was full, and it was almost as light as day. Perfect silence prevailed; in fact, so still was it, that one could hear the sentinels tread at a distance of four hundred feet, and the cry of "*All is well,*" on the vessels of the fleet, lying two miles away. It was the time for the sentry pacing his lonely beat, to commune with his own soul, to think of home and friends, and all that were dear to him, or perhaps longing that some favorite and loved one could be by his side. And yet to so many these were the enchanted dreams of the absent, none of whom he ever saw again. Such a night—to many a true and reverent hero was the time when he could look up to the placid moon and the radiant stars, and have his soul filled with glorious and holy thoughts of the world beyond, where the conflict of earth would at length be ended, and he should wear the conqueror's crown forever.

Thursday, June 27.—Regiment has been on picket about two miles from camp, in the woods, the reserve being stationed on a road. They constructed beautiful little huts with rails from the fences, and small trees and boughs, which formed very picturesque residences, and were hardly distinguishable from the forest surroundings. The round extended about one and a half miles in a thick forest of pine and oak. All was quiet except the different notes of the winged songsters, or the dropping of some small twig, which was duly noticed, the possibility that some lurking enemy might be near compelling constant vigilance. Above our embowered huts, rose the giant pines, some of them eighty or ninety feet in height. The men were on post four hours, and eight off.

When night came on it was somewhat dreary, but relieved by the mosquitoes, which were truly formidable. They swarmed in black clouds everywhere, and one of the boys that missed his fez cap in the morning, swore that the mosquitoes had taken it off, so that they could have more room to bite.

Friday, June 28.—Last night another of our Virginia torrents visited the camp, and flooded all the tents as usual, in some places the water being a foot deep.

Sunday, June 30.—A damp, disagreeable day; regiment again on picket duty; and Private Rouse, of Company G, accidentally shot himself through the hand. We lead a very active life, as we have done ever since the regiment was first organized, and have little time to ourselves. It is company, regimental, or brigade drills, inspections, dress parades, reviews, ditching, policing camp, picket and camp guard. Beside these activities, which keep our blood from stagnating, we have some howitzers and a brass piece, which we have been taught to handle, to which must be added the washing and mending of our clothes, and keeping our arms and equipments free from rust and tarnish. All these duties leave little time to play, but it is schooling a body of hardy, reliable, well-informed men, the stuff that veterans are made of, into what will be the best-drilled and most perfectly disciplined volunteer corps in the service.

It is astonishing how so many men can live in such a small space. The tents are about eight by ten feet; yet in these eight or nine men sleep, in addition to the stowing of knapsacks, haversacks, canteens, and accoutrements, with accommodations for an occasional visitor. Two Companies, I and E, have been presented with Sharp's rifles and sabre bayonet, but they will be obliged to do most of the skirmishing. Yesterday the regiment was inspected by a United States officer, and mustered in for two months' pay.

Wednesday, July 3.—All quiet, and we see and hear nothing of the enemy; details of men are building batteries beyond Hampton, and near the Ladies' Seminary on the banks of James River. To-day another regiment left for Newport News, leaving only four here, beside the garrison at the fort. To-morrow being the anniversary of our Independence, we would like to have a holiday, but there is no such thing in the code; in fact, we would hardly know when Sunday comes around, were it not from the inspection in the forenoon instead of a drill, and a dose of the Articles of War, which are read with due solemnity. The officers are more exacting every day, and the discipline is getting the men down to a "fine point."

Last night a large comet was in view. Toward morning it stretched half-way over the heavens. The men hope it is a harbinger of success to our cause. Just as the Sergeants were calling the roll, a bright light was seen on the bay, which proved to be the illumination from the steamboat *Cataline*, which was burned to the water's edge.

A little incident will serve to show the dry humor of the

Adjutant, from which may also be inferred some of the reasons why he is so well liked by the men. On an extremely warm day, the mercury being above the nineties, and the sun's rays fiercely hot, the writer was guarding some prisoners who were clearing up the ground about the Adjutant's quarters. Suddenly he heard a manly voice call out, "Young man, with auburn hair! come hither!" My head-gear not answering that description, I naturally looked at the prisoners to see if any of them had auburn hair, but not being able to discover any one, I turned in the direction whence the voice came, and saw the giant form of the Adjutant standing at the doorway of his tent. He was looking directly at me, and also motioning with his hand; seeing that he had attracted my attention, he gave the order, "Shoulder arms! March!" which I did, wondering what it all meant. "Right oblique! Halt!" and I found myself under the grateful shade of a large tree. Now, sentry," said he, "your orders are to stay under that tree, and watch these prisoners, and mind you that my orders are strictly obeyed," and immediately vanished into his tent.

Thursday, July 4.—Reveille just before sunrise, and a salute of thirty-four guns from the brass pieces in honor of the day. Three bunches of fire-crackers were set off, with all due ceremony, by one of the men. Being Independence Day, the powers that be had the independence to order the regiment out on picket, and they went. The men were called up every fifteen minutes after midnight, an attack being expected. They fell in with their rifles, the roll was called, when they turned in again, being consequently cheated out of their sleep, which occasioned some quiet grumbling.

Friday, July 5.—This morning we were relieved from picket duty and marched back to camp. In the afternoon the whole brigade, including Col. Baker's California regiment, which arrived yesterday, was reviewed by Secretary of War Cameron, Adj't-Gen. Thomas, and Gen. Butler and staff.

Professor Bartlett, of West Point, father of Capt. Bartlett, of Co. I, 5th New York, was present.

On returning to camp, it was nightfall, and the postponed celebration of the Fourth commenced with an illumination of the company streets, by placing bits of candles and pine-knots in the trees transplanted from the woods and set out in front of the tents. This made it look like a fairy scene. And now and then the distant shouts of the men—for the camp extends about 500 feet—announced that everybody was participating in the enjoyment except the solitary sentinels, who were pacing their lonely beats. On the color-line a fine display of fireworks, contributed by the munificence of the officers, fizzed away for an hour and added to the effect of the scene. At the head of each company street, immense bonfires were built, around which the "red devils" danced, sung, and yelled like so many Comanche Indians, and in their red breeches, looked, in fact, like so many red devils in Pandemonium. But it was all the exuberance of pure animal spirit, for not a drop of liquor was tasted, nor could it be had if desired. The different companies vied with each other in getting up the greatest and tallest blaze, and the most indefatigable exertions were made in the way of supplying fuel to attain this object. The palm of victory was finally awarded to Company G, many members of which were of the New York Volunteer Fire Department, who thus showed that they knew how to make "a big blaze," as well as to put one out. The scene defies description; the victors were joined by men from other companies in their dance of triumph around the huge burning pile, and such was the wild enthusiasm that if any of the celebrated Indian chiefs, from Osceola to the famous Sitting Bull himself, had been present, they would have dropped their dignity and joined in the excitement. It was a scene long to be remembered by those who shared in the festivities. Taps were delayed one hour, in order that the men might prolong their enjoyment.

Later in the night the officers had their own carnival. Three of the largest tents in camp were joined together, to form one marquee, in which were assembled the officers of the regiment, at the invitation of Col. Duryée, and as invited guests, Col. Townsend, of the 3d New York, and others. Speeches and toasts were in order, and Col. Duryée, Adjt. Hamblin, Capt. Hull, and other orators were heard from. Capts. Catlin, Cooper, and Smith, of the Third, made humorous and patriotic speeches. The music, which was supplied by the band of the 3d New York, added to the pleasure of the occasion. A bountiful collation was provided, and the festivities were prolonged until near morning. It lacked only one feature that would have completed the charm of the occasion—the presence of some of the far-distant women who were dreaming of us at home.

Saturday, July 20.—The Mechanics' and Traders' Fire Insurance Company have presented to Capt. Denike, of Co. G, $100, to be distributed among the men of his company, or for the purchase of any articles they might desire. A number of the men are obtaining their discharges on account of sickness, wounds, etc., camp life beginning to tell already, even on comparatively strong constitutions. Capt. Kilpatrick arrived to-day with a hundred new recruits, who look like a good body of men, although pale and sickly, alongside of those who are bronzed by service and exposure. The ladies of New York have kindly sent a supply of Havelocks for the whole regiment, which reminds the men that, although far away, they are not forgotten by the fair ones at home.

Col. Duryée, being Acting Brigadier and in command of this camp, the duty of drilling the battalion has devolved upon Lieut.-Col. Warren, who handles the regiment in a scientific manner. In field maneuvers the men are taught movements and tactics they never dreamed of before, and were never performed by the militia at home. He is very rigid with the officers, and requires them to know their duties thoroughly, and make no mistakes. The non-commissioned officers are also obliged to learn a lesson every day, and appear before Capt. Kilpatrick and recite it.

The regiment was reviewed on Monday by Mr. Russell, the famous war correspondent of the London *Times*. The regiment has received a beautiful stand of colors, which was the gift of some admiring ladies of New York. The following account is from one of the New York journals:

PRESENTATION OF A STAND OF COLORS TO COLONEL DURYÉE'S ZOUAVES.

"A beautiful stand of colors was presented on Tuesday, July 16, 1861, at Clinton Hall, to the Fifth Regiment, New York State Volunteers, commonly known as Col. Duryée's Zouaves.

"The Colonel being now stationed at Fortress Monroe, the flag was received by about 100 Zouaves recently recruited, who are about to join the regiment, and will have the distinction of presenting it to their commanding officer. The flag is a very handsome American ensign, of the regulation size and pattern, but distinguished by a scroll over the stars bearing the inscription, 'Above us or around us.' In lieu of the ordinary spear or eagle, the staff was surmounted with a fez surrounded by two folds of a turban (the regular head-dress of the Zouave), the latter in silver. The streamers (red and blue) were also inscribed with characteristic mottoes—the one, '*Fidele a Poutrance*'—the other, from the song of the Zouave, '*Ils possedent une baguette magique.*' The white streamer bore the inscription, ' Presented to the Fifth Regiment, New York State Volunteers, through Company H, July 16, 1861.' The flag was presented on the part of the ladies by Mr. Pyne, who alluded in a short address to the outrages our flag had sustained in the Southern seceding States, and the possibility that it might be the privilege of the Zouaves to redress them. Capt. Kilpatrick received the flag on the part of Company H, and subsequently presented it to Major Davies, as the representative of the regiment. 'The Star Spangled Banner' was then performed by the band, and the flag marched out into Astor

Place, where the company awaited the appearance of the ladies, and lowered the flag as they passed, by way of salute."

It is comparatively quiet in camp, but the men are not idle, being kept constantly employed at something when not on picket, camp guard, or drilling. They have much improved the appearance and comfort of the camp; have dug down the spaces between the rows of tents, or company streets, to about a foot in depth, and rounded and graded them off, cutting ditches on each side, which leave the tents on an elevation, so that when the heavy rains occur, they are not flooded as formerly. The company streets are kept scrupulously clean, it being one of the first duties in the morning for a detail of men to sweep them thoroughly, with brooms improvised from branches of trees. Capt. Denike is sick. The men hope that he will not be obliged to leave them, as he is one of the most patriotic officers in the regiment. The men lately have had some furious night skirmishes, and lost much blood, not, however, in fighting a human enemy, but (what is worse) in combating mosquitoes. It was reported the other night that they had carried off one of the men on guard, as he was not found for some time afterward. A search was made for him, expecting to find his bones clean picked, and his fez cap which they wanted to send home as a memento to his mother; but the lost was found at last, with his head in his haversack and a tremendous branch of a tree in each hand, belaying right and left, as if he was thrashing wheat.

Tuesday, July 23.—An important movement, which was expected to have been made by all the troops here, has been prevented by the news of the disastrous battle of Bull Run.

Thursday, July 25.—The regiment ordered to be ready to move in heavy marching order, and the men all very anxious to know their destination, with all kinds of rumors floating about camp. But this uncertainty was solved by the orders on the 26th to march to the Government wharf at Fortress Monroe, and embark on board of the steamer *Adelaide* for Baltimore, which was accomplished by 11.30 P.M.

Thus ended the first campaign of the Fifth in Virginia.

To sum up : If their sojourn there has not resulted in any brilliant success of arms to the Union cause, it has been of vast benefit in hardening, disciplining, and bringing the regiment up to such an efficient standard as to fit it eventually for greater and sterner trials.

CHAPTER VI.

LIFE AT BALTIMORE.

Arrival at Baltimore—Camp at Federal Hill—Zouaves at Large—Penalties for Pastimes—Making a Camp—Visitors—A Baltimore Journal Speaks—Running Guard—Joe Knott—Changes in the Regiment—A Revolt Subdued—The Guard-house and its Adventures—An Illumination—A Charge—Fort-Building—Rebel Recruits Disappointed—Our Bathing Ground—The Battle at the Pump—Camp Ballads of the Fifth—Colonel Duryee Promoted—An Unsuccessful Trip—Changes in the Regiment—Progress of the Fort—How the Days were Spent—Captain Hamblin's Departure—Regimental Dogs—A Loyal Newfoundland—Zouave Song by a Drummer Boy—Maggie Mitchel—Blowing out the Lights—A Drum-Major's Joke—An Expedition—Building the Barracks—Thanksgiving Day—An Elopement.

We arrived at Baltimore about 4 o'clock in the afternoon of Saturday, the 27th day of July, after a very pleasant sail up Chesapeake Bay, without anything of note occurring on the trip.

We marched through the streets under the wondering gaze of the citizens. It was evidently a novel sight, for the uniforms of the men were unlike anything they had ever before seen, and were stained and torn, from their previous camp life and service in the field. The regiment finally halted on Federal Hill, a commanding position within the suburbs of the city, and near the harbor around which the city is built. It completely commanded the city and vicinity, while the country beyond could be seen for a great distance, and the Peninsula on which Fort McHenry raises its time-honored walls was in plain sight. We could well understand from our position the emotions of the author of the "Star Spangled Banner," when he saw the old flag floating from its walls, after the fearful bombardment of the preceding night.

In fact, with artillery posted here, Baltimore itself could be laid in ashes, should occasion require it. It is almost inaccessible on two of its sides, and the exposed part could be easily defended by a body of determined men.

On the second day after our arrival, four companies were ordered to march to the New York and Philadelphia Depot to quell a riot. The mob dispersed before they arrived on the ground, having been informed of their approach.

The men were immediately employed in getting everything in order about the camp. It was at first supposed that we should make a halt of only a few days, and then proceed to Washington and report to General McClellan. But we were disappointed, for when the Colonel reported to General Dix, who had command of the district, he was ordered to encamp the regiment at this place, and remain until further orders; and, from all that was apparent to us, it looked as if we should remain for some time. The weather was extremely warm; there were neither trees nor any other shelter from the burning rays of the sun, except the slight protection of the tents. We felt it oppressively, but at times a refreshing sea breeze afforded great relief. Passes were given occasionally, so that men could visit the city, but only for two hours; and the men looked so shabby, some of their uniforms being almost worthless, they were ashamed to make their appearance in a civilized community.

The first night of our arrival some of the men rushed for the city, before a guard could be established. They were not only anxious to see the city itself, but to have a little unbending from the seclusion and rigidity of camp life. Some of them soon found they were in "secesh" districts, and made themselves masters of the situation. They would not allow anybody to walk on the sidewalks except themselves. The citizens either had to turn back, take the middle of the street, or be knocked down, and they cleaned out one or two bar-rooms kept by bitter secessionists. One of them got into a famous secession hotel, mounted a table, and gave vent to his Union sentiments in a speech. We wondered he was not shot. Some came back in the morning and were put in the guard-house; others stayed away for two or three days, were arrested, put in the guard-house, broke out again, and were away, and for a few days the camp was greatly demoralized; but soon all was quiet again, and the men were kept as close as if they were prisoners of war. Some were employed at hard labor, digging and making streets in the hot sun, and some of the most refractory were tied up for eight hours at a time, bound hand and foot, and suffered various punishments.

In a short time the regiment completed a fine-looking camp. At the head of each company street, they worked out of sod and clay of different colors the Goddess of Liberty, spread eagles, flags, etc., which had a very fine effect, and were much admired by the many visitors who daily came to inspect our camp. Our evening parades were usually witnessed by large numbers of citizens. One of the Baltimore papers spoke as follows :

"THE EVENING PARADE OF THE DURYÉE ZOUAVES.—There were not less than 2,000 ladies and gentlemen present on Saturday afternoon to witness the usual parade and drill of Colonel Duryée's Zouave regiment. The regiment drilled on Warren and other streets, and judging from the movements of the soldiers, they have paid strict attention to the lessons given them by their instructors. The drilling, as far as we could judge, was equal, if not superior, to any regiment which has pitched their tents near the city. The drilling for quelling riots was superb, and woe be to the secesshers, if they dare attempt another Pratt Street affair. Col. Duryée may well be proud of his gallant boys.

"In a few days the soldiers will be supplied with new uniforms, and it would be a great treat for our citizens to see the Zoo-Zoos making a full-dress parade through our streets. The masses then could see if we have been right or wrong in our conjectures concerning the efficiency of the Zouaves.

"We noticed, on Saturday last, that the Chaplain of the regiment, Rev. Dr. Winslow, was riding a splendid charger. We were informed that the animal was captured by four of the Zouaves while at Fortress Monroe. The Zouaves had been out on a private scout, and observing a rebel Captain seated upon the charger, the Zoo-Zoos surrounded him and made prisoners of both."

The Zouaves soon became great favorites with the ladies, who found that the majority could conduct themselves with as much propriety as other gentlemen, anywhere; and it was a common sight to see a well-dressed lady escorted through the camp by a Zouave, and conversing as if they had been old acquaintances.

It was a common remark, that every woman who came into camp was perfectly beautiful; but whether or no this be true, they must have appeared to be, for after seeing nothing but "colored ladies" for two months, the contrast was the more apparent. The officers were also becoming great favorites, and their acquaintance was rapidly extended among the best society in the city.

Whatever may have been the cause, a few weeks served to develop a great deal of dissatisfaction in the regiment. The discipline was rigid in camp, while outside of it lay a great city, with all its attractions and temptations, and the young men were free from the restraining presence of parents or relatives, or any one whose influence would be sensibly recognized, and it need not be a matter of surprise that some among them could not resist the opportunity to mingle in the social life of the city, even though they run the guard, or set authority at defiance. They liked the excitement, and the greater the risk, the greater became the incentive to outwit the guard and its officers. Sometimes men went out in a blinding storm of rain, and came in again, running the equal risk of capture in getting in as of going out, just for the adventure. The officers exercised all their ingenuity to keep the men within the lines, but notwithstanding a strong guard of one hundred men, on duty night and day, besides the provost guard, who patrolled the city, perhaps thirty or forty men would steal out at night after taps, and slip into camp again in the morning before reveille. By this course, as they did not miss a roll call, they escaped punishment, and nobody was the wiser. But the number of habitual guard-runners was comparatively few, compared to the whole number of men in the regiment. Of course all did not succeed without detection, and when any were discovered and arrested, their punishment was not light. Even the risk of being shot as a penalty did not seem to deter any of them when they had decided to go. The officers endeavored to discover where the weak places were by disguising themselves as privates; but the plan failed, for they were received with the most energetic and decisive challenge, by the innocent sentries. They hid themselves and watched from obscure and dark places, but they saw no one prowling about, made no captures, were not enlightened, and were left at their wits' ends.

It is all over now, and having no fear of the guardhouse before our eyes, or the contempt and execration of comrades, it will do no harm to explain. There was a tie among the men which led them to assist each other, and stand together, in their sympathies and interests. There were many among them who would as soon think of cutting their right arm off as to run guard themselves, or to permit anybody else to do so while on their beat, from a strict sense of military duty. But what transpired on the next post was none of their concern. If one of them was questioned by an officer, he never saw or knew anything that transpired on his neighbor's post. Very likely he did not; for if he suspected that anything irregular was going on, he promptly turned his back and intently looked another way. Then there were others, and good men too, who, in an enemy's country, were always foremost at the post of danger; on picket were alive and alert, and all that a good soldier should be, who, in such a camp as Federal Hill, would themselves run guard and also connive in the escape of others. In extreme cases, men passed out at the main sally-port of the fort, and in plain view of the officer of the day, by putting on a bold air, and giving the Sergeant at the gateway a slip of paper that looked like a pass, which he would pretend to scrutinize very closely, and then let him pass out. This, however, as I have said, was an extreme case. But to describe all the devices to get out of camp, which were many, would overtax the interest of the reader.

The men knew who they could trust, and some, who were a burden to the regiment, would be favored in their efforts by only a few. These generally took rough chances to get out, and sometimes made a bold rush for their liberty, trusting to their fleetness of foot, and running the risk of being fired at by a sentry. In all the guard-running during the protracted stay of the regiment in Camp Federal Hill and Fort Marshall, there was but one case in which a man was mean enough to betray a confederate. Out of all that suffered martyrdom in the guard-house, ball and chain, loss of pay, etc., by court-martial, only one proved treacherous to his comrades, and for the same offense he was himself thrust into confinement with ball and chain for thirty days. When he was released, he was shunned by all, and his life became so burdensome that he was actually driven to desertion. Above all things, soldiers despise a mean action among comrades. A regiment of men is like a large family—their interests are the same; they rely each one on the honor of the other for effectiveness and mutual protection; their obligations are reciprocal, and the tie is therefore very strong between them. They have no bolts and bars to lock up their slender effects; and when one happens to have a larger share of worldly goods than another, he cheerfully shares it with his messmates or anybody else who needs his help. They all know the penalties of infringing a military rule, and when they break one, do so with their eyes open, and, if caught, are satisfied to suffer the penalty; but they hate to be betrayed by one of their own number.

Who that was in Fort Federal Hill does not remember Joe Knott? He was on one of the favorite guard-running points one night when the officer of the guard was startled by hearing a shot, followed by a loud call for the Corporal of the Guard, No. —. The officer, Sergeant, and all that could be spared rushed frantically to Joe's post, when they were accosted with, "There they go! over in the ship-yard!" Down the declivity rushed the officer, sword in hand, followed by his men. They procured a lantern, and hunted and searched, but found no one. The truth of the matter was that Joe had let out about a dozen some ten minutes previously, when it occurred to him that he would have a sensation. He accordingly fired off his piece in the air and thus raised the alarm. He told the officer that while his back was toward camp, two men rushed by him like lightning, and he fired at them, and thought that he must have hit one of them, because he heard a voice cry out, "Oh!" The result of this vigilance on the part of Joe was different from what he expected; for after that, until he was laid up in the hospital, nobody could have that post, when he was on guard, but the faithful Joe.

It has already been mentioned that there was an undertone of dissatisfaction among the men, kept up by certain turbulent spirits, such as abound in all organizations, and it looked as if a storm was coming.

There was, in the first place, a slight misunderstanding between the two and three years' men, and they all wanted their pay, three months or more being due. Some of their families were suffering for the means to live, their only support being taken from them. Moreover, all of the regiments lying in the neighborhood of the city had been paid some weeks before, and the men were possessed with the erroneous idea that their pay was kept back by design of their commanding officer. On the contrary, he was using his utmost endeavors and influence with Gen. Dix to have the men paid. The great majority of the men were anxious to get hold of it in order to spend it while in the city. Some of the Captains and Lieutenants had been promoted to higher grades in other regiments. Capt. Bartlett received an appointment in the regular service; Major J. M. Davies, the Colonelcy of the 2d New York Cavalry; Capt. Kilpatrick, Lieut.-Colonel; Capt. H. E. Davies, Jr., Major in the same, and Capt. Swartwout had been appointed 1st Lieutenant in the 17th U. S. Infantry. Of course they left, being all first-class officers, and consequently the regiment was not in the best state of organization at the time. The uneasy feeling in the regiment at last culminated in an outbreak, which, however, was as short-lived as it was violent. The Captain of Co. E, (W.), who resigned on the 9th inst., which company was on the left of the line, made a visit to his old company. He was somewhat under the influence of liquor, and not on the best of terms with the Colonel. He made some remarks to his old command, and was cheered by the men. The Colonel approached him and ordered him out of camp. There was a little scene, but he obeyed. In the evening the men began to make a great deal of noise. Suddenly some one cried out, "*Clothes, money, or New York.*" It had an electrical effect, and the cry was taken up along the whole line throughout the camp. The officers looked distressed and anxious. The Colonel made some remarks, which the men listened to attentively, when the men of Co. E, and some others, cried out, "Three cheers for our old Captain," and "Three groans for his enemies." This made the excitement more intense. At this stage of the proceedings, Adjutant Hamblin, who was very much beloved by the whole regiment, and had not an enemy in the ranks, went through the different companies, and said that the Paymaster had gone to New York to get his drafts cashed, as there were no Government funds in Baltimore at the present time; and that requisitions had been made for clothing, all of which they should have as soon as possible. He pointed to his own uniform, and said that he needed a new one, but was willing to wait, as he knew the authorities were hard pressed with business, fitting out so many new regiments. This quieted the storm, and this slight unbending from the customary martinetism satisfied the men, and they quietly dispersed to their respective quarters. This affair was one of those sudden outbursts that will sometimes occur, in even the best regulated assemblages; it was all on the surface, and not the effect of a premeditated design; and when the excitement had abated, the men were all heartily ashamed that they had allowed themselves to be betrayed into such an exhibition of their feelings.

The next day the Paymaster opportunely arrived, and paid the men up to July 1st, with the promise to pay again on September 3d, or thereabouts. We had two drills daily, one in the morning, company drill for three hours, and a battalion drill in the afternoon with knapsacks, which were packed with all our extra clothing; overcoats, with blankets and ponchos rolled; after which we marched for an hour through the streets of the city, which were thronged with people, who showed a great deal of respect, either through fear or patriotism. In some localities we were greeted with cheers and the waving of handkerchiefs.

Baltimore was all right as long as the Zouaves commanded the Hill. At least this was the theory of the Unionist journals. It was divided into sections of Unionists and Secessionists. In the latter localities the feeling was intense against the Government, and even the little children cried out cheers for "Jeff. Davis" when a soldier happened to pass them. The ladies drew their skirts closer for fear of being contaminated, by the mere touching of their dress by a Yankee. In other sections, where the people loved the old flag, it was seen flying everywhere, and the Zouaves were often invited into handsome residences and offered refreshment, and were cheered by words of sympathy for the Union cause.

On August 19th, the regiment had been recruited up to 1,046 men, and five of the ten Captains had resigned, which made opportunity for promotions. The regiment was now drilled in street-firing almost daily by Col. Duryée, who had no superior in these tactics, and the men were very proficient in the exercise. (Col. Duryée was the author of several treatises on street-fighting. The latter was adopted by the New York State Legislature in the fall of 1857).

On Wednesday, the 21st of August, the Fifth was reviewed and inspected by Gen. Dix, and marched through part of the city with him, presenting a fine and soldierly appearance. Preparations were going forward for building a strong fort on this hill, which would undoubtedly serve to keep the men from demoralization by the *ennui* of camp life. But the prime object of erecting a strong work on the hill was prudential, as it would serve to overawe the secessionists in the city, and prevent them from attempting an uprising in conjunction with any attack that might be made by the enemy, if our arms should meet with a reverse; and also as a defense to the city itself in connection with the other forts.

The officers are determined to keep the men from running guard—the military vice of a city camp—or at least from staying out two or three days at a time. Handcuffs and the chain and ball were resorted to, but the officers found they had an erratic set of men to handle. But the majority of the guard-runners proved to be among the most efficient, and amenable to discipline when in active service in the field. One of them was asked by the Colonel, why he ran the guard, to which he replied that he could not resist the temp-

Life at Baltimore.

tations of the city while they were in plain view of it; "He enlisted to fight the enemy, and not to be cooped up in a fort."

The guard-house was a long, low building, formerly used as a bowling-alley. It was situated on the northern part of the hill, or bluff rather, for on this side it is almost perpendicular, more than one hundred feet. The other side is the parade-ground. The entrance was on the west end of the building, and there were windows in the side looking to the parade-ground and camp, which were barred with thick timber. Sentries were also stationed along that side. Toward the bluff there were no openings in the building, and consequently no sentries. On that side several men escaped who carried balls and chain, with the collusion of the other prisoners. They knocked a hole in the wall with the balls, while the others sung and talked loudly, so that the noise of the pounding was not heard, filed their irons, crawled out, and in some way found a path down the steep bluff.

The officer of the guard, and the guard reserve, had their quarters at the west end, and the prisoners generally harbored at the opposite extremity, but roamed up and down at will, to within a certain boundary at the west end. One day they purloined a lot of candles that happened to be too near their boundary-line. The prize lay in a box for the use of the guard. They were cut up into halves and quarters; and at night, when the officer in charge had gone to supper, each prisoner having his post allotted to him, placed them in rows each side of the long alley, and on a given signal, when they thought it was about time for the officer to return from supper, they were simultaneously lighted. It is easy to imagine the look of astonishment on the officer's countenance as he entered and saw the illumination, while the prisoners were all sitting in a very orderly manner at the other end of the building, singing, " Hail to the chief!" Sometimes they sang so loudly, the Colonel threatened to fire into them to make them desist. On one occasion the prisoners watched their opportunity when the guard was laying off, except the sentry on duty at the entrance, and at the order, "*Charge,*" all rushed yelling down the alley, as if to force their way out. The guard jumped up in a hurry, seized their muskets, and charged bayonets, when their leader called out, "*Retreat,*" and the reprobates scampered back to their quarters.

We had one man who defied all restraint when he wanted to go. The boys gave him the name of "Jack Sheppard." The last time he escaped, he was ornamented with bracelets to the extent of two pairs of handcuffs; a chain and ball were pendant from a leg, the chain being gracefully looped to the handcuffs. He told the officer of the guard that by 10 o'clock at night he would be free, a prediction which was taken as braggadocio. But he kept his word—at the time specified he was gone.

On Saturday, the 24th of August, active work was begun on the works to be built on the hill, under the superintendence of Col. Brewerton, of the U. S. Engineers, assisted by Lieut.-Col. Warren. Men were also detailed from the regiment to make drawings and profiles.

Captain Hiram Duryea, with a detail of forty men, had been sent out on duty on the 21st, and returned on the 24th. They had been to Point Lookout, at the mouth of the Potomac, St. Mary's County, where most of the inhabitants were bitter secessionists. It was learned that under pretense of having an excursion down the bay, some of the rebel element of Baltimore intended to carry down a body of recruits for the Confederate army, in the steamboat *Hugh Jenkins;* and at the same time to deliver the steamer over to the Confederates. The detail of the Fifth went aboard just before she sailed; after landing the passengers at Point Lookout, she steamed off the shore about one and a half miles and anchored. During the night they were approached by several suspicious-looking boats, but they were ordered off; and a steamer, supposed to be the *St. Nicholas,* which was seized by the Confederates some time previously, came over from the Virginia shore and displayed signal-lights of a suspicious character, but receiving no answer, put back. There could be no doubt that the rebel plans were thwarted in every way, in consequence of the presence of the Zouaves on board, and the reinforcement of the Confederate army was postponed. The *Hugh Jenkins* had a large share of patriotic interest taken in her good management after that date.

An agreeable change was made in the entire police guard regulations on the 28th, by which duty of the camp was to be performed by a single company in turn, instead of by details from each, as had previously been the practice.

Our regiment enjoyed a great advantage in having a very convenient and attractive bathing place, in the Patapsco, which was the source of much pleasure and delight to the men. The water was clear as crystal, flowing over a smooth sandy beach, and was the scene of uproarious mirth, as the different groups, under charge of non-commissioned officers, disrobed and plunged into the waves. Their games and races on the beach were invigorating, while the physique of many of them reminded one of the gladiators of old. This secluded spot was the scene of many a tough mill in the ring, fought according to the rules of the code, in a fair stand-up fight, to settle some rivalry or grudge that had been engendered in camp. A pass was never refused for such a purpose, but fighting about camp was strictly prohibited.

On one occasion, however, Colonel Warren permitted a little brush. It happened in this way: One day as he was passing by the pump, he saw two of the men wrangling as to who was entitled to fill his pail first, and he stopped and told them, if they couldn't agree, to put down their pails and fight it out. They accordingly, without any further words, clinched. In the course of the fight, the larger one attempted to take an unfair advantage of his opponent, when the Colonel, as umpire, interfered, and put him into the guard-house. Such little incidents tended to make him popular with the men, notwithstanding the strict discipline he always maintained in the path of duty, for as a body they liked fair play.

While on this subject the memorable battle between "Butch" Myers and H. may be mentioned. The former, some of my readers will remember, was not a very heavy or large man, was always quiet, a good friend, and well liked; H. was considerably taller and heavier, besides being a professed fighter. One day, by appointment with their seconds and a few friends, duly armed with passes, ostensibly to take a bath in the Patapsco, they sauntered out of camp, and near the beach, in a selected spot, fought for an hour and a half, the battle resulting in a victory for "Butch." His opponent had the most science, but could not conquer over the indomitable game of "Butch," and was obliged to throw up the sponge. They were both terribly bruised, but the conqueror was punished the most; his features were not recognizable to his most intimate associates, and he was obliged to lay up in "ordinary" for some days, by permission of the surgeon.

These and other similar incidents were only the by-play to the more earnest work of the pick and shovel, in which the men were obliged to take their part on the works which were being built. Each man's turn came every three days; it was hard work, as the great majority were not accustomed to it. The hours were from 7 A.M. until a few minutes before 6 P.M., omitting the usual dinner hour. After the day's work was over, the men were obliged to clean up and dress for evening parade. The clay soil was very hard and heavy to dig in some places, especially as there had been considerable rain, and the laboring forces were obliged to stand in mud and water ankle deep. Nevertheless they took it good-naturedly, and considered it all in the line of duty. As the different squads assembled to get their implements of labor, and before the word "Attention" was given, they had a great deal of amusement among themselves, by giving absurd orders, such as, "Right shoulder shift—Arms!" "Fix—pick-axes!" "Secure—spades!" Others would inquire very soberly what *ground* there was for such *grave* proceedings, when some one would answer, that "it was owing to *fort*-uitous circumstances. When the different squads passed each other on their way to work, they would salute one another after the manner of the New York firemen, with a "Hi—hi—hi!" The author has been favored with the following note by MIRON WINSLOW, of Company E:

"The occupation of Baltimore by the Federal troops, in the years 1861-2, was not, for the 5th New York at least, a mere idle or unlaborious task—a mere dwelling in barrack with no duties but those of drill parade and guard duty, as is apt to be the case with soldiers in winter quarters. The regiment from nearly its first arrival was engaged in the work of throwing up fortifications on Federal Hill, and it was some months before the soldier had any rest from the, to many of them, unaccustomed task of handling pick and shovel and spade from morning till night in digging the trenches, throwing up the ramparts, grading the glacis, forming the sally ports, the counterscarps, the bastions of that large and well-constructed fort, and mounting the heavy guns on its barbettes and in its bastions.

"It was the work thus performed by the soldiers, and the natural spirit of disinclination to that kind of labor, which was sometimes manifested by some of the men, which led to the composing of the two following parodies for amusement in the barracks after the hours of work, and though no merit is claimed for them on the ground of originality of thought or expression, they are reproduced here simply as a part of the barrack-life of the Fifth while quartered at Federal Hill."

5*

WORK IN THE TRENCH.

A Parody on "Mickey Free's Lament."

BAD luck to this grading,
This picking and spading,
While summer suns heat,
And winter rains drench;
I'm not come for a digger,
I'd as lieve be a nigger
As spend all my days
At work in the trench.

Then though we work well,
The why I can't tell,
The divil a farthing
We've ever yet seen;
Some say if we wait,
'Twill come soon or late—
On my faith, I think
They're confoundedly green.

From reveille beat
Till the welcome retreat,
They keep us at work
With our picks and our spades;
Let us long as we may
To join in the fray,
They give us no chance
To try our good blades.

Once done with this work,
And back in New York,
I'll stick to my trade,
Be it field, bar, or bench,
Not the Indies nor Spain
Could tempt me again
To enlist for a soldier
And work in the trench.

Bad luck to this grading,
This picking and spading,
While summer suns heat,
And winter rains drench—
There, the drums are calling!
The sergeant's a-bawling!
Och! the divil fly away
With this work in the trench!

M. W.

THE SONG OF THE SPADE.

A Parody on Hood's "Song of the Shirt."

WITH limbs all weary and worn,
  His temples throbbing with pain,
A soldier sat in unsoldierly mood
  Chanting a sad refrain—
    Work! work! work!
From morning till evening parade;
  And still, with tones in which sorrows lurk,
He sings the "Song of the Spade!"

    Work! work! work!
When the drums their reveille beat!
    And work! work! work!
Till we hear the welcome retreat!
  Oh, I'd as lieve be a slave
    Along with our Southern foe,
  Where one might at least find a grave,
    And an end to all his woe!

    Work! work! work!
Till the brain begins to swim;
    Work! work! work!
Till I ache in every limb!

  Spade, and mattock, and pick,
  Pick, and mattock, and spade
Till I sigh for the rest that Death would bring,
  And wish in my grave I was laid!

Oh, ye who rule the war!
 Ye who have children and wives!
It is not the foe you're fighting against,
 But your brave soldiers' lives!
   Work! work! work!
 From morning till evening parade,
We dig at once a trench and a grave,
 For here will our bones be laid.

But why do I talk of death?
 Can the thought any terror yield?
I would not fear his grizzly shape,
 If I meet him in the field—
 If I meet him in the field,
 For there is the soldier's grave;
O God! that I should be prisoned here,
 To work like a galley slave!

   Work! work! work!
 Our toil no resting knows;
And what are its wages? A paltry sum,
 Made up in curses and blows;
From one in authority dressed,
 With his epaulettes and sword,
Strutting about behind the redout,
 As if creation's Lord.

   Work! work! work!
From morn till dewy night,
   Work! work! work!
Like a slave in its master's sight!
 Pick, and mattock, and spade,
 Spade, and mattock, and pick,
Till my limbs grow tired, and my arms are numbed.
 And my very heart grows sick.

Work! work! work!
   In the cold December day,
      And work! work! work!
   In the sunlight's hottest ray,
When the air is like an oven's breath,
   While the sun like fire glows,
And as we bend to our toilsome task,
   We sigh for an hour's repose.

Oh, but to breathe the air,
   And to taste the joys of home,
To tread once more my native sod,
   Never again to roam!
To live as in days gone by,
   To be free as I once was free,
To wander whither I would,
   In childhood's sportive glee!

Oh, for a single day,
   A furlough however brief!
Not time to spend in pleasure or love,
   But only a moment's relief!
A glimpse of home would ease my heart—
   One hour of its peaceful rest
Would remove a share of the leaden care
   That burdens my wearied breast.

With limbs all weary and worn,
   His temples throbbing with pain,
A soldier sat in unsoldierly mood,
   Chanting a sad refrain:
      Work! work! work!
   From morning till evening parade!
And still in a tone in which sorrows lurk,
   He sings the song of the spade.

M. W.

One morning a party of laborers were refused admittance into camp because they were said to be of secessionist proclivities. They hailed from a section in the Eighth Ward, called "Limerick," which was thoroughly rebel in spirit. On August 31st the few laborers employed at the fort, after they left for their homes in the evening, had a lively encounter with another party, just outside of the works. It was Secessionist and Unionist, but no one was seriously hurt.

The Fifth was compelled to suffer a personal loss in the early part of September by the promotion of its commander to a higher duty. On the 10th we learned that Col. Abram Duryée, after whom this regiment was named, had been appointed a Brigadier-General of Volunteers. He therefore ceased his immediate connection with the regiment which he organized, and did so much to exalt in its efficiency, drill, and discipline. The country owes him a debt of gratitude for organizing in its service a body of men who rendered such service to the country during the war. He had the satisfaction of knowing that he could leave it without any anxiety as to its future career; for, under the leadership and training of the well-known and accomplished officer of the regular army who succeeded him in command, and to whom he was so greatly indebted for the discipline and drill of the regiment, its good name already acquired could not be lost. It must ever be a source of proud satisfaction for him to remember that *Duryée's Zouaves* were known throughout the Army of the Potomac as the best drilled volunteer regiment in the service; and for efficiency and discipline, was equaled by few and excelled by none.

On Tuesday, the 10th, Capt. Partridge, of Company A, two Sergeants, two Corporals, one drummer, and thirty privates were detailed to go to Rock Hall Landing, on board the steamer *Pioneer*, to arrest a company of secessionists, who were supposed to be drilling there, making an old school-house their place of rendezvous. The pilot, on account of some misunderstanding, carried them about fifteen miles from the place, and those having charge of the boat gave them no reliable information. The Captain ordered the boat to be stopped, arrested the crew, and then dropped anchor and had the fires put out. At half-past four the next morning, the engineer and firemen were released and ordered to get up steam, which was done, and at half-past five the boat was on the way to Baltimore, where it arrived at 10 A.M., and the party returned to camp.

Lieut.-Col. Warren was appointed Colonel of the Fifth on Sept. 11, 1861, and also Captain in the corps of U. S. Engineers; Capt. Denike, of Company G, resigned on the 6th. He was absent on furlough in New York, while all the recent changes and resignations of the officers were taking place, and being senior Captain, was entitled to either the Lieut.-Colonelcy or Majorship, which were both vacant. But in the reorganization two younger officers stepped into the vacancies. It was a new illustration of the old saying that "all is fair in war." The men of Company G were sorry to lose their Captain, who had proved himself to be their friend, a brave and good officer, and a Christian. Captain Denike was presented with a handsome sword, which cost $100, by the members of his former command, the presentation b ing made by a committee of six of the men.

Lieut. York was tendered, and accepted, an appointment as Captain in the regular infantry.

Captain Jacob Duryée, of Company G, son of our late Colonel, now General, was appointed Lieut.-Colonel of the 2d Maryland regiment, recruited in Baltimore. By this appointment we lost another brave officer.

The regiment having received new uniforms, made a grand parade through the city on the 15th of September, and were received with much enthusiasm.

As a contrast to the promotions and compliments of this month, we were compelled on the 18th to witness the dishonor of the flag by the dismissal of two of our men. The regiment was drawn up in line, and the culprits were drummed out of camp. One of them, James Nixon, was hung in the Tombs, New York city, a few years after the war, for shooting down a stevedore in Chatham Square in broad daylight.

From the memoranda made under date of October 10th, etc., the author copies a brief description of the fort as it stood at that date :

" The hill on which it is built is a very admirable site for a fortification. When standing on the parapet the visitor can have but one opinion as to its commanding position; and in the event of an attack, it could resist any force brought against it. It is an immense square fortification, occupying about two-thirds of the highest part of the hill, the space inside of the embankments being nearly four acres in extent. The earthworks would be half a mile in length if extended in a single line, thus affording shelter for a large body of men, who could keep up a fearful fire of musketry in perfect security, while the columbiads and other siege guns, stationed at regular distances in the bastions and along the curtain, were admirably planted for dealing out death and destruction. The breastworks were splendid specimens of engineering art, averaging, at least, fifteen feet through at the base, and sloping upward to about six feet across at the top. The height of these formidable banks is about nine feet at the highest point of the hill, running out on a water-level to the lower side, where it varies from fifteen to eighteen feet. They are not loosely thrown up, for every shovelful of clay which forms the mass was beaten down compactly with heavy paviors' pounders, and the outer sides are shaved off as smooth as a parlor wall. In addition to these is a ditch in front of the bank about eight feet deep, making, at the most exposed points, an escalade of at least twenty feet for a storming party to ascend.

" There are three large bastions, the guns of which command the river above and below, and every part of the city beyond; and as they throw eight-inch shot or shell, it is not difficult to imagine the havoc they will make if ever they are called into use. A lunette commands the approaches from the land side. The fort is entered upon its south-west face by a bridge and a huge gate, and the entrance is protected by a ditch. Within the fort is a well eighty feet deep, supplying excellent water in abundance."

An abstract from the author's journal will serve to show how the time was employed at this period:

"Reveille at 6 A.M.; directly after, roll call, when every one must be present and answer in person; if not, he is reported absent and unaccounted for, and subject to punishment; then 'Policeing Quarters,' which means to sweep out the tents, pick up the waste and rubbish lying about camp, even to the minutest bit of paper, and put everything in complete order.

"Breakfast call at 6.15, when the men fall in and repair in single file to the respective company cooks, who are enlisted men detailed from the regiment. A tin pint cup of coffee is served with no milk, with a piece of very fat pork or bacon to each man, which is thankfully received if it happens to be of good size. Then they repair to their respective tents, the cup and plate being private property (but the latter he rarely has), and sits down on the ground and discusses his meal.

"Sick call at 6.30, when all who are indisposed, their names having previously been entered by the Orderly Sergeant of each company in a book prepared for the purpose, repair to the surgeon's quarters (in charge of a Sergeant), who examines each man as his name is called, marks opposite his name the malady and the prescription, also a mark whether to attend duty or be excused. No Captain or Lieutenant can excuse a man from duty, unless first passed upon by the surgeon.

"Drill call at 8.30. When we assemble in company quarters, roll again called; then in charge of a commissioned officer, each company marches to some open fields about half a mile from camp, and go through the various evolutions, until 11.30, when the recall is sounded on the bugle.

"Dinner call at noon, when the roll is again called. This meal consists, without variation, day after day, of either boiled cabbage, or pork, bean soup, beef stew, and a small loaf of bread; the latter must last for three meals or go without. At 2.30 P.M., again fall in and roll called. Knapsack drill in the same place as the morning's drill, but it is a 'battalion' instead of company drill. Are formed into line of battle, charge over fences, etc., which generally results in some lofty tumbling and miscellaneous scratches, form squares, and march by either front—form column by division—drill in double-quick time, etc. At 4 o'clock or later, return to camp. Sometimes instead of the latter drill, we are formed in line on the parade-ground inside the fort. The drum beats, and immediately each company, without further orders, repair at a double-quick to their places behind the intrenchments, go through the movements of loading and firing, aim, etc. At the order *Charge*, every man jumps upon the parapet, and rushes to the edge of it with a yell, his bayonet pointed downward, as if to thrust at an enemy trying to scale up the sides of the fort.

"At 5, or 4.30 P.M., as the days are short, are assembled and roll called, and marched out for dress parade, which takes place outside the fort, if the weather is propitious, and is witnessed by hundreds of citizens, many of whom come in their carriages. After this performance, we have supper, which consists of a cup of tea or coffee and a piece of bread off the loaf, given out at dinner-time. This diet is sometimes varied by a ration of rice and molasses, which is considered a rare treat. At 8 P.M., retreat, roll call; 8.30,

FORT FEDERAL HILL.

taps. '*Lights out*,' cry the Orderly Sergeants, when every candle is extinguished except in the tents of the latter, and the quarters of the officers and guard. After this no talking or noise is allowed under heavy penalties. Thus closes the duties of the day, and silence reigns supreme, except the tread of the sentinel who is pacing his beat, or his sharp challenge, and the cry of 'Corporal of the Guard,' when perhaps he has caught some unlucky straggler trying to steal in or out of camp.

"*Wednesday, October* 16.—Captain Hamblin, of Company I, and his command have been on an expedition, about 50 miles from camp, and surprised a meeting of secessionists, surrounding them and capturing 17 muskets and 40 cartridge-boxes, and thoroughly dispersing the rebels.

"*Monday, November* 4.—The weather is now quite cold, and the sentinels exposed to it at night feel it keenly, notwithstanding their overcoats. We have had a very severe storm, the rain falling in torrents, and the wind blowing a fierce gale. It was impossible to drill, or rather, not necessary to expose the officers and men to such a storm, and consequently all not on necessary duty were housed in their tents most of the time for 30 hours, excepting at roll calls, meal times, and the never omitted evening parade, which was, however, in undress with overcoats.

"There are quite a number on the sick list and in the hospital with rheumatism, etc., while some have been discharged as unfit for further service. The citizens say that in winter Federal Hill is the coldest spot near Baltimore, and the men begin to think that 'public opinion' is quite correct on this point."

Captain Hamblin, the former Adjutant, and a great favorite with both officers and men, has accepted a commission as Major in the 65th New York Regiment, U. S. Chasseurs. All are very reluctant to part with him. He was a man of fine presence, standing about six feet four inches, with a voice like thunder; and I can not better describe the effect he produces on an evening parade than by quoting an extract from the New York *Times*, written by an officer of this regiment, which is as follows :

"Captain Hamblin would be easily remembered in New York by all who witnessed our march down Broadway, if they were told that he was the tall and colossal officer who marched along at such a seven-league pace, his good-looking phiz all smiling and joyful. Captain Hamblin, 'The Adjutant,' as the boys still love to call him, is a feature in our regiment, and would be sorely missed. We felt bothered when we no longer had Col. Duryée, but if in an evil hour we should lose 'The Adjutant,' God help the regiment, say I. You remember the description given by Kate Rocket, in the old comedy, of her fiery, blustering father— I forget the exact words—but still I never could hear little Miss Gannon describe his coming on parade with a stiff military air, frowning down the line, and pretending not to hear the 'God bless his old heart,' without tears starting in my eyes; and I never yet was on parade when 'The Adjutant' came thundering along the line without thinking of the similarity. He's a treasure to us. I could keep on all day telling you about his ways, although I have scarcely ever said a word to him in all my life, but I have no space; besides, it is hardly fair, and so I stop by saying that he is one of the funniest men you ever saw. He has, for instance, a huge dog, about the size of a small rat, and his kennel is an empty box of David's ink, about as big as one of those boxes of honey one sees in New York, while over it is a fearful placard—' Beware of the Dog !'"

The men of the regiment subsequently made up the sum of $600, which was appropriated to buy a stallion, which was presented to Major Hamblin, as a substantial token of their regard.

In speaking of dogs, the writer before quoted from, says :

"There are a great number of dogs now belonging to the regiment, picked up at Hampton among the deserted houses in that unfortunate village. These dogs have a home in some company, but they seem to have each a separate duty to perform. One always mounts guard; another gets in front of the drum corps at dress parade; there he squats gravely until the band has done playing; then as the drums strike up, he barks away to the no small amusement of the visitors; and, as at the instant the drum stops, the evening gun fires, over he goes in a back somersault, somewhat astonished, and not exactly understanding what makes the noise. This fellow is also detailed to go with the patrol that leaves every morning and evening for the city for the military prisoners.

"Another, a large black Newfoundland, better known as *Bounce*, the property of Co. G, but claimed by Lieutenant Jacob Duryée, used to attend all parades of the regiment until the Lieutenant was promoted to the Lieutenant-Colonelcy of the 2d Maryland Regiment, when he was carried off. All hands of course supposed that *Bounce* had forgotten his old corps in the enjoyment of his newly-acquired promotion. But fidelity in a dog is stronger than some people imagine, for the other day *Bounce* made his appearance on dress parade, as if nothing had happened, and I suppose he will remain a fixture—a regular Union dog—and an example to all would-be deserters.

"G. C."

Another canine who became a favorite attached himself to the regiment at Camp Hamilton. He was a little Scotch terrier, whom the boys named Jack. He took up his quarters at the guard tent, where he could constantly be seen on duty, following after the different reliefs. He would always return with them and remain until another relief was called out. The last that was seen of him was on the dock, the night the regiment embarked for Baltimore, having followed after his friends. The men felt the loss of Jack almost as much as that of a comrade, for he was a true type of a faithful friend.

Only one of the Captains (Winslow) who belonged to the regiment at its organization, now remained in that grade, and he was absent on a visit to New York, having accidentally sent a pistol shot through his foot. Col. Warren was sick and confined to his quarters at times for two months, but had recovered, and was also absent on a short furlough. The regiment was reviewed and inspected by Gen. R. B. Marcy, father-in-law of Gen. George B. McClellan, and Inspector-General of the Army of the Potomac, and the following day we were mustered in for pay.

We could now boast of a very fine band, under the leadership of Mr. Wallace, of New York. It was made up of professional musicians, and some very fine amateurs, who were detailed temporarily from the ranks. The drum corps, however, was our pride, and was under the charge of that veteran knight of the drum-sticks, John M. Smith,* who maintained strict discipline among his large corps, and took them to a distance every day and drilled them until their arms ached. They were such masters of their art that on parade they were greeted with much applause. They made a splendid appearance, for they were a good-looking set of lads, and commanded the admiration of all who saw them in their Zouave uniforms.

The following verses were written by one of our drummer-boys, which are worthy of preservation as one of the ballads of the time:

To the Fifth New York Zouaves.
By One of the Drum Corps.

A regiment once left New York to gain themselves a name,
Also to prove that they could fight and play the Yankee game.
At old Fort Schuyler they began their duties with a will,
And in a month they proved to all that they were some on drill.

CHORUS—Oh, Secessia, what's the use of funning,
    Don't you see the red breeches, look at them coming?
    On, Zouaves, on!

---

* Smith has been for years the Drum-Major of the 7th Regiment, and also of the Brooklyn 13th. One of his pupils (Jenks) acts in the same capacity for the 71st; and another (Strube) for the 22d Regiment; McKeever for a New Jersey Regiment.

Life at Baltimore.

To Fort Monroe by order sent, they quickly took their way,
They left New York one pleasant night, arrived up there next day;
When the rebels heard that they had come, it grieved them very sore,
For they never thought the " Red Devils " could land upon their shore. *Chorus.*

They did their duty faithfully, and " easy " slept at night,
Till one fine day they got " good news ; " it was to go and fight ;
On, on to Bethel, was the cry, nor did they ever tire,
Though on the double-quick they went to meet the rebel fire.
Chorus.

The Fifth drawn up in line, stood motionless and still,
They met the fire manfully, returned it with a will ;
But orders soon awake them, for " Warren gave the word,"
And in advance, on double-quick, they went to meet the herd.
Chorus.

Then next to Baltimore they went, another post to fill,
And very soon threw up a fort high on Federal Hill ;
They placed a flag-staff on their fort, aided by some " tars,"
And hoisted up their country's flag, the glorious Stripes and Stars.
Chorus.

They on an expedition went, down to old Accomac,
And very soon the rebels found the red boys on their track ;
So they took and pulled their tent-pins up, for they couldn't see the fun,
And the Fifth got into Accomac, and the rebels into a run.
Chorus.

They took some pretty trophies—cannon, muskets, swords, and shot,
Likewise some loaded shell, which the rebels had forgot ;
They took good care nothing to spare, but everything to bag,
And in Northampton County they took a rebel flag. *Chorus.*

The Fifth once made a grand parade through the streets of Baltimore,
And " Baltimoreans " said they never saw the like before ;

Their arms shone bright as silver, their step was firm and true,
While marching to the music of " Yankee Doodle Doo."
Chorus.

The Fifth have got a Drum-Major, a gentleman of ease,
He's a soldier, knows his business, believe me, if you please;
His pupils know his style, and obey him with a will,
But if they neglect his orders, why, he gives them extra drill.
· *Chorus.*

The bully Zouave drum corps are some upon a stick,
They understand their business, can go a double-quick;
When they are on parade the girls look at them shy,
And whisper to each other, How I'd like a " Drummer-boy."
Chorus.

And now my ditty's ended, as you shall quickly see,
And I've told you of the Fifth Zouaves, so happy and so free;
Three cheers for their brave officers, the noble sons of Mars,
Who swear to live or die beneath the glorious Stripes and Stars.
Chorus.

The drummer-boys, imitating their older companions, were continually hatching mischief and playing jokes. The bandmaster was a great admirer of Maggie Mitchell, the actress, who was a frequent visitor to the camp to witness the evening parades of the regiment, and as in duty bound, the officers always showed her great attention. One night the bandmaster marched his band with the drummers out of the fort and into the city, finally halting them in front of the hotel of the actress, intending to give her an agreeable surprise by a serenade. The music was delightful, and the affair was a success, but he had arranged that the drummers were to carry torches in order that his musicians could read their notes, and that it might be seen by the actress to whom she was indebted for this compliment. They, on the other hand, had arranged that when a certain one of their number counted one, two, where the number three came in, out should go the lights. The band-master was in the midst of his most enchanting piece, and he was performing his own part with the rest, his soul full of music and happiness with the thought that he was delighting the ear of the actress he so much admired. When one, two, puff, out went the lights, the music came to an abrupt termination, and the stillness was broken by three emphatic words not necessary to repeat, and his ears were saluted by the ringing laugh of the bewitching Maggie, who showed her appreciation of the joke by clapping her hands, and she probably enjoyed this episode which the mischievous drummer-boys had inserted in the performance, as much as she did the music.

It may not be out of place to chronicle one of the Drum-Major's practical jokes, perpetrated at the expense of a member of his own craft.

One day Adjutant Hamblin, Sergeant-Major Jack Collins, and himself, were dining together in the tent of the latter, when a knock was heard from without, on the tent pole. Smith called out: "Who is there?" "Drum-Major of the 4th Michigan," was the answer. "Come in! Drum-Major of the 4th Michigan;" and he went in. Of course he was invited to be seated and take dinner. After the meal was over, the conversation turned on the mysteries of the art of drumming. Fourth Michigan said that he had heard that Smith was a professor of the art, and he had come over to see him, and hear a specimen of his accomplishments in that line. Smith told him that he was mistaken as to his being able to drum; all he did was to walk ahead and flourish his stick; he understood how to do *that*. "But," said he, "I can appreciate good drumming when I hear it, and if you have no objections I should be very much pleased to hear what you can do with the drum-sticks!" "All right," replied Michigan, and he took the drum that was handed him, and putting the strap over his shoulders, he struck a position for business and asked what it should be. Smith said, "Let us have the long roll!" not thinking of the consequences. And now, thoroughly interested, down came the sticks, and out came the well-known alarm rattle. At the first sound, out rushed Smith, Hamblin, and Collins, leaving his astonished guest alone, and the startling conviction flashed on his mind that he was badly sold, and had committed a serious breach of military discipline. Some of the companies had jumped to arms, and the officer of the day rushed into the tent and caught the unhappy offender, "dead to rights," as the detectives say. He tried to explain, but it was of no use. He was sent to the guard-house. Smith was brought before the Colonel, and for some time matters looked serious. But it passed over, and after some time spent in durance, the musical interviewer from Michigan was released, and departed for his camp, thankful that he was not to be court-martialed and shot.

On Tuesday, the 12th of November, six companies of the regiment, under the command of Colonel Warren, left on an expedition to the eastern shore of Virginia. They took baggage-wagons with them. It was understood that some five thousand men were under orders for this service, and there was much disappointment among those who were left to guard the fort.

The carpenters, with the assistance of men of that trade detailed from the regiment, commenced work on the barracks. In the meantime, the men built large camp-fires to keep themselves warm, and around these they congregated when off duty, to talk and sing songs. Guard duty returned every four days while the other companies were away, and we had the usual drill the other three days. The fort was under the command of Major Hull, who kept the battalion under the usual discipline. Large quantities of cannon-balls were received, and they grew into regulation pyramids ready for use. There was no limit, apparently, to the number.

Sunday, Dec. 1.—Thanksgiving Day (Thursday) was celebrated by firing a grand salute of thirty-four guns with the thirty-two-pounders, which made the hill shake, while the concussion broke all the windows of the houses in the vicinity of the fort. After the salute the band played several national airs. The surgeon supplied all the men with oysters as a present from himself, and the sutler gave out cigars, so all were happy. Saturday a Volunteer Union Company of thirty-five boys, dressed in Zouave uniform, visited camp, drilled and went through different maneuvers very creditably, and in the evening at dress parade drew up opposite the battalion, after which they marched away.

A remarkable event of camp life which occurred just at this time, was described by a Baltimore journal as follows:

An Elopement.
Marriage of a Zouave—Exciting Affair.

THE greatest excitement of the season transpired in East Baltimore shortly after four o'clock on Sunday afternoon, the particulars of which we will give in as brief a manner as possible: Connected with the 5th New York Zouave Regiment, encamped on Federal Hill, is a handsome and brave volunteer, who in a few weeks after visiting our city fell in love with a sweet young lady residing on the Hill, but whose father is secesh to the back-bone. The daughter, however, entertained different opinions, and boldly declared that if ever she became a wife, a bold soldier boy should be her husband.

The Zouave, upon learning the sentiments of the old man, was sorely troubled, but nerved himself with the assurance that "Faint heart never won fair lady," and resolved to press his suit and carry off the prize despite the threats of the enraged parent.

For a while all went along smoothly, when red breeches learned that the father of his loved one had issued a proclamation that his daughter should wed a chap who was in heart as great a coward as ever lived, and in principle so mean that a clock would not tick while he was in the room.

The young girl, like a true heroine, detested him, and informed her Zouave beau how matters stood. The latter managed a stolen interview on Saturday morning, which resulted in the dear girl giving her hand to her sweetheart and agreeing to an elopement. The time named was half-past three o'clock Sunday afternoon at the house of a friend. The time arrived, and so did our hero with a horse and buggy. In a twinkling the loving couple were rattling over the cobble-stones at a merry rate in search of a minister to tie the Gordian knot. Up one street and down another the horse sped until the corner of Lombard Street and Broadway was reached. At this point the Zouave jumped from his buggy and inquired of a gentleman where a minister could be found that would render happy at short notice a couple anxious to get married. The gentleman could not impart the desired information, when our hero again sprang into the buggy and drove to the corner of Pratt Street, where his beating heart was quieted by John Randolph, Esq., who informed the Zouave that the Rev. Mr. Thomas, pastor of the Broadway Baptist church, would perform the ceremony. To the church sped the party (including the horse and buggy), and in a short time the blushing damsel and her companion were closeted with the minister.

By this time it became noised about that an elopement was on hand, and such an outpouring of marriageable ladies was never before witnessed on Broadway. Young ladies crowded about the church doors in great numbers, while the windows of adjacent dwellings were thronged with older persons, all anxious to catch a glimpse of the wedded pair as they emerged from the sacred edifice; and when they did appear, many were the well wishes for their future welfare that greeted them on all sides. Forcing their way through the crowd, the happy couple seated themselves in the buggy and passed rapidly up Broadway. Vive la Zouave! Vive la Elopement!

CHAPTER VII.

THE EASTERN SHORE—LIFE AT BALTIMORE.

THE EASTERN SHORE—OBJECTS OF THE EXPEDITION—A PROCLAMATION BY GENERAL DIX—" MARCHING ALONG!"—A SURPRISED ZOUAVE—REBEL SPIRIT AND REBEL SPIRITS—A SOLDIERS' REUNION—REBEL VISITORS SINGING THE STAR SPANGLED BANNER—RETURN OF THE EXPEDITION—RESULTS—A SOCIABLE PARADE—REBEL FLAG REVERSED—RECRUITING—OPENING THE BARRACKS—" FORT FEDERAL HILL"—SECOND YEAR OF THE WAR—OUR SURGEON—A SURGICAL DUELIST—RUNNING THE GUARD—" THE ZOUAVE HOUSE"—A MUSICAL MASKED BATTERY—FLAG PRESENTATION BY THE LADIES OF SOUTH BALTIMORE—ADDRESS BY JOHN WILLIS, ESQ.—COLONEL WARREN'S REPLY—A GRAND BALL AT HEADQUARTERS—FORT MARSHALL—WASHINGTON'S BIRTHDAY—AN INDIGNANT ZOUAVE—GRAND CITY BALL—A MILITARY EXECUTION—ATTACK THREATENED—THE MERRIMAC—CHANGE OF BASE—HO FOR FORTRESS MONROE!—FAREWELL TO BALTIMORE—'OUR FAREWELL ENTERTAINMENT—RELIEVED BY THE THIRD NEW YORK—FALLING INTO LINE—MARCH THROUGH BALTIMORE—EXCITING SCENES—FAREWELL SONG.

ON Tuesday, the 12th day of November, 1861, six companies, A, B, C, D, E, F, of the 5th Regiment, who were to act in concert with other troops, in all about five thousand men, left Baltimore on the steamer *Pocahontas*, for the purpose of invading Accomac and Northampton Counties, Virginia, the former Congressional district of Ex-Governor Wise, his country seat being near Onancook, Accomac County.

There were many Union people in the two counties, but they had been overawed by the secessionists, who were in the majority, and had been actively recruiting many young men from the ranks of the inhabitants for the Confederate army.

The two counties comprised about eight hundred square miles, with a population, including negroes, of about twenty thousand. There were about three thousand militia, who had assembled together in a camp, under a Colonel Smith, of the Confederate army, and batteries were being built to resist any advance of Federal troops into this territory. It was the object of General Dix to send such a large force against them as to either capture this body of men, or to overawe and disband them. Many of them were Unionists, but were compelled to enter the Confederate ranks by threats of personal danger and destruction of property; and it was anticipated that if troops were sent to their aid, and a firm, yet conciliatory po icy was adopted, the secession element would become demoralized, and the Unionists would not only be protected, but would remain firm adherents to the loyal cause. The command of the expedition was intrusted to General Lockwood, of Delaware, and consisted of detachments of the 17th Massachusetts, 5th New York, 21st Indiana, 6th Michigan, 4th Wisconsin, Nims' Battery, Troop of Cavalry, 2d Delaware Home Guards, and Purnell Legion.

On Wednesday, the 13th, the steamer on which the Fifth had embarked entered Pocomoke Sound and River, and got aground. The men were taken off the next day at 9 o'clock, by the steamer *Star*, and at 10 A.M. landed at Newton, Worcester County, Md., just above the Virginia line, and encamped. From this place General Lockwood sent a messenger under a flag of truce across the line into Virginia, and circulated a printed proclamation to the inhabitants, issued by General Dix, which called upon all in arms against the Government to lay down their arms and disperse, promising protection to the Unionists, and the penalties of the law against the disunionists if they continued in their treasonable acts, etc.

Upon receiving the proclamation, the Union people were wild with delight, and the camp of the secessionists began to melt away. On Sunday, the 17th, the troops crossed the boundary line into Virginia, the cavalry in advance, the 5th New York leading the infantry, and encamped, after a march of twelve miles, at Oak Hall. During the march they encountered many obstructions, designed to impede their advance; bridges had been burned, and trees were thrown across the roads, some of which it was necessary to remove, and deserted earthworks were found at Oak Hall.

November 18.—The cavalry advanced by a forced march to Drummondtown, and raised the Stars and Stripes on the pole on which the day before the Confederate flag had been flying.

November 20.—Marched to Knappsville, eight miles, and encamped.

November 21.—Marched fifteen miles, to a point seven miles from Drummondtown, and encamped. During this march we discovered another battery, mounting eight guns, almost new, of which we took possession. During the night rain set in, and the companies remained in this camp until Sunday, the 24th. Up to this time nine guns and one hundred flint-lock muskets had been seized. Colonel Smith, who commanded the troops at the earthworks, escaped; but we made prisoners of one Captain and two Lieutenants.

November 22.—During the night Captain Partridge, of Company A, and a squad of men, went in search of arms, and found a number of sabres and equipments which had been hidden in the woods, and Sergeant Pike captured a large Confederate flag.

November 24.—We marched to Eastville and encamped, being seventy-seven miles from Newton, from which place the expedition had started. A number of the 21st Indiana were put under arrest for foraging and committing depredations.

General Lockwood, before the expedition started, had issued an order that any one caught out of camp should be put in irons; but notwithstanding the imperative nature of the order, and the severity of the threatened punishment, some of the men of the various regiments could not resist the temptation to wander out of the lines.

One night after the regiment had gone into camp, one of the Zouaves ventured on a private errand as provider. He went to a house near by, and, without ado, approached and knocked on the door. "Come in," cried a manly voice. He thought it an encouraging summons, and forthwith opened the door; but much to his astonishment, he saw Colonel Warren and Captain Partridge warming themselves over the fire. If he ever disobeyed an order of his commanding officer during his two years' service, it was on this particular occasion. He not only refused to obey, but rudely closed the door and beat a hasty and disorderly retreat around the corner of the house. Seeing a cellar-door open, his first impulse was to disappear down that way; but luckily for his second thought, he did better by tumbling head over heels into a pig-sty conveniently near, regardless of pigs or mire. Out rushed the officers, who saw the cellar-door open, and concluded that the rascal had gone below. The Captain rushed back to get a light, while the Colonel stood guard, saying that he would cut the scoundrel down if he attempted to dash by him. Soon the Captain appeared with the light, and while they were looking into the cellar, "Phil" got out of the other side of the sty and made extraordinary time back to camp, thanking his stars for his narrow escape. "Phil" is now one of the shining lights of the New York Bar.

Two men, who afterward confessed that they had been officers in the Confederate army, after drinking freely, met some unarmed Zouaves out of camp, drew their pistols and pointed at them. They were arrested, and taken before Colonel Warren, confined for the night in comfortable quarters, and supplied with substantial meals from his own table; blankets were also furnished, and a good fire made for them. In the morning, when they were sober and penitent, and ashamed of their conduct, the Colonel explained to them the principles and the cause he was fighting for, and the madness and folly of their own false position, serenaded them with the "Star Spangled Banner," and dismissed them.

Wednesday, November 27.—Colonel Warren invited a number of gentlemen known to be bitter secessionists, some of whom were formerly rebel officers, to witness a drill and parade of the Fifth, and afterward join him in a soldier's supper. At the appointed hour they came in fine equipages, for they belonged to the wealthy and influential classes.

The Zouaves were encamped in a dense pine forest near the village of Eastville, adjoining which was a large and level meadow, which made an admirable parade-ground. The movements were performed under the order of the Colonel, in a most successful manner, and the gentlemen were astonished, never having witnessed anything like it before; afterward they had a splendid supper around a roaring fire. They were stretched in a semicircle about it, sitting and reclining on red blankets laid upon pine boughs, from which they could see the Zouaves flitting about their camp-fires in the pine woods across the meadow. The scene in the dusk of evening was enchanting and like a vision of fairy-land. After the bountiful repast, the Colonel sent for some fine singers of the regiment, and they were entertained for an hour by their performance. They then sung "The Red, White, and Blue," and the finale was the "Star Spangled Banner," in which all joined with great effect. The secession visitors got excited, and sang louder than any of them, swinging their hats in the air; after which they declared that, after all, they had an interest in the old flag—that one-half of it belonged to the South, and it was a shame to divide it. They wound up by proposing, and joining in, cheers for the flag, for the 5th New York, and for the Union.

Tattoo, with "Yankee Doodle," played with fife and drum,

cut short the entertainment. This little incident did more to overcome the secessionists, in spite of themselves, than a hard battle would have done.

Col. Warren invited Gen. Lockwood to witness a drill of the Fifth a few days afterward, as he did not seem to entertain very cordial feelings toward the Zouaves. But whether the question, "Who stole that goose?" which became proverbial in the regiment, had anything to do with it, has never been determined.

The regiment went through the movements with automatic precision in quick and double-quick time. The General was astonished, and said that he had never seen anything like it in the whole of "*Delaware*," and that it could not be excelled.

Monday, Dec. 2.—Marched to within seven miles of Ponateague, covering twenty-one miles, where more deserted intrenchments and obstructed roads were discovered.

Tuesday, Dec. 3.—Left the camping ground, and reached the steamer *Star*, lying at Ponateague, on the Chesapeake Bay, about noon.

Wednesday, Dec. 4.—Started about 6 A.M. on board the steamer *Star*, for Federal Hill, arriving at the fort on the morning of the 5th, after an absence of twenty-three days.

The companies had marched on this expedition over 160 miles, in heavy marching order, besides having severe drills while lying in camp. They found the majority of the people to be poor and ignorant, many of the women having neither shoes nor stockings, with their dresses unfashionably short. The negroes were allowed one coat, one pair of shoes, two shirts, and one pair of trousers for the year, and some of their clothes were so much patched that they looked like bed-quilts. At first the negroes were very much alarmed, and kept aloof, but having caught one, and given him a Union drill, by tossing him in a blanket, they soon had their hands full. They said that their masters had told them that the Yankees would cut their arms and legs off. They were greatly surprised and gratified to find that instead of being treated in that way, they were welcomed with "Union drills."

To sum up, the expedition seized ten cannon, eight of which were new, a thousand stand of arms, flags, etc., besides disbanding the drafted militia, restoring confidence to the Unionists, and demoralizing the secessionists.

Colonel Warren was much opposed to the policy of delay pursued by General Lockwood at first, and offered to take his battalion and Nims' battery, and push through to the end of the Peninsula. Had he been allowed to do so, there can be little doubt that Colonel Smith, the Confederate leader, would have been captured.

On the evening of Friday, Dec. 6th, the officers being again "at home," had a "sociable," in the Colonel's quarters, which were in a brick building, formerly used as a hotel, which was allowed to remain when the fort was built, and was situated inside the works, near the western embankment. The men also had an improvised concert, the band played at intervals, cheers were given for Colonel Warren, and expressions not very complimentary to General Lockwood or his military sagacity, were indulged. Altogether the entertainment was worthy of the occasion.

The following day, the weather being propitiously beautiful, all of the command that could be spared, marched out for a parade through the city, bearing the Confederate flag that was seized on the late expedition, upside down.

It was publicly presented to General Dix, at his headquarters in the city, after which the men gave three tremendous cheers for General Dix and the American Union. Doubtless the rebels growled and gnashed their teeth at the disgrace of their flag.

On Friday, Dec. 13th, several of the officers and a few of the men were sent to New York to obtain recruits.

It may seem strange, that regiments in the service, when they have not lost many men in battle, are obliged to recruit so often. The reasons are, that all comparatively new organizations lose many men, who, when first enlisted, pass a medical examination, but have not the stamina to endure the hardships and exposure to which they are subject. In addition to this, many desert. It is a hard school, and puts to the test all that there is in a man in the way of fortitude, patience, endurance, and all the hardier qualities, as well as moral courage. After the weaker ones are sifted out, there remains a body of strong, enduring soldiers, who can perform any duty, and submit to any hardship, who do the hard fighting in a battle, and are "mustered out" either by death on the field of battle, or with honor at the end of their term.

The attendance at divine service on Sundays was small, seldom exceeding over twenty; last Sunday quite a large number assembled, on account of some remarks made by Colonel Warren on the subject, and the men were drawn together at his request.

A few evenings since the men gave a concert, in one of the nearly finished barracks. A stage was erected at one end, and decorated as tastefully as the means at their command would allow; seats of plain boards were arranged for the audience, with camp-stools, borrowed for the occasion, to accommodate the officers. There were recitations and scenes from "Macbeth," etc., which were acted out in the most tragic manner. The Drum-Major gave an exhibition of his skill on the drum, and he made it speak in his hands. The good voices selected from members of the regiment, gave some very harmonious music, and the Colonel and officers were very much entertained and gratified.

On Monday, the 23d, the men struck tents, and moved into the barracks. "They were large and roomy, two stories high, with double verandas, supported by slight pillars, and facing inward toward the square. They occupied three sides of the quadrilateral, within the high embankments, and upon the fourth are situated a neat cottage of brick, commonly called the Colonel's quarters; a guard-house, and an unimposing building which affords ample accommodation for the commissary and quartermaster's departments.

"One building is occupied by the officers, and the others are divided into rooms ninety feet in length, each division furnishing ample accommodation for one hundred men. Three tiers of bunks occupy each side of the company quarters, and are arranged in the most convenient and approved manner. Company kitchens also occupy the ends of the large center building, and there are rooms in the same building for the band and the sutler. The buildings inclose a large parade-ground, sufficient in extent for ordinary military purposes; and the square is ornamented with native trees, which please the eye and afford an agreeable shade."

The company rooms were each heated by two stoves, which stood at either end, and the comfort of these quarters contrasted favorably with that of the cold and crowded tents. The day before moving was dreary and rainy; the wind blew a gale, and the tents appeared to lie in a morass of mud and water. It is needless to say that the change was immensely for the advantage of the men for health as well as comfort. The boys enjoyed themselves extremely in their new quarters, and after camping out so long, we felt somewhat domesticated in our new surroundings.

Thursday, December 26.—Our works have been named and are to be made historical by the title of "Fort Federal Hill." The armament of the fort is six 8-inch columbiads; two 10-inch mortars; two 8-inch S. C. howitzers; twenty-three 32-pound guns; five 24-pound howitzers (flank defense), and several 6-pound brass pieces. Stored in the three magazines were 10,000 pounds of cannon powder and 1,000 hand grenades. In addition there was in the fort over 4,000 solid shot, shell, grape and canister shot.

The Confederate flag captured in the late expedition to the eastern shore of Virginia, and presented to General Dix, was sent by him to the Mayor of the city of New York. The following is from the New York *Times* of December 27, 1861:

MAYOR'S OFFICE, *December* 26, 1861.
TO THE HONORABLE THE COMMON COUNCIL:

GENTLEMEN:—I have received a communication from Major-General Dix (a copy of which is annexed), accompanying a secession flag, captured in Virginia by the 5th Regiment of New York Volunteers (Duryée's Zouaves), under his command.

In compliance with the desire of Major-General Dix, it becomes my pleasant duty to transmit this trophy of a New York regiment to the appropriate custody of the municipal authorities of the city to which this gallant corps belongs. New York will preserve this relic with pious care, as a proof of the courage of her sons and their patriotic devotion to the cause of the Union. Let us receive it as an auspicious token, and as an earnest of the restoration of peace and the triumph of that Constitution which is the only safeguard of the true glory and happiness of our country. I recommend that the Common Council, in receiving the flag, pass resolutions congratulating the regiment of New York Zouaves for their gallant spirit, and thanking General Dix for his kindly remembrance of the city.

FERNANDO WOOD, *Mayor*.

On the receipt of the above message, the Common Council adopted a resolution returning the thanks of the city to the Fifth Regiment for the flag.

Friday Jan. 3, 1862.—With the opening of the new year winter had fully set in, and in the morning the air was very keen. The season was cold, and in addition we had the full force of the north winds on the elevated position we occupied. The surgeon, or "Opium Pills," as the men called him, whatever may have been his scientific attainments, was not fortunate as an officer or a humanitarian. He was tyrannical and cruel. It was his custom when the sick came before him, to commence business by asking his steward to bring him "some of those bitters," which was evidently nothing less than about five fingers of raw whisky. His loaded revolver was laid on the table at his side, and for some imaginary provocation he would fly into a towering passion, bring his fist down on the table with an oath, upsetting the ink and everything else, and either kick some poor fellow out of the room, or seize his revolver and threaten to blow somebody's brains out. One of the officers, Quartermaster Wells, took him at his word one day, much to the joy of the men. There had been some trivial dispute between them, and the surgeon (V.) challenged the Quartermaster. But he found that he had a new patient to deal with, and not a list of sick privates who could not resist his brutality. The challenge was accepted, the Quartermaster being a dead shot, and accustomed to making his fire tell, and the imperious surgeon was obliged to retire his challenge, and retire himself, by resigning his commission.

Passes to the city are again restricted, only one for each company being allowed every twenty-four hours. In consequence some of the men resume their guard-running practices, with the risk of being fired at by the sentries, besides being court-martialed when caught, or if they missed a roll call.

No harm will come now to any one to tell where the runaways often spent their time, and where the guard could have made a good capture not very far from the fort. The "Zouave House" will never be forgotten by the Fifth. A convenient trap-door led down into a dark cellar, where the carousers found refuge when their pickets gave the alarm; the trap was then covered over with the carpet, and a piano stood over the spot. It was a long time before this *cover* was *discovered* and our musical masked battery was abandoned.

Wednesday, January 8.—To-day there are about fifty boys

enjoying themselves outside the fort, coasting down the hill with their sleds. Sergeant F., feeling disposed to participate in the sport, borrowed a sled from one of the boys, and was soon going down the hill as fast as he could desire; but unfortunately for him, when he was about half the distance, he and his conveyance parted company; he slid about twenty feet in one direction and his sled in another, materially marring the beauty of his countenance. The men standing on the parapets of the fort gave a shout at his mishap, and he ever after bore the name of "Hunkey Slide."

The men had become very proficient in their drill, and were familiar with both the heavy and light infantry manual, bayonet exercise, heavy and light artillery, street firing, etc., and in addition one man was detailed daily from each company to learn the art of making cartridges. They were again allowed their full complement of passes to the city, and guard-running consequently decreased.

On Thursday, February 6th, the regiment was complimented by the presentation of a beautiful garrison flag, prepared by the ladies of South Baltimore. Although the weather was not very favorable, a large assembly was gathered within the fort, the ladies of South Baltimore, who manifested great interest and pride in the regiment that had built Fort Federal Hill, forming the principal part of the throng. The interior of the fort was placed in excellent order, and notwithstanding the alternate storms of rain and snow, afforded a fair promenade-ground for our fair visitors.

The following account of the presentation is from the *Baltimore American* of February 7, 1862:

"At half past two 'the assembly' was beat, and the regiment formed as for dress parade on three sides of the parade-ground. After formation, the regiment was closed at half-distance in front of the headquarters, Colonel Warren in front of his command, and the ceremonies of presentation commenced. The flag was brought forward by Messrs. Edward H. Price and

Joseph Brooks, the committee of arrangements on the part of the ladies.

"JOHN WILLIS, Esq., was introduced, and delivered the following presentation address:

"TO THE OFFICERS AND SOLDIERS OF THE FIFTH NEW YORK ZOUAVE REGIMENT:—I have been honored with the privilege, by patriotic ladies residing within the southern section of Baltimore, of presenting, in their name and on their behalf, to your regiment, the 5th New York Zouaves, this beautiful ensign of our country's nationality. Soon as man emerges from barbarism toward civilization, even in its rudest form, we find him naturally seeking some congenial association. It is not meet that he should live alone, as the fair donors of this exquisite gift would willingly attest.

"Combining thus for the better preservation of his own and his neighbors' rights; looking also through the light of reason, and in the exercise of those attributes which distinguish him above all other animate beings, he seeks the enjoyment of consolidated advantages vouchsafed in unity of purpose and of power.

"Associations thus formed naturally adopt their *insignia*, their mottoes, their emblems of faith, until each representation becomes the reflective index of an embodied principle. Thus from the small beginning of a rude circle, allied in plighted faith, looking toward the grand ultimatum of human happiness, we behold traced out the progress of civilization, until mighty nations have sprung into being, mapping the great globe congenial to their desired nationality.

"The revolutions of ages have brought us to the present momentous epoch in the world's history. The whole habitable face of our green earth is marked and countermarked with geographical and national divisions. These seem to have been the natural and almost unavoidable results of maturing and matured experience.

"Having therefore risen to the high dignity of nations, each with its integral though consolidated millions, has, in some form or other, adopted the ensign of its faith, not only to be respected at home, but to *command* respect abroad.

"There are some, in an individual point of view, whose patriotism, I regret to infer, has been so mildewed as to divert their mental visions from a true perception and translation of the real sentiment embodied in such ensigns.

"Looking, as they are prone to look, at our precious Star Spangled Banner under existing unfortunate circumstances, their frigid philosophy misleads them to pronounce it an unmeaning combination of colors and shreds.

"We envy not the heart from whose cold recess has vanished the sacred memories of this our country's ever-glorious flag. Would that the gladsome period be not distant when all such sluggish pulsating organs may be enabled to throb afresh with renovated patriotism, and that the bright image of this starry emblem may again live there to flourish, and blossom and bloom as the rose in the wilderness.

"The rainbow, with its tinted colors, in arching beauty spans the blue vault. We behold it with admiring eyes, are awe-stricken with its grandeur, and venerate Him who sprung it in the heavens. Nor this alone; for faith points to it standing there as an everlasting pledge of fidelity from God to man.

"It is not, then, the simple colors, so gorgeously blended, which fade, perchance, with the passing cloud, but our knowledge of their return to represent a sure pledge—a living eternal principle—that enchains the beholder's admiration.

"The golden-orbed sun invites us to his sinking in the purple west, leaving earth overshadowed with darkness and gloom; but hope points steadily to an auroral morn when he will arise again with the same promethean fire to assume meridian splendor. The moon and stars are hidden from visu range, yet they anon come forth, fresh as when first created, to illumine Niobe's pathway across the spangled heavens.

"It is the living embodiment of a sublime principle contained within the silken folds and clustering stars of this our nation's proud banner that wins our hearts and bids us reverence its holy memories. In youth we learned its history; in manhood's earlier years, its name was as an household word; in life's Indian summer, it gained deeper reverence; and as wintry age grows apace, the old heart becomes perennial in contemplating its glories. The Revolutionary patriot, and those who followed it through danger to victory in later struggles, never forgot, and *never can forget,* so sacred a thing as their country's flag.

"To us it is a legacy bequeathed from sire to son. It was baptized in the sacred blood of freedom, and still waves an emblem of untainted liberty.

"Almost a century has passed since our Revolutionary fathers proclaimed their independence and gave us this pledge of the wisdom, the power, and the grandeur of republican liberty. On land and sea, in storm and in sunshine, at home and abroad, in fertile valleys and on mountain tops, on lake and river, plain, island, or desert, we speak in reverence of Mount Vernon's holy shrine where Washington sleeps! Wherever civilization has planted *this banner* and fixed *these stars,* they are the faithful sentinels of human happiness.

"Under them we have grown up from partial obscurity to incomparable greatness, from seeming weakness to unconquerable strength; so that this day, under this banner, in its true constitutional meaning, it is ours to hold the world in admiration and in awe. No such word as defeat ever stained its folds, and, if we prove true to ourselves, never can.

"Pursuing the pathways of science in the light of its encouraging spirit, we have taught kingdoms and empires of the Old World, grown gray in years before ours had an existence, lessons of practical wisdom. That all-pervading subtle principle of electricity which fills the universe has been called from the thundercloud by American genius, and now speaks from *these shores* to our praise in all parts of the civilized globe.

"We have placed steam upon the mighty deep to plow its trackless billows, and given it locomotion on the outstretched arms of our countless railways. Genius in innumerable forms, emanating from us in our steady progress toward greatness under the ægis of this national ensign, has developed until we find its results stamped indelibly upon history's page.

"Is it, then, surprising, permit me to ask, that we, as Americans, are proud of the standard our nation has adopted?

"The true soldier whose spirit goes out amid the roar and carnage of battle, can close his eyes in peace, if their last gaze be fixed upon this hallowed ensign. Its azure and its constellated stars are but exchanged for the deeper blue and brighter gems that deck the brave warrior's celestial home.

"As the painter's brush transfers life to the canvas, making even the dead speak, bringing loved forms and past generations into our very presence, so may we behold the sentiment, the virtues, the life, and the pure intentions of Washington and his compatriots, speaking in resistless eloquence from this sacred banner.

"Interwoven with life's crimson current, as it gushes out from the heart in warmest pulsation, is commingled the undying love of cherished friends. Faces and forms once familiar are forever mirrored afresh in the vernal bloom of halcyon recollections. So it is with this banner. In early life and in maturer years it waved over us as a shield from danger. It has won our affections, and we would not, if we could, sever those ties.

"If, in the providence of God, He should kindly send His angels of mercy and of peace to stay the red arm of civil war, and bring us again to fraternal unity as a nation, to friendship and happiness as a people, *let the whole earth rejoice!*

"One of Maryland's gifted sons, whose spirit now, perchance, looks down from higher spheres, has interwoven this standard with garlands of poesy, and given it immortality in song. Presenting it, therefore, in behalf of our 'Monumental' ladies, to the gallant officers and men of this regiment, in appreciation of their soldierly bearing and gentlemanly deportment, allow me to say, as I hope and believe the author would now say, were he yet living amongst us,

"'The Star Spangled Banner, O long may it wave
O'er the land of the free and the home of the brave!'

No higher compliment can be desired than to know it has been bestowed by *fair hands and true hearts* upon those who are ever ready to preserve and protect so priceless a gift.

"Obedient, therefore, to the pleasing trust conferred on me, it becomes my high privilege to present your noble regiment, in the name of the ladies of South Baltimore, with this *our country's flag*.

Life at Baltimore. 141

"The address was received with applause, and followed by the 'Star Spangled Banner,' by the regimental band.

RESPONSE OF COLONEL WARREN.

"Colonel WARREN received the flag, and, transferring it to Major Hull, made the following brief and appropriate response:

"SIR:—Allow me to return, through you, to our fair friends of the city of Baltimore, the heart-felt thanks of this regiment for the friendly interest they have shown in presenting it with a national flag, the work of their own hands.

"It is impossible for us not to feel our patriotism glow afresh at this proof of their confidence. The unfortunate condition of our country brought us in your midst, and it is a source of unfailing gratification that in this gift they show that our true position is understood. We come as supporters of the American flag, and the beloved Constitution of which it is the chosen emblem, and not as conquerors or oppressors. (Cheers).

"We believe that the necessity which occasioned our presence here has now passed away, and trust that this fort, which we have aided in constructing, will hereafter be a safeguard against the future outbreaking of lawless violence. We hope soon to be called again to the active scenes of the now receding rebellion, and trust, as a part of the great Union army, to see this flag, endeared by the associations of to-day, waving in some place where our misguided brethren yet flaunt their rebellious banner. When that time comes, may the knowledge that this flag of our country was made by the ladies of a sister Southern State help to dispel the feelings of animosity engendered by the strife. Again I beg that you will present to the ladies our sincere thanks. (Applause).

"Major Hull called for three cheers for the ladies of Baltimore, which were given by the regiment with a will, and a 'tiger.'

"Major Hayward was then called on for a song, and gave one of his own composition, creating much laughter and applause by its amusing hits. The regiment joined in the chorus with vim.

"At the close of the presentation the regiment was dismissed for a short interval (which was well filled by the fine music of the band), and again assembled for drill in the bayonet exercise.

The parade-ground not being large enough to drill the whole regiment at once, the right and left wings were brought on one after the other. The bayonet exercise resembles, in many respects, the exhibitions given by the Ellsworth Zouaves, but is put in a more serviceable form for practical use, and without the claptrap additions which made those exhibitions more of a theatrical than a military display. The exercise, when participated in by four or five hundred well-drilled men, is a splendid sight, and impresses even the unmilitary beholder with the conviction that the bayonet is the best offensive and defensive weapon in the world. A regiment drilled in its proper exercise would have over one not thus drilled, supposing the numbers and bravery of both to be equal, an advantage that would enable it to defeat its opponents with slight loss.

"It is impossible to describe in words the exercise, but it may be said to make the soldier and his weapon one. It places him first in the best position for attack or defense, and by a series of movements, based on scientific principles, enables him to guard every exposed part—to throw off the lunge aimed at head, breast, or thigh, and by a dexterous shortening of his own weapon give the deadly thrust before his opponent recovers; in close quarters it enables him to convert his gun into a club; and again, by a series of rapid movements, to act in front or rear, to the right or left, and in retreat or advance. While it accomplishes all these purposes, the exercise develops the physique of the soldier, gives him suppleness and wind, and a confidence in himself and weapon that in the field would be of the greatest advantage. After the right wing had been drilled by Colonel Warren, the left wing was put through the exercise by Major Hull. Both did so well that it appeared to the unprofessional spectators that it would be impossible to decide with which the greater merit rested. A light artillery drill, with all the loadings, firing, changing positions, etc., followed next, and had time and opportunity allowed, we might have had drill with the heavy guns, in the management of which the regiment have also been instructed.

"After the drill, the Committee of Arrangements, a number of the ladies, and the friends of the officers, were hospitably entertained in headquarters.

"Not the least pleasant feature of the occasion was the fine music of the band. Under its present leader, Mr. Wallace, it has been brought up to a high degree of excellence.

"As for the drum corps, it is *the* drum corps, and Drum-Major Smith is *par excellence* the Drum-Major.

"The display ended with the usual evening dress parade, Lieut.-Col. Hiram Duryea commanding. Capt. Winslow acted as Officer of the Day."

On Sunday, the 9th, the resignations of Lieuts. C. W. Wright and Dunham were read off as accepted. Col. Warren was absent, and Lieut.-Col. Hiram Duryea was in command. Miss Mitchell, the actress, visited the fort to witness the dress parade.

On Friday, the 14th, a ball was given at the officers' quarters, which did not terminate till daybreak. It was a select affair; all the guests came and went in carriages. The men during its progress were restricted to their own quarters.

Immediately after breakfast, on Wednesday, the 19th, four companies, B, E, G, and —, were ordered to be ready in heavy marching order, and in the afternoon they fell in line on the parade-ground, and were marched through a heavy rain-storm to Fort Marshall, which was about five miles by land from Fort Federal Hill. It was a similar structure, but did not cover as much ground, but mounted thirty-three heavy guns. It was situated on a high, bare hill, about two hundred feet above the level of the sea. It was about half a mile from the limits of the city, on the side of the harbor opposite to Fort McHenry, and commanded that post.

The detachment arrived about dusk, wet through, covered with mud, hungry, and with nothing to eat. Coffee, which was our only supply, was served about 9 P.M.

Saturday, Feb. 22d, being the anniversary of WASHINGTON'S BIRTHDAY, all the forts fired salutes in honor of the day. In the afternoon a grand parade of the military was made through the city. The Fifth was the principal attraction, and their bayonet exercise was viewed by thousands of spectators. Everybody seemed to observe the day in a very patriotic manner, except the secession element, of which there was a large representation yet in the city, plotting their schemes of rebellion in secret. They were no worse than the "copperheads" in the North, who, like the reptile they represent, were ready to sting their protectors behind their backs—the men who were risking their lives to defend their property, and to keep from coming true the prophecy of their South Carolina *friends*, "The grass will grow in the streets of New York."

One evening two or three of the boys, while out in the city, were in a store where they found a brace of secessionists, who were very open in their expressions against the Government and its hirelings. No notice was taken of them or their conversation for some time, but it was continued so, long that one of the boys became impatient, and turning around, he suddenly caught the man nearest him by the neck, and run him out of the place, vigorously applying his boot lest he might think it was only a joke. Before he was really sensible of the ignominious situation in which he was placed, he found himself lying in the street, when his companion concluded it was prudent to retire, and slunk out. Our boys waited some time, but they did not come back to wreak their vengeance on "Lincoln's hirelings."

A grand ball was held on the evening of Monday, the 24th, in the city, at which were present the Mayor and Common Council, General Dix, and many distinguished people. By request, one of the events of the evening was an exhibition of the bayonet exercise by a detail from the Zouaves.

The detachment from the Fifth sent to Fort Marshall under command of Lieut.-Colonel Duryea, who was a very severe disciplinarian, was kept constantly at fatigue duty or on drill.

On Friday, March 7th, the whole regiment was called out in compliance with the following General Order :

HEADQUARTERS, DIVISION,
BALTIMORE, Md., *March* 5, 1862.

GENERAL ORDERS, No. 6.

I. The several regiments and commands of this division in the vicinity of Baltimore, except those guarding the railroads, will be paraded at Fort McHenry at 12½ o'clock P.M., on Friday, the 7th inst., for the purpose of witnessing the execution of Private Joseph Kuhns, 2d Maryland Volunteers, who was found guilty and sentenced to be hung by the neck until he be dead, by a general court-martial, for the capital crime of shooting to death, without provocation, his superior officer, Second Lieutenant J. Davis Whitson, 2d Maryland Volunteers. . . . .

By command of Major-General Dix.

Official: D. T. VAN BUREN,
   WILSON BARSTOW,   *Assistant Adjutant-General.*
   Aide-de-camp.

The detachment at Fort Marshall, excepting the camp guard, returned in heavy marching order to Federal Hill, and then the regiment marched to Fort McHenry, where was assembled the whole of General Dix's command. The troops were drawn up in a hollow square, in the center of which stood a gallows. In a few moments a man walked up briskly and mounted the scaffold, and stood for five minutes with a rope around his neck, apparently unmoved, before he was launched into eternity. He was a private belonging to the 2d Maryland Regiment. To avenge a grievous wrong that had been done to himself, and to one who was dear to him, he had sworn vengeance against a Lieutenant of the company to which he belonged. Accordingly, one evening when his regiment was drawn up on parade, he stepped out of the ranks, leveled his musket, and deliberately shooting the officer, who fell dead on the spot, he threw down his piece and gave himself up, with the remark that he was satisfied.

It was necessary, for the sake of military discipline, and as an example to others, that he should die.

After the regiment returned to Federal Hill it was obliged to supplement the execution with other disagreeable duty in the cases of several of its own members. After being drawn up in line, six men who had been lying in irons in the guard-house for several months, were marched before them, having one side of their heads shaved, dressed in the most ragged and wretched suits of citizens' dress that could be obtained. It was a painful and degrading sight. Their heads hung down like felons, with the guard behind and before at charge and reversed bayonets respectively, and drum and fife playing the "Rogue's March." But this was not all; some of them were to be sent to the Washington Penitentiary to serve out terms varying from six to twelve months, and one of them to the Dry Tortugas. They also forfeited all pay and allowances due, or that would become due, to them. Several others were waiting similar penalties, who had been lying in irons for several months. These unfortunate men had violated the military laws so often, proved so incorrigible, that it became necessary to inflict the severest punishment known to the service.

Just after dinner, on Sunday, the 9th of March, there was great activity in the fort; men were ordered to fall in with spades and picks, and were put at work strengthening the fort on the water-side; others were drilling at the heavy guns and the ammunition was inspected. Information had reached headquarters that the Confederate ram *Merrimac* had run the blockade, in which event it was expected that the first place she would visit would be the flourishing city of Baltimore. At Fort Marshall the men worked all night strengthening the banks and shifting all the heaviest guns from the land-side to the water-fronts of the fort. It was laborious work, the guns weighing four or five tons each; ammunition was arriving all night, and the next day details were employed in filling shell, and oiling the wheels and screw-levers of the guns and carriages. The men were assigned their posts of duty, to which they were to repair at the first alarm-roll of the drum ; and Company K, from Federal Hill, and several companies of the 17th Massachusetts Regiment, were sent in as reinforcements. All kinds of rumors were afloat—one to the effect that General Banks had been defeated and the enemy were marching on Baltimore. It appeared certain, in any event, that something important had occurred, and all were rejoiced when the news came that the " Cheese-box" had defeated the *Merrimac.* But, on the other hand, they were disappointed when it was realized that they were not to try their guns on the enemy.

On Tuesday, the 25th, the regiment was reviewed by General A. Duryée, at his request, and he took leave of it, his brigade having been ordered to Washington. A Baltimore journal of the 25th, announced the event as follows :

"About 11 o'clock this morning a large concourse of people assembled on Broadway near Baltimore Street, on what is known as 'Fairmount Hill,' to witness a dress parade of the 5th New York Regiment, Colonel Warren (Duryée's Zouaves). A hollow square was formed of pickets, when the regiment proceeded to execute their peculiarly beautiful drill, which was gone through with in a most creditable manner. The bayonet exercise elicited the warmest applause from the spectators, and was certainly as near perfection as it can well be brought. The regiment has been stationed for several months at Federal Hill, and by their constant drill practice, have obtained the reputation of being the best drilled regiment in the service, which they certainly merit. The evolutions in double-quick time this morning attracted great attention, and whilst it was very exciting, it was novel and interesting. A large force of police was on hand, who kept down all excitement and difficulty."

The days passed on in the usual manner, when a rumor was

heard, at the close of the month, that the regiment had been ordered to Fortress Monroe, and all appearances indicated a move in some direction. The detachment from Fort Marshall returned on the afternoon of Thursday, the 27th, and all were on the alert. The rumor was confirmed. It was announced officially that the regiment was destined for Fortress Monroe, to join General McClellan's army, now moving by vessels to Old Point Comfort. There was much joy and excitement occasioned by the tidings.

All was bustle and confusion; the men talked like bedlamites, and a spectator would think, from the pleasure expressed by their countenances, that they were ordered to New York, instead of to the front, to enter on an active campaign, where they could expect nothing but hard usage, privations, and dangers. Officers and privates all felt a pride in their regiment, and were determined to keep up its good name in whatever position it might be placed.

It was determined to give a farewell entertainment, to be held in the fort, the preparations for which had been in the hands of a committee for some time, in anticipation of a change of base. The programme was as follows:

THE GRAND FAREWELL FESTIVAL

BY THE

FIFTH REGIMENT, NEW YORK ZOUAVES,

AT

FORT FEDERAL HILL,

On Friday Evening, March 28, 1862.

CONSISTING OF A FIRST-CLASS

CONCERT OF CHORUSES, GLEES, AND SOLOS,

COMIC AND SENTIMENTAL.

Choice Selections from the Standard and Local Drama—both Tragic and Comic, together with a variety of Select and Instrumental Music by the

BAND OF THE REGIMENT.
The whole under the direction of
MR. FREDERICK ROUSE, COMPANY F.

STAGE MANAGER.................................. *W. R. Bailey, Co. A.*
SCENIC ARTIST..................................... *Wm. McIlvaine, Co. A.*
MUSICAL DIRECTOR .... *E. N. Bull, Co. E.*
TREASURER.. *J. H. Pierce, Co. D.*

ADMITTANCE FREE.

PROGRAMME.
PART I.

GRAND OVERTURE.............................. *5th Regt. Band.*
OPENING CHORUS................................ *5th Regt. Glee Club.*
COMIC SONG....................................... *Brown, Co. F.*
BALLAD .... *Carroll, Co. E.*
DANCE... *Tucker, Co. H.*
SONG... *Bailey, Co. A.*
SCENE FROM TOODLES......................... *Dobbs, Co. H.*
BALLAD.. *Collins, Co. B.*
DRAMATIC READINGS. .... *Southwick, Co. F.*
MOCKING-BIRD SONG, with Imitations... *Bull & Hern, Co. E.*
COMIC SONG .... *Sapher, Co. B.*
BALLAD .... *Tierney, Co. A.*
GROUND AND LOFTY TUMBLING.......... *Leddy, Drum Corps.*
SONG .... *Matthews, Co. D.*
DANCE .... *Murphy, Co. F.*
BALLAD.. *Mulligan, Co. I.*

PART II.

OPERATIC SELECTION......................... *5th Regt. Band.*
FAVORITE GLEE.................................. *5th Regt. Glee Club.*
COMIC DUET...................................... *Carroll & Mathews, Co. E.*
BALLAD.. *Verney, Drum Corps.*
DRAMATIC READINGS....................... *Southwick & Rouse, Co. F.*

COMIC SONG	*Bailey, Co. A.*
BALLAD	*Williams, Drum Corps.*
DANCE	*Clark, Drum Corps.*
COMIC SONG	*Sapher, Co. B.*
DRAMATIC READINGS	*Sheffrey, Co. K.*
COMIC SONG	*Brown, Co. F.*
BALLAD	*Tierney, Co. A.*
COMIC SONG	*Carroll, Co. E.*
BALLAD	*Bull, Co. E.*
COMIC SONG	*Rouse, Co. F.*
BALLAD	*Mulligan, Co. I.*
DONNYBROOK SCENE	*Company.*

During the intermission between the parts, by particular request, the

GLADIATORIAL AND SCIENTIFIC DISPLAY OF MUSCLE

will be repeated.

To conclude with the National Song and Chorus of the

"RED, WHITE, AND BLUE."

By the entire Company and Audience.

The performance passed off with great *éclat*, notwithstanding some things occurred that were not down on the bills, but they rather added to the enjoyment instead of marring it. At one time, when one of the men was performing on a banjo, the floor of the staging gave way, but the performer was undisturbed, landed erect on his feet, and continued his playing amid the wreck, which elicited much applause and laughter, for the break-down was occasioned by the mischievous "Butch" Sapher, who had crawled under the staging and upset one of the wooden horses on which it was supported.

Sunday, March 30th, the regiment fell into line on the parade-ground inside of the fort. It was raining hard, and every one looked sad. The men felt as if they were leaving home, as they had made many acquaintances and won many friends in Baltimore. We were relieved by the 3d New York, who were to take the place of the Fifth, and to them we cheerfully surrendered our lofty position. Notwithstanding the rain, the fort was crowded with friends, all looking very sorrowful, and some of them pressed the men to take money for future wants. Finally the order to march was given, and the men stepped off. They had buckled on their armor, and were marching forth to join that immense armed host which had been assembling and preparing for months to hurl themselves against the enemies who would disunite a free and happy people, and deluge our fair land in blood.

As the Zouaves marched through Baltimore Street in the rain, the band playing "The girl I left behind me," they received an ovation at every step; the street was crowded with men, women, and children; the windows of the houses were full, the men cheered, and the ladies waved handkerchiefs and flags. But the hearts of the men told them it was no holiday parade; for many of them were bidding farewell not only to a friend, but to one where there was a stronger tie, for some had found partners for life among the fair sex; and there were others to whom the plighted troth had been given, and they were leaving those they should, perchance, never see again.

The scene was an impressive one; the Zouaves ever and anon kissed their hand to some fair friend, or nodded adieu to some male acquaintance, who were recognized in the crowd of spectators, and were saluted in return; the women wept, and the men cried, "Good-bye! good-bye! God bless you!" Eight months before they had made their entrance among strangers, with the mailed hand, to stand guard at their very doors; they were now taking their departure as friends, bound with ties which should be surrendered only by death.

Thus they marched, about nine hundred strong, through

the crowded streets to the wharf, and embarked on the steamship *S. R. Spaulding* at 4 P.M., and bore away amid the applause of thousands; the Zouaves mounted the rigging and highest spars, and waved their turbans with wild huzzas. The rain had ceased, and the sun shone brilliantly on the scene; the piers were full of people, many of whom were ladies, who stood wherever they could obtain a foothold, waving their handkerchiefs, and there were countless numbers of small boats, with their living freight, gliding about in the stream. The 3d New York, on Federal Hill, mounted the ramparts of the fort, and added their cheers to the general leave-taking. The sailors on the United States gunboats and sloops of war in the harbor manned the rigging and united their cheers with the rest. As they steamed by Fort McHenry they received their last cheers from the 4th Regiment (Scott Life-Guard) and the regulars; beyond lay the broad Chesapeake Bay.

The following verses on the occasion were written by MIRON WINSLOW, of Company E:

FAREWELL TO BALTIMORE.

Farewell, Queenly City!
   Before we depart,
I would bid thee farewell
   From the depths of my heart;
With gratitude fervent,
   Our bosoms expand
At thought of the kindness
   Received from thy hand.

With our ardent desire
   To join in the strife,
And our longing to live
   A more soldierly life,
Is blended the sadness
   That parting still lends;

We came to thee strangers,
  You received us as friends.

Our country is calling;
  We eagerly go,
To meet with new vigor
  The traitorous foe;
But where'er we may be,
  Whatever our lot,
Thy kindness and friendship
  Shall ne'er be forgot.

Farewell, Queenly City!
  Thou'rt lost to our sight;
Thy dim shores are wrapped
  In the mantle of night;
But memory still
  Weaves its magical spell,
And our hearts beat response
  As we bid thee farewell!

CHAPTER VIII.

THE PENINSULAR CAMPAIGN—YORKTOWN.

THE TRIP TO VIRGINIA—SCENE AT HAMPTON ROADS—CHANGES—CAMP MISERY—PEEP AT BIG BETHEL—PRIME RATIONS FOR SIX—*N. Y. Times* CORRESPONDENT—GEN. MCCLELLAN'S REPORT—CAMP SCOTT—CORDUROY AND DITCH—HEADQUARTERS—CALIFORNIA JACK—THE 4TH MICHIGAN—FIRST DEATH BY SICKNESS—GEN. MCCLELLAN'S HEADQUARTERS—AN OFFICER'S LETTER—LETTER FROM A PRIVATE—FIRE AND FUN IN THE DARK—A STRATEGIC PIG—SIEGE PREPARATIONS—BATTERY NO. 1—GEN. BARRY'S LETTER—CAMP WARREN—AFTER THE BATTLE—CAMP BUCHANAN—A PROMISE OF BATTLE—MARCH IN THE SHADOWS—MAGNIFICENT SPECTACLE—A NIGHT VIEW OF THE CAMP AT PAMUNKEY RIVER—DROOPING SKIES AND A DRIPPING ARMY—REVIEW BY HON. WM. H. SEWARD—DESERTED TERRITORY—NEARING THE WHITE HOUSE—STRAGGLERS—"DR." WARREN AND HIS "PILLS"—THE SICK-LIST—THE COLONEL'S ORDER AND A DONKEY'S REPLY.

Monday, March 31, 1862.—Out of Maryland and into the waters of the Old Dominion. The steamer was a staunch vessel, and sailed well, and our passage was made in good time, and would have been much more pleasant but for the inconvenience to which men are subject in an overcrowded ship. We were closely packed in the holds and on deck, without sufficient room; only a part could lie down, those who enjoyed that luxury being obliged to use the decks, and sandwiching themselves between cordage and comrades, and remain in one position until they were satisfied. The darkness between decks added to the discomfort of the trip.

As the ship sailed into Hampton Roads the scene was enlivening in the extreme; it seemed to us that we were nearing a large seaport. The offing was crowded with transports, thronged with soldiers, horses, stores, artillery, and everything that is required for a large army. The *Monitor* was pointed out, but one could scarcely believe that such an in-significant-looking affair—for vessel it could hardly be called —caused the rebel monster, the *Merrimac*, to skulk back into the port from which she had sailed so defiantly.

The regiment landed in the afternoon of Tuesday, April 1st, and marched about two miles beyond Hampton and bivouacked. It was almost impossible to recognize this locality as the same which the command had left eight months before. There was not a tree, fence, or landmark left, with the exception of the seminary, and stretching miles beyond was an immense camp. There appeared to be no limit to the artillery, cavalry, and infantry, moving day and night. We remained in this camp five days, bivouacking at night, not yet being supplied with tents. The men called this stopping-place "Camp Misery," for the reason that the rations were very short, while a cold north-east rain-storm, which continued day and night, during the second, third, and fourth days, made it impossible to keep our clothing dry. The fires would not burn, and the smoke hung close to the ground like a thick cloud, affecting the eyes, and surrounding us with a suffocating atmosphere. On the fifth day the sky cleared, and the air was warm, but the roads were in a very bad condition.

We left camp at 6.30 A.M. on Tuesday, April 6th, without any regret, and marched through mud a distance of twenty miles toward Yorktown, passing through Big Bethel, which was an interesting spot to the old members of the regiment, as the various objects reminded them of their previous encounter with the enemy. We remained in "Camp Starvation" the 7th, 8th, 9th, and 10th, living on one or two crackers a day. Heavy details were sent out every day to work on the roads, and help the wagons along the muddy highway.

The sojourn here was very disagreeable, as it rained the greater part of the time, and we had no shelter except such as could be improvised from "ponchos," or branches of trees plastered over with mud. There were, however, about half a dozen men, composing two messes, that had an abundance to eat and to spare; one of each having dropped out from a fatigue party, and hidden in the woods until the coast was clear, and then went on a foraging expedition and struck a placer. They returned to the vicinity of the camp, and hid their spoils in the bushes until night, when they brought in to their starving messmates one pail of molasses, about two pounds of sugar, haversacks full of the best of pilot biscuit, half a pig, one sugar-cured ham, two pounds of the best smoking tobacco, some fresh beef, and a canteen of peach brandy! It was a royal banquet! How and where they made their levy it would take too long to relate; suffice it to say that they came very near being ambushed by guerrillas and losing their lives.

The regiment was singled out while in this camp from the rest of the volunteers, and attached to General Sykes' brigade of regulars, with which corps they remained through their term of service. It may be of interest to the reader to know how this was brought about. The Fifth not being encamped in a situation favorable for exercise in drill, Colonel Warren asked permission of General Sykes to give his regiment a drill on the field used by the regulars. The request was granted, and they marched out and went through all the most complicated battalion movements in quick and double-quick with so much spirit and precision, that we soon had a large audience of the regulars, upon whom it made a very favorable impression. General Sykes himself was viewing it from his tent. Subsequently Colonel Warren's request to move his camp nearer the regulars, which had been previously denied, was allowed, and we were permitted to draw rations from his Commissary.

The New York *Times* correspondent said:

"The 5th New York Regiment, Duryée's Zouaves, are considered the finest drilled regiment in the army of Yorktown, and

The Peninsular Campaign—Yorktown.

have been assigned the post of honor, being the only volunteer regiment with the regulars."*

Another journal spoke as follows:

"Constant drill at the artillery, bayonet, and rifle, together with recitations for officers and soldiers in the regulations of the army tactics—both artillery and infantry—soon brought this body of soldiers to the highest state of perfection, so that on the 30th day of March, 1862, when leaving Baltimore and joining the Army of the Potomac, on the Peninsula, the honor of being assigned to duty with the regulars was granted to this regiment, and the 'red legs,' as they were called, were not slow in convincing the regular infantry that they were not to be outdone by them, either in drill, marching, or under fire. This reputation gained has always been maintained by them while in the field."

The Prince de Joinville,† in his comments on the volunteer organizations, makes special mention of the regiment as follows:

"Thus, a young Lieutenant of Engineers, named Warren, was marvelously successful with the 5th New York Regiment, of which he was Colonel. This regiment served as engineers and artillery at the siege of Yorktown, and having again become infantry, conducted itself like the most veteran troops at the battles of the Chickahominy, where it lost half of its force. And yet these

---

* " McClellan's Report and Campaigns " (p. 54). Regulars—" The advantage of such a body of troops at a critical moment, especially in an army constituted mainly of new levies, imperfectly disciplined, has been frequently illustrated in military history, and was brought to the attention of the country at the first battle of Manassas. I have not been disappointed in the estimate formed of the value of these troops—I have always found them to be relied on ; whenever they have been brought under fire, they have shown the utmost gallantry and tenacity. On the 30th of April, 1862, they numbered 4,603 men. On the 17th of May they were assigned to General Porter's corps for organization as a division, with the 5th Regiment of New York Volunteers, which joined May 4th, and the 10th New York Volunteers, which joined subsequently. They remained from the commencement under the command of Brigadier-General George Sykes, Major 3d Infantry, United States Army."

† " The Army of the Potomac, its Organization, its Commander, and its Campaign." By the Prince de Joinville. Translated from the French, with Notes by William Henry Hurlbert.

were volunteers, but they felt the knowledge and superiority of their chief."

We left camp about 10 A.M. on Friday, the 11th of April, marched three miles over very bad roads toward Yorktown, and went into bivouac at Camp Winfield Scott, within two miles and a half of that historical place. It is proper to give the reason why the army did not move faster after assembling at Old Point. The only road was in a very bad state, in consequence of the frequent rains, and the numerous ditches and pits, men sometimes being obliged to wade up to their knees in mud and water. It was necessary to repair and corduroy it in many places, to enable the miles of wagons, ambulances, and artillery to pass over it. It should also be remembered that each man carried about fifty pounds weight in addition to the clothing they had on their persons, as they were in heavy marching order. Then, after a day's march, where were the means, not to say comforts, which would give a soldier the necessary rest and recuperation? If not ordered off on guard, a soldier will make his bed on the wet ground, his knapsack his pillow, and a blanket for his covering; his supper is a hard cracker or two and a piece of fat salt pork, often eaten without being cooked, and thankful oftentimes to get that. If he needs a fire he must go to the woods and cut down the timber; or, if already cut, haul it for some distance over ditches and fields, to his stopping place. Then, after considerable perseverance, he may succeed in getting his fire to burn, when he can have a cup of coffee, which he boils himself in his tin cup; after which he smokes his pipe and is as happy as the case will allow. On such roads as those just passed over by the army, the procession of wagons, miles in length, could not make more than six or eight miles a day, and the men were obliged to lie by occasionally for them to come up; hence the delay. "Citizens" and "Home Guards" thought we ought to move faster, but the "citizens" who had become soldiers knew the reasons and the roads too well.

On Saturday, the 12th, we were detached temporarily from the brigade under a special order, and reported to General W. F. Barry, Chief of Artillery. The officers and men were employed in building siege-works, and some of the companies placed on duty in the batteries to work the heavy guns, and at the landing on York River, transporting and mounting the siege guns and mortars. This duty was all performed under the heavy fire of the enemy's artillery, and required nerve as well as experience to perfect the work.

While staying in this camp we had liberal supplies, pleasant weather, and good tents. The troops built a good road to Shipping Point, the extremity of which was about eight miles from camp, where the stores were landed when brought up the York River from Old Point Comfort. The men had no idle time; they were constantly employed on fatigue duty of some kind, making corduroy roads, etc., and gabions to fill with earth for siege-batteries. A detail of the Fifth put up General McClellan's tents and laid out the grounds about them, and a detail was made up every day for guard duty over his quarters, which were near the regimental headquarters.

A continual bombardment was kept up, and at almost any time of the night or day, the shell of the enemy could be seen bursting in the air, sometimes appearing to be directly overhead. Pickets were shot hourly, and skirmishes between the outposts were continually occurring, by which additions were made to the list of killed or wounded. At night it was grand to hear the roar of the heavy siege-guns, and listen to the rushing shell as they died away in the distance, and carried destruction into the enemy's stronghold. California Jack, the famous sharp-shooter, who was out at the front all the time picking off the enemy's gunners, made a visit to camp, being out of ammunition. Capt. Winslow furnished him with a liberal supply of cartridges for his Sharp's rifle, two of the companies being armed with the same weapon. He thanked him and said he wouldn't waste them, "you bet."

On the night of the 17th, the infantry firing was quite sharp. It appeared that the enemy came out and attacked one of the new intrenchments, and the 4th Michigan, one of the finest regiments in the service, drove them back and took three hundred prisoners. The men were ordered to have their canteens filled with water every night, and always one day's rations on hand, so as to be ready at a moment's notice.

A private of Company E died of typhoid fever in the hospital. It was the first death from disease that has occurred in the regiment since its organization, which was remarkable, although many had been discharged for physical disability, some of whom had subsequently died.

The following is an extract from a letter written to, and published in, the New York *Times* by an officer of the 5th Regiment:

CAMP WINFIELD SCOTT, before Yorktown, Va,
Monday, April 21, 1862.

We are constantly occupied in military exercises, in studying the tactics, in enforcing or submitting to the discipline, and in performing the daily duties incident to our connection with the present movement; and we see the officers and men of other regiments encamped near us engaged diligently in the same kind of labors. We hear the booming of cannon daily on our right and on our left; we see bombs bursting in air, and varicolored rockets shooting across the sky; we see artillery, cavalry, infantry proceeding hither and thither; we see aides-de-camp galloping by; we see balloons ascend and descend; we see baggage-wagons and ambulances on the road; rumors come to us of a fight in this or that part of the lines, and beyond this we know nothing of the progress that is making. We lie down on the ground at night prepared to respond to the first summons. Sometimes we are awakened by the thunders of artillery and the rattling of small arms, and lie listening to the noises of a deadly conflict somewhere. We endeavor to conjecture what corps are engaged, and picture to ourselves, as we follow with the ear, the fluctuations of the strife, "now high, now low, like the sound of music which the wind still alters," the scene and incidents of the fray. Now there is a lull, and now the combat thickens. For a while all is still as death; doubtless our brave fellows are advancing to the charge, and we strain to catch the clash of steel. Suddenly again comes the roar of cannon; the battle evidently now is fiercely raging. Now the discharges are less frequent; a solitary shot is heard, and now all again is quiet. Which has won the victory? Who of our dearest friends has fallen? We might not go forth to seek him if we knew he was gasping on the field. But we are warriors, not women. Let the dead be buried, and lead us against the foe! And so the soldier gathers his blanket around him, and in a moment is asleep again. And with all this disturbance in the distance, no alarm is sounded in the camps near by. No one thinks of obeying the impulse to rush forth and join in the fight. All await orders, and when they come, the battalions that are called for quietly form in line and are marched to the point where one mind decides that they are needed. Such is the discipline in the Army of the Potomac, attained by much training during the season of "inactivity," which they who knew not its value were inclined so much to complain of.

The 5th New York Zouaves, whose friends at home will read this, are undergoing no unendurable hardships here, and are much happier just where they are than any individual of them could possibly have been had he endeavored to content himself at home in a season in which his country called for his services in the field. And here we are, just where we want to be, with a leader in whom we have confidence to conduct us against a foe that lies immediately before us. We occupy a beautiful camping-ground near the marquee of the Commander-in-Chief. Our regiment has been complimented by being brigaded with the regulars—the only volunteer regiment so honored—and with them it constitutes the chosen corps which General McClellan keeps always with him. Brigadier-General Sykes is its commander, the same who, with 1,300 regulars, covered the retreat of the army at the first Bull Run. Lieutenant J. Howard Wells, the Quartermaster of the Fifth, has been transferred to the regular service. He now holds the position of United States Commissary with the rank of Captain, and is stationed at Baltimore. Lieutenant A. L. Thomas is his successor, and a very worthy one he is.

We have had very heavy rains here recently—such rains as in New York are entirely unknown. The roads are exceedingly heavy. Those who sit at home carping at delay should be compelled to travel over them in a loaded baggage-wagon once. They would soon get an idea of the difficulty of moving large armies in a country like this, and in such a season. G. C.

The following extract from a letter written home by the author, also tells part of the story:

CAMP WINFIELD SCOTT, NEAR YORKTOWN, VA.,
5TH REGT., N. Y. V., DURYÉE'S ZOUAVES,
Monday, April 21, 1862.

We still remain in camp, and are as comfortable, that is, for soldiers, as circumstances will admit. Our tents are of good material and keep out the rain, and the camp is situated on rather high ground, therefore the water runs off. To the south of our portion of the ground is a small ravine through which a small stream runs, supplied by pure springs, from which we get plenty of water or drinking and cooking purposes. In the stream itself we wash our clothes and ourselves. On the banks above the ravine there was a thick wood of pine, with its ever-green foliage; elm-trees, which were soon robbed of their bark to satisfy the chewing propensities of the men; sassafras bushes, the roots of which are pleasant to eat, and are therefore pulled up without regard to quantity; but the wood is now getting thinner every day, falling a sacrifice to our axes, and used by the cooks to keep up their fires, and by us as a means to warm ourselves when it is necessary. We can see the balloon make its ascensions every day, and often hear a report up in the air. We look up and see a ball of smoke, resembling a small cloud, which tells us that a shell has burst; but it is of such frequent occurrence that often we do not notice it. A few shells have landed in camp, one of which killed a mule; another was filled with rice, so they say; one fired yesterday cut a man in half while he was in the woods; but we are comparatively safe, all things considered. But about a mile further to the front the situation is different, as they have sharp practice there on picket. Some of the companies are detailed in turn to drill on the mortars, and one of Company C was wounded in the head a few days ago. We see very little of Colonel Warren; during most of his time he is with General McClellan and staff, by whom he is highly esteemed, making observations, etc. Many of the regulars know him, having seen him out West and in other places, before the war. They say that he understands his business. We all like him as a man and a soldier; he is strict, but he knows all the wants of a soldier from experience, and seldom taxes our endurance too much.

Our men are on details night and day, building batteries and roads in every direction; one can not tell at what time of night he may be called up to shoulder his musket and march off on a detail. Saturday night, the 19th, I was on fatigue duty; we marched about three miles to the mouth of Wormley's Creek, York River, where they are putting up a battery.

Part of the road has been built by our army, leading over a creek through which a solid road has been built. As we came out of some woods at one point we could see a deserted rebel fort in the middle of a swamp to the right of the road. It was built square and in a substantial manner, with barracks inside of it, a ditch nine feet deep all around it, filled with water, and an abatis, bushes, and stumps of trees. Near it was an inferior work, partially masked; the place could not have been stormed. Further on we went through the camp of the 1st Connecticut Heavy Artillery, a regiment fourteen hundred strong.

We were astonished to see the heavy guns that have been sent to this point for the purposes of the siege. We next passed through the most extensive corn-field that I ever saw, and came to a large peach-orchard, which was in full blossom. Emerging from the latter, we came upon the grounds of one of the first families, on which was built a fine large house, with a water front on the York River. The battery we are building is a little way from the house.

The owner of this large estate is said to be a Lieutenant in the Confederate army now at Yorktown, and owns five thousand acres of land hereabouts. This place is certainly the handsomest one I have yet seen in Virginia. I, with others, was trotted off to the corn-field, to await our time to be called upon to take our turn at the pick and shovel, which was to be in about four hours.

We accordingly stacked our arms, and sat down on the soft and yielding soil, to take it easy. In company with some others, I lit my pipe, and we sat there talking, trying to worry through the time, but it was not long before a storm, that had been threatening for some time, burst upon us in all its fury. It was rough enough for us, notwithstanding the joke went around as usual, and all tried to be merry, but it was under aggravating circumstances. We were obliged to stand up at the side of our muskets and take it all. The furrows between the hills of corn were filled with water, and we were all soaked through, men and muskets.

The latter is always a source of anxiety to a soldier, as he is aware that, with a wet, rusty weapon, he would stand a poor chance in case of an attack. Finally our turn came; we fell in, and were soon hard at work in the mud and water, with very little light, so as not to attract the attention of Johnny Reb. We worked about three hours, and were relieved, when I, with some others, succeeded in getting into a sort of kitchen of the mansion; we found a roaring fire in an old-fashioned fire-place, but every spot that a human being could squeeze into was occupied. The boys were stowed away on shelves not over six inches wide, snoring away as if they had not a trouble in the world; some were sitting on barrels, asleep in the cellar, which led off from the room; others on the window-sill, and I saw one fellow trying to crawl under a refrigerator; in fact, it would have taken a New York detective to have ferreted them all out. In one corner of the room sat H., looking full of mischief; he is one of the leading spirits. Butch, the "head devil," was not to be seen; he was doubtless stowed somewhere in a comfortable place, if there was such a thing to be found. Fuel becoming short, and the boys having burnt up several cot bedsteads, H. said, "George, just put that mantel-piece on the fire; there are some more of them up-stairs, I will bring them down." No sooner said than done; the mantel-piece threw out its cheerful blaze on the scene. Just then a crowd of officers of all grades filled the doorway, with alarm depicted on their countenances, saying that the chimney was on fire. The boys looked at one another, as if to say, "We have done it this time." We did not care whether the whole house was burned to ashes or not, as far as its loss was concerned; but, in truth, it was a dangerous accident, for the rebels, guided by the light, could have shelled us easily to our great loss. The chimney, however, was soon burnt out, and everything fortunately went on without interruption.

A little while before this, the innocent H. and the missing "Butch" had been "scouting" on their own account to see if anything could be made. They found a pig-sty with a squad of the boys asleep in it, but no genuine pigs. They soon after discovered the pigs running about at large. They ran one down; H. seized it, and "Butch" drew his knife across his throat in the dark. H. loosened his hold, saying, "He is a dead pig," when the bristly quadruped made off on the "double-quick." "Butch" discovered that, in the hurry and darkness, he must have used the back of his knife. They turned back to find the others, but they were all missing.

Trotting along, not in very good humor at the loss of fresh meat, "Butch" spied a blind horse in a field. Determined to have a sensation at least, he drove him into a barn where a lot of the boys were sleeping in the stalls and on the floor. Roused by the new-comer, and half frightened out of their senses, it was some time before they could believe that the enemy were not upon them, and that they were not all prisoners. This is the way in which some of the "red devils" amuse themselves at every opportunity that is presented either for frolic or mischief.

The battery we were working on is one of great importance; it is supported by gabions, and will mount two two-hundred and five one-hundred-pound Parrotts. It was commenced and put up within two or three days, and was masked. The guns are brought up at night by a large truck drawn by from fifty to one hundred horses, and will be mounted by to-morrow. Although it has stormed a cold north-easter, with rain for two days, the work has been carried on unceasingly, and, in fact, everybody is busy doing something, etc.   D.

Soon after the arrival of the regiment in front of Yorktown, John G. and two others slipped out of camp, and went on a foraging expedition on their own account. In their rambles they discovered a barn, under which a half-grown hog had taken refuge; they tried all their artful and winning ways to induce him to come out, but he was evidently a shrewd pig, as all their allurements failed, and only elicited a knowing grunt. Finally, a bright idea occurred to John, who was a famous forager. He went off, and soon returned with half a dozen ears of corn, one of which he placed about two feet from the barn, and several more at intervals of a few feet further away. The trio, armed with clubs, John having a stout whiffletree in one hand and a dirk-knife in the other, took up strategic positions around the corners of the barn, and waited patiently for further developments.

Presently the pig was heard approaching the nearest ear of corn, with grunts of satisfaction, and cautiously advancing, seized it, and retreated, having soon devoured it. He came from his covert the next time with more confidence, and munched on the other ear further from his base of retreat; and not seeing anything alarming in the situation, finally went for the others. At the proper moment the trio made a grand charge to cut off the porcine retreat, but he was on the alert, and retired on a run. They threw their clubs at him, John throwing his with more energy than skill, which sent him sprawling on the ground, his club doing more harm to the side of the barn than to the pig; but he scrambled along on all-fours, and succeeded in catching his victim by the hind leg, and in his anxiety to secure him, commenced stabbing him in the only part of the animal that was presented to his view, but which did not happen to be a very vital one. This undignified proceeding called forth from the pig a protest shrill enough to wake the dead. But reinforcements were at hand, and the pig was dispatched. He was cut up, skinned and divided, and John made for camp with his share of fresh pork ; but, unluckily for him, he ran across an officer of the provost-guard. He was halted, and asked where he got his meat. "Bought it ; where do you think I should get it?" That was "too thin," and John was put under arrest; but soon after he saw S. going by, who had been out on a little forage for himself, but was returning empty-handed, not having met with any luck. He called to him, and at the same time threw his meat toward him ; the officer called to S., and said that if he took the meat he would arrest him also. But S. took chances, grabbed the pork, and legged it. John was put under guard in a tent ; but after half an hour's detention, seeing an opportunity, he crawled out under the rear of the tent, and made his way back to camp. He did not eat any army rations that day or the next, but ate pork-chops morning, noon, and night, to repletion, and thought that it was the sweetest meat that he had ever eaten, because, as he said, "it was corn-fed."

Tuesday, April 22.—The siege operations were somewhat delayed by the frequent and heavy rains, but the preparations proceeded with unwearying industry, rain or shine, night and day, without cessation. The battery No. 1, which the Fifth and 1st Connecticut erected on the bank of York River at the mouth of Wormley Creek, in front of the Fairnholt House, was the heaviest mounted of them all. It commanded the water-front of Yorktown and Gloucester Point, and the extreme left of the enemy's massive works. It was distant 5,000 yards from Gloucester; 4,800 from Yorktown wharf; 4,000 from the center of Yorktown, and 3,800 from the enemy's "big gun." It was garrisoned by a detail from the 1st Connecticut Artillery, under the command of Captain Burke and Major Kellogg. This regiment was under the command of Colonel Tyler, and was justly considered one of the finest organizations in the service.

We were visited by a north-east storm which lasted two days, and directly afterward by a south-easter, which flooded the country and made our camping-ground a large pond part of the time; but it was well ditched immediately afterward, and made comfortable. All of the companies that could be spared were detailed to corduroy the road to Shipping Point, as it was full of deep holes, in some of which the mules sunk breast deep.

On Thursday, the 24th, some of the companies were detailed to make gabions. The weather was cold and the sky overcast, and appearances indicated the approach of one of the usual hard rains. We were also short of rations, and had only one cracker apiece, a cup of coffee and a small piece of bacon for breakfast, with small prospect of having any hard-tack for dinner or supper.

On Tuesday, the 29th, four companies of the 1st Connecticut were relieved from the duties of unloading shot, shell, and mortars at the landing by two companies of the 5th New York; battery No. 10 was garrisoned by two companies of the Fifth, under command of Captain Winslow. This work was situated in the middle of the first parallel, between "Right Branch" and York River. It was distant from the fort 2,550 yards; from right redoubt, 2,150 yards; from high redoubt, 1,500 yards. Its armament was three 100-pounder Parrotts; one 30-pounder do.; and seven four and a half inch rifled siege guns. One company of the Fifth garrisoned battery No. 11, and were employed in getting out timber and hewing the same for sea-coast mortar-platforms. It was situated at the head of a ravine, distant from Gloucester 4,700 yards; from Yorktown wharf, 3,650 yards; from the fort, 2,600 yards; from exterior works, 2,400 yards; from Wynn's Mills, 3,300 yards. Its armament was to consist of four 10-inch sea-coast mortars.

On Wednesday, the 30th, at 2 P.M., battery No. 1 opened for the first time, and thundered its eloquent protests against treason with a power worthy of the cause in which it spoke. The fire was first directed at the wharf at Yorktown, where the enemy were busily engaged in discharging six or seven schooners; the vessels were soon driven off. In all, thirty-nine shots were fired, which were replied to by the enemy, twenty-three of whose guns could be brought to bear on this work; but such was the engineering skill expended in its construction, that the fire of the enemy produced no effect of a damaging nature. One shot per hour was fired during the night, and morning of May 1st, to prevent the enemy's transports, which had been driven away, from landing. Companies G and F were ordered to proceed to Cheesman's Landing, about three miles from camp, and assist the other two companies there in unloading shell and mortars from the vessels, for the purposes of the siege. One company was ordered to garrison battery No. 12. It was situated on Peninsular plateau, behind "Secession Huts," and was distant from exterior earthworks 2,000 yards; from fort, 1,600 yards; from burnt house, 925 yards. Its armament consisted of five 10-inch and five 8-inch siege mortars. The enemy kept up a continuous fire on the men in the trenches at the front.

On Friday, the 2d, battery No. 13 was garrisoned by two companies of the Fifth, under the command of Captain Cambrelling. It was situated right of Boyau, in front of Moore's house, and was distant from Gloucester Point 3,000 yards; from exterior works, 2,400 yards; from fort, 1,300 yards. Its armament was six 30-pounder Parrotts. Sixty shots were fired during the day from battery No. 1 with effect. The largest gun in the enemy's works, a rifled sixty-eight, exploded on its twenty-eighth discharge.

Saturday, the 3d, found the men still hard at work at their posts of duty; they were hungry and rations were scant. Thirty-four shots were fired from No. 1; two of the shells, which were badly directed, dropped into battery No. 10, one

of which exploded, fortunately without injury to any one.
During the night the enemy kept up a heavy fire of artillery,
and at the same time were evacuating their works, which
were occupied at daylight, on Sunday, the 4th, by the Union
troops. Some of the Fifth who were detailed in battery No.
13, at the front, were among the first in the Confederate
works, not by orders, but on their own responsibility, while
the rear guard of the enemy were discharging shell into the
evacuated works. "Brockey," of Company E, had hold of
the halyards that hoisted the Stars and Stripes on the staff,
where a few hours before had floated the rebel ensign.

General Magruder had under his command at Yorktown,
fifty-three thousand men.

The enemy left fifty-three heavy guns, all of which they
had spiked, besides several that had burst; also a large
quantity of cotton, tobacco, flour, beans, and other stores.
Torpedoes that had been planted in the ground exploded,
killing and wounding a number of the soldiers.

The 6th day of May, at daylight, was the time that had
been appointed to open a general bombardment of the
enemy's works from all the fourteen batteries, and it was
the opinion of the experienced officers of the engineer and
artillery corps that the works would have been untenable in
twelve hours thereafter.

On Monday, the 5th, the scattered companies of the
Fifth were united once more, and the regiment received two
months' pay from Major Hoops, the Paymaster, and their
clothing account was settled.

Brigadier-General W. F. Barry, Chief of Artillery, says in
his report:

"The difficulties attending tne placing in position the unusually heavy machinery used in this siege were very much increased by the peculiarities of the soil, and by the continuance
of heavy rains during the greater portion of the operations.
Oftentimes the heavier guns, in their transportation of three

miles from the landing to the batteries, would sink in the quicksands to the axletrees of their traveling carriages.

"The efforts of the best trained and heaviest of the horses of the artillery reserve were of no avail in the attempts to extricate them, and it became necessary to haul this heavy metal by *hand*, the cannoneers working knee deep in mud and water. In these labors the officers and men of the 1st Connecticut Artillery and the 5th New York Volunteers exhibited extraordinary perseverance, alacrity, and cheerfulness. It finally became necessary to construct a heavy corduroy road, wide enough for teams to pass each other, the whole distance from the landing to the dépôt.

"In conclusion, I beg to present the names of Colonel Tyler, Majors Kellogg, Hemmingway, and Trumbull, and Captains Perkins and Burke, 1st Connecticut Artillery; Major Alexander Doull, 2d New York Artillery; Colonel Warren, Lieutenant-Colonel H. Duryea, Major Hull, and Captain Winslow, 5th New York Volunteers, as conspicuous for intelligence, energy, and good conduct under fire."

The following letter was read off at evening parade:

OFFICE CHIEF OF ARTILLERY, ARMY OF POTOMAC,
CAMP WINFIELD SCOTT, before Yorktown, Va.,
May 5, 1862.

COLONEL G. K. WARREN, *Commanding New York 5th Regiment Volunteers:*

COLONEL:—In transmitting to you the enclosed copy of Special Order No. 135, Headquarters Army of Potomac, relieving your regiment from its temporary service with the siege train under my command, it gives me great pleasure to state that the duties which have devolved upon it, in landing, transporting, and placing in position the extremely heavy material to be employed in the siege of Yorktown, have been performed with cheerfulness, alacrity, and intelligence. The highest praise is due to yourself, your officers, and enlisted men, for the very creditable manner in which your very arduous (and at one or two points hazardous) labors have been performed.

Should circumstances again render siege operations necessary, I shall be much gratified to have your regiment again placed under my orders.

     I am, Colonel, very respectfully,
       Your obedient servant,
        WILLIAM F. BARRY,
     Brig.-Gen., Chief of Artillery.

We received orders at tattoo to march at 1 A.M., with four days' rations. A battle was raging, and heavy and continuous firing was heard in the direction of Williamsburg. We marched at about midnight. It was raining, and was so dark that one could not see the man in front. After proceeding a short distance, sliding and slipping about in the mud and water, the order to march was countermanded, and we returned to camp.

At 3 o'clock on the morning of Friday, the 9th, the reveille was sounded, and we marched at seven. We passed by three separate burying-grounds, where some four or five hundred pine slabs denoted the resting-places of as many soldiers. While marching through Yorktown, the men were surprised at the extent, strength, and beauty of the enemy's fortifications. The weather was very sultry, and the roads were dry and dusty, and as the men carried about sixty pounds weight on their backs, their sufferings were great. The hot sun beat down on their heads, and quite a number of them were sun-struck. On the march we passed the different fields where skirmishing had taken place on the preceding days. The action at Williamsburg was very severe, the place being strongly fortified, and many a gallant fellow was cut down before the enemy was dislodged. The trees on the outskirts of the open plain in which the enemy had built their works, and which partially protected our forces, were completely riddled with bullets, and the small saplings were cut down entirely. The hospitals and churches of Williamsburg were still filled with the wounded and dying. The regiment marched through the latter place in company front, and the men were much amused at the looks of disgust which were portrayed on the faces of many of the inhabitants.

There were also some sad sights. A lady dressed in mourning, and holding a little child by the hand, stood viewing the troops from a balcony, as they passed by, and was weeping; she had probably lost a husband or some near relative in the late battle.

The command was halted for the night about four miles beyond the city, having marched twenty-two miles. After spreading their ponchos on the ground, and wrapping themselves in their blankets, all, except the pickets and camp guard, were soon fast asleep.

Saturday, May 10th, we turned out at sunrise, wet and cold from the heavy dew, and somewhat stiff from the previous day's exertions; marched at 8 A.M., at rather a dragging step at first, and halted at 2 P.M., after traveling about eight miles, and went into bivouac at Camp Warren. A squad of men were detailed for guard at General Sykes' headquarters.

Sunday, May 11.—The wagons arrived last night, and for the first time in three days we were blessed with the sight of coffee. At 1 P.M. we slung knapsacks, marched about four miles and bivouacked at Camp Buchanan, six miles from West Point. The men made their coffee in their tin cups, feasted on hard-tack, smoked their pipes and chatted, and then spread themselves on the ground and went to sleep.

Monday, May 12.—There was a heavy dew during the previous night, which wet the blankets and chilled the men. They made coffee and awaited orders. The reveille awoke the regiment at 3 A.M. on the 13th, and we marched at six. In the afternoon we fell into the wrong road, were halted suddenly, and ordered to unsling knapsacks, which were left in the woods; after which we were ordered off down a road for some distance on a double-quick, and into an open field to the left, where the regiment was quickly drawn up in line of battle, facing a wood, to support the cavalry who had encountered the enemy, and deployed skirmishers. We remained under arms in readiness for two hours, our interest stimulated by squads of cavalrymen who kept filing in from the front, each and all agreeing that the enemy were in force. At dark we were relieved by some infantry and artillery, and countermarched to get the knapsacks. Our gait was considerably accelerated by the sight of dense clouds of smoke which arose from the vicinity of the spot where they had been placed, and alarmed for their safety, as it was soon discovered that the woods were on fire. Fortunately, the knapsacks had been cared for by some of the drum corps, drummers Jenks and Verney being complimented by Colonel Warren for their efforts in saving them.

The regiment resumed the march, and after a tedious stretch of thirteen miles, running well into the night, we suddenly struck the camp at Cumberland, on the banks of the Pamunkey River. It was a magnificent sight as it burst upon the view of the weary men.

Below them, stretched over an immense plain, were encamped an army of eighty thousand men. Innumerable camp-fires could be seen in every direction, which became smaller as the eye scanned them in the distance, until at the outline they seemed like mere star points of light. We arrived in camp about 11 P.M., and immediately went into bivouac. A storm which lasted two days came upon us, which made the men extremely uncomfortable, as they were without shelter. On the 15th, all the troops were drawn up in an immense square, and reviewed by Secretary SEWARD. It was a splendid spectacle, notwithstanding the rain.

The country through which the regiment marched to this camp was desolate and deserted. Not a cow, horse, or cart were to be seen on the farms, nor indeed a living animal of any kind. Many of the houses were dismantled and deserted, and the few that were occupied were inhabited by old men, women, or invalids, who hung out a white rag for protection; but not an able-bodied man or a grown boy was to be seen. They were all in the Confederate army. Very few negroes were found, nearly all having been driven into the interior by their owners. While staying in this camp, considerable traffic was kept up by a few soldiers of trading dispositions. They obtained passes to the landing on the river, and laid out their money in cakes, cheese, and butter, and on their return disposed of their commodities to their comrades at a profit of five hundred per cent. So eager were the men to buy, at any price, that they fought, pushed, and shoved their way through the crowd, with their money in their fists, and exchanged it for the coveted luxuries without regard to long or short measure. Their principal anxiety was to get something, reckless of cost. One of the men managed to buy a barrel of cider, on which he cleared about fifty dollars when it was only two-thirds gone. A raid was made upon it by some of the "red devils," who tumbled him, with the cider and all of his customers, into a promiscuous heap, and in consequence none of the raiders got enough to wet their lips with.

On Saturday, the 17th, we marched five miles, and bivouacked near the White House. General Sykes' division of regulars, including the Fifth, were assigned to the Fifth Army Corps, under command of General Fitz John Porter. Seven wagoners were killed by guerrillas between New Kent and Cumberland.

Who were the guerrillas? When the army was marching along a road, occasionally an old, grizzly-bearded man might be seen hoeing away at a patch of ground near his cabin, apparently so much absorbed in his work as to scarcely notice anything else; nor did he attract any attention in return. But the main body having passed along, were followed by the stragglers, at first numerous, but gradually decreasing in numbers until now and then only one perhaps might be seen at considerable intervals. Now, that apparently harmless old man has dropped his hoe for his rifle, perhaps the same that his grandfather used in the Revolutionary struggle for independence. He is lying in wait, behind some stone wall or convenient clump of bush, or perhaps near his barn, where some belated or sick soldier may seek rest for the night.

At the company roll call in camp next morning a man is reported missing. He is never heard of again by comrades, family, or friends. He is on the army records as a "deserter." That is all that will ever be known of him on this earth; but that old man could solve the mystery if he would.

One morning, just before the regiment started on its day's march, Colonel Warren said he had a remark to make to the men, which was about as follows: He had noticed on the previous day a great deal of straggling, and it must not occur again. "Now, to-day," said he, "I intend to act as doctor, and for such as are disposed to lag behind, I have some pills which are a sure cure," and he tapped his revolver significantly as he said it. It is needless to say that there were very few sick men that day, and it was astonishing how well the regiment kept together.

To those who have never been in the army, and may chance to read this, it may be said that on a march there are many who drop out from choice as well as from exhaustion. The surgeons and some of the field officers always follow in the rear of a regiment, brigade, or division; the former examine those who are sick, and if, in their judgment, they are not good enough for a few steps further, they are put in ambulances and brought along. But there are some men of strong wills who would not give in even when dangerously ill, until compelled to do so by a surgeon. The camp guard are also in the rear, and they drive the stragglers along; if they escape them, they are liable to be picked up by the brigade, division, or corps provosts; and last of all comes the Provost-General of the army, with at least a regiment of regular infantry and a squadron of cavalry, who scour both sides of the road, looking into farm-houses, barns, etc. In an engagement, all of the provost guards pick up the men who fall to the rear, and form them into battalions, and they are marched again to the front and assigned a position, often the very worst that can be found.

Reveille started us from our slumbers at 2 A.M., on Monday, the 19th. After bolting some coffee and hard-tack, we started off on our march, and at the end of two miles we halted to await the construction of a bridge. While patiently tarrying for this purpose, we were visited by a heavy shower of rain. After several hours spent like chickens under the bushes to keep as much sheltered as possible, we resumed the march, and at night halted in a swamp near Tunstall's Station, about five miles distant from our starting-place. The men built slight shanties and slept on the muddy ground, but endeavored to convince themselves that they were comfortable. This effort required too vivid an imagination, and they finally gave up in disgust and fell back on their fortitude.

On Tuesday, the 20th, we remained in camp, and dined luxuriously on boiled beans, not overdone. At dusk we were favored with the usual music of heavy firing in the distance. On the 21st we marched seven miles and bivouacked for the night. On the 22d we marched six miles and bivouacked at Cold Harbor. It was reported that General Sykes' negro servant was shot dead by guerrillas while watering a horse. The latter wandered back without its rider, and two cavalrymen, who went to see what had become of him, were fired at. It occurred about half a mile from camp. On Saturday, the 24th, it commenced to rain, and the men built shanties, but had scarcely completed them when they received orders to pack knapsacks, which was done in the midst of a beating storm. We marched five miles through the mud and water, and halted at Old Church, where a cavalry skirmish had taken place during the previous night.

The men are beginning to feel severely the effects of sleeping on the ground without any covering except a blanket or overcoat, exposed to the mists and heavy dews. There are about one hundred sick in the regiment, a few cases being sun-strokes, but the majority are suffering from malarial diseases.

During the march lately the regiment passed some beautiful residences and flourishing farms, all seemingly abandoned and deserted except by a few negroes. It is a well-wooded country, and most of the marches have been made over roads through the woods. There was no scarcity of water, the country abounding in fine springs; but, on the other hand, the bill of fare clearly showed that there was no danger of being overfed. Sometimes "Yankee Doodle" was served for breakfast, "The Red, White, and Blue" for dinner, and "Hail Columbia" for supper. The roll calls took the place of sandwiches to fill up with, all day long while in camp, and a general inspection of arms every night at 6 P.M.

Colonel Warren was now in command of a provisional brigade, consisting of the 5th New York, the 1st Connecticut Heavy Artillery (at the time acting as infantry, about 1,000 strong), the 6th Pennsylvania Cavalry (Rush's Lancers), and Weeden's R. I. Battery. In all the marches of the Fifth, either before or after this period, the 1st Connecticut was the only regiment, besides the regulars, that put their endurance to a test, and between them and our boys it was a close match.

On the 25th, Colonel Warren rode into camp in great haste, and the brigade was put in readiness to march; but after lying on their arms a couple of hours, three companies of the Fifth were ordered on picket, and the rest of the troops were dismissed.

The position which Warren's brigade now occupied was on the right and rear of the army, to guard against guerrillas and detachments of the enemy from cutting off supply trains.

We were obliged to be very vigilant to avoid a surprise or to be ready if attacked, and pickets were detailed in all directions.

On one of the recent marches during the night, the Colonel gave strict orders for the men to make as little noise as possible, on account of the nearness of the enemy; but he had hardly ceased speaking when a jackass, on which the band-master was riding, having scented water somewhere, set up a discordant "he-haw." It is needless to say that the Colonel was excited! in fact, that word would not do justice to his feelings; and he did not stop to place the few words which escaped from his lips in the most studied and graceful language. To make matters worse, "Saxey" and another of the drummer-boys, who could not resist the opportunity for a frolic, managed to apply some horse-chestnut burs to the flanks of the brute, who made a jump for the woods, and threw his rider into the brush, from which he emerged with his face and hands much scratched and clothing torn, besides losing his rosinante.

CHAPTER IX.

THE PENINSULAR CAMPAIGN—(*Continued*).

Pamunkey Bridge—Crossing the Bridge—Killed at his Birthplace—The Rebels Retire—Rebel Communication Broken—An Astonished Negro—A Descendant of Patrick Henry—Return to Camp—Hanover Court House—Captain Griffin's Brazen Pet—After the Battle—Burying the Dead—Result—A Raid and a Capture—A Reconnoissance—Back to Old Church—What we Fought for at Hanover—The Chickahominy—New Bridge—A Donation of Flour—A Speculation in Doughnuts—Sal Eratus and what She Did—A Pair of Shoes—Sleeping under Arms—General McClellan's Address to the Army—General Sykes' Speech—Picket at New Bridge—Review by General Prim—Masking a Battery at Night—Stuart's Cavalry on a Raid—What they Did

Monday, May 26, 1862.—Four companies of the Fifth, A, G, H, and —, in company with a squadron of Rush's Lancers and a section of artillery, under the command of Colonel Warren, marched early in the morning from camp near Old Church to a place called Pipping Trees, Pamunkey River, a distance of nine miles. As the Lancers approached the river they were discovered by the enemy, who were a detachment of the 4th Virginia Cavalry guarding the bridge at this point. A skirmish immediately ensued, in which two of the enemy were wounded. The detachment of the Fifth hurried forward and drew up in line of battle on the high ground overlooking the bridge. The enemy commenced firing on them, but with defective aim.

Company H, under the leadership of Lieutenant-Colonel H. Duryea, was ordered to charge the bridge. They approached as near as possible under cover of the woods, and then made a dash for it on the double-quick. The enemy's cavalry on the bridge, who were dismounted and acting as infantry, retreated to their reserve on the other side of the river. One of them halted at about the center and took deliberate aim, but before he could discharge his piece there were half a dozen shots fired at him almost simultaneously, and he fell shot through the body, mortally wounded. He was picked up and carried to a farm-house that stood near the approach to the bridge, which proved to be the same in which himself and his father were born. He died like a brave man, fighting for what he probably thought the right, and literally in defense of home and fireside.

Private Woodfall, of Company H, was wounded by a shot at about the same instant that this man received his death wound. The company, followed by the cavalry, kept on over the bridge, and the latter deployed in battle array for a charge. The rebel cavalry in the meantime kept up a running fire, and were flying like the wind on splendidly mounted horses; the Lancers followed, but were left far behind in the rear.

After a portion of the battalion were stationed as pickets to avoid a surprise, and as a guard over the stacked arms, the rest of the men commenced the destruction of the bridge. It was substantially built of oak and pine timber, and was of great benefit to the Confederates, as it connected the great highway used for the transportation of supplies to Richmond from that part of the country.

Colonel Warren directed the men how to pull it down in a scientific manner, and under his instructions there was soon nothing left of it but the fallen trestles and supports, floating in the rapid current. Fires were built on each shore to burn portions of the timbers. An old slave stood looking on in wonderment, rubbing his hands together, in evident glee, when finally he spoke up and said, that the "Squires were ten years in argufying about, and buildin' dat dar sucumstructure, but yuse massa Lincums' sojurs had dun gone and spiled it in ten minits." When its destruction was completed and the battalion were making preparations to march again, it was discovered that James R. Murray, of

Company A, was left on the other shore, but luckily he was able to work his way over by jumping from one piece of floating timber to another.

The men had captured some half a dozen citizens of the upper class, at various houses on the march, to avoid intelligence of the movement being made known to the enemy. One of them, a Doctor Henry, who wore a high silk hat and a black frock coat, was a fine old Virginia gentleman. He was questioned by the Adjutant as to the whereabouts of the enemy and other matters that might have afforded valuable information; but he was self-possessed and secretive to the utmost. Finally he was informed that he would be shot if he did not answer. He drew himself up, and raising his hat, said: "I am an old, gray-haired man of sixty years. My name is Henry, a direct descendant of PATRICK HENRY, of Roanoke. I was born and reared near this spot, where the illustrious patriot spent his youth and manhood; and I will say, that I have never been guilty of doing a dishonorable act in my life, nor can you compel me, with all the force at your command, to do so at the present time." He was taken to Colonel Warren, who treated him in a noble and generous manner, and soon put him at his ease. The object of the expedition having been accomplished, the detail returned back to camp, having marched about eighteen miles.

Several of the companies were sent out on picket at dark, one of which was Company F. The latter constructed shanties while the rain fell heavily. At midnight the outposts were ordered to fall back on the reserve. The night was so dark it was impossible to see a yard ahead; the mud was knee deep, and they floundered back, slipping, sliding, growling, and cursing. They had no shelter from the heavy rain, but nevertheless managed to catch a little wretched sleep, sitting with their backs against the trees. In the morning they floundered back to camp in a miserable condition, and had coffee made, but had scarcely touched it, when they were ordered to duty with the rest of the command.

Early on the morning of Tuesday, the 27th, the regiment was ordered to fall in, in light marching order, which was significant to them of prospective fighting, and they felt at this time that a brush with the enemy would be a great relief to their unquiet temper, for they were not in the most amiable mood. They moved from camp near Old Church, through a heavy rain, and over bad roads, on a route leading to Hanover Court-house, parallel to the Pamunkey River. After marching some miles, Colonel Warren took the Lancers and pushed on some distance to the northward, and destroyed some bridges leading over the Pamunkey, and captured a number of prisoners and rejoined the command.

The force kept on their march to join General Porter and a portion of the Fifth Corps. On arriving at a large field, we were halted and ordered to load, and the cavalry were sent forward to reconnoiter. They had scarcely returned when, at a little distance, the booming of cannon was heard. They built a bridge over a creek, crossed, and moved at a quick step in the direction from which the sound came. But for the inevitable delay occasioned by building the bridge, the brigade would have been among the first to engage in the battle of Hanover Court-house.

General Emory, with the 5th and 6th U. S. Cavalry, Benson's 2d U. S. Artillery, and General Butterfield's brigade, had come upon the enemy, who were composed of North Carolina and Georgia regiments, under the command of General Branch, at a point about two miles from the Court-house, where the road forked to Ashland. General Emory was joined by the 25th New York and Berdan's Sharp-shooters. These regiments deployed with a section of the battery, and advanced slowly toward the enemy until reinforced by General Butterfield, with four regiments, when the enemy was charged and routed, the 17th New York capturing one gun of Latham's New Orleans battery, which had become disabled by the fire of Benson's battery. The firing here lasted one hour. The cavalry and battery were ordered in pursuit, followed by Morell's infantry and artillery, with the exception of Martindale's brigade.*

At this stage of the battle, the 5th New York came up, and followed on after Morell's division in the direction of the firing, over an immense field of wheat about one and a half miles in width. A wooden farm-house stood at about the center of this field, which had been the scene of a severe struggle. They advanced as far as Hanover Court-house. Suddenly aides, on horseback, came flying by, and the troops were ordered to return. General Porter and staff passed by, and ordered us to quick-march. A Major of the staff informed our Lieutenant-Colonel, H. Duryea, acting in command of the regiment, that we were outflanked by the enemy in force.

The Fifth faced about and hurried back again to the wheat-field. They were immediately formed in line of battle, facing toward the south-west, and advanced by the double-quick.

The sun had come out in the meantime with scorching heat, and the men were exhausted by their fifteen-mile march in the morning, over execrable roads in the rain, and a few fell down in the field from sun-stroke. It appears that Confederate troops had come up on cars from Richmond as reinforcements, and were formed in line of battle near Peake's Station, on the Virginia Central Railroad, and on the Ashland road, near the scene of the first engagement, and were in the rear of the troops following the enemy.

It is not my purpose to describe all the movements of General Porter's command, but he immediately ordered all the troops in the pursuit to face about and retrace their steps.

---

* See General McClellan's Report (pp. 206–7.)

The enemy attacked General Martindale, who had with him the 2d Maine, 25th and 44th New York, with a section of Martin's battery, on the New Bridge road facing his own position of the morning, and who held his ground against large odds until reinforced by the 13th and 14th New York and Griffin's battery.

The "Fighting 9th" Massachusetts, and the 62d Pennsylvania, of McQuade's brigade, pushed through woods on the right (our original left) on the flank of the enemy. Butterfield, with the 83d Pennsylvania and the 16th Michigan, advancing by the railroad and through the woods, further to the right, completed the rout of the enemy.

When the 5th New York arrived near the scene, it had become quite exciting; batteries dashed along the roads on a *sharp run*, and the infantry were going at a *double-quick* through the fields, and they were surprised to see so many troops, and wondered where they had all come from, not knowing when they started from camp in the morning where they were going or what was required of them. All was excitement and activity; they were moving on in quick time to attack the enemy, who had just shown themselves on the edge of the woods that skirted the field to the southward. Presently the music commenced, with the prolonged rattling that continuous musketry-fire produces. The artillery had not yet got to work, nor was it needed until the enemy had got on the retreat. General Butterfield came dashing up in front of the Fifth as they were going on the double-quick in line of battle, battalion front, for the woods. He took off his cap and waved it above his head, and said : "Go in, boys ! and I ll see you supported !"

In a few moments they had reached the wood, which was entered with a Zouave cheer. The sulphurous smoke hung so thick that it was almost impossible to see any distance. They relieved the 25th and 44th New York, who had stood the brunt of the engagement, and had suffered severely.

The last regiment (Ellsworth's Avengers) was one of the finest bodies of picked men in the service, morally as well as physically. The men advanced through the woods, stepping over the Union and Confederate dead and wounded, who lay thick, and out of the woods to the Ashland road; down the road to the railroad cut, and after some difficulty climbed up the bank and advanced over an open field. The enemy had reached the cover of a wood the other side of the field in full retreat, and the men could not get at them. Night coming on, they were recalled, and marched back, very much disappointed at losing the opportunity to grapple with the enemy as compensation for their long and laborious tramp. As the regiment passed the men who had been in the thick of the fight in the woods, just in advance of the Zouaves, some of them said that as soon as the enemy saw our red breeches coming through they beat a hasty retreat, and a Confederate officer who was taken prisoner also stated that when they saw the Zouaves charging in a steady, unbroken front toward them, they thought there was too much steel for them. The sight no doubt hastened their movements.

As the men passed down the Ashland road after coming out of the wood, they saw Captain (afterward General) Griffin, of the 5th United States Artillery, sighting his guns personally, and was patting one of them on its side, which had just blown up one of the enemy's caissons, and killed several horses at the same time. He exclaimed, " A good shot! now another like that." In the wood and at the side of a fence on the border of the road by which the enemy retreated, the dead and wounded were very numerous. Some of them had ghastly wounds and were still struggling with death. Others lay dead without the sign of a mark on them, with faces upturned, their stony eyes glaring at the sky. A father and his son were found lying side by side, wounded and bleeding freely; the old man was crying, while the son endeavored to console him. In another place two or three were found dead, whose appearance led one to think they had died talking to one another; others reclined against the fence, among whom was a powerful fellow, with a portion of his forehead torn away and his brains exposed, who was still breathing. A splendid bay horse lay rigid in the road; he had cleared his last fence. All night long we could hear the groans of the wounded and dying at the temporary hospital in a house near by. That night we bivouacked on the field, and as the men were without ponchos or blankets, and the ground damp and cold from the heavy dew, we passed a wretched night.

On the morning of the 28th, when the men awoke, some of them found that they were lying among the dead; it was after dark when they laid down the previous night, and what they supposed were soldiers sleeping with blankets over them, were dead men. Details were made from some of the regiments, including the Fifth, to bury the dead. Trenches were dug large enough to hold twenty-five. The detail from the Fifth buried twenty-five Confederates as decently as their circumstances would allow. They were all placed in a single trench with an Orderly Sergeant at their head, the post he occupied when alive; at each corner of the plot they placed stakes, and at one end of it, cut on the trunk of a tree, "25 N. C. X killed."

The result of the battle was two hundred of the enemy buried on the field; about eight hundred prisoners captured; one twelve-pound howitzer and caisson, a great number of small arms, and two railroad trains loaded with a large amount of tobacco, were captured and destroyed. The Union loss was less than four hundred in killed and wounded. One wing of the Fifth and the Lancers went about four miles and captured an entire company of the enemy, besides paroling many wounded who were in houses on their route. The next day, Thursday, the 29th, Colonel Warren, with the Fifth,

1st Connecticut, the Lancers, a section of Weeden's battery, and other detachments, went on a reconnoissance on the Ashland road, about seven miles. It was the same path by which the enemy retreated. We found knapsacks and clothing strewn along the road. The advance was cautiously made, with skirmishers deployed ahead and on the flanks, as we might come upon the enemy at any time, or run into an ambush. At one time we laid in line of battle.

Colonel Warren, with the cavalry, finally pushed forward and entered Ashland, the birthplace of Henry Clay, capturing some prisoners, and obtaining information of General McDowell's advance. We then marched back to camp, and after resting two hours, we were again on our way to Old Church, which we reached about midnight, having marched fifty miles since we left it on the 27th. The men suffered greatly for the want of food, and straggled, limping along the road toward camp. By some mismanagement of the Commissariat the men had received no rations since leaving camp. In the railroad trains captured on the battle-field there was a large quantity of tobacco, from which the men filled all the available pocket-room they could command. They improvised the art of cigar-making, and produced some prize specimens of mammoth size.

The object of the battle of Hanover Court-house was to clear away the enemy from the right and rear of the army, and to leave no obstacle in the way to the junction of Gen. McDowell's First Corps, which was lying south of Fredericksburg, with the right of General McClellan's army besieging Richmond. If he had been allowed to advance, the march could have been easily accomplished in two days, and in all likelihood the seven days' retreat, a month later, would never have occurred, and General McClellan would have been promptly in Richmond. At all events, that was the belief of all in the Fifth Corps, and of the Confederates themselves.

The smooth-bore rifles, heretofore in use by eight companies of the regiment, were exchanged on the 30th for Springfield rifles. The command expected to march the same day at 4 P.M., but a terrible thunder-storm coming up, it was delayed. The thunder and lightning were grand in the extreme, and at times truly terrific; it rained in torrents, and continued until late in the night. It seemed ominous of the storm of battle which was about to open about Richmond.

The next morning, reveille roused us at two o'clock and at five o'clock we marched four miles, the roads all under water and muddy, and were ordered back again; and finally, after covering six or seven miles, encamped upon an evacuated camp-ground near Cold Harbor, joining the rest of the division.

In the afternoon an engagement took place on the other side of the Chickahominy. There was a constant roar of artillery, and the roll of the musketry was incessant. The division was held under arms, and all ready to move when wanted. The engagement alluded to was the battle of Fair Oaks, and the division would have been sent across the river, and probably engaged, had not the bridges been carried away by the unprecedentedly high flow of the waters, occasioned by the recent heavy storm of rain already mentioned.

Sunday, June 1.—The conflict commenced again at daylight, but in a few hours appeared to recede in the distance. Our forces drove the enemy and approached to within five miles of Richmond. The aggregate losses on both sides in killed and wounded was 12,500 men. We marched at 4 P.M. about two miles, and encamped in a dense pine wood near New Bridge, which was an admirable spot for a camp. The firing on the other side of the river led the men to expect that they would be called upon at any moment to take part in the great struggle which appeared to them would perhaps decide the fate of one of the two great armies. We were so near the enemy that no drum or bugle call was allowed to be sounded.

On the 2d the weather was very warm, and the sound of battle was almost entirely subdued, very little firing being heard during the day. A small detail was made up and employed in digging about the camp. Colonel Warren supplied the men with a quantity of flour, and bread-baking was the order of the day. Those who had tin plates were the favored ones; the rest were obliged to wait and borrow them from their comrades. The flour was simply mixed with water and made into unleavened cakes and baked; but the men relished them with great satisfaction, as it was an acceptable change in the diet to which they had been accustomed; and at times was heard from some epicure who could not restrain from giving vent to his satisfaction, the expressive, but not very elegant remark, "Aint this bully."

Two of the boys (of Eastern Shore celebrity in mischief) procured about a bushel of flour, and some sugar and saleratus, borrowed a sheet-iron kettle of one of the officers' servants, obtained a lot of fat salt pork, and went into business. They first washed all the salt from the pork, tried it out, mixed their flour with sugar and saleratus, let it rise, and then made some of the finest doughnuts, as they supposed, that were ever served up; at all events they were "done brown." When they had made a great pile of them, they opened shop, and never before was there such a rush to procure some of those elegant doughnuts. The pile was soon gone at five for twenty-five cents, and the demand far exceeded the supply. Occasionally a man was found who had the temerity to express the opinion that they were rather tough, and were good specimens of home-made India rubber; but he was immediately frowned down as a barbarian, and a man devoid of epicurean tastes. The sale kept up so briskly that by night the batter was almost exhausted, and the firm closed up their business for the day, estimated their profits, and talked over their plans for the future. But they were in a quandary. The batter was nearly gone, and no more flour could be obtained within range of their guns. Suddenly the contracted brow of H. relaxed from its thoughtful aspect, and his face lit up with a genial smile. He had struck an idea, and was like a gold-miner when he pans out a rich lot of " pay-dust." " Eureka !" he exclaimed, quoting Archimedes. They had still on hand a quantity of saleratus, which up to this time was looked upon as dead stock, but now it was worth its weight in gold. "What idea have you struck, pards?" asked H.'s colleague. "Why, you noodle-head, its very plain—put in more saleratus !" " That's the cheese. Why didn't you think of that before?" The saleratus was added in generous quantity, and they turned in and went to sleep, probably dreaming of light doughnuts for the million—so light, in fact, that a piece of dough the size of a walnut would turn into a doughnut the size of a pumpkin. At all events, they must have dreamed on promiscuous subjects, for they had partaken liberally of their own stock in trade to show their faith in home manufactures. I am not positive that this was the identical night that the whole camp was aroused by fearful screams, and the men grasped their rifles, and the officers rushed out of their tents clad in Georgia costume, swords and revolvers in hand, supposing at first that the enemy had captured the camp and were bayoneting the men in their tents, until it was discovered that a somnambulist of Company F had jumped up in a nightmare and was trying to climb a tree before he was awakened, having dreamed that one of Hood's Texan Rangers was trying to scalp him. At all events this was the camp where this identical thing happened, and this naturally ought to have been the night, for never before were the men's stomachs so full.

In the morning the firm were roused from their dreams of

wealth by the reveille, and jumped up in a hurry. But what a sight met their eyes! Dough, dough, dough everywhere! The fact of it was, their stock had risen about one hundred and fifty per cent. above par, and kept on rising. The floor of their tent, blankets, rifles, cartridge-boxes, and everything else, were covered with a layer of dough, and they could be traced out to the line for roll call by a string of dough. This was something that had not entered into their calculations. They, however, did well in business that day, and added saleratus, as their batter decreased, until the compound was so sour that all the sugar they could beg, borrow, or steal was not sufficient to sweeten it enough to suit the most depraved taste. Accordingly one night, after a very dull day's trade, they buried what remained of their stock in a hole outside of their tent, in the company street. But their astonishment was great in the morning at finding that the stuff refused to stay buried, and had burst through the crust of earth over it, and, like a fountain, was sending out its streams, whereupon they were obliged to heap several bushels of dirt over the spot to prevent its resurrection. The next morning they looked out of their tent with anything but confidence, expecting to see a new eruption. They were agreeably disappointed, and thus ends the long, but true story of the "Zouave" doughnuts.

As the regiment was about to assemble for evening parade, one of the drummer-boys made his appearance in his accustomed place barefoot, his shoes having mysteriously disappeared. The Drum-Major dismissed him with the admonition to present himself in just one minute and a half decently shod, or suffer the consequences. He hurried off in great anxiety as to what he should do; for, being a small boy, he had great doubt in his mind about being able to borrow a pair from any of the men off duty that would be anywhere near a fit. But time was precious, and seeing a contraband, one of the officers' servants, who wore number fourteens, he prevailed upon him, with tears in his eyes, to lend him his brogans. He made his appearance in the niche of time, and as he shuffled down the line with the drum corps, for he could not raise his feet for fear of losing his shoes, trying to put on an unconscious air, as if there was nothing extraordinary in his appearance, it was as much as all could do, from the Colonel down, to keep a straight face. Such enormous feet were never seen before on a small boy, outside of a negro minstrel show, and I venture to say that had he been shot, he would have died upright, for nothing short of an earthquake could have destroyed his equilibrium, with such a broad and lengthy foundation.

At night we slept under arms, and during the following day, the 3d, the division was drawn up on parade, and General McClellan's battle speech was read. It was, in substance, that the army was about to go into battle, and that when it marched, knapsacks, baggage, and wagons were to be left on this side of the Chickahominy. All that the men were to carry would be their arms and accoutrements, haversack, with three days' rations, and canteen of water. He said the enemy were now at bay before their citadel, and that he would be with his men in the hour of battle. General Sykes said that he could add but little; but that little was said to the point. He spoke about as follows: "Soldiers of Connecticut and New York! We are about to go into battle, and if there is any hard work to do, *we have got to do it*. We must stick by our General, and march by his side into Richmond." Cheers then rent the air, and the troops were marched back to their respective camping grounds.

The rain fell in torrents at night, and continued to do so the whole of the next day. The Chickahominy had risen to an unprecedented height, and overflowed the swampy ground on its borders, and it was feared that the flood might endanger the communications between the right and left wings of the army. Blankets and overcoats were wet through; for, having no tents, the only shelter the men had, was one of the most temporary kind. They were troubled with diarrhœa and malaria; there were about forty new cases of fevers in the regiment; many of the officers were absent sick, and others had sent in their resignations. Whisky and quinine were given out night and morning as a tonic. There were about 650 men present for duty.

The regiment went out on picket on the morning of Thursday, the 5th, on the Chickahominy, at New Bridge. The enemy opened with their batteries, and it was not long before three of our batteries were replying; the artillery duel continued for two hours, which made the position of the men on picket and the reserve anything but agreeable. They were obliged frequently to shift their positions from the road leading to the bridge, as the guns of the enemy completely commanded it, and nothing could live there a moment. Finally the Confederate guns were silenced. They wounded some of our men, killed three horses, and did other damage.*

Two Confederates who were on picket deserted their post and came over and delivered themselves up to George Finley, of Company H. They were fired at by their comrades, but escaped injury. The Confederate and Union pickets were quite close, being in plain view of each other, and sometimes made an agreement not to fire on one another. If an officer made his appearance the men jumped for cover, as they were not included in the armistice, and a general fusilade follows from both sides. One shot breaks the truce, and this may continue for some days, until they renew the agreement.

The next morning we were relieved from this duty, and several of the pickets that relieved the Fifth, were shot by the rebels, who received similar compliments in return. On the 7th three men died in the camp hospital, of fever. We

---

* General McClellan's Report, (p. 227): "NEW BRIDGE, *June* 5, 1862.—Enemy opened with several batteries on our bridge, near here this morning; our batteries seem to have pretty much silenced them, though some firing is still kept up."

were joined by the 10th New York, from Fortress Monroe. On Sunday, the 8th, after the usual inspection, the men occupied themselves in mending and washing their clothes.

On the 9th, the division was reviewed by General Prim, of Spain, the Count of Reus and Castillejos, accompanied by General McClellan and staff. General Prim paused before the Fifth, and appeared to be highly delighted. He was astonished to see a regiment uniformed exactly like the 2d Regiment of French Zouaves. He inquired respecting their organization, and complimented Colonel Warren personally on their appearance, offering him his hand in acknowledgment of his gratification. After the review the Zouaves went through a drill, bayonet exercise, etc. General Prim attentively watched the unity and precision of their movements. He clapped his hands enthusiastically, and the men felt highly complimented.

Orders were sent us on Thursday, the 12th, to be ready at a moment's notice in light marching order. We left camp at 7 P.M. and marched to the Chickahominy with other troops, numbering in all about 1,500 men. Arms were loaded and ambulances in attendance. After posting strong pickets and reserves, the remainder were set to work throwing up an earthwork to protect a battery, which they also masked; it was finished just before daylight, and we marched back to camp. If the enemy had been aware of what we were doing, they certainly would have attacked us.

On the following day, about 5 P.M., the regiment fell into line, loaded rifles, and stepped off in light marching order, without waiting for rations or evening coffee, after Stuart's cavalry, about 1,500 strong, with four guns, who made a dash by the right flank of the army and got in its rear. They attacked two squadrons of the 5th U. S. Cavalry, under the command of Captain Royall, near Hanover Old Church, and overpowered them. The first squadron was surprised and dispersed; the second charged vigorously, without regard to the enemy's numbers. Capt. Royall killed the commander of the first squadron of the enemy with his own hand, and was himself wounded in several places a moment after. It was feared the enemy might damage the railroad by which the supplies for the army were transported from White-house Landing. We bivouacked near Old Church, after a forced march of thirteen miles. A detail from the regiment, who were stationed as an outpost, and guard of protection over Mrs. Robert Lee, her daughter-in-law, the wife of Colonel Lee, and two nieces, who were living in Ruffin's house, saw all the enemy's cavalry pass along on the other side of the river a few hours before the regiment came up. This was the residence of Edmund Ruffin, the Virginian who went to Charleston and begged the honor of firing the first gun at the opening of the attack on Fort Sumter. A few weeks after the close of the war, with that insane hatred of the Union and the flag which animated so many at the time, and determined that he would never again live under the Stars and Stripes, he deliberately loaded his pistol and fired a bullet into his head, falling dead on the spot. It was the last tragic act of the Rebellion.

When the troops first arrived in this part of Virginia, about May 24th, a squad of the Fifth, under an officer, were detailed to search Ruffin's house, under the supposition that papers containing valuable information for the Union cause might be discovered. The search was submitted to with an ill grace by Mrs. Lee, and as the officer was about to depart, the following note was placed in his charge, addressed to the General in command of the division:

SIR:—I have patiently and humbly submitted to a search of my house by men under your command, who are satisfied that there is nothing here that they want, all the plate and other valuables having long since been removed to Richmond, and are now beyond the reach of any Northern marauders who may wish for their possession. WIFE OF ROBERT LEE,
General C. S. A.

Instead of not noticing her insulting and impudent communication, a guard was established over the house and grounds for the protection of the property as well as for herself and family.

After two hours' sleep we continued the march, and arrived at 1 P.M. on the 14th, at Tunstall's Station, about five miles from the White House, having marched eleven miles under a scorching sun. The enemy turned off from this point, and finally crossed the Chickahominy by Long Bridge, having made the entire circuit of the army, thus exposing the weakness of Gen. McClellan's right. They killed several teamsters and cavalrymen, and a sutler; burned fourteen army wagons and their contents, and two schooners laden with forage; cut the telegraph, and commenced pulling up the railroad track. They also fired into a train of our sick and wounded. This was about the whole of the damage done by Stuart in his celebrated raid, beside exposing the weakness of our right wing.

After a short rest, the regiment started back to camp, the lame and laggard left to follow at will, as it was a forced march throughout. Notwithstanding this, we were left in the rear of the enemy as witnesses of the burning wagons they left in their path. We halted at three o'clock in the morning, cooked some coffee, and continued the march, arriving in camp at forty minutes past 7 A.M. of Sunday, the 15th, having marched about forty-six miles in thirty-six hours. The morning was a beautiful one; the moon rose about midnight, and there was a cool, refreshing breeze. The troops on this tramp, besides the Fifth, were the 10th New York, 1st Connecticut, Rush's Lancers, and four pieces of Weeden's Rhode Island battery.

CHAPTER X.

THE SEVEN DAYS' RETREAT — BATTLE OF GAINES' MILL.

ANNIVERSARY OF THE BATTLE OF BUNKER HILL; THEN AND NOW—FREEDOM AGAINST SLAVERY—SANITARY CONDITION OF THE REGIMENT—PICKET DUTY—A SABBATH JOURNAL—DEATH OF SERGEANT REYNOLDS—SEVEN DAYS' RETREAT—FIFTH CORPS ENGAGED—BATTLE OF GAINES' MILL—DEATH OF CAPT. PARTRIDGE—COLOR-SERGEANT BERRIAN—A CHARGE IN THE WOODS—A REBEL TRICK—THE FIELD AT NIGHT—LOSSES—TESTIMONY OF THE OFFICERS—OFFICIAL REPORTS — CONFEDERATE REPORTS — INCIDENTS—WM. McDOWELL— "DAVE" BURNS — WALTER S. COLBY — FRANCIS SPELLMAN — SAD SEPARATIONS—COLONEL WARREN'S REPORT—GENERAL SYKES' REPORT.

Tuesday, June 17, 1862.—The anniversary of the battle of Bunker Hill was, to our regiment, one of comparative inactivity, nothing having occurred to give special significance or importance to the day distinguished in the history of the Union for a conflict which gave so much of character and impress to the impending struggle for independence and liberty. Yet no one of all the great army was an indifferent observer of the day. The American soldier remembered the story of Warren and his heroes, and the soldier of foreign birth, who was fighting for his adopted home, learned, if he had not before, the meaning of the event, and felt stronger for the struggle before him. The century was nearing its close, and the feeble colonies of that day had grown up into a nation of independent States, whose power, grandeur, and civilization rivaled that of the oldest nations of the world, and commanded the unanimous homage of mankind.

All around us and covering the adjacent plain for miles was an immense camp. There were assembled here scores of thousands of brave men waiting and watching another army of equally brave men, in about equal numbers, and preparing for some great encounter which might decide the issue of the momentous question which had brought them from homes and firesides, and from the progress and splendid developments of peace to the cruel and barbarous arbitration of war and blood. There were assembled in other camps, and on other fields in various parts of the Union, vast numbers of men not less brave and not less determined, and the armies who thus were flashing their blades in the sunlight were more in number than all the able-bodied men in the colonies who rejoiced over the achievements of Bunker Hill. But the issue of to-day was not less vital than that of the fourscore years passed away, and the people of the next century will no less honor the men who surrendered their all on the altar of their country. The interests of slavery that inspired the war were compelled to surrender to the grander behests of freedom; and while hundreds of thousands of brave men died in obedience to the imperialism of their leaders in behalf of slavery, it can never be forgotten that slavery made the attack, and in the contest perished. The system, which was itself a perpetual war against humanity, fell in its attack upon the free institutions under which it had grown into such colossal strength. Although we were idle for the day in camp, amid its routine the sound of distant thunder, borne by the winds, told us that the struggle was continued by some other portion of our wide-spread army of freedom.

On Wednesday, the 18th, some of our companies returned from picket. They were posted on the Richmond side of the Chickahominy, within eighty yards of the enemy's pickets. As soon as they were posted, the enemy opened from different points, but the men kept themselves sheltered behind old trees and logs, some of them being up to their waists in water, but none of them were struck, though the balls whistled very close, often striking within a few feet. The firing was continued by both sides during the day, and toward evening an additional interest was given to the scene by an artillery duel, which took place to the right. The firing was continued all night at intervals, and until they were relieved in the morning. While passing over the brow of a hill on their return to camp they were made a target for the enemy's shell, but none were injured.

The sanitary condition of the regiment continued about the same as usual. Some of the officers were absent on the sick-list, and a number of the men were in the hospitals. The locality in which we were placed, and the want of shelter, day or night, with the continuous exposure to the heavy rains alternating with scorching heat, and the dense malarial atmosphere, made an ordinary sanitary condition an impossibility.

On Thursday, the 19th, we were blessed with a supply of shelter tents, giving room for two men in each, but open front and rear. From the time the regiment landed on the Peninsula, with the exception of the three weeks spent in front of Yorktown, they had been destitute of shelter, except such as could be improvised from the branches of trees lashed together and plastered with mud for mortar, or by spreading their ponchos over low branches of trees and lying under them.

Picket duty for nearly the whole of the regiment was ordered on Friday, the 20th. Seven companies went into the swamps for twenty-four hours. In this service the artillery had a part, and a duel between the opposing batteries was almost always inevitable. The armies were very close, and a general engagement might ensue at any moment, and great vigilance was necessary to guard against a surprise. Six shell dropped into our camp, which was hidden from the view of the enemy by the woods, but their fire may have been guided by the smoke of our camp fires rising above the trees. The first shell went directly over the camp, and passed so close that some of the men dropped down, expecting it to burst. It killed a regular. Another shell burst in the 1st Connecticut camp, lying near the Fifth, and killed one of their men. About 7 P.M. Companies G and H were ordered to move in light marching order, with details from other regiments to build a battery for the protection of the artillery on picket. The rifles were loaded as usual, and ambulances in attendance, as they were liable to a sudden attack at any time. They succeeded partially without accident or discovery, but the day dawned before it was quite completed, and obliged them to discontinue their labors, to avoid being discovered by the enemy and shelled. After masking it with small trees and boughs, they retired.

Sunday, the 22d, gave us rest from the bloody work of war. There was very little picket firing, and the day was unusually quiet. The regiment was very much reduced in numbers, and had not over five hundred men fit for duty out of the nine hundred who left Baltimore to enter on the campaign. Many were mere shadows flitting about camp. Private Hunter, of Company A, died in the morning, of typhoid fever, and the funeral, which took place in the evening, was largely attended. General Sykes and staff, Colonel Warren, and other officers were present. His death was soon followed by that of our color-bearer, Sergeant Wm. T. Reynolds, of Company K, who died on Monday, the 23d. His remains were sent to his friends in New York, who were wealthy. At 1 A.M., on the 24th, a fearful thunder-storm burst over the camp, by which everything was thoroughly drenched, and soon afterward the men were called out and ordered to hold themselves in readiness, under arms, to repel an attack threatened to be made by the enemy at daylight, but which did not occur, although firing was heard in the direction of Mechanicsville. The camp remained quietly listening to the reports of the distant guns that were occasionally heard, until the 25th, on which day we were favored with a strong breeze, which made the atmosphere cool and refreshing. About noon we were ordered to fall in, in light marching order. We stacked our arms, and felt assured that there was earnest work before us.

On the morning of Thursday, the 26th, the clear sky and refreshing breeze were a pleasant prelude to its duties. We received orders to pack knapsacks and be ready to move with three days' rations. Various orders were received during the day, showing a state of uncertainty as to the movements to be made. There was very heavy firing in the afternoon about 3 P.M., which lasted until 9 P.M., on the extreme right, where an engagement was going on. Sykes' division was at length ordered to march. We left camp and went in the direction of the firing, which was at Mechanicsville, carrying overcoats, but leaving knapsacks in camp, under the charge of the provost guard, and laid in a corn-field under arms until about 4 A.M. of the 27th, in support of our forces engaged. In the early evening the firing was very heavy. The night was beautiful, a full moon casting its beams over the field, which was to many gathered there the scene of their last hours on earth. On the morrow, at the same hour, that same calm, peaceful moon, if not hidden by the passing clouds, would probably shine on thousands of the ghastly dead and the mangled forms of the wounded. As the night advanced, the din of battle at a short distance ceased, and all was quietness and seeming peace. But it was only the prelude of the storm which was to follow on the morrow, and hurl all its power and fierceness on the Fifth Corps. Many of the 5th Regiment, who were lying there that night, full of life, health, and strength, at the same hour on the morrow's eve were lying in the sleep of death, to wake not again until the last reveille. Some of them had a premonition of their fate. Captain Partridge appeared to be in an unusually serene frame of mind; he would exclaim at times to Lieutenant McConnell, as he lay gazing at the moonlit scene, " Oh! is not this beautiful! Is not this a glorious night!" He had given directions as to the disposition of his body in the event of his falling on the field, and remarked that he would not live to fight in many battles.

The morning of Friday, the 27th day of June, 1862, broke hot and sultry, and found Generals Porter and McCall (the latter of whom and been fighting the day before) stripped and ready for the fight. The wagons and heavy siege-guns had nearly all been removed to the other side of the Chickahominy during the previous night, and it now remained for General Porter to select his ground and place his troops in line for the deadly affray. The position selected was a strong one. A small, curving stream (Powhite Creek) empties into the Chickahominy, the banks of which are, in most places, bordered with a fringe of swamp, but in others rise steeply, the bed of the stream forming a ravine. East of this the ground rises in a gradual slope, crossed by gullies, and spreads into an undulating plain, with patches of woodland and clearings. The line of battle was formed on the higher ground, on the left bank of the stream, and was in the shape of the arc of a circle, covering the approaches to Woodbury's* and Alexander's Bridge, which connected the right wing of the army with the troops on the opposite, or Richmond, side of the Chickahominy. Butterfield held the extreme left of the line extending to the swamp of the Chickahominy, which was swept by our artillery on both sides of the river; then came Martindale, occupying the edge of the Powhite wood ; then Griffin, deployed across the forest ; all these belonging to Morell's division. On the right of them was Sykes' division, which, partly in woods

---

* Woodbury's Bridge, named after Colonel D. P. Woodbury, of the 4th Michigan Regiment, was the most extensive structure of the kind built during the siege. It was, with its approaches, a mile long, and in width fifteen feet ; and was constructed by his regiment in six days, during three of which it rained in torrents.

and partly in open ground, extended in rear of Cold
Harbor. It was composed of Warren's brigade (the 5th
and 10th New York) on the left, and next to Griffin, next
to whom were the two brigades of regulars; this composed
the first line. Behind this was McCall's division of Pennsylvania troops, composed of Meade's brigade on the left,
with Reynolds' on the right, observing the road that led from
Cold Harbor and Dispatch Station to Sumner's Bridge;
Seymour's brigade on the right and rear in reserve to the
second line; General P. St. G. Cooke, with five companies
of the 5th Regular Cavalry and two squadrons of the Pennsylvania Lancers, were posted behind a hill in the rear near
the Chickahominy to aid in watching the left flank and defending the slope to the river. Sixty pieces of artillery were
advantageously posted in the intervals between the divisions
and brigades upon the surrounding eminences, in addition to
Tidball's Horse Battery, which was posted on the right of
Sykes, and Robertson's on the extreme left of the line in the
valley of the Chickahominy. The line of battle extended
for more than two miles, and Porter had in all under his
command at this time, including infantry, artillery, and
cavalry, about 27,000 men. "It was, in fact, 27,000 against
60,000, an overweight of opposition that lent to the task
assigned to Porter almost the character of a forlorn hope."*

The Confederates marched to the attack in three heavy
columns, Longstreet's and A. P. Hill's divisions, numbering
24,000 men, parallel with and near the Chickahominy River,
Hill in advance. D. H. Hill's division, 10,000 strong, about
a mile further inland, bore toward the Confederate left to
join Jackson, and formed a junction with the latter at Bethesda Church; while Jackson, 30,000 strong, moved directly
toward Cold Harbor. In addition there were about 2,000
cavalry, under Stuart, making in all, according to Confederate reports, nearly 70,000 men.

---
* Swinton (p. 148).

About 2 P.M., A. P. Hill's division, 14,000 strong, advanced to the attack.

The Fifth Regiment was ordered back to camp in the woods, at daylight on the morning of the 27th; slung their knapsacks, and about 7 A.M. turned off on the road which led toward Cold Harbor, passing over familiar ground. The men did not know the reason for this change, but supposed that the enemy were making a movement to get in the rear of the army.

After marching and countermarching about four miles, and making several halts, they reached a piece of high ground, where a large number of troops were getting into position. Colonel Warren, in command of the 5th and 10th New York regiments, which composed the Third brigade of Gen. Sykes' division, Lieutenant-Colonel H. Duryea, acting in command of the Fifth, took up a position well to the front of the regulars, facing the line of the enemy's approach, the Tenth being on the left of the Fifth. The 3d, 4th, 12th, and 14th regiments of United States infantry, First brigade, under the command of Lieutenant-Colonel Buchanan, formed a second line of battle on the slope of the high ground to the right and rear. The 14th infantry were posted in an orchard to the extreme right; the Twelfth to their left front, and the 5th Zouaves to the left front of the Twelfth, and nearest to the enemy, and consequently were the first to be attacked. Between the 5th and 12th regiments there was a large interval.

Colonel Warren selected his position with great care, placing his brigade just below the brow of a slight eminence in open ground, there being a small depression in the rear of his line, through which ran a stream of water bordered by marshy ground. The rifles were sighted to reach a pine wood in front at an easy killing distance. The provost guard, which was under the command of Lieutenant Whitney, who had been left behind for the purpose of burning the officers' and sutlers' tents, and any property that could not be removed, joined the regiment, and reported that the enemy shelled the camp before they left. The sick turned out in a hurry and were obliged to hobble to the rear as best they could; some of them, however, were able to make excellent time. We were now certain that a battle was imminent. All the fighting men on any detail joined their companies voluntarily, among whom was James Tuits (the butcher), from the Quartermaster's Department, with his Sharp's rifle; Sergeant Joe Vail and Jack Whigam, of the Provost, who determined to take their full share of honor in the victory, or suffer their share in any disaster that might happen; and Luke Gilligan, from the hospital tent, who was recovering from typhoid fever. His body was weak, but his spirit strong, but ere night it had fled, and his lifeless body was lying on the battle-field.

On the right of the pine wood was a clump of evergreens, and beyond them and in the woods was a ravine. Beyond the evergreens, and stretching back about four hundred yards, was an open field, bordered on its further side by woods, and at some distance from our extreme right were thick woods running perpendicular to our line, and to the rear toward the position of some regular battalions.

Company E, under the command of Lieutenant John Collins, were deployed as skirmishers, and went out into the evergreens and wood on the right, and before long the sound of their rifle-shots fell on the ears of the men. Company I, commanded by Captain Partridge, occupied the pine woods directly in front of our position.

After waiting in line of battle a short time, a Confederate officer and staff were seen to ride to the edge of the further woods beyond the open field, and directly after them a battery* dashed up, unlimbered, and a puff of smoke was fol-

---

* Crenshaw's, which was roughly handled during the engagement.

lowed by the rushing sound of a shell. In the meantime the skirmishers of the regiment had encountered the enemy in force lying behind a ridge, who opened fire upon them, which was returned. Lieutenant Collins ordered them to fall back on the regiment, but in endeavoring to do so he lost his way, and was conducting his company toward his right, where they would all have been taken prisoners had it not been their good fortune to meet Lieutenant Porter, in command of the skirmish line of the regulars, who had just been wounded by a shot from the enemy posted in the direction that Collins was leading his men. Being warned in time, they turned to the left through the woods, and struck a narrow road, which they took, and passed around the left flank and rear of the regiment, and took their proper place in the line on the right.

The correspondent of the New York *Times*, in speaking of the battle, stated that "the Duryée Zouaves were the first attacked."

A. P. Hill, commanding twenty-six regiments and six batteries, distributed in six brigades, says in his report:

"I had delayed the attack until I could hear from Longstreet, and this now occurring, the order was given. This was about half-past 2 P.M. Gregg, then Branch, then Anderson, successively became engaged. Branch being hard pressed, Pender was sent to his relief. Field and Archer were also directed to do their part in this murderous contest. . . . . Gregg having before him (what he pleases to mention as) the vaunted Zouaves and Sykes regulars. . . . . General Maxcy Gregg's brigade in advance, made the handsomest charge I have seen during the whole war."

It was composed wholly of South Carolina regiments, viz.: the 1st Rifles, Colonel J. Foster Marshall, about 537 men; 1st regiment, Colonel D. H. Hamilton; 12th, Colonel D. Barnes; 13th, Colonel O. E. Edwards; 14th, Colonel S.

McGowan. The 1st Rifles had 81 killed and 234 wounded, nearly all their officers being among the number. The 1st Volunteers were badly cut up, after fighting bravely, and obliged to retire. All of their color-guard having fallen, the brave Colonel Hamilton bore the colors himself; their Lieutenant-Colonel, Smith, was mortally wounded. The Twelfth was routed after severe loss, and Colonel Barnes severely wounded in the thigh. The Thirteenth, in support, also suffered heavily, and the Fourteenth, which came up in the thick of the battle, reported a loss received here and subsequently of 200, their Colonel, McGowan, receiving a wound from which he died, and their Major and many officers were killed and wounded. The loss in the brigade was over 900 in killed and wounded.

The shot and shell now began to fly in rather dangerous proximity, and the rushing sound they made was anything but agreeable music. The men were ordered to lie down, which they did, in an effort to make themselves as diminutive as possible. There was not a man in the line that could complain of being too thin at this particular time. A section (2 guns) of Captain Edwards' 3d U. S. battery of 10-pound Parrotts moved up close to the right of the line and opened in return, but they were too much exposed, and were ordered to withdraw to their original position on the hill in the rear. Colonel Warren ordered the men of Company E to try and pick off the enemy's artillerists; as they were armed with Sharp's rifles, their fire appeared to have some effect. The men placed their knapsacks in front, hoping they might be of some slight protection from the pieces of flying shell. The solid shot, shell, grape, and canister plowed up the ground around them, throwing the dirt and sand into their faces; while shell, bursting in the marshy ditch in the rear, threw the mud thirty feet in the air. A number of the men were killed and wounded, and many had narrow escapes. A solid shot struck the stock of the rifle of Sergeant Chambers, dash-

The Seven Days' Retreat—Gaines' Mill. 209

ing it to pieces, and tumbling him and Lieutenant Eichler over one another, covering them with dirt, but, strangely enough, without any injury to either. About the same time Lieutenant Agnus received a severe wound from a piece of shell, and commenced rolling over like a barrel toward the regulars in the rear. The men watched him occasionally with much interest until they saw him get into their lines, where he was taken care of. One of the men had a favorite dog that had followed him from camp, who amused himself by chasing after the solid shot, but he was wounded and retired from the field.

During this time, Edwards', Weed's, Martin's, and other batteries opened on the enemy's guns and infantry, some of them firing very close over the heads of the men of the Fifth. The shrieks of the balls through the air were continuous, but the men kept cool, for they knew there was no recourse but to lie still and obey orders. The enemy advanced at one time toward our right, but a vigorous fire by companies, and then by file, drove them back. They did not seem inclined to advance and begin the long-expected attack at close quarters; but some of them had crept up into the woods on the right, and were picking off the men. Sergeant S. B. Parker had received a severe wound; Soden, of Company E, a mortal wound from a piece of shell; Lieutenant Collins had also been struck, and Winslow's arm fell powerless by his side, yet he made a strong effort to again load his piece, but it was out of his power. The Confederate battery was doing so much execution that Colonel Warren ordered the command to march by the left flank through the depression in the ground in the rear to a cut in a road that led along at right angles to the former position. There was not room for the whole regiment to lay in line and keep covered in this cut, so one wing was doubled behind the other. On top of the bank was a brush fence, through which they could watch any movement of the enemy if they came out into the open ground.

Martin's Massachusetts battery of Napoleon guns was posted on the bank to the rear of the new position, and were firing over the heads of the men, who were repeatedly admonished to keep their heads down ; but several of them, not heeding the advice, were placed *hors du combat* by the canister shot from these guns. One of the Captains went to Colonel Warren, who was sitting on his horse to the left of the regiment, on the top of the bank, and told him that their own battery was killing the men. A remonstrance was made to the Captain of the battery, about which there are so many versions, that I decline to state any of them. In a little while a column * of the enemy were seen marching by the flank in formation of fours, through the strip of woods on the other side of the field that ran along toward the position of the regulars. Captain B. reported it to Colonel Warren, who replied, " Yes, Capt. B., I am very much obliged to you for the information, but have I not eyes as well as you ? " The Captain returned to his company, and at the same instant the guns poured their grape and canister shot into the flank of the enemy's column, and they beat a hasty retreat, where they were out of range of the fire.

Soon after, Lieut.-Colonel Hiram Duryea, acting in command of the regiment, said that the enemy we had already faced were coming out of the woods, and were in the open field where he wanted them ; but it was only a line of skirmishers. They were, however, followed up closely by their first line of battle, who made their appearance advancing at double-quick out of the wood and over the open ground. The men watched them through the brush fence. After they were well out in the field, Colonel Duryée cried, " Now, men, your time has come ; get up and do your duty ! " The regiment jumped up as one man, and down went the fence on the bank in front, and the order was given to left wheel. On account of one wing being doubled behind the other in

---

* Eight companies of the 12th South Carolina.

the road, the order was given for one wing to march double-quick by the flank and form on the other, to make one line of battle, which was performed in good order in the face of the enemy, who were within about five hundred feet. In the meantime, Company I, on the left, charged over the field in advance of the main body to the other side of the ditch or gully, along the borders of which were bushes, to draw their fire; they waited until the enemy had got quite close to them, and then, by order of Captain Partridge, they picked out their men from right to left and poured in a murderous volley from their Sharp's rifles, which cut large gaps in their ranks and made them come to a sudden halt. They immediately fell flat on the ground, but suffered severely in turn, from the enemy's fire, but then loaded again quickly and jumped up and gave them another volley; this was repeated four or five times, the enemy closing up and then made a charge on Company I. Captain Partridge, before this, had given them orders when they fell back, to join the regiment according to their best judgment if they got scattered, either on the left or the right of it, whichever was the nearest point. He had just given the order, "Skirmishers, retreat!" when Sergeant Strachan saw him lift his hand to his side; he jumped for him, but the Captain fell, opening his mouth as if to speak, out of which rushed a stream of blood; he was shot through the heart.

Hannon had seen a Confederate, wearing a long beard, taking aim at the Captain, but could not cap his piece in time to fire at him before the fatal bullet sped on its errand of death. As the Captain fell, Strachan and ten others turned instinctively and fired at the Confederate, and he fell dead; and it was afterward ascertained that his breast was pierced by eight balls. The Captain's death was avenged. His body was afterward taken charge of by Lieutenant McConnell and carried to the rear, and delivered to Quartermaster Thomas. On his person were found some important papers, which were placed in the hands of Colonel Warren.

While Company I was so nobly acting its part, the regiment had formed in line of battle, and the order rung out to charge with the bayonet, when the men made for the Confederate line at a double-quick to come to close quarters. The ditch broke up the order of the line somewhat, but the regiment quickly formed again under the fire of the enemy, and after delivering a destructive fire, the order was given, "Advance the colors! advance the colors! Charge!" The men rushed forward with a yell, and the enemy appeared to be paralyzed; they evidently had not come out of the woods to be driven back, but to make a charge themselves. They stood for a moment, but the boys not wavering under their fire, and showing that they were determined to bayonet them, the remnant commenced to waver and break, and finally ran for the cover of the woods, completely demoralized and in a panic. Some of them stood until the Fifth were within thirty yards of them, firing steadily, and with good aim. They were nearly all shot down, as many of the men had reserved their fire; moreover their right wing received the fire of a portion of the 10th Regiment, on our left; they already had suffered severely, especially in officers, from the fire of artillery and sharp-shooters, in their advance over open ground, before they reached the cover of the pine wood. This regiment was the 1st South Carolina Rifles, and were armed with Enfields.

It appears, from Confederate reports, that Col. Marshall, who commanded the 1st Rifles, was ordered to charge the battery we were supporting. He says:

"Before giving the order to advance, I called upon the regiment to remember the State from whence they came, to put their trust in God, and acquit themselves like men. At this awful moment there was not a quiver or a pallid cheek. . . . . There was a calmness, a settled determination on the part of every man to do or die in the attempt. I gave the command, 'Double-quick, march!' and, as soon as we had gained the old field, 'Charge bayonets,' at the same time deploying six companies to the left,

The Seven Days' Retreat—Gaines' Mill. 213

supporting the entire line of skirmishers. As soon as we emerged from the pines, we were met by a most destructive fire from the enemy in front and on our left, and as soon as we had cleared about 100 yards of the old field, two heavy batteries, on our left, about 600 yards off, poured into our ranks a deadly fire of grape and canister. Here it was that my Adjutant, J. B. Sloan, was shot down by my side, while gallantly aiding me and urging on the charge of the regiment. Here, also, fell Capt. R. A. Hawthorne, gallantly leading his company. A few paces further fell Capt. Henagen, another noble spirit, leading his company; close by his side fell his gallant Lieutenant (Brown), and farther fell the gallant and patriotic Lieut. Samuel McFall, and near him fell Sergt.-Major McGhee, nobly cheering the men on to the charge. My men, although now under three cross-fires, and falling thick and fast from one end of the line to the other, never once faltered. Finding no battery, they dashed on to the woods in front," etc. " Here my men got the first chance to exchange shots," etc.

"While this successful movement was going on, the left wing of my regiment was about being outflanked by about 500 New York Zouaves, who came down upon my left in a desperate charge. . . . .

"I ordered my regiment to fall back . . . . to the edge of the wood, where we entered, and then filing to the right, conducted them in safety down a road, where I formed the remnant under cover of the hill in front of the Zouaves. Just as I was forming, a North Carolina regiment came up, and assisted us in giving a complete check to any further movement to the enemy in this quarter. Thus ended one of the most desperate charges I ever witnessed; and I feel thankful to a kind Providence that so many of us escaped to witness the most complete triumph of our arms in the hardest contested battle before Richmond, and the one which decided the fate of the Yankee army."

Among the losses Colonel Marshall mentions, in addition to those already noticed, Major J. W. Livingston, wounded in the side severely; Captains J. J. Norton and F. E. Harrison, wounded; Captain Miller, wounded, and thirteen men of his company killed; Captain G. W. Cox, wounded, and sixteen men killed; Lieutenants William C. Davis and Latimer, wounded, the latter mortally.

The Fifth now occupied the ground beyond, where the numerous dead and wounded Confederates lay, facing and near the wood. It was now their turn to suffer severely; they received a volley from the second and stronger line of the enemy, who were drawn up in the edge of the wood. The whole regiment was actively engaged, firing very rapidly, and aiming low, two of the companies, I and E, being armed with Sharp's rifles, the others using a patent cartridge, which did not require to be torn open by the teeth, as usual, hence saved time, consequently their fire was continuous and rapid. But the fire from the enemy was also incessant and well sustained, and the battle raged fiercely, but the men of the Fifth obstinately held their own and fought desperately. At times they were forced back and obliged to give ground, but it would be for only a moment, as they immediately re-formed and charged forward again and recovered their former position at the point of the bayonet, which tended to demoralize their opponents, and saved loss to themselves. But flesh and blood could not stand such a fire much longer without one side or the other giving way. Yet the Fifth had no idea of being the first, as long as there was anybody left to fire a shot. They, however, beheld, with dismay, the long line of their own killed and wounded, and their rapidly decreasing numbers, while there was no slackening of the heavy fire from the pines, which seemed to increase instead of diminish, and there were no signs of any direct relief coming. It was a critical moment, when Sergt. John H. Berrian, who carried the regimental colors, strode firmly thirty paces in front of the regiment, planted the staff in the ground, and looked defiantly about him.* He was immediately joined by Sergt. Allison, who bore the United States flag.

---

* John H. Berrian enlisted as a private May 9, 1861, and rose to be Color-Sergeant in charge of the regimental colors. In the severe action of Gaines' Mill, he showed

The Colonel and officers shouted to them to come back, fearing that the enemy might make a sudden onslaught from the wood, and capture the flags; but they were idle fears; they could only have been taken over the bodies of scores of brave men, who would have fought with the bayonet to the last to preserve them. When the men of the Fifth saw the bravery of this action, they gave a terrific yell—" a yell never heard off the battle-field, so demoniac and horrid that men in peaceful times can not imitate it "—and without orders, of one accord rushed like demons into the wood with the bayonet, and never paused until they saw the enemy's line completely broken and shattered, and flying to the rear, some of them being bayoneted in the retreat, their officers trying in vain to rally their commands. Some of them had even thrown away their arms, and our men made the best of their time in picking them off as fast as they could. On our right the 12th regular infantry had become engaged, and the Sixth moved up to our support, and were placed in position by Colonel Warren.

It was now after 4 P.M.; the recall was sounded, but some of the Fifth did not come out of the wood for some time. The enemy, in the meantime, had taken refuge in and beyond the ravine. A long line of the Pennsylvania Reserves were advancing in line of battle, and had nearly reached the wood, and were about to open fire, when the Zouaves that remained behind were obliged to go through their lines to get to the rear. As they returned through the wood and

---

such coolness and bravery, that he received a commission as Second Lieutenant, but being stricken with the malarial fever, he reluctantly sent in his resignation, at the earnest solicitation of his parents, who had two other sons in the regiment, one of whom was killed in action, and the other subsequently enlisted again in the Second battalion, and was also killed. Lieutenant Berrian (the survivor), for thirteen years has been a faithful guardian of the peace, and for some years has been specially entrusted to watch over and guard the treasures of a very large Savings Bank, and from his distinguished record as a soldier, it is needless to say that those whose treasures he watches over could not have selected a better or more faithful guardian of such a trust.

over the open field, they were surprised at the carnage, for it had been an obstinate fight on both sides, of over two hours; a long row of red uniforms marked the place where they first charged, besides little knots of them lying here and there, while just beyond in groups, and in the wood, lay the deluded, but *gallant* sons of the South.

The correspondent of the Cincinnati *Commercial* thus describes the conflict on this portion of the line:

"Again he gathered his columns, supported them by fresh troops, again advanced, extending his lines as if to flank our right, and renewed the attack with greater ferocity than ever, to be again repulsed with terrible slaughter. Sykes' Regulars and Warren's brigade, in which are the Duryée Zouaves and Bendix's 10th New York regiment, played a brilliant part in this portion of the engagement, the Zouaves especially fighting with a desperation and tenacity only to be expected from such superior men."*

---

* Compte de Paris (2d V., p. 96): "Hill was repulsed by the right of Morell's division, and by the brigade of the young and valiant Warren."

B. J. Lossing (1st V., p. 421): "A. P. Hill attacked at 2 P.M. The brunt of the attack fell first upon Sykes' division, who threw the assailants back in great confusion and heavy loss."

A. H. Guernsey: "It was past 2 P.M. when Hill was directed to begin the assault. For two hours the battle raged with equal obstinacy on both sides. The Federal troops gained ground, and from being assailed became the assailants. Hill was defeated, crushed, and almost routed. Some of his regiments stood their ground; others threw themselves flat on the earth to escape; others rushed from the field in disorder." He says: "The defeat at this point is fully shown in the Confederate report," as follows:

"Lee (Report 8), and Hill (*ibid.* 176), affirms it in generl terms."

"Archer (*ibid.* 256), says: 'My troops fell back before the irresistible fire of artillery and rifles. Had they not fallen back, I would myself have ordered it.'

"Pender says (*ibid.* 253): 'My men were rallied and pushed forward again, but did not advance far before they fell back. The enemy were continually bringing up fresh troops, and succeeded in driving us from the road.'

"Whiting, of Jackson's command, who came to the relief of these troops, says (*ibid.* 154): 'Men were leaving the field in every direction, and in great disorder; two regiments, one from South Carolina and one from Louisiana, were actually marching back from the fire,' etc. 'Near the crest in front of us, and lying down, appeared the fragments of a brigade,' etc. 'Still further on our extreme right, our troops appeared to be falling back. The troops on our immediate left I do not know, and I am glad I don't,' etc., etc."

The Seven Days' Retreat—Gaines' Mill.

The now thinned ranks of the Fifth marched a short distance to the rear, and rested after their long fight, in the meantime supporting a twenty-pound battery, the fire of which was doing great execution in the ranks of the enemy, and there seemed to be a slight lull in the din of battle, but it soon commenced again and raged as fierce as ever. The spent balls flying around them thickly, many of the men received stinging blows from them. All the troops were now engaged. The Confederates generally advanced in three lines, the first firing a volley and dropping flat, the next line firing over their heads, while the first line reloaded. "The din and noise of the contending forces was terrific, and amid the roar of one hundred and twenty guns, and the crash of ninety thousand muskets, could be heard the shouts of the Union forces mingled with the rebel yell."*

Guernsey says: "Whiting does great injustice to the troops of Hill. They were indeed defeated and broken, but it was after two hours of desperate fighting under every disadvantage of position, against a force quite equal to them, as the record of their losses shows. Thus, the regiment from South Carolina which was actually marching back under fire, must have been the 1st Rifles, South Carolina Volunteers. Of this regiment its Colonel, Marshall, reports (*ibid.* 502): 'In that charge we sustained a loss of 76 killed, 221 wounded, and 58 missing. Early on the morning after the battle, I made a detail from each company to bury their dead, and so severe was the work of death in some of the companies that it took the detail all-day to bury their dead, and of those missing in the morning, all but four rejoined their regiment.'"

"Hill, after acknowledging the repulse, says (*ibid.* 176): 'My division was engaged full two hours before assistance was received. We failed to carry the enemy's lines, but we paved the way for the successful attack afterward, and in which attack it was necessary to employ the whole of our army that side of the Chickahominy. About 4 P.M. reinforcements came up on my right from General Longstreet, and later, Jackson's men on my left and center, and my division was relieved of the weight of the contest.'"

* Guernsey says: "Jackson now arrived upon the scene, D. H. Hill on the extreme Union right, Ewell and Whiting on his left, with Lawton (4,000) a little in the rear, and a general advance was ordered. Porter's line was so severely pressed at every point, that he was obliged to divide Slocum's division (9,000), which arrived about half-past four o'clock, sending parts of it, even single regiments, to the points most threatened."

General McClellan's Report (p. 248): "On the left the contest was for the strip of woods running almost at right angles to the Chickahominy in front of Adams' House, or between that and Gaines' House. The enemy several times charged up to this wood, but were each time driven back with heavy loss. The regulars of Sykes' division, on the right, also repulsed several strong attacks."

"The enemy attacked again in great force at 6 P.M., but failed to break our lines, though our loss was very heavy."

Soon the sound of the musketry approached nearer and nearer, and the men knew that our forces were being driven. The regiment had not rested long apparently (for in a battle it is difficult to judge of the flight of time), the men every moment expecting further orders, when Colonel Warren came dashing up, and cried out: "Fall in, men! Fall in!" "Fall in!" was repeated by Lieutenant-Colonel H. Duryea and the other officers; the men jumped up with alacrity, and were hurriedly marched off by the flank to the right, through volleys of canister shot that raked the field, after some minor movements, and the regiment "told off," and the companies equalized under a heavy fire, faced in line of battle, and Lieutenant-Colonel Hiram Duryea gave the order, "Forward, guide center, march!" In a moment the regiment found themselves on a ridge of ground facing a long line of the advancing enemy. They opened a vigorous fire by file upon them, and brought them to a halt. Upon receiving our fire the enemy called out, "Don't fire on your own men;" at the same time they did not return the fire, but waved what resembled, as seen through the smoke, the "American colors." At this admonition from supposed friends, the majority ceased their fire, thinking that possibly they might be *friends*. But it was only a Confederate trick. Just then Colonel Warren dashed up, and cried out: "Blaze away! blaze away, men! If they are our men, they have no business there." At the same time a terrible volley, fired by our supposed friends, swept over and through the ranks, dealing out death and wounds. Again our rifles flashed, and the Confederate colors fell. A battery of six Napoleon guns (Platt's United States), concealed behind the ridge, and which was unobserved by the enemy, opened with double-shotted guns on their column, now advancing again on a charge, and they were repulsed with great slaughter.

The sight from the ridge was appalling; the view extended over the hard-fought field, which was enveloped in smoke;

on the far left the troops were falling doggedly back, fighting for every foot of ground, pressed back by overwhelming numbers of fresh Confederates, and there were no reserves on the Union side to put against them; every available man had been, or was, fighting, and the trying hour had come in which the steadiness and discipline of Sykes' division, now much reduced in numbers, but the most reliable in the service, was to be taxed to its utmost. The salvation of our shattered army on the left bank of the Chickahominy depended upon its efforts, until reinforcements or night should come to their relief, to stay the advance of the Confederate columns which were pressing on to drive our forces into the swamps of the river.

The battalions of regulars had been, and were, fighting desperately to the right, as had also the Eleventh infantry on our left. They stood as firm as a rock, meeting and foiling the desperate onsets of Ewell's, D. H. Hill's, and Jackson's troops to outflank and crush the right.

A battery of Parrott guns on the right of our line near McGee's house, had been creating terrible havoc in the enemy's ranks; two regiments charged and took it, one of them, the 20th North Carolina, losing their Colonel and Lieutenant-Colonel and more than one-half of their men in the attempt; but it was retaken again.

Up to this time the Confederates on this part of the line were held at bay. Lawton now appeared on the scene, and pressed forward through the broken ranks of the Confederates in one continuous line of 3,500 men, armed with Enfield rifles. General Ewell seeing this strong body of fresh troops coming to his assistance, waved his sword over his head and cried out, "Hurrah for Georgia!" The temporary stoppage of the fire of the battery on the right was taken advantage of, and General Winder pressed forward with eleven regiments, the Hampton Legion, 1st Maryland, 12th Alabama, 52d Virginia, 38th Georgia, and the 2d, 5th, 33d,

27th, 14th Virginia, with the Irish battalion, and attacked the regulars on their flank and rear; and they were compelled to fall back. When the Confederates had approached to within two hundred feet, the battery was withdrawn, leaving two of the guns in the hands of the enemy, the horses being all shot down. The regulars fell back about three hundred yards, fighting for every foot of ground. Colonel Allen and Major Jones, of the 2d Virginia Confederate regiment, both fell mortally wounded. While this was transpiring on the right, the Fifth was to the right of the left of the division supporting Platt's battery.*

Men separated from their regiments, lost, stragglers, and wounded, were continually passing to the rear; there was nothing left in front but Stonewall Jackson's legions, every available man of them pressing on with the bayonet to be in at the death. The masses of our broken organizations were thronging toward the bridges that crossed the Chickahominy in the rear. Officers drew swords and revolvers and placed themselves in front of their retreating troops and soon rallied them. The men of the Fifth intelligently made the most of their position, which was an advantageous one, or otherwise they would soon have been too much decimated by the flying bullets to maintain it. Some of them lay down

---

* Guernsey says: "It was now half-past six, an hour before sunset. The whole Confederate force on this side of the Chickahominy was brought into action. Jackson, Longstreet, and the two Hills, with the exception of Kemper's brigade of '1,433 muskets,' of Longstreet's division, which was held in reserve; opposed to them was only Porter's (two divisions), and McCall and Slocum's divisions. Making allowances for losses on each side up to this time, the Confederate force on the field numbered about 56,000; Union, 33,000." [This estimate does not allow for stragglers on both sides, which were numerous.—A. D.]

Lossing: "At six o'clock, brigade after brigade hurled against the line in rapid succession, hoping to break it. For a long time it stood firm, but weakened by carnage," etc., etc.

Swinton (p. 152): "The right held its ground with much stubbornness, repulsing every attack. The left, too, fought stoutly, but was at length broken by a determined charge led by Hood's Texan troops." [They captured fourteen guns; the horses all being shot, they could not be removed in time, but Hood, according to his own accounts, lost 1,000 men, killed and wounded, in the charge].

The Seven Days' Retreat—Gaines' Mill. 221

behind the ridge, others were partially shielded behind trees, and were firing at the enemy with steady aim and deadly effect, some of them making the colors of the regiments the focus of their fire. During this part of the engagement three times the Confederate colors were seen to fall. There were only about two hundred of the Fifth together at this time supporting the battery, which was doing its best. A few of the 10th New York were also there under the command of Colonel Bendix. The Confederates were advancing, as seen indistinctly through the smoke, in line after line, but their fire was not very destructive, as, according to their own reports, many of their regiments were out of ammunition, and their heavy force was pressing on with the bayonet; some of our men who had faced the worst up to this time drew out. The majority of the Zouaves had stripped off their knapsacks, expecting a hand to hand conflict; to save the battery, or to keep from a rebel prison—a fate worse than death. There were some there who were determined never to be taken prisoners, unless too much disabled to defend themselves; a fact which can be verified by men now living.

The double-shotted guns of Platt's and Griffin's batteries were pouring deadly discharges of canister into the masses of the enemy; the regulars and the 16th New York, of Slocum's division, were delivering terrible volleys to check their onsets, and the remnants of the Fifth and Tenth added their fire. Sykes' division was indeed doing its hard work, and its war-worn and indomitable chief was with it, cool and steadfast in its time of peril, standing like a lion at bay.* The Commander-in-Chief of all our forces on that bloody day, General Fitz John Porter, was there. It was during

---

* General Sykes graduated from the United States Military Academy, West Point, and was commissioned Brevet Second Lieutenant in the regular army July 1, 1842. He served with distinction in the Mexican war, and has been on active duty ever since. General Sykes is a man of few words, but when hard work is required he is the man to do it.

their charges on this part of the battle-field that so many Confederate officers fell while animating their exhausted men and bearing the colors of their regiments in their hands.

We were now passing through some awful moments; suddenly we heard the shouts of men in the distance toward the rear, which at first threw us into a fearful state of excitement, but was somewhat allayed when it was ascertained that instead of an enemy, the shouts came from friends. We answered them lustily, and knew that relief was coming, but it was yet far away, and the minutes were testing our ability to stand until succor should arrive. The Duke of Wellington did not long for Blucher to appear, with more agony, than did those present on that ridge for the coming up of French, and Meagher with his fighting sons of Ireland. Colonel Warren moved about regardless of the missiles of death; word came to him that the ammunition of the battery was nearly expended, and on'y two or three rounds remained; he answered, "Let them fire all they have; I will stand by them." It seemed at this moment as if the sun stood still, but he was slowly creeping below the horizon, veiled by thick clouds of sulphurous smoke; the glories of his crimson hues were paled, as if he shrank, with averted face, from the sight of the gory field.

Colonel Hiram Duryea stood by our little band, cool, but anxious; said he, "I wish to God we had help!" and it was time. In a few moments, if we did not fall back, we must either cross bayonets with overwhelming numbers, or be surrendered as prisoners of war.

It was now sundown, and the battery fired its last round, and, as current rumor has it, rammers and all, almost into the faces of the Confederates, and moved off down the ridge with every gun. The Fifth, worn and tired, filed off by the flank in its rear, missing many a familiar face. Just as they passed down the road a rebel farewell, in the shape of a shell, came hissing over their heads, and burst in the side of a barn, not twenty feet away, tearing a great gap in its side; and as we marched and disappeared in the gloom of the woods, in the fading twilight, the air was rent with the shrill rebel yells as they swarmed over the vacated ridge.*

"No battery was lost, or any part of it near our regiment (5th New York) at Gaines' Mill, nor did the enemy break our line (Sykes' division) from where we were on the left of it to the right of it. We were on the field till dark, and then were withdrawn without molestation by the enemy."†

It was now quite dark; after marching a short distance, the Irish brigade were met, which, with that of French's, came up on a double-quick, and cheering loudly. These fresh troops charged the skirt of the field, and their opportune arrival had the moral effect of checking the further advance of the enemy, who were much exhausted by the long contest.

D. H. Hill says:

"It was now fairly dark, and hearing loud cheers from the Yankees in our immediate front, some 200 yards distant, I ordered our whole advance to halt, and wait the expected attack of the enemy. Brig.-Gen. Winder, occupying the road to Grapevine Bridge, immediately halted, and the whole advanced columns were halted also. The cheering, as we afterward learned, was

---

* Compte de Paris (p. 100): "At 6 P.M. Jackson attacked with 40,000 men. Ewell attacked the regulars, who made it a point of honor never to yield before volunteers, whatever may be their numbers." (p. 102): "Attacked in front and menaced in flank, Sykes fell back defending the ground foot by foot. The regulars do not allow Hill to push his success along the road leading from Cold Harbor to Dispatch Station, by which he could have cut off the retreat of the enemy.

"Fearfully reduced as they are, they care less for the losses they have sustained than for the mortification of yielding to volunteers."—(p. 103): "Stuart, near Cold Harbor, does not know how to make his excellent troops play the part which appertains to cavalry on the eve of a victory; he allows himself to be held back by the resolute stand of the regulars and some few hundred men bearing the flags of Warren's brigade."

† General G. K. Warren.

caused by the appearance of the Irish brigade, which was sent forward to cover the retreat. A vigorous attack upon it might have resulted in the total rout of the Yankee army and the capture of thousands of prisoners. But I was unwilling to leave the elevated plateau around McGee's house to advance in the dark along an unknown road, skirted by dense woods in the possession of the Yankee troops."

The sanguinary battle of Gaines' Mill was over; a few scattering shots were heard up to 9 o'clock, when quietness prevailed; both sides were about exhausted by the terrible ordeal through which they had passed. The regiment was formed in line and counted by the Adjutant, and numbered seventy-three files, or 146 men. Besides those killed or disabled, there were some who fell out from exhaustion; others had assisted their wounded comrades to the rear and failed to return, and a detail under Lieutenant Eichler were guarding a number of Confederate prisoners. The number whose hearts failed them were comparatively few, and these managed to elude the officers and file-closers, and retire to the rear.

Through the blackness of night little lights could be seen dancing about in the distance, looking like twinkling stars. They were borne by the good Samaritans, and those who had been transformed from demons into angels of mercy, and were seeking and succoring the wounded of Union and Confederate alike, who lay together like one great family. As soon as the ranks were dismissed, the men dropped down on the bare ground without covering, and were soon in deep slumber, with their rifles by their sides, ready to clutch at the first alarm. But many a soldier misses his mate, who may be lying wounded in the hands of the Confederates, or being jolted over a rough road in an ambulance to the rear, or mayhap lying on the battle-field, wearing the laurels of the brave, though his spirit has fled in glory from its earthly tenement, and taken winged flight to Him who gave it.

The orders had been obeyed. General Porter had held the

left bank of the river till night. Notwithstanding their desperate efforts, the flower of the Confederate army, comprising, at least, 130 regiments of infantry, and 84 guns, under command of the two Hills, Longstreet, Ewell, and Jackson, all under the personal supervision of General Lee himself, and also encouraged by the presence of Jeff. Davis, had driven the Union troops only about one mile. They had reaped a barren victory.

General Fitz John Porter fought this battle with 51 regiments of infantry, besides his batteries, which was all his force. He commanded in person throughout, and directed all the general movements; and the obstinacy with which the troops held their ground, and the masterly manner in which he directed their movements, foiled the well-laid plans of the Confederate Generals, and withstood till night the furious onsets of the enemy.* This delay gave General McClellan twenty-four hours' start in which to forward his miles of wagons, containing army stores, ammunition, etc., and his heavy siege guns, to the new base on the James River.

The field officers of the Fifth acted their parts with the greatest heroism and bravery, and throughout the battle remained mounted, and were at every point where their services were most required; and how they escaped serious wounds or death is miraculous. Colonel Warren received a contusion from a spent ball, and his horse was wounded. He was everywhere conspicuous on the field, and not only directed the movements of his own brigade, which he handled with consummate skill, and placed in the most advantageous positions, where they could produce the most effect on the enemy, but directed the movements of other regiments.

Lieutenant-Colonel H. Duryea, acting in command of the regiment, rose from a sick couch to take part in the action

---

* Compte de Paris (p. 104): "Had fought with great vigor, and it was no disgrace to Porter's soldiers that they had to succumb in such an unequal struggle."

when his services were most required, and did not make his bodily ailments an excuse, as some others did, to shirk danger and responsibility and win glory without earning it. He set a good example to the men by his bravery, coolness, and gallantry. Captain Winslow played a noble part as a field-officer. Surgeon Doolittle was wounded in the course of the action, and his horse was killed under him. The other officers, with a few exceptions, won honor by their cool behavior and fidelity. Of the men, an officer high in command said that every man who stood supporting that battery at dusk deserved a commission. Another (a General) officer said the next day as the regiment passed by him on the march, in reply to the remark of an officer who stood by his side, " Did well! why, I could hug every man of them."

The New York *Herald* of July 1, 1862, says: "Duryée's Zouaves fought, as did all the regulars, under General Sykes, in whose brigade they are attached, with undaunted courage."

In concluding his narrative of the battle, the correspondent of the Cincinnati *Commercial* says:

"The conduct of the entire force that day was admirable. The regulars, who had previously complained of restraint, had full scope, and they re-established their ancient fame. Duryée's Zouaves, clad in crimson breeches and red skull-caps, emulated their regular comrades, winning the admiration of the army. But volunteers and regulars alike won glory on that bloody field."

Extract from General George B. McClellan's report to the Secretary of War, Hon. Edwin M. Stanton:

HEADQUARTERS ARMY OF POTOMAC, SAVAGE STATION,
June 28, 1862—12.20 A.M.

On the left bank our men did all that men could do, all that soldiers could accomplish, but they were overwhelmed by vastly superior numbers soon after I had brought my last reserves into action. The loss on both sides is *terrible*. I believe it will prove to be the most *desperate* battle of the war. The sad rem-

The Seven Days' Retreat—Gaines' Mill.

nants of my men behave as men; those battalions who fought most bravely, and suffered most, are still in the best order. *My regulars were superb;* and I count upon what are left to turn another battle in company with their gallant *comrades of the volunteers.*

Abbott speaks of this battle as follows:

"It was now night—a night of awful gloom. The second day's battle—the battle of Gaines' Mill—had ended, and silence succeeded the thunders of war, which all the day had shaken the hills. Even the darkness could not conceal the harrowing spectacle of death's ravages. The dead lay upon the field in extended windrows. The wounded were to be counted by thousands. Their heart-rending cries and groans were audible on all sides."

Colonel B. Estvan, of the Confederate army, says:

"In by-gone days I had been on many a battle-field in Italy and Hungary, but I confess that I never witnessed so hideous a picture of human slaughter and horrible suffering."

General McClellan, in his report (p. 249), says:

"Our loss in this battle, in killed, wounded, and missing, was very heavy, especially in officers, many of whom were killed, wounded, or taken prisoners while gallantly leading on their men, or rallying them to renewed exertions. It is impossible to arrive at the exact numbers lost in this *desperate* engagement, owing to the series of battles which followed each other in quick succession, and in which the whole army was engaged. No general returns were made until after we had arrived at Harrison's Landing, when the losses for the whole seven days were estimated together,"

The Compte de Paris, of General McClellan's staff, who distinguished himself in this engagement, informs us in his History, that out of the 35,000 engaged, the loss was nearly 7,000, and that the assailants suffered still more.

The Confederate losses from their own estimates Guernsey places at 9,500. "Jackson's loss alone was 3,284, and the other corps in the same proportion would make the Confederate loss about 10,000."

The Fifth Regiment lost more than one-third of its officers and men, killed and wounded, including nearly all of the color-guard. Out of the 450 men engaged, 56 were killed or died of their wounds; 3 were missing, 110 severely wounded, making the total casualties among the officers and men 169. Besides the above, there were about 50 who received contusions in the course of the engagement, which, although in most cases painful, were not of such a serious nature as to be classed in this regiment as wounds, or to incapacitate the recipients for duty.

The Tenth lost 114, in killed, wounded, and missing, out of 575 men engaged; among whom were Lieutenants James R. Smith and George F. Tate, wounded.

As an instance of the different effects of gun-shots produced in battle, the losses in two instances may be mentioned. Company H had twenty-one severely wounded, some of them having several wounds, but *none* of the wounds proved mortal. Company K had nineteen hit, out of whom eleven were killed or died of their wounds.

INCIDENTS.

After the regiment was relieved by fresh troops, and after the latter had become engaged, William McDowell, the Orderly Sergeant of Company G, remained on the field wholly regardless of flying bullets, and employed himself in picking up rifles and throwing them into the ditch. He also took off his shoes and stockings and bathed his feet, and then rejoined the main body of the regiment, who were resting, as already mentioned, loaded down with the rifles he had collected. If others had been as thoughtful, the enemy would have gleaned less booty in the matter of abandoned arms.

When the men lay in the cut of the road, Sergeants Forbes, Law, Tiebout, and a few others crept out under fire to the open field and secured their knapsacks, which had been left with those of the majority of the regiment. The others secured theirs afterward, but most of the men supporting the battery, the second time they went in, which was late in the afternoon, were compelled to lose them.

Dave Burns, of the Fifth, had a long argument while the battle was raging with a wounded Confederate, who, it appears, was an Irishman. His attention was attracted to him, by seeing that he had a revolver in his hand. He asked him what he was doing with "that," and was answered, it was for protection from being bayoneted. Burns waxed wroth at the idea of one of the Fifth doing anything so cowardly, and berated him soundly; getting warmed up, he wished that the Confederate was a well man, and he would knock all the secesh blood out of him; that he was a disgrace to the Irish people for fighting against the flag, etc. Finally, he took the revolver away from him, and removed the caps, but the man begged so hard for it, as it was a present from one of his officers, he gave it back to him, and also a drink of water, and went at the fighting again, as if he had merely stopped work for a few moments to have an argument with a friend.

In the battle, Walter S. Colby, a native of New Hampshire, and a member of Company G, received a wound which shattered his leg, and he fell. He supported himself as well as he could, pulled his cap off his head, waved it in the air, and gave three cheers for the Union and the American flag, and fell down again. Several of the men went to his assistance and offered their aid, but he declined it, saying that "he would have to lose his leg, and that meant, in his poor health, his life; that they could testify that he died in a good cause and died 'game.'" He told them to look after themselves and let him lay.

No other information of him has ever been obtained from any source, and the only inference is that he died like a hero in the hands of the enemy, and sleeps in an unknown grave. He was troubled with a racking cough in Baltimore; and when the regiment left Federal Hill, he was left in the hospital. He was offered his discharge, but refused it. After the regiment was on the march up the Peninsula, beyond Yorktown, the men of his company were surprised to see Colby appear among them, knapsack and all, fully equipped; he looked thin and emaciated. One of the boys said: "Why, Colby, we never expected to see you again." He replied: "You didn't! Well, I expected to see you again; and I mean to go home with the regiment, or go home in a box," and there was not a man in the company but knew that Walt Colby meant what he said. He had an iron will, and his decision once made, as they knew from experience, was unalterable. The writer had him for a messmate on the march up to near Richmond, and was often kept awake by his violent coughing. One night, being very tired and sleepy, after a long march, a rather petulant remark was made, which the writer has ever since regretted. The poor skeleton, for that was all there was of him in the flesh, flared up with, "I'll live to stamp on your grave," and bounced out of the shelter that I had rigged; nor could any persuasion on my part induce him to come back that night, but he laid outside on the ground, without any covering, in a drizzly rain. As long as he lived, no matter how long or hard the march, be it rain or shine, there was Colby at its end, with what was left of the regiment. While strong men were strewed all along far in the rear, he was never known to drop out, and his limbs were wasted away to skin and bone. He did not aspire to any higher position than that of a private, although evidently of good social rank, and had seen much of the world. When he enlisted he was handsomely dressed. He once told the writer that when he enlisted he was only on a visit to New York, and had dined with a friend at the St. Nicholas Hotel, and bid him good-bye, the friend to go South for the purpose of joining the Confederates. He himself strolled off, went into the quarters in Canal Street, and entered the Fifth. He always had plenty of money to spend or to lend, but who he was or who his friends were, he would never divulge. And this invincible hero, unknown to his comrades, further than is narrated above, sleeps in an unknown grave in Virginia. He deserves a better tribute than mine to the decision and character of a soldier who had no superior for loyalty and heroism in the army.

Sniffin, of Company B, was one of the first men killed in the first charge. He was one of the comical characters of the regiment. Skipping out over the turf, he said: "Johnny on the green! here comes a ball from Brooklyn," then, "Here is one from Coney Island;" but one came from a Confederate, as if in mockery, and poor Sniffin dropped dead.

One of the color-guard, Spellman, was overcome by the heat during the height of the action, and fell as if dead; he was carried to the house used as a hospital, on the hill to the rear. His "chum" found time to run over and see how he fared, after the regiment was relieved the first time, and discovered him lying unconscious. He asked a surgeon to do something for him, who said it was of no use, as he was as good as a dead man. Finally, another surgeon was induced to examine him, but he also gave him up, and said that he must use his time on those he could save. When the enemy shelled the hospital building, the crash of the shell partially aroused Spellman, and his comrade raised him up and half dragged him from the building. All those who could move were crawling off, and a great many stragglers were going to the rear. Spellman opened his eyes, and glared about him for an instant, as if his consciousness was returning. "What does this mean?" he asked. He was answered that the battle was going all right; those are the stragglers. "Cowards!" exclaimed Spellman, and again he went off in a swoon. His friend succeeded in getting him into an ambulance, never expecting to see him again, and rejoined the regiment. On the march to Malvern Hill, the men were surprised to see Spellman coming over the fields to join them. We will see what a "dead man" was made of on a future occasion.

We rested as well as it was possible to rest, after the sanguinary struggle of the day, and early in the morning of Saturday, the 28th, before daylight, the men were ordered from their slumbers, and crossed the Chickahominy, over Woodbury Bridge, to the Richmond side of the river, and took a position on Trent Hill, which overlooked the stream. The regulars crossed about 6 o'clock, and blew up the bridge behind them. We remained here, with the rest of Sykes' division and the reserve artillery, serving also on picket along the river till 6 P.M. We then started about dusk and marched to Savage's Station, and destroyed by fire a large pile of knapsacks and other property, to prevent them from falling into the hands of the enemy.

At this place there were about 6,000 wounded and sick, about 2,500 of whom, the last troops that left on the succeeding night, were compelled to leave from inexorable necessity, as there was not sufficient means of conveyance to remove them all. The army marched on its way, accompanied with the thousands of disabled and afflicted comrades upon whom the blow of war had fallen, but with heavy hearts that so many were left behind to take the hospitalities or the revenge of the enemy, at whose hands they had received their wounds.

Rev. J. J. Marks, D.D., in the "Peninsular Campaign in Virginia," p. 243, describes the scene on the evening of the 29th, in the following language:

"I beheld a long, scattered line of the patients staggering

The Seven Days' Retreat—Gaines' Mill. 233

away, some carrying their guns and supporting a companion on an arm, others tottering feebly over a staff which they appeared to have scarcely strength to lift up. One was borne on the shoulders of two of his companions, in the hope that when he had gone a little distance he might be able to walk. One had already sat down, fainting from the exertion of a few steps. Some had risen from the first rest, staggered forward a few steps, and fell in the road; but after a few moments in the open air, and stimulated by the fear of the enemy, they could walk more strongly. Never have I beheld a spectacle more touching or more sad."

Also an eye-witness* of this painful episode in the events of the campaign, tells his observations as follows :

" A very affecting scene was now witnessed as the troops bade adieu to their sick and wounded friends, whom they were compelled to leave behind, to abandon as prisoners to the rebels.

" Up to this time the disabled had not known that they were to be left behind; and when it became manifest, the scene could not be pictured by human language. I heard one man cry out, 'O my God ! is this the reward I deserve for all the sacrifices I have made, the battles I have fought, and the agony I have endured from my wounds?' Some of the younger soldiers wept like children; others turned pale, and some fainted. Poor fellows! they thought this was the last drop in the cup of bitterness, but there were many yet to be added."

REPORT OF COLONEL G. K. WARREN,

3d Brigade, 2d Division, 5th Corps, of the Battle of Gaines' Mill.

HEADQUARTERS 3D BRIGADE, SYKES' DIVISION,
PORTER'S CORPS, *July* 4, 1862.

SIR :—I have the honor to report the operations of this brigade from June 26th to July 3d, 1862.

The brigade consisted, on the 26th ultimo, of the 5th New

---
* Rev. John S. C. Abbott's " Change of Base."

York Volunteers, commanded by Lieut.-Col. Duryea, numbering about 450 effective men for duty, and of the 10th New York Volunteers, commanded by Col. Bendix, numbering about 575 men for duty. The 1st Connecticut, Col. Tyler, had been relieved from my command for duty with the heavy artillery.

The conflict having begun on the right of our army, at Mechanicsville, on the afternoon of the 26th ultimo, we were ordered out with the rest of the division, and remained in line of battle all night. At 2.30 A.M. on the 27th, we marched back, as directed, and took up our line so as to defend the crossing of Gaines' Creek while the trains and artillery effected a passage. This having been accomplished, we again marched forward to a new position, about half a mile from the last, where it had been determined to prevent the further advance of the enemy.

The line assigned to my brigade, forming the left of the division, had its left resting upon a forest, which, I was informed, was held by Griffin's brigade, and our line of battle was in an open, plowed field, along a gentle slope, in a measure hiding us from the observation of the enemy, though affording but little shelter from distant curved firing. In front of us, distant from 200 to 300 yards, was a belt of woods, growing in a ravine, through openings of which a view could be had of an extensive, open field beyond. These woods I occupied with a company of the 5th New York Volunteers as skirmishers. From 300 to 400 yards to the right of my line was another forest bordering the open field, and running nearly in a direction perpendicular to our line. This I guarded by a company of the 5th New York Volunteers, deployed as skirmishers. Major Clitz's battalion of the 12th Regular Infantry was on my right, on a line nearly perpendicular to mine, with a large interval between us. Our artillery was posted to the rear and to the left of my line.

About 10½ o'clock A.M. these arrangements were complete, and we waited the approach of the enemy. The weather was very warm.

About 12½ P.M. the enemy forced the passage of Gaines' Creek near the mill, and cheering as they came, appeared in force at a distance in the open field beyond the wooded ravine in my front.

About 1 o'clock P.M. they advanced in several lines, and at my request, Captain Edwards brought up a section of his battery on my right, and opened on them, and a fierce fire was carried on between them over our heads, in which we suffered considerably. Captain Edwards steadily kept up his fire, though opposed by several batteries, till the enemy having driven in our line of skirmishers, I advised him to retire. The enemy now advanced sharpshooters to the edge of the woods to pick off our artillerymen, posted behind us, but our rifle-firing compelled them to retire.

One of our batteries having opened with shrapnel, the premature explosion of these shells behind us caused so much loss that I was compelled to change my line by throwing the right to the rear along the road, and the left more toward the enemy, and along the woods to our left.

The enemy's fire ceasing for a time, our artillery also ceased, and there was a lull, so that we began to think the enemy had retired. But under the shelter of the woods he had formed a column to attack the position occupied by Major Clitz, to the right of my first position, and as soon as it appeared, the rapid firing of our artillery dispersed it in a few moments. Again there was a lull, but this time he had planned his attack on the position occupied by myself, and where our artillery could not be used without endangering us.

I should think it was now nearly 3 o'clock P.M. Suddenly a regiment burst from the woods with loud yells, advancing at double-quick upon us. The 5th New York Volunteers, which had been drawn back to be out of the fire of our own artillery, rapidly re-formed to meet them on our first position. The enemy received a portion of the fire of the 10th New York Volunteers as he came rapidly on, and when he neared the 5th New York Volunteers we charged back, turning his charge into a flight, killing and wounding nearly all of those who fled. This charge of the enemy had also been accompanied by a vigorous attack on our position in the woods, and as we advanced we received a heavy fire from the enemy stationed in them. Our men, nothing daunted, continued to advance, and drove them from it. The brigade was re-formed (as well as the confusion produced by this charge would allow) in its first position, and again it successfully repulsed the advance of the enemy, driving him back to the woods in front, up to which point the colors of the 5th New York were twice carried. During this part of the fight, the artillery on both sides was silent. The enemy continued to throw forward fresh troops. The gallant and lamented Major Clitz engaged them on the right.

The 6th Regular infantry came to reinforce me, and I placed them in position. General Reynolds also came up now with his brigade, and I withdrew my shattered regiments. Besides the exhaustion of the men from their efforts, and the bad condition of the arms from the firing we had done, about one hundred and forty of the 5th New York Volunteers, and about fifty of the 10th New York Volunteers, were killed and wounded.

The battle had now become general all along our lines, and the artillery had resumed its fire. I took up a position supporting a twenty-pounder battery, just to the rear of the first position, and maintained it, though suffering continually from the enemy's fire, which now reached all parts of the field. To our left was the 11th U. S. Infantry, also supporting batteries. Toward evening the enemy succeeded in forcing back the division on our left, when the batteries we supported were withdrawn, we throwing in all the fire our diminished numbers would permit. We here witnessed the firm stand of the 11th U. S. Infantry on our left, and the charge of the 2d U. S. Infantry on our right. The advance of the enemy on our front was thus effectually checked. We then took up a position supporting one of the batteries under Captain Platt, which position we maintained till darkness put an end to the firing, and the battery was withdrawn.

We were much concerned as to the cause of the cheering which took place in our rear, by the regiments of French's and Meagher's brigades, fearing they were a rebel force that had succeeded in getting in our rear. From the beginning of the battle, till night brought it to a close, we were almost constantly under fire, of which fact I believe the General was a witness.

. . . . Among the killed was Captain William T. Partridge, who fell nobly leading on his men to the charge. Among the wounded were Captain George Duryea, Lieutenant Thomas W. Cartwright, Jr., Lieutenant Felix Agnus, and Lieutenant Ralph E. Prime. Lieutenant-Colonel Hiram Duryea was everywhere conspicuous in the fight, mounted on his horse, and inspired

The Seven Days' Retreat—Gaines' Mill. 237

every one by his gallantry. Major Hull's horse was shot in the first charge. Captain Winslow was acting as field-officer, and mounted. Both acted most bravely. Colonel Duryea speaks of the gallant conduct of the following-named officers, to which I can also add my own testimony: Major H. D. Hull, Captain C. Winslow, Captain William T. Partridge, Captain George Duryea, Captain H. H. Burnett, Captain C. J. Cambrelling, Captain W. F. Lewis, Captain C. Boyd, Lieutenants C. J. Montgomery, G. O. Hager, H. G. O. Eichler, J. McConnell, J. H. Lounsbery, Charles Sergeant, T. W. Cartwright, Jr., R. E. Prime, F. Agnus, S. W. Wheeler. I refer you to the list of meritorious non-commissioned officers and privates in Colonel Duryea's report submitted herewith, and also to it for the names of the killed and wounded.

Three of the officers of the 5th New York Volunteers left the field, it is believed unnecessarily, from the effects of contusions made by spent balls. Their conduct will be made the subject of official investigation. I received a bruise on my knee by a spent ball which gave rise to the report of my being wounded, and my horse received two balls in his neck, but he carried me all through the fight.

.... Colonel Bendix has not furnished any report of those distinguished for meritorious conduct. I have only to say that the Colonel himself behaved in the most cool and efficient manner, always at his post, always ready to execute my orders with promptness, and always with his regiment under fire. I must also mention the gallant conduct of Surgeon Doolittle, whose horse was killed under him and himself bruised, but who has been constantly with the command to this day.

. . . .

Very respectfully, your obedient servant,
(Signed), G. K. WARREN,
Col. 5th N. Y. Vols., com. 3d Brigade.
LIEUTENANT SAMUEL A. FOSTER,
Aide-de-camp, and
Act. Asst. Adjt.-Gen., Sykes' Division.
[*Official Copy*].
R. C. DRUM, *Asst. Adjt.-General.*
A. G. OFFICE, *October* 29, 1878.

The following extract from the official report of General Sykes was furnished for publication in these pages through the courtesy of the Hon. George W. McCrary, Secretary of War:

HEADQUARTERS SYKES' DIVISION,
CAMP NEAR HARRISON'S LANDING,
July 7, 1862.

SIR:—The events taking place since the 26th ultimo have followed each other so rapidly that they may well be included in one general summary, which I have the honor herewith to submit: . . . .

About 11 A.M. (June 27th) the enemy appeared in some force beyond the ravine in front, and with his artillery endeavored to shake the center of my line of battle. From this hour till 2 P.M., his battalions being constantly strengthened, he made repeated attempts on the flanks and center of my line, and was as often driven back to his lair.

At noon Tidball's Battery of Horse Artillery reported to me, and taking position on the right of Weed, these two batteries broke up every attack of the enemy on our right flank, and finally sent him scampering to his main body on our left. Matters now remained quiet for an hour. It was only the lull that precedes a storm.

At 3 P.M. I directed Colonel Warren to throw forward his skirmishers and feel the enemy in the ravine. Desultory firing began, which soon deepened into a continuous roar, unvarying and unceasing, until darkness set in and the conflict ceased.

In this interval, between 2 and 3 P.M., the enemy had brought up his reserves, replenished his ammunition, and, under cover of the forest heretofore mentioned, marshaled his legions for a grand attack. It was not one, but many, each of which was met and repulsed with a steady valor that could not be surpassed.

In these attacks the *5th New York Volunteers*, under *Lieutenant-Colonel Duryea*, and 2d, 6th, 12th, and 14th U. S. Infantry were especially conspicuous. The *5th New York Volunteers* were the peers of any troops on that hard-fought field.

The 12th and 14th U. S. Infantry, under Major Clitz and Captain O'Connell, advanced in the most perfect order in line, hero-

The Seven Days' Retreat—Gaines' Mill.

ically aiding Warren's brigade (5th and 10th New York Volunteers), drove the enemy from our left and center far into the woods beyond.

In connection with this movement the 3d U. S. Infantry, under Major Rossell, was thrown from its original position to the right and rear of the 12th and 14th, and while in this exposed situation, boldly resisting the foe, the gallant Major lost his life. . . . .

(Signed), GEORGE SYKES,
Brigadier-General Commanding Division.

ADJUTANT-GENERAL'S OFFICE,
WASHINGTON, *Nov.* 27, 1878.

Official:
R. C. DRUM, *Assistant Adjutant-General.*

CHAPTER XI.

THE SEVEN DAYS' RETREAT—MALVERN HILL—HARRISON'S LANDING.

White Oak Swamp—Charles City Cross-Roads—General Kearney—Malvern Hill—A Desperate Struggle—Rebel Repulse—Retreat from Malvern Hill—The Rain and the Roads—An Incident—A Life Saved by a Stratagem—Report of Lieutenant-Colonel H. Duryea—Letter from Surgeon Joseph S. Smith—Harrison's Landing—The Camping-Ground—Want of Water—A Review by President Lincoln—Moving our Camp—Reviewed by General McClellan—Resignation of Captain Camerelling—Changes—Health of the Army—Hospital Grounds—A Death by Poison—Improved Diet—A Rebel Salute—Death in a Tent—Pine Woods Experience—Knapsacks Forwarded—A Night March—Crossing the Chickahominy — Negro Messenger Shot—Soldiers' Hospitality Refused—Newport News—The March to Manassas Junction—On the Battlefield.

WE marched during the night, leaving behind us the blood-stained field, the silent graves of our departed comrades, and the multitudes of the sick and wounded, and at length found a brief repose on the road through White Oak Swamp. The next day, Sunday, the 29th of June, we completed our passage through this part of the exodus. It was a terribly dreary pilgrimage. The heat was almost insupportable; there was not a breath of air, and we suffered intensely for the want of water, of which none could be had but the black, stagnant water of the swamp through which we were wading. Having again stepped upon firm ground, we formed in line of battle at Charles City Cross-Roads, pulled down the fences in front, and sent out pickets. The shots of skirmishers were heard in the vicinity. We remained here, guarding this important point, until General Kearney arrived with his division to relieve General Sykes. General Kearney looked

The Seven Days' Retreat—Malvern Hill. 241

like a Knight errant of old; his face was bronzed by exposure, and as he sat on his horse, straight as an arrow, with his strongly-marked and stern countenance, holding the reins in his teeth, he was a perfect picture of a soldier.

At 10 A.M. Sumner's corps were attacked by the enemy at Allen's field, but were repulsed. At 4 P.M. Sumner's and Franklin's corps were attacked near Savage's Station, and fought until 9 P.M., when the enemy retired.

We continued our march on Monday, the 30th, to Turkey Bend Creek, near Malvern Hill. At this point we were formed in line of battle, sent out pickets and skirmishers, advanced through a wood, and the skirmishers reached an immense corn-field on level ground, outside of the wood. Sergeant William Hoffman about 5 P.M. discovered the enemy in force over a corner of the corn-field, in the edge of a wood, with artillery in position. Colonel Warren was immediately notified, who ordered Lieutenant Dumont, of the Fifth, on detached service with the signal corps, to signal the gun-boats *Jacob Bell*, *Galena*, and *Aroostook*, which opened over the heads of the Fifth, where they rested on their arms in the wood, and created great havoc in the rebel ranks, thereby preventing them from advancing.* Sergeants Forbes, Wilson, Jack Taylor, and Hoffman, and some others were stationed in the corn-field and elsewhere, to signal where the shell struck, so as to regulate the aim of the gunners. Some batteries and infantry also opened from the Hill, and drove the enemy back, leaving two guns of Graham's battery, with their caissons, in the hands of Colonel Warren. The guns were subsequently spiked, and the spokes of the wheels cut with axes, leaving them entirely unserviceable. About half a barrel of whisky and a quan-

---

* While engaged in this duty, Lieutenant Dumont was stationed on the roof of a large house situated on Malvern Hill, and was much exposed to the fire of the enemy's batteries. He was highly commended for his good conduct.

tity of prime pork were also seized, the latter being distributed among the men.*

When the hundred-pound shell from the gun-boats came rushing over our heads, they conveyed the impression that flour barrels were flying through the air, and it required considerable nerve to listen to their roar without being moved, especially as a mistaken signal or a short fuse would bring a shell in our midst. The discharges from one gun especially were rather unreliable, and it was with a sigh of relief that we heard its shell go beyond us. The crash, as they burst in the woods among the enemy, was terrible. During the night the Fifth and Tenth were in line of battle in the wood, expecting an attack. Some cattle were slaughtered, and small pieces of tough meat were distributed, but as there were no means of cooking, fires not being allowed, it was of no benefit to us whatever.

The enemy attempted to follow the army across White Oak Swamp, and attacked General Franklin's corps about 1 P.M., but were repulsed. At night, after a desperate engagement of five hours near the Charles City Cross-Roads, and after driving McCall's division, the enemy were again repulsed by Generals Hooker and Kearney, aided by General Sumner's corps. These continual encounters had kept the army in unceasing activity, and the month of July opened wearisomely upon us, for the men had passed the previous twenty-four hours without sleep.

Remaining in position, Porter's corps held the left of the line with many batteries; Sykes' division on the left, with

---

* General McClellan's Report (p. 268): "At about this time, 4 P M., the enemy began to appear in General Porter's front, and at 5 o'clock advanced in large force against his left flank, posting artillery under cover of a skirt of timber, with a view to engage our force on Malvern Hill, while with his infantry and some artillery, he attacked Colonel Warren's brigade. A concentrated fire of about thirty guns was brought to bear on the enemy, which with the infantry fire of Colonel Warren's command compelled him to retreat, leaving two guns in the hands of Colonel Warren."

The Seven Days' Retreat—Malvern Hill. 243

Warren's brigade on the extreme left on low ground, which was swept by the fire of the gun-boats. It was a vital point, for if the enemy could force their way in here, they would be enabled to cut off the line of retreat to the James River, hence their desperate efforts during the battle to force back the left flank. About 9 A.M. the enemy commenced the attack with their artillery, the batteries on the hill replying. In the afternoon, the Fifth and Tenth were advanced to the edge of the wood facing the corn-field, the Fifth on the extreme left, the Tenth on their right, which rested on the Richmond road, running along by the "Hill," and the regulars on their right.*

The men were ordered to build barricades of logs and stones from the fence, and whatever other material they could make available, and two men were placed together about fifteen feet apart behind each barricade. Their orders were to hold their posts to the last man. About noon the enemy made a demonstration on our left, as if they intended to attack us, but the fire of our battery and from the gun-boats drove them to cover.

About 3 P.M. a heavy artillery fire was opened by the enemy on Kearney's division, and their infantry advanced against Couch's division on the right of General Porter, but they reserved their fire and drove the enemy back in disorder. Shortly after 4 P.M. the firing ceased along the whole line, but it was only the calm that precedes the storm. At 6 P.M. the enemy suddenly opened with the whole of their artillery, soon after which brigade after brigade started on a run from the cover of the woods, and across the open ground

---

* General McClellan's Report (p. 269): "From the position of the enemy, his most obvious lines of attack would come from the directions of Richmond and White Oak Swamp, and would almost of necessity strike us upon our left wing. Here, therefore, the lines were strengthened by massing the troops and collecting the principal part of the artillery. Porter's corps held the left of the line (Sykes' division) on the left (p. 270). One brigade of Porter's was thrown to the left on the low ground, to protect the flank from any movement direct from the Richmond road."

to storm the batteries stationed on the left, supported by Porter's and Couch's commands; but they were met by such a withering fire of grape and canister shot, that they were mowed down in heaps. Still did these brave men sweep on, when the infantry, who had reserved their fire, opened with such terrible volleys, that their columns broke, and the remnants went back reeling and tottering like drunken men. In the meantime the terrible shell from the gun-boats fell among them as they were gathering in the edge of the wood for their reckless and desperate charges, which were without a parallel almost in history. General Porter had sent to General Sumner about 6 P.M., who was the chief in command, for reinforcements, who sent to him Meagher's, Richardson's, Sickles', and Patterson's brigades, who relieved such of the troops as were out of ammunition. By the steady, cool fire of the infantry, aided by the batteries, the enemy were driven back to the cover of the woods, leaving the ground in front heaped with their slain. The loss of the Union side was comparatively small as compared to that of the Confederates. The enemy in large force at one time advanced against Warren's brigade on the extreme left; Pollard says: "Holmes' division were frustrated from cutting the enemy off from the river by the severe fire of the gun-boats." We could plainly see the flashing of their bayonets on the opposite side of the corn-field. The continual roar of artillery and musketry during the battle was like long rolls of thunder, and did not slacken until 9 P.M.

The men remained in their positions in the barricades all night, and were worn out and almost dead for want of sleep. They felt as if they had heavy weights fastened to their eyelids, but they were kept awake by the consciousness of the great responsibilities resting upon them; knowing also that the penalty of sleeping on their posts in such a position was death. Moreover, one-half of the regiment, who were on reserve, went the grand rounds, under command of Major

The Seven Days' Retreat—Malvern Hill. 245

Hull or Captain Winslow, every half hour. The enemy appeared to be desperate enough to undertake any movement to destroy the Union army, and it was probable they might attempt to accomplish, under the cover of darkness, what they had failed to do by day. Besides, as was currently reported, they had been plied with whisky, and could be led into the jaws of death itself, and it was necessary to be vigilant.

On the right of the Richmond road was stationed James W. Webb, of Company F, a trusty and reliable soldier, and on the left of it was William Higgins, of the same company. The clatter of a horse's hoofs were heard coming from the direction of the enemy, and soon the form of an officer on horseback loomed up over a slight hill on the road. He discovered Webb at the same time he was sighted, and immediately pulled rein and came to a sudden halt. He called out and inquired where General Whiting's headquarters were situated; Webb pulled his cap off and said, "Come forward, they are a short distance in the rear." But unfortunately at this moment Sergeant F., who was a few feet in the rear of the picket, jumped into the road and said, "You are my prisoner." The officer turned his horse about in almost a second of time, and disappeared over the brow of the hill. Webb and Higgins fired their rifles at him as quick as they could, but he did not fall from his horse. Thus, by the want of forethought on the part of the Sergeant, the capture of an officer with, in all probability, important dispatches, was frustrated.

After the battle the army commenced to retreat again, and wagons, troops, artillery, and ambulances were leaving all night as their convenience dictated. The covering of the retreat was left, as usual, to Sykes' division. On the morning of Wednesday, the 2d, about 4 o'clock, a heavy storm of rain began, which continued the entire day. The balance of the troops were retreating from the hill in a disorganized mass, fleeing from a beaten and demoralized foe. They became blocked up on the road among the ambulances and wagons; many of the sick, weak, and wounded were knocked down and trampled upon, notwithstanding their cries of anguish. When Lieutenant-Colonel Hiram Duryea saw this, his soul revolted at the sight. He also knew that if he marched his regiment into such a disorganized mass of moving humanity it would be impossible for them to keep their formation, and he would lose all control of their movements; he therefore ordered a halt, and remarked that "before he would take his command into such a mob, he would face the whole Southern Confederacy." An aide soon came to him with orders to move, but he took the responsibility of acting on his own better judgment; an aide came a second time with orders to move, followed in a few moments by Colonel Warren. Lieutenant-Colonel Duryea explained, in a few brief words, the situation of affairs, and pointed to a train of wagons on the hill, apparently abandoned by their guard, that should be moved off. Colonel Warren took in the situation at a glance, and looking toward the retreating crowd, exclaimed, "This is disgraceful!" He called the officers together, and, after a brief consultation, turned and surveyed his men for a moment, when he called out, "Unfurl your colors;" "About face! Forward, march!" and the regiment moved down the Richmond road, toward the enemy, formed in line of battle on the hill, and there they stood alone awaiting orders. Colonel Warren sent an aide to order up a battery. In a few moments a fine battery of artillery came up, the horses on a run, unlimbered, and the men stood by their guns, prepared for action. In the meantime some of the regiment were detailed to gather together a lot of abandoned shell and ammunition which was lying near, and throw it into a ditch, that it might be of no service to the enemy. When the regiment was ready to move the first time, Colonel

Warren ordered Lieutenant —— to see to it personally that all the men on picket were called in. As the regiment was about to march, the Colonel discovered a Zouave (Corporal James R. Murray, of Company A) standing a good distance off alone, who had not been relieved, but, like the Roman centurion of old, would not forsake his post without orders. He dashed up to the Lieutenant, and asked him if he had obeyed his orders in reference to the men on picket, to which the officer answered in the affirmative. "Then," said the Colonel, "what is that man doing out there; is that the way you forsake my men? is that the way you obey orders? Draw your sword and defend yourself," at the same time he half unsheathed his own sword, for he was very much vexed.

The regiment remained in this position, the Tenth not having halted, until the road was clear, in the meantime manifesting much interest in the skirmishing of the cavalry with the enemy in the edge of the woods on the other side of the plateau. Finally they were ordered to march, and when they came to a little bridge that led over the creek, they found that its supporting timbers were nearly cut through, as well as the trees each side of the road near it, and men with axes in hand stood ready to put the finishing strokes as soon as the rear guard had passed over. There were no troops left behind at this time but Colonel Buchanan's brigade of regulars, a battery, and Colonel Averill with the 3d Pennsylvania Cavalry. This was nearly 7 A.M. These troops were the last to leave. "Sykes' division could have held the hill if ordered to do so."

The men experienced this day the hardest marching they had ever endured. They had been without sleep for forty-eight hours; a cold north-east storm had set in, and it was raining in torrents. The road was cut up by the wheels, so as to be almost impassable. The men forded innumerable small streams and ditches, often nearly waist deep. At the numerous halts, the road and fields being blocked very often, they could not sit down without being content to rest in mud a foot deep; the fields on either side of the road were all under water, and the men were continually slipping and falling down. They were very much weakened in their condition, for, be it remembered, this was the seventh day in which they had been deprived of their sleep, except the few hours now and then snatched at intervals; they had nothing to eat except a little hard-tack, and were almost starved and thoroughly reduced. Moreover, they were obliged to form in line of battle after every mile's march, and wait for the wagons to pass on.

Beside all these trials of endurance, the continual excitement of battle and suspense night and day, and the never-ceasing rattle of musketry and thunder of artillery, of which there seemed to be no end, there was added the doubt as to where they would come to rest. Such was the indifference on this day, that a colored man who had been run over, and was lying in the road, was left to his fate, no one taking the trouble to pull the body out of the way; wagons and artillery passed over it, as if it were nothing but a dead dog. Finally, at night, we reached Harrison's Landing, with an unbroken organization as a regiment, one of the very few, outside of Sykes' division, of which the same is recorded, in the 5th corps. A large ration of whisky was given to each man, and the whole army were soon vigorously recounting their experiences; but they laid down in the mud and water and, notwithstanding the rain, which continued all night and until noon of next day, slept soundly. We had no covering but the sky, for nearly all in the regiment had lost their knapsacks, and all they possessed was on their backs.

The loss during the seven days, in Morell's, Sykes', McCall's and Slocum's divisions, the same that fought the battle of Gaines' Mill, was 8,500 in killed and wounded alone. If all the divisions in the army had lost in the same proportion, it would show a total loss of over 25,000 men.

One instance, out of many, will serve to show the straits to which the men were reduced on the retreat.

One of the drummers saw Drum-Major John M. Smith, of the Fifth, sitting on a log at the side of the road, completely worn out and not able to go any further. He told the drummer that he was starving, not having eaten a mouthful in three days. The latter was possessed of a few crackers, and gave him two or three, and told him not to move a foot from where he was, and he would get him some meat. The drummer started off with not the slightest idea where he was to obtain it; but fortunately he saw a colored man toasting a piece of bacon over a fire. He immediately accosted him, and asked him whose servant he was; to which the negro replied, giving the name of a well-known General. J., nothing abashed, said that he was a cousin of General McClellan. "Shuah?" said the cook. "Shuah," said J., "and I would be very much obliged to you if you will fill my canteen with water, as I am wounded in the leg, and it is hard work to move; in the meantime, I will toast your bacon." Off went the innocent on his errand to do a favor for the cousin of the General of the army, and, of course, as soon as he was out of sight, off went J. with the bacon. Smith ate the whole of it, and it probably saved his life.

The following is the report of Colonel Duryea on the service of the regiment from June 26th to July 2d:

REPORT OF LIEUTENANT-COLONEL HIRAM DURYEA,
Commanding the 5th Regiment—Seven Days' Retreat.

HEADQUARTERS 5TH REGIMENT, N. Y. V.,
CAMP NEAR HARRISON'S LANDING,
July 4, 1862.

SIR :—I have the honor to respectfully submit the following report of the movements of this regiment from June 26th to July 2d, inclusive.

Thursday at 4 P.M. moved out of camp to the support of McCall's division on the Mechanicsville road, bivouacked that night in line of battle in an open field, where we remained until about half-past four on Friday morning, when we returned to our camp, slung knapsacks, and moved on the road toward Coal Harbor. About daybreak formed a line of battle on the skirt of a wood in rear of Gaines' Mill, where we remained for about two hours, then moved forward in the direction and to the left of Coal Harbor, where we formed line of battle in an open field about half-past 10 A.M. Here we rested until about noon, when, in accordance with your order, we changed our position forward, our line resting under the crest of a hill about two hundred yards from a piece of woods, where, after remaining about half an hour, the enemy appeared in force opposite our right, advancing in successive lines of battle. Shortly after making their appearance they posted a battery on our right and opened fire through an opening in the woods, throwing shrapnel, shell, grape, and canister with accuracy and effect. Company E was then ordered to the front as skirmishers, to pick off the gunners from the batteries, which was done with considerable effect; they were driven in by an advance of the enemy in force, which was met by a fire by companies along the whole regiment, followed by fire by file, which had the effect to check the enemy and drive them back into the woods. They did not appear again for about an hour; the batteries meanwhile continued to play upon us, thinning our ranks perceptibly. Agreeable with your orders, we again changed position, forming line of battle in the road. Shortly after the enemy emerged in force from the woods on our left, and we then resumed our former position on the crest of the hill. Of the charge which the regiment then made, in which Colonel Warren and all the field officers, mounted, took a part in leading, it is unnecessary for me to report. Suffice it that the enemy were driven in confusion from the field, and the fugitives were nearly annihilated by our fire. The enemy with fresh troops now opened with musketry from the woods.; the most deadly fire being carried on by both sides, they several times appearing on the field in force. They fought bravely and contested the ground with great stubbornness; our line was several times forced to yield, which it did in good order, before a greatly superior force, but as often advanced and

Report of Lieut.-Col. H. Duryea. 251

regained the ground at the point of the bayonet. We occupied the ground till reinforcements came to our support and held it; when we were relieved and ordered to support batteries of field artillery on our right, which we did until 8½ P.M., delivering an effective fire whenever the enemy approached, and suffering considerably. Night having set in, and firing having ceased, the batteries were withdrawn, and we retired from the field. We were in the engagement about eight and a half hours, the greater part of the time under a very severe fire.

Colonel Warren having charge of the brigade, left but two field officers to the regiment, and Captain Cleveland Winslow, of Company E, was detailed to act as Major. During the action the following changes took place in the commands of companies:

Lieutenant C. S. Montgomery, of Company C, was assigned to the command of Company B. The two remaining officers of Company C being subsequently wounded, Lieutenant Eichler, of Company H, was assigned to the command of that company; Lieutenant Lounsberry, of Company K, was assigned to the command of Company E.

I wish to mention the gallant conduct of the following officers: Major Hull, Captain Winslow, Captain Partridge, Captain Duryea, Captain Burnett, Captain Cambrelling, Captain Lewis, Captain Boyd, First Lieutenant Montgomery, Lieutenant Sargent, Lieutenant Hager, Lieutenant Cartwright, First Lieutenant Eichler, Lieutenant McConnell, Lieutenant Lounsberry, Second Lieutenant Prime, Second Lieutenant Wheeler, Second Lieutenant Agnus. Their coolness was particularly shown in preparing for the last charge, just previous to which, the regiment being very much thinned, the ranks were closed and told off with great coolness under a most terrific fire.

Captain Wm. T. Partridge, of Company I, behaved with great bravery and coolness, commanding the admiration of the entire regiment. He was nearly the whole day advanced with his company as skirmishers in a very exposed position, and was killed while gallantly leading his company in a charge.

I must also call attention to the following non-commissioned officers and privates whose meritorious acts come under the notice of myself and officers:

Color-Sergeant Andrew B. Allison, who bore the National

Flag, which was pierced by eight balls, one of which nearly severed the staff.

Color-Sergeant John H. Berrian, who bore the Regimental Standard, which was pierced by eleven balls, one of which entered the staff. Color-Corporal George L. Guthrie, Company D. Orderly Sergeants Patrick Gilligan, Company A ; John H. Reilly, Company D ; John Frie, Company E. Sergeant Thomas R. Martin, Company D. Corporals John McKenna, Company D ; Jos. H. Pierce, Company D. Sergeant John S. Raymond, Company E. Orderly Sergeants Andrew Whitehead, Company H ; Wm. McDowell, Company G. Sergeant Wm. H. Chambers, Company H. Privates Wm. H. Manderville, Company F ; James E. McBeth, Company H ; John McGeehan Company E ; Drummer-boy Robert Daly, Company D.

We went into action about 450 strong.

[For list of killed, wounded, and missing, see Appendix].

You will observe that our loss amounts to thirty-six per cent. of the number that we took into the field. Dr. Owen Munson, Assistant Surgeon, remained with the sick and wounded at Savage Station, and no doubt fell into the hands of the enemy. He is the officer reported missing.

Of the missing enlisted men, some are supposed to have been wounded and left on the field, and all are supposed to have been taken prisoners. After leaving the battle-field, we proceeded to near Woodbury's Bridge, where we bivouacked and remained until three o'clock Saturday morning, 28th, when we crossed the Chickahominy and remained supporting the artillery, defending the passage of the stream till about 5 P.M. We then proceeded in the direction of Savage Station, marching all night, crossing the White Oak Swamp on the morning of the 29th, halting on the Charles City Cross-Roads in the direction of Richmond. Monday morning took up the march and halted about noon at Turkey Creek, near James River. Here we took a position on the Richmond road along the river. About 3 o'clock P.M. the enemy appeared in force of infantry, cavalry, and artillery. The latter opening fire upon us, we prepared to give them battle, advancing our skirmishers along the edge of the woods ; when the enemy being fired upon by the gun-boats and artillery on our right, he retired.

Report of Lieut.-Col. H. Duryea.

We remained on the ground that night, and in the morning were reinforced by a section of artillery. About noon the enemy, force of cavalry and infantry, again made their appearance advancing along the Richmond road. We opened fire on them from our battery, and succeeded in driving them back; they afterward appeared several times during the day, but were as often driven back. In this position we were very much exposed, shell often falling inside our lines. The entire regiment remained on picket till 1 o'clock Wednesday morning, July 2d. Marched through a cold and drenching rain to near Harrison's Bar, where we arrived and bivouacked about 5 P.M.

During all these trying scenes the men under my command have maintained a spirit of cheerfulness and determination, yielding none of their discipline or soldierly pride.

Very respectfully,
Your obedient servant,
H. DURYEA,
Lieutenant-Colonel Commanding 5th N. Y. Vols.

To Lieutenant A. S. MARVIN, JR.,
Assistant Adjutant-General,
3d Brigade, Sykes' Division.

The following letter from Surgeon Jos. S. Smith speaks for itself:

HEADQUARTERS, ARMY OF POTOMAC,
July 28, 1862.

COLONEL G. K. WARREN:

Dear Sir:—While within the Confederate lines I was much gratified at often hearing the highest praise bestowed upon your gallant regiment by the enemy.

From their Generals down through all grades they all coincided that they never had seen the superiors of the "red legs" for unflinching courage and coolness.

Yours, with respect,
JOS. S. SMITH,
Assistant Surgeon, U. S. A.

July 29, 1862.

The above was sent to me by Colonel Warren, then Acting

Brigadier-General, I being in command of the regiment in the actions referred to.

H. DURYEA,
Lieut.-Col. Commanding 5th N. Y. Vol. Infantry.

HARRISON'S LANDING.

Wednesday, July 3.—In the morning we were saluted soon after reveille by the report of cannon, and some shell dropped into camp. The regiment was ordered out into line of battle, and after advancing and standing under arms for some time, the firing ceased. The battery was charged and captured by the 5th Maine, and was found to consist of two rifled pieces. The cannoneers and an officer were taken prisoners.

The next day, the 4th, a salute was fired in honor of the day at sunrise, and in the afternoon we were reviewed by General McClellan and staff, and a Major-General's salute fired by the artillery in each corps. His address, which was very eloquent and patriotic, was read to the men.

Some of the companies in the Fifth were in command of non-commissioned officers and Second Lieutenants, most of the officers having resigned, or were on the list of sick and wounded. This loss of officers made room for many promotions. Many of the officers and men had contracted the fever peculiar to the swamps of the Chickahominy, which made a large portion of them invalids for life. Three of the former were under arrest, and awaiting trial by court-martial, for their unsoldierly conduct in the late retreat. The regiment numbered in Baltimore, when in the height of its organization, 1,000; only about two months previous. We mustered on the 4th for duty only 350 men.

Harrison's Landing was favorably situated for a large camp, easily defended, and supplied with the necessary provisions and forage by way of the James River. The Fifth was encamped about two miles back from the river, on the borders of a narrow strip of timber, through which flowed Herring Creek, a narrow stream which emptied into the James River, suitable for bathing and washing clothes, if the men had any to wash. But there was one great deficiency: the cause of constant delay, trouble, and vexation—the absence of pure water for consumption. Much of the time was spent in waiting turn on the line at the only spring in the camp. Most of the men had lost their knapsacks in the recent "change of base," and were obliged to bivouac with star-rays for mantles, and pillows of turf from the sacred soil. Requisitions for knapsacks, clothing, etc., were made, but some time elapsed before their arrival. Many of the men had scarcely anything left of their uniform but rags, and there were very few who did not carry these fluttering badges of their late hardships. All they had was in daily use, and if they wanted to wash a shirt or pair of socks, they were obliged to go without until they dried; or, if ordered on duty, put them on wet and let them dry on their persons. They had, however, already become accustomed to these laundry eccentricities.

The enemy was now at some distance, and the remnants of the bands played at times, and the drum was heard for the first time since the evacuation of Yorktown.

General McClellan complimented Colonel Warren, and said that men never fought better than his regiment did, and that they did their share toward saving the right wing of the army at Gaines' Mill. General McClellan's address was read at parade on Sunday evening. It was eloquent and true. But eloquence and eulogy were swallowed up in the stern realities of the dead and dying, the wounded on the road, the sick and wounded left behind to be made prisoners, the unknown and unremembered graves, and the individual suffering of every survivor. Each man had an experience of his own, and the battle of a life-time is epitomized in a short ten days of such experience.

But such is a soldier's life ; he accepts it as a part of the inevitable experience that he must pass through sooner or later; and he can say with R. H. Dana, Jr., from his experience of two years of sailor life, and his view of it, will apply in one sense to that of a soldier's life in the field, viz. : " It is at best but a mixture of a little good with much evil, and a little pleasure with much pain. The beautiful is linked with the revolting, the sublime with the commonplace, and the solemn with the ludicrous."

The regiment dragged out the weary hours of camp life, one-third on the sick-list, and the rest half sick, while faith and hope kept them up, and that is about all that could be said, for there was no enjoyment in the mode of living at that time. The ringing laugh was seldom heard, but men slowly paced along with sad and care-worn faces, with nothing to do but to kill time, answer roll calls, or occasionally do a little fatigue duty, each man doing as little as possible. The weather was intolerably hot and water was difficult to obtain.

The men all had great confidence in General McClellan, and would fight to the last and die under him if necessary, but they knew that the army needed strengthening by new recruits, and that Richmond would never be taken unless we were reinforced. The Confederates fought desperately, and were on their own ground, and had an extensive territory to maneuver in. The union forces were compelled to go through a country where every man, woman, and child was opposed to them, and as they advanced they grew weaker and their opponents stronger. They were obliged to look well to their communications for the army supplies, and this necessity demanded the care of a large fighting force.

On Friday, July 12th, the whole army was reviewed by President ABRAHAM LINCOLN, who made us a brief visit. The men were all glad to see him, and noticed that he was a keen observer, and asked a great many questions of the officers in his escort. He left a good impression with the rank and file, and convinced them that the "powers that be" took some interest in their welfare.

The regiment had a thorough inspection to-day by Lieutenant-Colonel H. Duryea. The sick were also inspected. We went out at 9 A.M. and the work lasted till noon. The sun was very hot, but the men considered only three hours' standing nothing at all. The weather continued very hot. The time was occupied quietly with company drill in the early morning, and then continual details. Knapsacks and uniforms in part, with a change of underclothes, were distributed on the 21st, making nearly a month since we had a change of underwear.

We had moved our camp the day before about one hundred yards, to a better location, and were hard at work all day, grading and ditching, to keep the camp dry as possible when a rain-storm set in. There were two companies in line which were called a division, and between them and the next line of two companies was a space, to assemble for roll call or other duty. We built temporary arbors over each division to screen the shelter tents from the sun, which gave the camp a pleasant and inviting appearance. In fact, not to be outdone by other regiments in this respect, under the superintendence of Colonel Warren, we succeeded in making our camping-ground, all things considered, the most inviting of any in the army, with one exception.

On Saturday, the 27th, the division passed in review before General McClellan, and the following day the whole corps was reviewed. Captain Cambrelling resigned on account of ill health. He was much beloved by all, and the men felt that they had lost a good friend.

He had not an enemy in the regiment, and that fact is a high testimony to his conduct as an officer and a gentleman. At this date there was only one of the original Captains, with the exception of our Lieutenant-Colonel, who entered at the organization of the regiment—Captain Winslow, and only two or three of the original Lieutenants. The health of the army improved somewhat in the new encampment, as we were not living in the miasmas of the swamps; but there were funerals every day, and the three rounds of musketry told that the last ceremony was performed, and another soldier had been mustered out of the service of his country.

Lieutenant Fowler resigned, having been sick for some time. Lieutenant-Colonel Duryea was on the sick-list, not having been able to be on duty for several days, and Captain Winslow was in acting command of the regiment.

During one of the heaviest thunder-storms that we ever witnessed, one of the regimental hospital tents blew down; in it were patients suffering with typhoid fever and other complaints, who were too weak to help themselves, and they were obliged to lie still until the tent could be put up again. There was great mortality in the hospital, and the tents under the personal superintendence of Colonel Warren were removed to higher ground further to the rear of the camp, where the sick were in good condition and comfortable.

A lamentable mistake occurred in the 10th Regiment. A bottle containing sugar of lead and whisky, used as a prescription by a member of the regiment to bathe his limbs, was left exposed. It caught the eye of three of the men, who drank out of it, and one of them died in consequence. A new spring was discovered on the banks of the creek, and a cracker-box was sunk, as a basin, to hold the water. It was of service only during low tide, as it was flooded when the water rose. The loathsome insects which dropped down into the spring, from the bank above it, at low water, were scooped away from the surface.

The general health of the men slowly improved with rest and better diet. They fared well for soldiers, occasionally having a stew made from fresh beef, potatoes, and onions; sometimes cabbage, beets, and vinegar. For breakfast and supper we had nothing but "hard-tack" and coffee; occasionally rice or stewed dried apples were served for supper. These variations in our bill of fare were very gratifying to the "Boys in Blue" as well as to the "Boys in Red" in our regiment.

The whole army was aroused at midnight on the 1st of August, by the thunder of very heavy cannonading in the direction of the James River. At first it was supposed that the Confederate rams had come down from Richmond and attacked the gun-boats. For about an hour there was a tremendous noise. The fire of the Union gun-boats could be easily distinguished, by their loud reports dying away in the distance with a long roll, like thunder. The reserve artillery lying by the river also opened, and the enemy's batteries soon ceased their work. They had posted forty-one guns under the command of Colonel W. N. Pendleton, at Coggins' Point, on the other side of the river, and their fire killed ten men and wounded fifteen, besides killing some horses. The shell looked very grand going through the air, as the night was extremely dark; but the spectators would have been just as well satisfied if they had not opened the performance, as they did not know but that with the morning's light an attack would be made in front.

At this time two Corporals of Company I were returned to duty from the hospital; but the officer in command of the company was convinced that they were not strong enough to drill. On the second day thereafter, which was the 25th of July, when their company came in from evening parade, they found one of them lying dead in his tent; he had breathed his last while they were out on parade.

One of the men saw an apparition in the woods moving along toward the creek, and not being superstitious, he went over to make an investigation, and discovered one of the hospital patients, who was delirious with fever, making his way to the water to drown himself. Besides the patients in the camp hospital, there were two hundred and fifty absent, sick and wounded. This left only a small number able to perform the necessary duties, but it was noticeable that at dinner-time there was a pretty large muster.

"*Sunday, August* 10.—The weather is now oppressive, and the steady heat, day after day, without rain or clouds, is very trying in its effects on the troops.

"On Friday last several companies were detailed to cross over to the south side of the James River to cut down trees and work on the batteries. Men have been sent over every day since the rebel bombardment of the shipping. After a pleasant sail across the river on the steamer *Long Branch*—which reminded several of the men of a sail on this same steamer in former years on a more auspicious occasion—they set about their work, but could not continue it more than three hours in the pine woods. The temperature was over one hundred degrees, and some of them fainted. We arrived at camp about 7 P.M., having suffered more from the heat than at any time or place in all our experience."

On Monday, the 11th, our knapsacks were sent away, which was premonitory to us of an early movement. This took place on Thursday, August 14th, when we left Harrison's Landing at 9 P.M., in our accoutrements, with a blanket looped, tied at the ends and thrown over the shoulder; we did not see our knapsacks again for ten weeks. We marched till midnight, and after resting about two hours at Charles City Court-house, we resumed the march, crossing the Chickahominy at Barrett's Ferry, near its mouth, over a pontoon bridge nearly 1,000 feet in length. We limped into a bivouac in the woods two miles beyond the river, at the side of the road, at 3 o'clock in the afternoon of the 15th. This was one of the most trying marches the regiment had at one stretch, being about thirty miles. The men tried to sing and be cheerful, but toward the latter part of the march, the fatigue and strain had a very marked effect upon their tempers, as they had not yet mounted their marching legs. On a long march, when the men get tired out, they will move along for half an hour, or longer, at times in perfect silence, but let one of a company happen to stumble and only touch the man next to him, then it seems as if bedlam is let loose. He is asked if he is too lazy to hold himself up, and if he wants to ride on somebody's back? This brings a retort, and in five minutes the whole company are likely to be engaged in a "war of words," the formulæ of which are not usually found in dictionaries or works on military tactics.

While bivouacking here the men were startled by a shot, just back of the spot where they were lying, and a cry of "Oh! I'm shot!" but hearing nothing further, they went to sleep again. The following morning, the 16th, we ascertained that Corporal Frank Hyatt, of Company G, was called by one of the pickets. He went to him and took charge of a negro, who had been stopped in an effort to pass through the lines in the direction of Richmond. He was bringing him in to the guard, when the negro shied off into the woods. He was called back and warned not to try it again ; but the messenger was determined to accomplish his errand if possible, and a second time darted off on his way, when Hyatt shot him dead. He had a carpet-bag containing papers, which were delivered over to Colonel Warren. It was supposed that he was conveying important information to the enemy.

Marched at 6 A.M., and having reached a point about two miles beyond Williamsburg, we bivouacked twelve miles distant from our resting-place the night previous. While passing through the town, a young woman called out that we were going the wrong way. One of the men answered, he guessed not. "Oh, yes, you are!" "Why, what makes you think so?" "Because that aint the way to Richmond!" was the reply. He had to acknowledge that the young lady was right.

Sunday, August 17th, about 6 A.M. we renewed our march; passed through Yorktown, and bivouacked about eight miles beyond at Smith's Mills, having traveled twenty miles. The 8th New York militia garrisoning the works at Yorktown had dinner and coffee prepared for the regiment, but Colonel Warren refused to stop; probably on account of orders to reach a certain point. This refusal to accept the hospitality of friends, after a long march under a burning sun, and over dusty roads, provoked the ire of the men, and brought out curses not loud, but deep. Monday, the 18th, we started at 5 A.M., and passed through Big Bethel to Newport News and bivouacked, after a march of sixteen miles. We spent two days at Newport News, where we saw the hulk of the frigate *Cumberland*, sunk by the Confederate ram *Merrimac*. We enjoyed the luxury of salt-water bathing in the James River, and were joined by about 100 recruits. We left Newport News on Wednesday, the 20th, about 6 P.M., on the steamer *Cahawba*, for Aquia Creek. It rained all day on the 21st, notwithstanding which everybody was cheerful. After a much crowded voyage, there being two regiments, the 5th and 10th New York, packed on the steamer for forty-two hours, we arrived on the 22d off Aquia Creek, and were finally landed by a steam-tug in detachments. While being ferried to the dock by the tug, some of the men found their way to the storehouse and helped themselves, and were supplied with sugar-cured ham enough to last a week. At Aquia Creek we were put in baggage and on platform cars, like so many cattle, some of the men sitting with their legs dangling over the sides, there being no railings, while the center of the platforms was crowded with men.

We reached Falmouth Station about 11 P.M. on the 22d, after a trip of an hour and a half, and the regiment went into bivouac. While waiting here a " Union " man came around with a wagon and a barrel of cider, which he was selling to the men at five cents a cup. Some mischievous fellows took out the pin that fastened the front axle to the body of the wagon, and on his starting, the fore wheels moved out, and down came wagon, cider, and man, to the astonishment of the latter.

On the 23d we marched two miles, and halted near Falmouth; Sunday, the 24th, we started at 4 A.M. to Deep Run, and bivouacked under arms after a march of ten miles; the 25th we reached Ellis Ford (four miles), and bivouacked under arms; the 26th, left at 6 A.M., and after a march of about ten miles, we joined the division about six miles from Bealton, and bivouacked under arms.

On Wednesday, the 27th, we moved at 4.30 A.M., and marched to Catlett's Station, twelve miles, and bivouacked under arms. We resumed our march at 4 A.M. on Thursday, the 28th, eleven miles to Bristoe Station, and bivouacked under arms. As we approached this place, we saw numerous ambulances, and wounded men were lying near a house under the care of surgeons. Details were burying the dead slain in an encounter between Hooker's division and Ewell's forces that had taken place the day previous. Some Confederates were lying dead alongside of the railroad track in their gore; also a number of their wounded were lying about in the sun, and Colonel Warren ordered some of the men to place boughs over them to shield them from its burning rays. Two locomotives, their trains, and the bridges had been destroyed by the enemy. We fell in line and marched at 7 A.M. on Friday, the 29th, and after moving as expeditiously as possible, halted at Manassas Junction. The destruction of property at this point was enormous; large numbers of locomotives were ruined, and long trains of cars were burnt, and damaged stores for the army were lying about in promiscuous heaps. After marching and countermarching all the afternoon up and down a narrow road, leading through woods, looking for a fight—the men in a bad humor at what to them looked like useless exercise—the regiment drew up in line of battle in the afternoon on an elevated position, from which the country could be seen at intervals for a long distance. In front of us the ground sloped off into a little valley, and was cleared of timber. The opposite heights were covered with dense woods. General Porter was observed at one time pacing backward and forward over a little clearing a few yards from the road. A battery stationed within a few yards of us fired about a dozen shell into the distant timber, but there was no response; although from the reports of stray skirmishers the woods were supposed to mask an enemy; if so, it would have been very poor judgment for them to expose their position, as any force marching to or through the woods could have been taken at a great disadvantage. We heard heavy firing late in the afternoon, apparently a few miles to our right, and it was the general impression among the rank and file at the time that an engagement was going on; but as to the firing heard, it was nothing unusual, as we had been accustomed to hearing it in various directions for several days, and the common talk had been that Jackson was in a bag, and all that remained to to be done was to pull the string and secure him. Finally, after having traveled *over* about twelve miles of ground since morning, we laid down at night on the side of the road and slept under arms. There was no movement of the regiment during the afternoon that could be misconstrued as a retreat.

The following will show the position of the forces under General Longstreet at this time, as described by his own pen:

NEW ORLEANS, LA., *July* 30, 1870.

GENERAL F. J. LIPPITT, Boston, Mass.:

The head of my column reached the field of the second Manassas about 11 o'clock A.M. on the 29th of August. The forces were advanced and deployed as rapidly as possible, and I think

On the March to Manassas.

that I was fully prepared for battle by 1 o'clock P.M. . . . . There were twelve brigades, Anderson's division of three brigades coming up after dark on the 29th.*

Extract from a letter to the Philadelphia *Weekly Times* of Feb. 23, 1878, written by General Longstreet:

". . . . When the head of my column reached that field it was about 12 o'clock on the 29th. As we approached the field we heard sounds of a heavy battle, which proved to be General Jackson very severely engaged with the enemy. As my column deployed on the field, the enemy at once withdrew in good order, however, and took up a strong position a little in the rear of where the heaviest fighting had been going on. During the lull that succeeded, General Lee rode up to where I was and told me that he had determined to attack the position taken by the enemy, and indicated his purpose to have me open the fight. My men were then arranged for battle, but I asked General Lee to withhold the order for attack until I had made a careful reconnoissance and determined exactly how the troops had best be handled. He consented, of course, to this, and I went forward to make the reconnoissance. After a careful examination of the ground I rode back to General Lee, and reported that the position was very strong and the prospects hardly such as to warrant the heavy sacrifice of life that a serious attack would involve. General Lee was not satisfied, however, but seemed disposed to insist upon an attack. He began to suggest moves by which an advantageous assault might be made. Before the question was at all decided a dispatch was received from General Stuart, giving us notice that a very strong column was moving up against my right. General Lee ordered me at once to reinforce that part of my line and be ready to repel the attack. I ordered the reinforcing column to the march, and rode out rapidly in advance that I might see precisely what was needed. The threatening column proved to be *General Fitz John Porter's command.* After seeing it I reported

---

* *Atlantic Monthly* for September, 1878. Pope's "Virginia Campaign," and Porter's part in it, by Francis J. Lippitt. Letter from General Longstreet.

back to General Lee that it was too light a column, in my opinion, to mean a real attack. This presumption was correct, and the advance soon halted, and then withdrew. General Lee then recalled the question of an immediate attack upon the main position of the Federals. I was thoroughly convinced that the position was too strong to be taken without very severe loss, and I suggested to General Lee that the attack be postponed, and that we make a forced reconnoissance just at nightfall, and that we could then prepare to attack at daylight, if it seemed advisable, after thorough investigation, to make the attack at all. He consented very readily to this, and I left him to prepare for the forced reconnoissance. The reconnoissance was successfully made at nightfall. During the night several of my Brigadiers came in, and they all agreed in reporting the position very strong. At about midnight Generals Hood and Evans, and possibly one or two others, came to my headquarters and made similar reports, expressing apprehensions as to the result of the attack. Everything developed by this closer reconnoissance went to confirm the impression made upon me by my reconnoissance during the day. I therefore determined not to make the attack, and ordered my troops back to the original line of battle."

On the other hand, in referring to General Porter's conduct on the 29th, General Pope says, in his official report, dated at New York, January 27, 1863:

". . . . I do not hesitate to say that if he had discharged his duty as became a soldier under the circumstances, and had made a vigorous attack on the enemy, as he was expected and directed to do, at any time up to 8 o'clock that night, we should have utterly crushed or captured the larger portion of Jackson's force before he could have been, by any possibility, sufficiently reinforced to have made any effective resistance.

". . . . I believe—in fact, I am positive—that at 5 o'clock in the afternoon of the 29th, General Porter had in his front no considerable body of the enemy.

"I believed then, as I am very sure now, that it was easily practicable for him to have turned the right flank of Jackson, and to have fallen upon his rear; that if he had done so, we should have gained a decisive victory over the army under Jackson before he could have been joined by any of the forces of Longstreet. . . . ."

It is an undoubted fact that General Pope was unaware that Longstreet had arrived on the field, and expected General Porter to advance and attack Jackson, who was opposed to himself, on his right and rear. Jackson's right was within a few miles of Porter at this time, and it is alleged that the latter did not receive General Pope's order to make the attack until it was too late in the day to obey it. Also we have seen by the testimony of General Longstreet himself, that if Porter had advanced, he would have encountered his overwhelming forces, which had made a junction with Jackson's right, and as he (Longstreet) testifies before the board of officers appointed for the rehearing of the court-martial proceedings against General Porter: "In view of the impenetrable woods, it would have been very hazardous for General Porter to take his command around the road to Groveton, and if he had attempted it his force would have been broken up. General Porter's position checked the forces of the witness till it was too late; if General Porter had attacked that day any time after 12 o'clock, the forces of witness would have annihilated him, for the Federal lines were then too much extended and disjointed."

General Porter's infantry force this day and the following one consisted of but twenty-four skeleton regiments, Griffin's brigade not being present. These regiments, although nominally composing five brigades, only made in reality, as compared to the enemy's similar organizations, four and one-half; as Warren's brigade of two regiments was smaller by one-half than any brigade in the Confederate army. On the other hand, General Longstreet's infantry force that he mentions as being present on the afternoon of the 29th, was twelve brigades, to which were added, by the arrival of Anderson's division during the night, three more, making in all an infantry force of sixty-five regiments. Jackson had under him at this time only about fifty regiments, while, on the other hand, General Pope had *in hand*, exclusive of Porter, about one hundred.

CHAPTER XII.

SECOND BATTLE OF BULL RUN.

THE FIELD—DISTRIBUTION OF FORCES—THE HENRY HOUSE—POSITION OF THE FIFTH—GENERALS JACKSON AND LONGSTREET—THE FIFTH ENGAGED—FEARFUL SLAUGHTER—ALLISON, THE COLOR-BEARER, KILLED—ANNIHILATION OF OUR COLOR COMPANY—BALD RIDGE—THE TEXANS—"DON'T LET THEM TAKE MY FLAG!"—OVERPOWERING NUMBERS—"LET THERE BE NO FALTERING IN THIS LINE!"—A ZOUAVE TARGETED—A ROUT—A TERRIBLE SCENE—THE REMNANT OF OUR REGIMENT AFTER THE BATTLE—COLONEL WARREN'S REPORT—GENERAL POPE'S REPORT—PERSONAL SKETCHES AND INCIDENTS—SPELLMAN—CHAMBERS—MCDOWELL—WILSON—HAGER—SAPHER—HUMANITY—STONEWALL JACKSON—JAMES CATHEY—A STRANGE COINCIDENCE—A RIFLE SHOT—JAMES PATTERSON—POLLARD'S TESTIMONY—BULLWINKLE—STURGESS—TYNDALL—STRACHAN—HUNTSMAN—A WALK AMONG THE GRAVES—FAULK'S LETTER—CONFEDERATE TESTIMONY—MARCH TO FAIRFAX—MCDOWELL'S BROTHER—GENERAL MCCLELLAN'S RETURN TO THE COMMAND—NEAR FREDERICK CITY.

ON the morning of Saturday, August 30th, the men of the Fifth arose from their bivouac and took up their line of march to the rear and right, *via* the Gainesville and Sudley Springs roads, to the scene of the previous day's engagement of General Pope's forces, which took place near Manassas Plains, and known by the name of the battle of Groveton. As the regiment marched toward the front, they passed by a large number of troops who had bivouacked in the fields each side of the roads (among whom was recognized King's division), many of whom cheered our regiment as they marched by them; and they noticed that the cannon were begrimed with powder, as if they had been recently in use, while the soldiers wore that general look of weariness and lassitude which is the habitual and natural reaction from the excitement of battle. As they neared the front, they met many details of men carrying off the wounded and dead of the previous day's fight. Among them were recognized the uniform of the Brooklyn 14th, some of whom were lying on a hill in sight at the front. Our brigade (the 5th and 10th New York) took a position well to the front, on the borders of a hill running up in front of them. The Warrenton turnpike, at the point where the engagement took place, known as the Second Bull Run, or Manassas Plains, intersected the Union lines at their center, and ran in a westerly direction. It was the great highway, in this immediate vicinity, by which the army must advance, or, if defeated, retreat, as it led in their rear over Bull Run Creek across a stone bridge, the river being difficult to ford, and the banks on each side quite steep. "As the road approaches the battle-field, going west, it goes up the valley of a little rivulet of Young's Branch, and through the battle-field is mostly close to the stream. The ground rises from the stream on both sides; in some places, quite into hills. The Sudley Springs road, in crossing the spring at right angles, passes directly over one of these hills, just south of the Warrenton pike, and this hill has on it a detached road, with fields stretching back away from it some hundreds of yards to the forest. This is the hill on which the Henry House stood," which was the key to the Union position, particularly in case of a retreat. If the enemy could gain possession of it, the result would be disastrous to the Union forces, as it would drive them from access to the turnpike. To the west of this hill was the Bald Hill, so called; between the two hills was a small stream, a tributary of Young's Branch.

The Confederate line of battle was in the shape of an "obtuse crescent," at least five miles long, the apex of the crescent convexity toward the west. Jackson was on the Confederate left, his extreme right about one-fourth of a mile from the Warrenton turnpike; Longstreet's command, fifteen brigades, extended from a point north of the turnpike near Jackson's right, far to the right beyond the line of Manassas Gap Railroad. In the interval, to the rear, between

Jackson's right and Longstreet's left, the Confederate artillery was placed, eight batteries, on commanding elevations behind a ridge; front of it was open ground between two forests, which stretched on each side of the Warrenton turnpike, the space between opening like the letter V, and about half a mile between them. At the apex facing the open ground the Confederate artillery was placed.

General Pope's army, comprising, besides batteries, at least one hundred and forty skeleton regiments of infantry, was in the following position :

General Heintzelman (3d corps) was on the extreme right of the Union forces; General McDowell (1st corps) on the extreme left; Fitz John Porter, Sigel's corps, and a division of Burnside's corps (Reno's) were placed in the center north of the pike. Porter's corps, composed of less than two divisions, Morell's (Griffin's brigade not being present) was on the left center, pushed forward in the concave crescent, facing west, and on the north side of the pike, with two brigades (Sykes' regulars), their left resting on the Warrenton pike; Morell's two brigades, Butterfield's and Martindale's, were on the right of the regulars; Warren's brigade was held in reserve, with the batteries of Weed, Smead, and Randoll. Reynolds' division of Pennsylvania reserves was on the left, or south of the pike.

As Warren's brigade remained in this position, batteries posted on the left and the right of them were throwing their shot and shell in the direction of the enemy. They returned the fire, and their shot and shell came whizzing about us, sometimes compelling the men to lie down. While this was transpiring they made their little fires and boiled coffee in their tin cups, which was their principal nourishment during their long and tedious marches. After lying in this position some time, they were advanced to the top of the hill in front, supporting a battery which still kept up a rapid fire on the enemy. The regulars were now further to the right, supporting batteries.

General Porter having received orders from General Pope to attack Jackson, on the supposition that he was retreating from his position, ordered General Butterfield to attack. While he was making his preparations to do so, General Reynolds, who held the left of the line, withdrew, by orders, two of his brigades (Meade's and Seymour's) to a position in the rear, nearer the pike. It was at this juncture that Warren, seeing the wide gap on the left flank of Porter, leaving the approaches to the turnpike open and exposed, advanced his little brigade, about one thousand strong, to occupy the position, and also to protect Hazlitt's battery, which had been ordered to the left and was without support. The brigade, accordingly, was marched to a hill on the left, and in advance of the former position.*

While marching up the slope of this hill they met a stray skirmisher, belonging to Reynolds' division, who was unaware that his division had moved; he came from the wood in front, and as he passed on to the rear, he reported that the enemy were advancing in force. A battery was posted

---

* General Sykes' Report, "Pope's Campaign" (No. 35, p. 146): "The Pennsylvania reserves, under General Reynolds, had been posted on my left, south of the Warrenton pike. Just previous to the attack these troops were withdrawn, leaving my left flank entirely uncovered, and the Warrenton road open. Colonel Warren, 5th New York Volunteers, commanding my 3d brigade, seeing the paramount necessity of holding this point, threw himself there with his brigade, the remnants of two regiments, and endeavored to fill the gap created by the removal of Reynolds."

Swinton (p. 190): "General Reynolds' division was detached from the left of Porter by McDowell, and, with a portion of Rickett's division, placed sc as to check a flank maneuver that menaced to seize the Warrenton turnpike, which was the line of retreat of the whole army. Some other troops should have been taken rather than remove Reynolds from that position. But the detachment of Reynolds from Porter's left for that purpose, had an unfortunate result; for it exposed the key-point of Porter's line.

"Colonel G. K. Warren, who then commanded one of Porter's brigades, seeing the imminence of the danger, at once, and without waiting for orders, moved forward with his small, but brave brigade of about one thousand men, and occupied the important position abandoned by Reynolds," etc.

on the right of the brigade, and a little to the rear, and continued its fire over the open space, between the woods before mentioned, on the enemy's batteries beyond.

This new move of Warren's placed the brigade on the south side of the turnpike, which was on his right, and some distance from it, to the extreme left of our assaulting columns. On a hill to the rear, commonly called Bald Hill or Ridge, about twelve hundred feet away, was Colonel McLean, commanding a brigade, consisting of four regiments and a battery of four guns, and in his vicinity was Colonel Anderson, in command of Jackson's brigade, Reynolds' division, composed of four regiments and a battery.

The 5th Regiment was drawn up facing a wood which ran down near their position to a distance of from thirty to ten feet, and again to the rear on the left ran along at nearly right angles. Company I, on the left, were mostly in the wood; a little to the right of the regiment was the boundary of the timber land, and then came the open space stretching back some distance, and also across to the wood on the north side of the pike.

Directly to the rear was an open field, which sloped down to a brook, the banks of which were quite steep. The water varied in depth from one to six or eight feet, and was skirted by some light timber on the other side of the stream; then came Bald Hill or Ridge, on the slopes of which was scattered a scant growth of bushes.

Six companies of the 10th New York were posted in the woods, in front of the left wing of the regiment. The remaining four companies were sent out as skirmishers. About this time Butterfield, on the north side of the pike, having made his arrangements, moved toward the enemy with his own and Martindale's brigade, of Morell's division, and attacked them with great spirit, supported by Sykes' regulars; but instead of being on the retreat, the enemy were strongly posted in an old railroad cut, which shielded

12*

them to a great extent from his fire; and although he maintained himself with great gallantry for some time, aided by the regulars, and made three assaults, he was finally obliged to retire, suffering a loss of one-third of his command. At the most critical moment of this attack, the Confederates on the left, under Longstreet, who had been masked, biding their time, opened a heavy fire of shot and shell from a battery posted on a commanding eminence, which enfiladed his line, and which decided the contest, so far as his attack was concerned.*

As we have seen, nearly all of Longstreet's command, lying in concealment, was south of the pike, facing the left wing and flank of the Union troops; and, according to Confederate reports, the general disposition of their troops was as follows: Law's brigade, of Hood's command, four regiments, was on the north side of the pike, his right resting on the pike. During the subsequent charge it crossed over to the south of the pike and joined Hood's Own brigade. Hood's Own, composed of the 1st, 4th, and 5th Texas, 18th Georgia, and the Hampton Legion, was lying south of the pike, its left a short distance from it; and Evans' brigade, under the command of Colonel P. F. Stevens, was a little in the rear, with the left resting on the pike and in support of Hood. These three brigades were closely supported by Anderson's division of three brigades. On the right of Hood were the divisions of Kemper and Jones, three brigades each. The remaining three brigades were advantageously placed, and also took part in the action.

At the decisive moment of the repulse of the attack by Porter's troops on Jackson's right and center, Longstreet's phalanx commenced its terrible charge, under cover of a

---

* Pollard's History (p. 460): "The infantry attacked Jackson, whose men were concealed behind an excavation on the railroad, two crack corps of the Federal army, Sykes' and Morell's, but it was not in human nature to stand unflinchingly before that hurricane of fire."

heavy fire from all his batteries posted on the commanding ridges on his right and rear, and which played over the heads of the charging columns. This charge was only checked at night, after nearly all our whole army, and many batteries, had been engaged. The first to meet it was Warren's little brigade, which happened, by the exigencies of war, to be occupying the position of a *forlorn hope*,* being pitted against overwhelming numbers, and obliged to hold on to the last to enable the rest of Porter's corps to withdraw from Jackson's front.

The enemy had kept so quiet on the left, that it struck the men that either some mischief was brewing, or that they were retreating. A few rifle-balls had struck the ground a little while previous, pretty well spent. It looked mysterious, as not a Confederate was to be seen. It was not long before some shots were heard close in front, fired rapidly. A body of the Tenth came in all in a huddle, excited and somewhat demoralized, breaking through the lines of the Fifth, on their left, and cried out that the enemy had come out of the ground, as it were, and were coming on in heavy force, and were right on top of them and on the flank. An order was given by Colonel Warren to change position, but the thoughts of the men were so intensely engrossed on the movements of the enemy, that their principal anxiety was for the Tenth to get out of their way as soon as possible, so that they could make their fire tell, and get to close quarters; they pretended not to hear any orders, or did not wish to comprehend them.

The balls began to fly like hail from the woods, and the Texans were yelling like fiends; their fire directly increasing into one unceasing rattle, the air was full of deadly missiles;

---

* Pollard (p. 460): "In the meantime, Jackson's left had advanced more rapidly than the right, and were pressing the Federals back toward the turnpike. It was now the opportunity for Longstreet to attack the exposed left flank of the enemy in front of it."

Lee's Report: "Hood's two brigades, followed by Evans, led the attack."

it was a continual hiss and sluck, the last sound telling that the bullet had gone into some man's body. On account of the companies of the Tenth who were in front of the left wing, and who had not all got away from their front, the Fifth returned the fire with difficulty, and that only by obliquing their aim, but Company I, on the extreme left, with their Sharp's rifles, and G Company, were doing well, and could not fail to bring their man every time, they were so close.

The Tenth having thus been surprised by overwhelming numbers, without any warning, were forced to fall back to save themselves from annihilation or capture. The majority of them passed through the right and center of the Fifth; but before they could extricate themselves from their perilous position they suffered a loss in a few short minutes, killed, wounded, and missing, of one hundred and fifteen. Owing to the very heavy fire, and being somewhat scattered in breaking out of the woods, it was impossible for them to rally and re-form on that part of the field. But no blame should be attached to them for retiring, as no regiment in the service would have hesitated to do the same, under similar circumstances; moreover, they would have received the fire of the Fifth if they had not fallen back.

But notwithstanding the desperate situation, which was enough to demoralize almost any regiment, particularly under the heavy fire they were receiving, and their own men falling like autumn leaves, not an able man in the Fifth left the ranks, and the regiment stood as firm as a stone wall. In fact, they had so much pride in their organization, and were so well disciplined, that they did not require any officers to urge them on.

About this time Sergeant Andrew B. Allison, formerly a soldier of the British army, who carried the United States flag, received a ball through his wrist, and gave the flag to one of the color Corporals, but immediately took it again,

and fell shot through the heart, the colors falling with him.*
They were immediately raised again, and how many took them
during the seven minutes that the regiment stood alone, to be
slaughtered, and before they were brought off the field, will
never be known. Lucien B. Swain, of Company K, was the
brave hero who brought them off, holding them on high, but
was wounded in the attempt, and went to the hospital, where
he remained until mustered out. The flag came to the regiment the next day. Around the colors nearly all were cut
down; it looked like a slaughter pen. Four of the color
guard besides Allison were lying dead; two others of the
eight were wounded, and the color Company K was almost
wiped out; the men kept closing up toward them, trying to
fill up the gaps, but it was in vain; they were swept down as
if mown by a scythe. Sergeant Francis Spellman, of Company G, who carried the regimental flag, was bleeding at
every pore, yet regardless of pain or his own life, still clung
to his flag.

All along the line the fire was murderous; the enemy were
on the front and flanks, and were pouring in a terrible cross
fire on the men, and were endeavoring to surround and take
prisoners the remnant of the regiment. Captain Winslow, in
command of the regiment, who was acting nobly, fell with
his horse, which had received seven wounds, but fortunately
the brave Winslow was spared. Captain Lewis, of Company
D, acting as field officer, who a few moments before had
been begged by his men to dismount, fell from his horse,
dead, while one foot was still in the stirrup, and his body was
being dragged over the field. Lieutenant Wright, of the same
company, its only remaining officer, had received his mortal
wound. Adjutant Fred Sovereign and Captain Hager, of
Company F, and its only remaining officer, were both dead.

---

* It is to be regretted that a likeness of Sergeant Allison could not have been preserved in this work, as he was equally deserving as Spellman. But all efforts to obtain his photograph were futile.

Lieutenant Martin, of Company G, and its only officer, was wounded in the leg, but scorned to leave his command. Lieutenant Raymond, of Company H, wounded, and with Captain McConnell, the remaining officer, soon to become prisoners. Captain Boyd, of Company A, wounded, and soon to become a prisoner. Lieutenant Keyser, the remaining officer of the company, wounded and left the field. Captain Montgomery, of Company I, also soon to become a prisoner, and Lieutenant Hoffman, the remaining officer of the company, suffering from three wounds. The foregoing include, with Colonel Warren and one other officer, all the officers that were present with the regiment. Colonel Warren still stood by the regiment which he had cherished with so much care, and was not the man to forsake his troops in the hour of need, although he would have been justified in doing so, as he was only exposing his life to no purpose, before as murderous a fire as ever fell to the lot of soldiers to. endure. It was not in his power to aid them, and he was forced to look on and see the flower of his regiment swept away. Nearly all of the new recruits who had just joined had fallen, and the remainder broke out to the rear. Some of the non-commissioned officers at first attempted to shove them in again, until Sergeant Forbes sung out: " Let them go! let them go!" and the men were receiving deadly volleys from an unseen enemy on their left and rear, at close quarters, as well as on their front, into their faces, from Hood's brave, but ragged, barefooted, half-starved Texans, who now swarmed in their front within twenty paces, yelling like fiends. Had the Fifth not been overwhelmed by such vastly disproportionate numbers, they would have shown them a trick with the bayonet which they did not understand. Our men had such confidence in themselves from the rigid training in the practical use of the bayonet, first introduced by Colonel Warren, and such pride in the honor of their regiment, that it never entered into their heads that any force could drive them, nor could they have been forced, except under the circumstances in which they were placed. Here was a regiment of 490 men standing alone, without support, against two choice brigades of Confederate troops, meeting the first onset of Longstreet's famous charge, that drove several divisions of our army before it was finally checked on Henry House Hill by Sykes' regulars, who were the bulwark of the army on many a field. They belonged to the Fifth corps, General Fitz John Porter, who had saved the Army of the Potomac by his skill and obstinacy in fighting at the battle of Gaines' Mill. His military sagacity had saved his corps from useless slaughter, and perhaps annihilation, on the afternoon of the 29th, only to be ordered forward the next day, without support, to be slaughtered, while the efforts of the innocent victims were treated by those responsible with slight and disparagement. If General Porter committed a fault on the 29th, who was responsible for the disaster of the 30th, when a small force was ordered to attack an enemy supposed to be retreating, while an immense reserve was held back in the rear at a safe distance?

It now became apparent that the only hope of saving a man was to fly and run the gauntlet, for in three minutes more there would not have been a man standing. The only alternative was to fly or to surrender. But the men of the Fifth did not understand the latter movement; they had never been taught it by their officers. All hope having vanished, and being without officers, the remnant of the once proud regiment broke and ran for their lives. They were nearly annihilated, but not conquered or disgraced, and bore away with them all of their flags, and many of their wounded. Their heroic stand had not been in vain. Butterfield on the right had been enabled to withdraw, as well as Hazlitt's battery, which the regiment was supporting. . "The latter had greatly impeded the enemy's movements on our right by an enfilading fire."*

As soon as Colonel Warren saw that his men were trying to save themselves, which he had ordered them to do before, he put spurs to his horse and escaped by dashing down the slope and jumping him over the brook at the foot of the hill, but turned again as soon as over to meet his men.

When the remnant of the regiment turned toward the rear, the enemy were coming on in a long line without a break, and were not over twenty feet distant, with others pouring out of the woods that ran along on the left and rear of their position. It was ascertained afterward from wounded men left on the field, and who subsequently returned to the regiment, that they were followed closely by a second and third line. On the right toward the turnpike was another long line of Confederates, led on by their officers. But here and there were some of the Fifth who scorned to turn their backs or to surrender, and fought to the last. They were all shot down.

The Confederates came charging on, a division strong, with yells and cheers for Jeff. Davis and the Southern Confederacy, and giving vent to all kinds of profane and obscene epithets. All this time they were pouring in their deadly fire at short range, picking out their victims as they ran down the slope to the brook; men were falling on all sides, canteens were struck and flying to pieces, haversacks cut off, rifles knocked to pieces, and still the enemy came on and swept everything before them.

Alluding to General Butterfield's attack, General Sykes says:

"The enemy seeing its failure, and that our weak point lay on my left in front of Warren, poured upon his little command,

---

* A. H. Guernsey says, in "Harper's Pictorial History of the War": "Warren's desperate stand had not, however, been unavailing. To all seeming, it saved the defeat from becoming a rout.'

under cover of the forest, a mass of infantry that enveloped—almost destroyed—him, and completely pierced our line."*

Captain Smead, a regular officer and a graduate of West Point, who commanded one of the batteries, was killed. Hazlitt's battery, which the regiment was supporting, and which the enemy expected to capture, was saved while our men were standing, receiving their fire; but the artillerists suffered severely.

There were about ten men of Company H who were among the last to fall back, among whom was Sergeant William H. Chambers, formerly a soldier of the British army and of the Crimean war. He saw Color-Sergeant Spellman (Regimental), while coming off the field, very badly hurt, with one of his hands pressed to his side, his body turned half around, with his face looking toward the rapidly-approaching enemy, who, with vile epithets, were calling upon him to surrender. With the other hand he was holding up his flag, and looking the very picture of distress. When Spellman saw him, he called out, "*Chambers! For God's sake don't let them take my flag!*" and to use the words of Chambers himself (who,

---

* Swinton (p. 191): "Warren occupying the important point he had seized, held on stoutly and against a fearful loss till all the rest of Porter's troops had been retired, and only withdrew when the enemy had advanced so close as to fire in the very faces of his men."

Compte de Paris (p. 297): "There remained only about 1,000 men, Warren's brigade, to form the left. The young chief of this brigade, with that war instinct for which he was always distinguished, had not waited for orders to place himself at the most important point of the line, which Reynolds had stripped by moving toward Bald Hill. In this position when Porter made his great attack, Warren had stubbornly covered the left flank of his chief. But the reverse sustained by the latter obliged him to fall back with the remainder of the corps."

Pollard (p. 461): "Hood's brigade charged next the turnpike. In its track it met Sickles' Excelsior brigade, and almost annihilated it. The ground was piled with the slain."*—[* He is in error; it was Warren's brigade. Sickles' brigade was composed of five regiments—in Hooker's division of Heintzelman's corps, which held the extreme right at least two miles from Warren, who was on the extreme left. See Pope's Campaigns, Heintzelman's Report (p. 56): "General Hooker's division now advanced into the woods near our right, and drove the enemy back a short distance," etc.]

as all of the old members of the Fifth know, was a brave man and could appreciate a brave deed), he replied: "*I won't if I can help it,*" and brought it off safe, but, as he says, "It was the narrowest escape I ever had in my life." He had been a soldier all his life; when he enlisted his profession was recorded as that of a soldier. Chambers yet bears the scars on his face and body where he was scratched by the bullets of the enemy. Flave Carr was the only Color-Corporal that came off the field. After the men crossed the brook they saw a few regiments in a kneeling position, and further back a battery, but they were, from appearances, beginning to receive a deadly fire.*

In fact, there was little to stop Longstreet, who was performing one of those flank movements for which the Confederates were ever famous, and had force enough to walk over the few troops that were ready to oppose him.†

The men of the Fifth kept on after they got across the brook, but the bullets followed as they went. Many of them

---

* "Pope's Campaigns" (Report No. 13, p. 101): "Colonel N. C. McLean, commanding 2d brigade, 1st division, Sigel's corps, four regiments of infantry and a battery, occupied the Bald Hill. 'I could, by this time, see the enemy advancing on my front and a little to the right, driving before them a regiment of Zouaves..... They came on rapidly, when some troops advanced to meet them from behind a hill on my right; these troops were also driven back in confusion,' etc. After fighting hard a short time, the enemy were on his flanks and rear, and he was compelled to fall back."

Colonel Anderson, commanding Jackson's brigade of Reynolds' division, four regiments, and a battery of four guns, to the right and in advance of McLean, was overwhelmed, and lost his battery. Some other regiments were also driven.

† McDowell's Report (No. 2, p. 49): "The attack on the Bald Ridge line had been too severe for the troops to hold it long under the hot fire the enemy maintained upon it. Jackson's brigade, of Reynolds' division; McLean's, of Schenck's, and Towers' two brigades, of Rickett's division, were, after heavy losses, little by little compelled to yield it, General Schenck and Tower receiving severe wounds."

Pollard (p. 462): "Hood has already advanced his division nearly half a mile at a double-quick, the Texans, Georgians, and Hampton's Legion, loading and firing as they run, yelling all the while like madmen."

"The din was almost deafening, the heavy notes of the artillery, at first deliberate, but gradually increasing in their rapidity, mingled with the sharp treble of the small arms, give one an idea of some diabolical concert in which all the furies of hell were at work."

now endeavored to assist their wounded comrades who had succeeded in getting thus far.

The remnant of the regiment rallied on Buchanan's brigade, in the rear of the plateau of Henry House Hill, where they found their regimental flag, the staff of which was planted in the ground by Chambers, who was standing on guard at its side, with Colonel Warren, who was dismounted, his horse having been disabled from wounds. The Colonel formed the men in line as they came up, but there were only about sixty of them that got together. The remainder were mostly engaged in assisting the wounded to the rear. They were joined by lost members of other organizations, and Colonel Warren took command of them again, saying every few moments, as the shell and bullets came over their heads, "Don't dodge, men! don't dodge!" They were glad to see their colors safe, with the remnant of stout hearts yet left, rallying around them. There were a few of the Tenth whom Lieutenant-Colonel Marshall was exhorting and encouraging, with tears in his eyes, to be brave and resolute, come what will. . . . .

This stand was made on one of the camp-grounds, and as a proof of the rapid advance made by the enemy, the camp-kettles were boiling over the fires. Lest the meat therein might be wasted, a few of the Zouaves picked out pieces and stowed them in their haversacks, not meaning to starve to death, whatever else might happen, notwithstanding the bullets were continually flying around and overhead. Among these provident men was "Jake" Lowns, of Company G, at present in the regular army, where he has been for eight years or more, who filled the writer's haversack with the meat, his own having been shot away.

At this time the wounded came limping along in squads, covered with blood, some being assisted by comrades and others carried in blankets, a man holding each corner, and all intensely excited.

The field everywhere presented to us, at least, one of the worst pictures of the chances of war. The wounded reeled about from one place to another, some of them groaning with pain; infantry and artillery flying, the horses galloping as if they were mad, with drivers bewildered; officers with drawn swords and revolvers, shouting, cursing, threatening in the confusion, striving in vain to rally their commands; bullets were flying and shells bursting; the rattle of musketry and the roar of artillery made a fearful din, while everything was enveloped in smoke, and aides and orderlies rode back and forth in wild confusion, or endeavoring to convey the orders of their chiefs. This was, in fact, what is called a "rout." All this commotion was as sudden as a storm at sea after a calm. We stood here excitedly looking on all this scene, in an agony of suspense as to the fate of our army, and what the effect would be on our cause. The little band stood with but one will, to obey orders; *but minutes were ages.* Finally, they saw General McDowell, with some other officers, ride along the front amid the storm of bullets. After making some motions with his hand, he dashed away again. Soon a long line of men were seen through the smoke advancing rapidly along the ridge in front. The men went onward at double-quick, and with a cheer; at the end of the line was one of the Fifth going with them, although he had no business there. It was never ascertained who he was, and he probably left his body on the field, and his name is on the rolls as missing in action, or, mayhap, among the names of the deserters, as many another man who lost his life in the service of his country stands to-day. This line of troops was a brigade of Sykes' regulars, who were sent to the rescue. The fate of the army, and, for all we then knew, perhaps that of the Union, depended upon their success in staying the onward rush of the enemy.*

---

* Bald Ridge having been carried by the enemy, they were making an attempt to capture Henry House Hill, the key to the Union position. Lieutenant-Colonel

A general officer's voice rang out clear and loud above the din, "*Let there be no faltering in this line!*" Immediately after, a fearful rolling crash, as the whole brigade poured in their volley, succeeded by a fierce yell, told that the brigade had commenced the work of death; at the same time several batteries stationed on the hills opened with grape and canister on the Confederate hordes. But darkness was fast spreading her mantle over the scene, and the army was saved. The regiment now only a company, with the rest of

---

Chapman, commanding the 2d brigade, regulars, and a volunteer brigade and battery, held that vital point for three-fourths of an hour; Sigel's corps and other troops were also engaged at this time on other parts of the field. The regulars were deserted by some of the volunteer troops and the battery, but they succeeded in keeping the enemy from flanking the position and in checking their onward career. Meade's and Seymour's brigades also came up and did valiant service; but the latter, being hard pressed, about six o'clock Lieutenant-Colonel Buchanan's 1st brigade of regulars was ordered forward.

Swinton (p. 191): "Longstreet kept on and carried the 'Bald Hill,' held by Reynolds and Ricketts; and it then became doubtful whether even the 'Henry House Hill' could be maintained so as to cover the retreat of the army over Bull Run, for Longstreet had thrown around his right so as to menace that position. The regulars saved it, until relieved by the brigades of Meade and Seymour and other troops, that maintained the position and permitted the withdrawal of the army across Bull Run by the stone bridge."

Compte de Paris (p. 298): "Hill, crowned by the Henry House, checked by Buchanan's brigade of regular infantry, whose unfaltering stand under a terrific fire, vindicated the reputation of the troops *d'elite*, of which it was composed. They were afterward reinforced by Tower's brigade of Ricketts' division, Meade's and Seymour's brigades of Reynolds' division, forming a nucleus around which grouped regiments and batteries that had preserved their organization amid the disorder" (p. 299): "In checking the offensive movement of Longstreet, the gallant defenders of the Henry House had saved the Federal army from a terrible disaster. They held their ground until night."

Lieutenant-Colonel Buchanan (Report No. 37, p. 153): "I can not omit calling the attention of the Brigadier-General commanding to the firm and gallant manner in which my brigade held the enemy in check on the extreme left for such a length of time, and finally prevented his turning our flank."

"Pope's Campaigns" (No. 50, p. 175). Extract from a letter of Lieutenant-Colonel Buchanan to General McDowell: "I did not lose one inch of ground after I got my brigade together, which I did immediately by moving this latter portion to the left, but held the enemy at bay for an hour; and, instead of being 'forced back,' I maintained my position until ordered to fall back. In the sense of General Milroy's report, he would have obtained possession of the *stone bridge;* and what would have been the result? You are well aware, our defeat would have been disastrous."

the army, under the cover of night commenced their retreat.

From the time the first shot was fired at the regiment, to their getting off the field, it was not over fifteen minutes. It stood in line receiving the murderous fire only about seven minutes, yet in that short space of time *one hundred and thirteen* were killed or mortally wounded; four missing, who were never heard of, and one hundred and eighty wounded; a total of two hundred and ninety-seven, out of the four hundred and ninety engaged. Many of the wounded were struck more than once, and of those who escaped the tempest of bullets the majority could show scratches, and bullet holes through their clothing, some having no less than seven. No other regiment suffered an equal loss in so short a space of time, on the Union side during the war. The Fifteenth Massachusetts, mentioned in Pollard's "Southern History of the War," nearly equals it. They lost at the battle of Antietam in twenty minutes, eighty men dead on the field, and two hundred and twenty-four wounded, out of a total of five hundred and fifty-six men engaged.

The following report by Colonel Warren is from General Pope's report (No. 36, p. 149):

HEADQUARTERS THIRD BRIGADE,
SYKES' DIVISION, *Sept.* 6, 1862.

SIR:—I take leave to present herewith a sketch of the field of action of the 30th August, as it appeared to me, with an account of what I witnessed and the part sustained by my brigade, consisting of the 5th New York Volunteers, about 490 strong, and the 10th New York Volunteers, about 510 strong. (Diagram) ..... Smead's and Randoll's batteries in the road near me. Hazlitt's rifled battery was executing an order from General Porter to take up a position at where Reynolds had been, (Hazlitt's battery was without support, and our whole left flank was uncovered). I immediately assumed the responsibility of oc-

Second Battle of Bull Run. 287

cupying the place Reynolds' division had vacated, and make all the show of force I could.

For this purpose I deployed three-fifths of the 10th New York Volunteers to hold the edge of the woods toward the enemy on our left, and keeping the 5th New York Volunteers in reserve, out of view of the enemy's battery.

Notice of this movement of mine I immediately sent, by an officer, to General Sykes or General Porter. He found the latter, who directed me to hold on, and sent me mounted orderlies to keep him informed. He was, I believe, near where Weed's battery was placed. From the point where Hazlitt's battery was placed, I probably had the best view of what followed that the battle-field presented. As soon as General Butterfield's brigade advanced up the hill, there was great commotion among the rebel forces, and the whole side of the hill and edges of the woods swarmed with men before unseen. The effect was not unlike flushing a covey of quails. The enemy fell back to the side of the railroad, and took shelter on the railroad cut and behind the embankment, and lined the edges of the woods beyond. Butterfield's advance beyond the brow of the hill was impossible, and taking his position, his troops opened fire on the enemy in front, who, from his sheltered position, returned it vigorously, while, at the same time, a battery, somewhere in the prolongation of the line, E, B, opend a most destructive enfilading fire with spherical case shot. It became evident to me that without heavy reinforcements, General Butterfield's troops must fall back or be slaughtered, the only assistance he received being from Hazlitt's battery, which I was supporting, and Weed's, (near N).

After making a most desperate and hopeless fight, General Butterfield's troops fell back, and the enemy immediately formed and advanced. Hazlitt's battery now did good execution on them, and forced one column that advanced beyond the point of the woods at (A), to fall back into it. Unwilling to retire from the position I held, which involved the withdrawal of this efficient battery and the exposure of the flanks of our retreating forces, I held on, hoping that fresh troops would be thrown forward to meet the enemy now advancing in the open fields ; well knowing, however, that my position was one from which I could not retreat in the face of a superior force. Reynolds' division, on my left, probably aware of the superior force of the enemy gathering in his front, fell back from I toward P. The enemy advanced with rapidity upon my position, with the evident intention of capturing Hazlitt's battery. The 10th New York was compelled to fall back, scarcely arriving at the position held by the 5th New York, "before" the enemy; and in such a manner as to almost completely prevent the Fifth from firing upon them. While I was endeavoring to clear them from the front, the enemy, in force, opened fire from the woods on the rear and left flank of the Fifth with most fearful effect. I then gave the order to face about and march down the hill, so as to bring the enemy all on our front; but in the roar of musketry I could only be heard a short distance. Captain Boyd, near me, repeated the command, but his men only partially obeyed it. *They were unwilling to make a backward movement.* He was wounded while trying to execute it. Adjutant Sovereign carried the order along the line to Captain Winslow, commanding the regiment, and to the other Captains, but was killed in the act. Captain Winslow's horse was shot; Captain Lewis, acting field officer, was killed; Captain Hager was killed; Captains McConnell and Montgomery were down with wounds, and Lieutenants Raymond, Hoffman, Keyser, and Wright were wounded. Both color-bearers were shot down, and all but four of the Sergeants were killed or wounded.

Before the colors and the remnant of the regiment could be extricated, 298 men of the Fifth, and 133 of the 10th New York were killed or wounded.* In the 10th New York, Lieutenant Hedden was killed, and Captain Dimmick, Lieutenant Deweyick, Lieutenant Mosscross, and Lieutenant Cuthane wounded.

We assisted from the field 77 wounded of the Fifth and 8 of the Tenth. The remainder fell into the hands of the enemy. Among these were Captains Boyd, McConnell, and Montgomery, and Lieutenants Wright and Raymond of the Fifth.

Braver men than those who fought and fell that day could not

---

* A later report states the loss in the 10th New York as 115.

be found. It was impossible for us to do more, and as is well known, all the efforts of our army barely checked this advance.
Very respectfully your obedient servant,
G. K. WARREN,
Colonel 5th New York Volunteers,
Commanding Third Brigade.

Lieutenant HEYWARD CUTTING,
Acting Aide-de-Camp and Acting Assistant Adjutant-General, General Sykes' Division.

General Sykes, in his report ("Pope's Campaign," p. 148), makes the following statement of the occurrences on the field :

"I desire to call the attention of the Major-General commanding to the services of Colonels Warren, Buchanan*, and Chapman,† United States Army, commanding brigades of my division. Their coolness, courage, and example were conspicuous. Their claim to promotion has been earned on fields of battle long prior to that of the 30th of August, 1862." " Had the efforts of these officers, those of Generals Reynolds, Reno, and Butterfield, been properly sustained, it is doubtful if the day had gone against us." " Warren's command was sacrificed by the withdrawal of Reynolds' troops from my left, and their non-replacement by others. The enemy masked and concealed his brigades in the forests south of the Warrenton pike. His presence was unseen and unknown until he appeared in sufficient strength to overpower the infantry opposed to him."

Many of the old and experienced members of the regiment ran zig-zag when escaping from the enemy, to distract their aim, who were picking their men at close range. A number of new recruits were on the way to join the Fifth, but little could they imagine what their trials and troubles were to be. Second Lieutenant Thomas R. Martin, in command of Company G, which lost 34 men killed and wounded

---

* See Appendix.   † See Appendix.

out of 50, stood at his post to the last encouraging his men, although himself wounded in the leg, ably assisted by Sergeants Forbes, Law, Jack Taylor, and Wilson. They, and the remnant of the company, which was next in line to the left company, did not leave until the enemy were within a few feet of them, and all hope had fled of making any effective resistance. There were present with the regiment after this engagement only about eighty privates of the two years' men who were at Fort Schuyler when the regiment was first organized; the rest had been killed or wounded, sick in hospital, discharged or deserted. Had this little remnant been so unfortunate as to become engaged in another similar struggle, it would have been wiped out as a thing of the past. It was a fearful conflict, and seemed to be one of extermination. The Confederates fought hard and with the greatest determination, and the prisoners taken seemed to be confident of success in the end. They persisted that the South would never yield. One of the Texans drawled out, in a conversation with Jack Whigam (whose brother was killed in this battle), one of the men detailed with the flag of truce to bury the dead and look after the wounded: "We will foute you until we are all dead, Yanks! and I reckon the women will foute you after that." The people of the North were too much disposed to underrate them. Many of them did not seem to reflect that the Southerners were fighting for what they were brought up to believe was their right, and for their homes and firesides, and were of the same flesh and blood as themselves; and I venture to say that the proportion of native born was much larger than in the army opposed to them. They were the descendants of the men who, under Generals Greene, Sumter, Marion, Morgan, and the immortal Washington himself, fought and suffered in the struggle for independence against the power of Great Britain, and in the wars in which the country had since then been engaged.

FRANCIS SPELLMAN.

Sergeant Francis Spellman the writer had every opportunity to know well, as he was one of his messmates for some time in Baltimore. Afterward, when there was a vacancy in the color-sergeantcy, he conversed about it; he was very quiet and calm when he spoke, and with a resigned air, as if he should never think of refusing any duty that might be imposed upon him as a soldier. He said: "Several of the men have been talked of for the vacancy on the colors, and I am one of them. I don't care for the honor, but *I won't refuse*." That sentence was the utterance of his nobility and courage; for he knew that the position entailed, besides the honor, almost sure death, sooner or later. In all his associations, in the mess or out of it, he never had a quarrel or a cross word with any one. He was no ordinary man; being quiet and reflective, spending his leisure hours in reading or discussing military questions from Hardee's "Tactics," and was very quick to see through their complications; and if he had lived, his merit and ability to command would have been discovered by such an observant officer as Colonel Warren. He was always gentlemanly, and there was nothing vulgar in his composition; extraordinarily neat, his rifle always shone like silver, and he was one of the most perfectly drilled men in the regiment. But beneath his outward and even-toned temperament, one could see in the deep blue eye that lighted his face the truest kind of courage. When he was discovered in a hospital in Washington (by what means he was conveyed there was never learned), his right arm had been taken off near the shoulder. He was shot through the side in several places, and had a ghastly wound through the neck, his throat being so much swollen that he could only make a humming noise. The following letter was written by a friend and former messmate of Spellman, Alonzo Ameli, of Company G, and addressed to his brother; and was copied from the original by the author:

BALTIMORE, *Jan.* 30, 1863.

Last week I received a letter from the Rev. W. W. Winchester, who attended FRANK SPELLMAN in his last moments, and he said that being interested in him, he strove to learn his name, and mentioned over several names to him, to all of which Frank shook his head; then taking his memorandum book he held it up, and feeble and trembling poor Frank tried to write his name upon it. When he got through he said, "Francis?" and he nodded yes; then he wrote again, and the minister said "Spellman?" receiving an affirmative nod. He said he tried to find out where he lived, but the left hand fell upon the bed, and he said he could not urge the poor, brave man to any more exertion. Then he prayed with him, and when he left, Frank was humming a tune very faintly, which he says was a hymn. In a few hours he called again, and he found him sinking rapidly from his severe wounds, but he was happy, and soon after died. Noble Frank! He was indeed a true friend, a cheerful companion, and a brave soldier. I have copied his name just as he wrote it upon the leaf of the memorandum book.

Spellman died a few days after the battle, and sleeps in a soldier's grave, near Washington, among an army of others who died under the old flag, for the honor of which they gave up their lives. He had not a relative or a friend in this country outside of his army comrades, and there was no one at home to watch his career, or who would feel proud of his honorable deeds, and from whom he could expect paens of praise, or who would mourn over him if he should fall. All the honor he could expect would be that from his comrades in arms and his officers, and the consciousness that he was performing his duty. His actions proved that his whole thought was nobly fixed on the trust he had accepted, when he singled out from those around him a comrade whom he knew to be a brave man and a soldier, and who would accept the flag he was no longer able to defend. And in his agony of mind, far above his bodily pain, he called out: "Chambers! for *God's sake, don't let them take my flag!*"

A monument should be erected to his memory, and no more fitting words could be inscribed upon it, than the dying words of the hero, as an example to future generations.

ILLIAM H. CHAMBERS.

William H. Chambers enlisted, when he was only seventeen years old, in the English army, and in the course of his service was in the Crimean war. He came to this country a short time before the breaking out of the Rebellion, and immediately enlisted in the 5th Regiment as a private, and was mustered out with it as a Major by brevet, May 14, 1863, having never been absent from sickness or serious wounds—an honor accorded only to one other Captain. Re-enlisted with the 5th Veterans as a private, commanded by Colonel WINSLOW. He was promoted on the field for bravery, and served till the end of the war, and was again breveted Major. He was offered the position of Orderly Sergeant in the regular army, with the promise that he should be promoted to a commission at the first opportunity, but he declined to accept anything but a commission.

I omitted to state that the first officer he met after crossing the brook with the flag he had saved, was Lieutenant Hoffman, who was wounded; the next was Colonel Warren.

WILLIAM MC DOWELL.

Among those who lay dead on the battle-field, was William McDowell, the Orderly Sergeant of Company G, to which position he was appointed from the ranks, thus stepping over all the intermediate Corporals and Sergeants, and no man better deserved it. He had been offered, and refused to accept, an inferior appointment. He was a member of Washington Truck Company, No. 9, Volunteer Fire Department, New York City, when he enlisted, in April, 1861. (Three members of this fire company were killed in this battle). He belonged to a family noted for their fine physique, and stood six feet two and a half inches in height, and was well-proportioned. He was as brave in the hour of need as he was kind and gentle in his social relations among his comrades and friends. A large party of members of the Volunteer Fire Department enlisted together, one of whom was Wm. McDowell, and it was their fortune to serve together in Company G. When he became Orderly, it soon began to be understood among his former associates that they must not presume on old acquaintanceship to shirk any duty, or expect any partiality, even among his own messmates, in the line of duty. When a man's turn came to go on a detail of any kind, go he must, no matter who or what he was; and often when a man tried to evade it by managing to be in some other than his own quarters, I have seen McDowell take a spade or pick in his hand and stand in the shirker's place until he could be hunted up, rather than put a man to duty outside of his regular turn. When the delinquent was found, he would quietly remind him of his duty in such a way as to make him thoroughly ashamed, and the men of the company soon began to dread a lecture from "Billy," or "Pop," as he was sometimes called, more than they did the guard-house. He very seldom reported any one, because under his management it was not necessary. When off duty it was just the opposite; anything that he possessed he would share with the men, but the majority respected him too much to attempt to take any undue liberties with him, and those who were wanting in the latter quality, did not care to rouse his lion nature, as he was known to possess great physical power and undaunted courage. He had a fine sense of honor, and would never run guard himself nor allow any one to pass him when he was a private on post.

At the second battle of Bull Run, McDowell was one of the number that would not run or surrender. It was seen that he was wounded in the body, and had fallen back a few

Second Battle of Bull Run. 295

paces, and was facing the enemy when they came out of the wood. After the most of the remainder of the regiment had made for the rear, a ball struck him in the forehead, and he fell dead, with his feet to the foe, and in this position he was found and buried by Jack Whigam, of the same fire company, who went with the detail under flag of truce. Thus died as brave and noble-hearted a man as ever lived. The men of his company felt his loss keenly, and mourned for him, as they looked up to him as their father. They could have another Orderly, but there was only one Sergeant McDowell.

The following tribute to the memory of Sergeant McDowell appeared in the New York *Leader :*

"THE LOSS OF ANOTHER GALLANT FIREMAN AND SOLDIER.

"We notice that in the battle of Bull Run, at the head of his company, Wm. McDowell, First Sergeant of Company G, Duryée's Zouaves, fell, nobly leading his command. He was one of nature's noblemen, well known in the Department, standing over six feet two inches high, of heroic courage, possessing an innate modesty and kindness of heart that made each one love the man. A native of this city, he possessed the confidence of his employers, and the highest esteem of his brother firemen as a member of Washington Truck Company, No. 9.

"His towering frame might have been seen in the front rank of the Duryée Zouaves on leaving New York, one of the very first to go forward to guard the emblem of our country, and to put down the traitors to his beloved flag and the institutions he adored.

"His company was in many battles. He was foremost in encouraging his comrades, offered promotion for his gallantry, but ever declining. He died like the brave ever like to die, and he now fills a patriot's grave, leaving an aged mother to mourn the loss of an affectionate and brave son. God protect and console the widowed mother! His companions deeply mourn his loss, and will ever hold his memory in grateful remembrance."

Another of those who would not leave the field, was Sergeant Philip L. Wilson, of Company G. He was a direct contrast to McD. in size, social position, and education. Coming from the higher walks of life, and though still suffering from his wounds, is at present a lawyer of standing in N. Y. City. He stood to the last, and had received two scratches, and as the enemy were coming from the woods, fired at one of them, and saw him clap his hands on his abdomen and fall. He went about forty paces further to the rear, at the same time endeavoring to load his rifle, and the charge was partially down in the barrel, when he heard a Confederate officer give vent to an opprobrious epithet, and exclaim: "My children, kill every Yankee you can find." This stirred Wilson's blood, and he turned toward them, at the same time endeavoring to ram home the charge, for he was determined to kill that officer if possible, when his right leg was knocked from under him, and he fell with an ugly wound, which permanently crippled him.

Before the regiment went on the field of battle they came to a halt and rested on the banks of a beautiful stream of water. Many of the men availed themselves of the opportunity to wash themselves, among whom was Captain Hager, of Company F, who was the only commissioned officer in the regiment at the time who wore the full Zouave uniform. After he had washed and completed his preparations, he said to the company, "Boys, how do I look?" "You look nobby," said one; "You look bully," said another. "Well," replied the Captain, "don't you think I'd make a fine-looking corpse?" A short time afterward he was lying dead on the battle-field. He was a favorite with his company, and a brave, cool soldier. He enlisted in the regiment as a private.

The irrepressible "Butch" Sapher was in the most serious difficulty of his whole service, and he was awaiting sentence of court-martial for striking an officer at Harrison's Landing, and the probabilities were, that notwithstanding his many good qualities as a brave and cool-headed soldier, and the life of the regiment, that he would be shot. Notwithstanding his dilemma he must have his amusement. He had on an old white-felt hat he had picked up somewhere, with the crown torn out, his hair, or "scalp lock" rather—for that was all he would allow to grow—was standing up above it, and over his shoulder was a stick, with a bundle tied to the end of it; this was just before the battle, and he had "come up to take a hand in." A shell came bouncing along, and struck close by him; he did not budge a hair, but taking off his apology for a hat, he bowed very gracefully, saying, "Good-morning; may you all strike in the same spot," which made a laugh all about him, among the officers as well as the men. For two or three days after the battle nothing was seen of "Butch," and it was supposed that he had either been killed or had disappeared to avoid the sentence of the court-martial. When the regiment arrived at Hall's Hill, a strange character was seen approaching at a distance, but on getting closer, it was perceived that it was our missing "Butch," mounted on a mule, with three or four rifles strapped to his back, together with a surgeon's knapsack of medicines. He had taken them from a cowardly hospital steward who had run away, and been captured by "Butch," who stripped him of the stores, and it appears he had been rendering invaluable services to the surgeons and among the wounded. The first words he said were, "Come here, all you that are sick, and I will give you physic." Nothing more was heard of the court-martial. He was a very powerful man, and had served an apprenticeship in the navy, before the war, and was marked in India ink with the usual devices of anchors, ships, etc. He could hold a fifty-pound shot at arm's length, with ease, in either hand, and was always full of fun and mischief; could sing comic and sentimental songs, etc., and was a great favorite with officers and men.

One of the wounded who was lying on the field stated afterward that the Confederate General, "Stonewall" Jackson, came over the ground where the regiment had been engaged, and he heard him say to the Confederates, "Be careful not to hurt any of the enemy's wounded, as they must be regarded as our friends."

Charles Taylor, of Company G, was lying badly wounded near the brook, and he asked one of the Fifth, who laid down under the enemy's fire and became a prisoner, to fill his canteen with water from the brook a few feet off. He replied that he was afraid that the enemy would shoot him. A Confederate came along, and not only filled his canteen, but bathed his wounds himself.

Among the recruits who joined the regiment at Newport News, twelve days before the battle, was James Cathey, a young man of high spirit and strong principle. The last words he said were to Patterson, who stood near him in the line, and who knew him and his family in New York, before they went into the field. They were these : "Look out for Siss." He was killed.

A prominent member of the Masonic fraternity, who is proprietor of a well-known house of refreshment in the upper part of New York City, and was also well acquainted with Cathey, told the writer that the day he left for the front, he came into his house in full uniform, and bade him and some friends good-bye. Before he went, he took out a copper cent from his pocket, and cutting a nick in it, said, "Keep this until I come back." The barkeeper stuck it up on the wall behind the bar. On the day of the battle, and at the precise hour, as was afterward ascertained, that young Cathey's spirit had fled, a few friends were talking about the war and the absent ones ; among them were mentioned the many good qualities of Cathey. They were commenting on the circumstance of his leaving the penny when he went away, which was still sticking on the wall, when, without any apparent cause, it dropped to the floor. They thought it was ominous of evil at the time, and in a few days their forebodings were verified. Cathey was dead.

A ball passed through the canteen, haversack, a blank book (three-fourths of an inch thick), a tin plate, and a large piece of pork, and embedded itself in the hip of First Sergeant Geo. A. Mitchell, of Company F, occasioning a painful, but not dangerous wound. This circumstance, trifling as it may appear, shows at what close quarters the men received the fire of the enemy.

James Patterson, of Company G, was lying with four wounds made by one ball, and perfectly helpless. A Confederate cavalryman came along, and was robbing the dead, and not even sparing the wounded. He said to Patterson, "You won't live anyhow, and I guess I'll take what you have got." He took his shoes off and two dollars in money. The wounded man begged him to fill his canteen with water, but he refused, and said that he didn't need any water, as he could not live anyway, for he was all shot to pieces. As he left, the rebel told him that Jackson was in Washington, and waving the bill in his face, said, "I am going there too, and will not fail to drink your health with this note when I get there."

Pollard in his history says :

"The scenes of the battle-field were rendered ghastly by an extraordinary circumstance. There was not a dead Yankee in all that broad field who had not been stripped of his shoes and stockings—and in numerous cases, been left as naked as the hour he was born. Our barefooted and ragged men had not hesitated to supply their necessities even from the garments and equipments of the dead. So numerous were the wounded Yankees, that in four days' 3,000 had not been attended to."

The following is from a narrative by a Confederate Lieutenant :

"The fight was by far the most horrible and deadly that I have seen." "Their dead (Union) on the field were left in such numbers as to sicken even the veterans of Richmond and the

Shenandoah Valley;" "they left 2,000 dead, rotting clay, and almost innumerable wounded." "Their discipline and night saved them from a rout."

The Confederate losses, by their own reports, were 1,090 killed, 6,154 wounded, in the one hundred and fourteen regiments of infantry, and among their artillery battalion, engaged. The greatest loss appears in the brigades that first charged, especially among the officers; the 5th Texas lost 239 in killed and wounded, among whom were all of their field and acting field officers, and after the battle the regiment was under the command of a Captain. The loss in Porter's twenty-four regiments in killed, wounded, and missing, was 2,164, about one-fourth of the number of his forces engaged.

The dead of the Fifth Regiment had not generally been stripped, as their uniform was not of any use to the Confederates, but they took their shoes and stockings in most instances, and in many cases their fez caps, and of course whatever money or valuables any of them chanced to have on their persons. The badly wounded lay on the field for two or three days, among the festering corpses, before they were removed by their comrades, who were sent to their relief under a flag of truce. The latter buried 79 of the Fifth, and there were others who could not be recognized on account of the loss of their uniforms, or who had crawled into the woods and died there, whom they could not reach, as they were restricted by a Confederate guard to a certain boundary. But the number killed and wounded that I have heretofore stated—297, the names of whom appear in the Appendix—have been taken from the company rolls, and no pains have been spared to have them verified by comrades. It is generally supposed that the loss was even greater, as some names appear on the rolls as dropped for desertion from the date of the battle, who have never been seen since by any of their comrades or friends.

Sergeant Henry Bullwinkle, one of the original members of the regiment, and who served all through with it, was as cool as he was brave, as all those that served with him can testify. He was one of the last to leave the field on the left, as the enemy came out of the woods. He had received one bullet through his fez cap, grazing the side of his head. As he fell back, he took deliberate aim at a color-bearer, and saw him fall. As he was running off, he received a shot through his pantaloons, grazing his thigh; another cut through a leather leggin grazing the bone, and the balls whistled lively about his ears. Something struck his blanket, which was rolled up and hanging over his shoulders, (all of the men were carrying their blankets in this manner, having left their knapsacks at Harrison's Landing). He could hear the cursing and abuse of the enemy. He fell on the ground and they stopped their fire, but he jumped to his feet again and succeeded by great agility in crossing the brook at the foot of the hill. He halted in the bushes on the other side, and reloaded his piece, when seeing a group of mounted officers he took steady aim and fired, and had the satisfaction of seeing one of the officers fall from his saddle. He then ran toward a battery of four guns on a hill, the men of which were making frantic gestures for him to get out of the way, as they were about to fire. He succeeded in reaching it and going by it, and the battery immediately opened on the enemy, who were now at close range.

Reuben P. Sturgess, a young man, only eighteen years of age, and one of the first to enlist in the regiment, picked up Colonel Warren's cap, which had fallen to the ground, and handed it to him. This was about the time of the crisis of the onslaught of the enemy, and the men had been ordered to fall back, but they would not leave. Colonel Warren asked him his name, and what company he belonged to. He replied, "Company C." "Well; you get to the rear; this is no place for Company C;" instead of retreating he fired a shot at the enemy, and stood, and again re-loaded his piece. The remnant of the regiment were now trying to save themselves by falling back. The next day, Colonel Warren inquired for young Sturgess. "Missing," was the answer. "Then," said the Colonel, "that brave young man is dead or wounded." It was too true—he had received a mortal wound.

Joseph H. Tyndall, of Company D, finding himself surrounded by the enemy and unable to escape, threw down his rifle at the feet of a Confederate, who was charging upon him with the bayonet, in token of submission. The latter, however, contrary to the rules of civilized warfare and the common instincts of humanity, was about to run him through, when Tyndall by a quick movement eluded the thrust, seized the weapon, and by a powerful movement wrenched it from his grasp, amid the jeers and gibes of the Confederate's companions.

Sergeant Robert Strachan, of Company I, supported James Cochrane, who was bleeding from four wounds, to the rear, and endeavored to halt one of the ambulances on the road, which were all full and moving off at a rapid pace. But none of the drivers would take any notice of his urgent appeals. Finally, one of them dashed rapidly by him, drawn by four horses. He called to the driver to stop; but the only response he received was a curse. Strachan was a determined man, and feeling that he must adopt a decided course of action, knowing that there was no time to spare, as the enemy were coming on, he leveled his Sharp's rifle at the head of the driver, and said, "Halt! or I will drive a bullet through your skull." This mandate was obeyed, and he lifted "Jim" by main strength and threw him into the wagon on top of the wounded, and the ambulance dashed off. By this means Cochrane was saved from being left to fall into the hands of the enemy, and probably owes his life to Strachan's decision.

Corporal George Huntsman, a young man of great promise, who was receiving an academic education before his enlistment, left his pleasant home at Flushing, Long Island, and went alone to Baltimore and enlisted in the 5th Regiment, October 19, 1861, to serve for three years, or during the war. He was promoted Corporal for good behavior and soldierly conduct, May 11, 1862, and was in active service with his company up to the engagement of Second Bull Run, August 30, 1862. In this battle he received a mortal wound, and died four days thereafter in the Wolf Street Hospital, Alexandria, Va. His remains were transported to his parents' residence at Flushing, and the funeral took place on September 11th.

This young patriot, an only son, whose life was thus sacrificed at his post of duty at the early age of nineteen, was beloved and respected by all his comrades. Sergeant E. L. Pierce said: "He was one who shared with me the perils of campaign life, and who by his pleasant and brotherly manner, endeared himself to me and made it much easier to bear."

On a beautiful monument erected in the town park by the citizens of Flushing, in memory of those who fell for their country's sake in the war of the Rebellion, may be seen engraved with eighty-six others, the name of Corporal George Huntsman.

He was a son of Professor George Washington Huntsman, of the College of the City of New York. His great-grandfather on his father's side fought in the war of the Revolution, to establish the Independence of the States against the unjust exactions of Great Britain; two of his uncles were in the war of 1812; and his cousins on both sides were in our late war. His mother's grandfather was Samuel Neilson, one of the noble Irish patriots who was imprisoned and exiled during the closing years of the last century by the British Government, the truths they maintained not being agreeable to the power that strove to annex Ireland to its empire.

George Huntsman Post, No. 50, Grand Army of the Republic, of the town of Flushing, was named to honor the memory of our deceased comrade.

Let us look at this field one year later through the eyes of one of the three years' members of the old Fifth, who was transferred to the 146th New York Volunteers to serve out the remainder of his time. The letter from which the following extract is made was addressed to the writer under its date:

CAMP NEAR NEW BALTIMORE, VA.,
October 22, 1863.

DEAR D..... When we arrived at Centreville we struck off again and marched (you would hardly guess where) to the old Bull Run battle-field, about three hundred yards from where our regiment had the fight last year. As soon as I had my supper I started over, and in five minutes I stood by the graves of our departed comrades. Graves, did I say? it would be a disgrace to call them such! Graves! if a few handfuls of dirt strewn over skeletons can be called such; but I don't. I tell you, D., it was a heart-rending sight, to see their skulls kicked in every direction, and the feet and bones of the dead sticking above the ground. There was one grave this side of the creek which took my attention. The rain had washed the earth away from where one of his knees must have stuck out, and covering this joint was part of his red breeches; there was quite a crowd around the grave, and they almost all took a piece of what was left of the cloth. While one of the men was looking around, he overturned one of his jacket sleeves; it had on a Sergeant's gold stripes; at first I thought it was Billy McDowell's body; we looked again, but could not find any diamond, so we all came to the conclusion that it must be Sergeant Allison, the color-sergeant. We were going to make out a detail the next morning to properly bury the remains, but we marched again at 2 A.M.

JOHN MURRAY.

The remains of those who were buried on this field, as

Second Battle of Bull Run.   305

well as those in other fields, were all collected and removed to cemeteries established by the Government authorities soon after the close of the war.

> "On Fame's eternal camping-ground
> Their silent tents are spread,
> And memory guards with solemn round
> The bivouac of the dead."

An admirable description of the battle was published in *The Soldier's Friend*, August, 1866. It was written by Paul K. Faulk, one of the "Left-armed Corps," late of the 11th Pennsylvania Volunteers, Hartsuff's brigade, which was badly cut up in the Second Bull Run engagement. He very justly places the Zouaves in the front—where they fought—in the following extract :

"During many a lonely hour visions of that bloody day have trooped up from the dim mist of the dreamy past, and mingling in the imaginary fray, I have passed again through the gory drama and fought the battle over anew. . . . . Three thousand bayonets gleamed in the sultry rays of the sun ; a grim determination compressed the muscles on the dusty-bronzed faces of the toil-worn brigade ; the starry flags fluttered proudly and defiantly ; and amid the wreathing smoke, and shaken by the deafening thunders of musketry and artillery in the fiery front, the devoted battalion pressed forward into the valley of death. No martial music cheers the weary ranks ; only the wild excitement of battle sustains the half-wavering column, as the rebel batteries vomit forth their deadly iron hail, and the terrible zip, zip, of the minie ball is quenched in blood. Streams of stragglers pour from the smoke-curtained front, and the wounded pass on to the rear, faltering and bleeding at every step. A great many of them wore the *red breeches of the Zouaves.*" . . . .

TESTIMONY FROM THE ENEMY.

Charles F. Ballou, formerly a member of the 44th New York Volunteers, who was wounded, and lay on the field of battle, told the writer that while conversing with a Confederate soldier, the latter made the remark that there was one Yankee regiment that would stand a bayonet charge; he knew it because he had fought against them at Gaines' Mill; and they wouldn't budge. Ballou asked him what regiment it was; he replied, "*Them Zouaves.*"

An officer of high standing thus expressed himself in regard to this battle:

"The 5th army corps were treated on that day, by *whoever was responsible*, in a way that should be his everlasting disgrace, for they were made to assault twice their numbers in a good position, under the false idea that they were in retreat, and while they went up to be butchered, the rest of the army at a safe distance were mere spectators."

After dark, on the day of the battle, what remained of the regiment fell back to Centreville; a wearisome march, especially so after the trying ordeal through which they had passed on that day. The road was blockaded with wagons, ambulances, stragglers, etc., and many of the commands were mixed up. But the men kept together, notwithstanding nearly all the companies, or rather squads, were under the command of Sergeants and Corporals, preserving their formation perfectly, the same as they did through the seven days' retreat, and could have formed a small line of battle of about 100 men at any moment. They showed a marked contrast, in this respect, to many of the other organizations on the march that had not suffered near as much loss, thus reaping the benefit of the severe training they had received from the first under Colonel Warren, assisted by such severe disciplinarians as Colonel Hiram Duryea, Winslow, and others.

Colonel Warren, from his long experience, was thorough master of the details of military service in all its branches, and of the science of war. He was severe, but just, to the men as well as to the officers, and held all alike in their different spheres to a strict attention to their duties. We finally arrived at Centreville and bivouacked outside of the works.

The Fifth numbered, on the morning after the battle at Centreville, less than 100; Companies F and D, mustering 17 men, were under the command of First Sergeant George A. Mitchell, of F; Sergeant William H. Chambers took the command of H and B; Sergeant Forbes held Company G; Sergeant Brogan, Company I; and the other companies were under the command of Lieutenant Gedney, and Lieutenants Whitney and Chase, who had not been in the engagement; and remained about the same until they reached Hall's Hill, where the few stragglers rejoined us, and we were increased by the addition of some new recruits.

Sunday, August 31.—We went inside of the works and sent out a detail, under a flag of truce, to bury the dead and look after the wounded. They suffered greatly for the want of food while performing their sad duties, as the scanty supplies they were able to procure were given to the wounded.

We left Centreville September 2d, about 1 A.M., and marched to Fairfax Court-House, rested until 3 P.M., and then resumed the march, and bivouacked at Ball's Cross-Roads.

While on the road near Fairfax during a brief halt, a regiment came marching by, and an unusually tall and well-proportioned man stepped from the ranks; it was noticed that he carried the colors. He inquired for Company G and William McDowell, and was answered that he was lying dead on the battle-field. The tears started to his eyes, and for a moment he was quite overcome, until suddenly becoming conscious that men were looking at him, he dashed his hand across his eyes, and joined his regiment, which was the Anderson Zouaves. He was the brother of our own lamented Sergeant.

Shortly after the regiment had gone into bivouac at the

side of the road, some of the men discovered General McClellan, with three orderlies and an aide, riding up toward us. He was on his way to the front from Washington, having been reinstated in the command of the army, now that Washington was in danger. It was after dark, but the men recognized him at once, and turned out and gave him three rousing cheers. He stopped, and asked if they had suffered much in the late engagement, and seemed sorry at the reply, as he held the regiment in high esteem, and always put it forward before distinguished visitors to the army.

During the march from Centreville, the enemy were running a race on roads parallel to the route of the Union army for Washington, and did get in the rear, on the line of retreat at Chantilly, where the lamented Generals Kearney and Stevens lost their lives in the battle that ensued to dislodge them. When General Jackson, the Confederate leader, saw the body of the former, he uncovered his head, as did those about him, and said: "You have killed the bravest officer in the Union army; this is General Philip Kearney, who lost his arm at the gates of the City of Mexico." It was a tribute of respect paid by one brave soldier to another, although an antagonist. The men could see the reflection of the sun on the enemy's bayonets at times as they marched, and skirmishers were out on the flank of the column. A diminutive Lieutenant of the regular army had charge of those detailed from the Fifth, and the boys worried the poor man's life out, hunting them out of farm-houses on the route where they were trying to find a square meal.

The movements for about ten days may be stated very briefly as follows:

We marched at about 6 A.M., on Wednesday, the 3d, some five miles, and occupied Hall's Hill, and were joined by a large number of recruits, sent on from New York. The appearance of the men did not tend to raise their spirits much, as we were all in rags and dirt. On the 4th and 5th we re-

Second Battle of Bull Run. 309

mained at Hall's Hill, and were visited by citizens from Washington. 6th, marched at 9 P.M., and crossed the chain-bridge over the Potomac, and bivouacked near Tenallytown, having marched nine miles; and on the 7th we transferred our camp to the other side of the road. 8th, started at 7 P.M., moved six miles and joined the division near Rockville. 9th, marched at 7 A.M., passing through Rockville, and bivouacked. 11th, marched at 9 A.M, eight miles and bivouacked near Seneca Creek. 12th, marched at 10 A.M. eleven miles to Hyattsville, and bivouacked outside of the town. 13th, marched at 6 A.M., thirteen miles, crossing the Monocacy, and bivouacked two miles from Frederick City.

CHAPTER XIII.

BATTLE OF ANTIETAM.

THE CONFEDERATE SUCCESSES—VIRGINIA *versus* THE COTTON STATES—THE BATTLE OF ANTIETAM—THE ENEMY RETIRES—GENERAL MCCLELLAN'S REPORT—CROSSING THE POTOMAC—BATTLE OF SHEPARDSTOWN—TENTH NEW YORK REGIMENT TRANSFERRED—SCARCITY OF SUPPLIES—A MIXED UNIFORM—PENALTIES OF OLD CLOTHES—A BREAD SPECULATION—A WHISKY SMUGGLE—A DRILL CHALLENGE ACCEPTED—CROSSING AT HARPER'S FERRY—COLONEL O'ROURKE OF THE 140TH NEW YORK—SNICKER'S GAP—WARRENTON—A SECESSIONIST TOWN—FAREWELL REVIEW BY GENERAL MCCLELLAN—GENERAL BURNSIDE IN COMMAND—THE 146TH NEW YORK—WARRENTON JUNCTION—SPOTTED TAVERN—THE HENRY HOUSE—RESIGNATION OF COLONEL HIRAM DURYEA—CHANGES IN THE REGIMENT—BEFORE THE BATTLE.

THUS far the prestige of success on the Peninsula appeared to rest with the Confederate army. The commanding officer, the military chief of the Rebellion, was a Virginian, and many of his most effective Generals were proud of the same distinction. They were not only in deep sympathy with the objects of the war against the Union, but they were thoroughly familiar with the country which was made the great arena of this stubborn conflict. They were VIRGINIANS, and the State pride which corrupted all the politics of the South, and which gave to the Union a secondary place, intensified their determination to carry the war to the extremity almost of extinction rather than surrender to the armies which contended for our national life. They were thus, in one respect, masters of the situation. They were fighting on their own soil, for their own heritage, in a latitude and under a climate where the Northern troops suffered great losses by sickness and death; the latter were decimated in localities and in an atmosphere which to their antagonists were healthful and invigorating. The immense disadvantages of the Northern troops, who, under other circumstances, would have achieved a succes-

Battle of Antietam. 311

sion of victories, gave to the Confederates the substantial fruits of triumph, and of repeated disaster to the loyal arms ; and whi e these events did not dampen the ardor of the latter, they inspired the Confederates with greater confidence and determination. Their purpose was to annihilate the Army of the Potomac, and this accomplished, either the possession of the national capital, or their own terms of separation, they assumed to be a certain event.

One special feature of the contest was always apparent. Whatever amount of zeal and bravery were shown by Virginian and North Carolina regiments on the field, they were fully equaled by the impetuous, wild, and determined dash and tenacity of the troops from the South and South-west. The regiments from South Carolina and the States whose shores were washed by the Gulf, showed an ardor and a stubbornness of will together with a bitterness of hatred that made them difficult foes to meet in the field. They had a motive kindred to that of the Virginians, but it was one of supreme selfishness.

The leaders of "*the* South," the cotton-growing States, were resolved that the fate of the Confederacy should be decided on the battle-fields of the Border States.

Maryland, Virginia, Kentucky, and Missouri were to be the camp-grounds and the arenas where the question should be determined, and while the men of the Border States fought for their own soil, the Cotton States men fought *that the battle should not be transferred to theirs.*

Virginia especially was to be made the great theater of war, and by massing all the power of the Confederacy on her soil, the rest, and especially the more remote States, could " continue to grow cotton in peace." The Old Dominion was the victim of a bloody stratagem of statesmanship, when the capital of the Confederacy was transferred from Montgomery to Richmond.

The resolve to break the power of the Union, and to dic-late terms of separation, at the doors of the national capital, for the sake of preserving the rest of the Confederacy from the ruin and waste of war, gave to the Peninsular campaign the extraordinary fury and the sanguinary and fearful disasters of that dark period in our history.

How high the price that was paid for these hopes, and how disastrously they were ultimately defeated, was written in the broad and bloody seal of death, and the heaps of slain who gave up the bounding life-blood of their heroic hearts, and laid down to die on the field or the highway, to be intrenched in the numberless graves, dug in a momentary pause by other thousands who were rushing on to fall into kindred cemeteries on other fields. If nations and governments have moral responsibilities, where does the responsibility rest for these?

Each day's march found us further from the scenes of Bull Run, and brought us nearer to the impending struggle, in which, at least, the tide of success of the Confederate arms was to be tested and turned.

On Sunday, the 14th of September, we took up our line of march at 8 A.M., proceeding eight miles, passing through Middletown, and bivouacked. On the march the battle of South Mountain was raging, and we could see the smoke as it floated into the blue sky over the field, while the diapason of the booming guns was heard a few miles in advance on the road. We passed General McClellan on the march, who was enjoying a cigar, and observing the troops as they filed by. He said to us: "Boys! we are pressing the enemy back, and will keep doing so."

Early on the morning of the 15th we resumed our march through Turner's Gap, South Mountain, where the Confederate dead of D. H. Hill's division lay behind a stone wall which ran along on the top of the mountain, at right angles with and commanding the road. They also were lying on the main road on the other side of the pass. They were piled in heaps, lying three or four deep at the intersection of the road and turnpike. It was an impressive reminder of the words of LONGFELLOW—

> " Art is long and time is fleeting,
> And our hearts, though stout and brave,
> Still like muffled drums are beating
> Funeral marches to the grave"—

and we could not help the consciousness, that in all probability before another setting sun many of us would be lying on the bosom of mother earth in the silent companionship of the dead.

After marching about nine miles, the division deployed on the left of the Sharpsburg turnpike, near Antietam Creek, being on the left of Richardson's division, which was the first to arrive in advance.*

The Fifth deployed as skirmishers, and advanced through woods on the left. The enemy had opened with their artillery, and were throwing shell, some of which fell among us, but fortunately did not burst. Tidball's 2d United States and Petits' 1st New York artillery returned the fire. The enemy were posted in a strong position on the high ground on the opposite side of the creek, front of and to the right and left of Sharpsburg, which town was in the rear of their center; their flanks and rear being protected by the Potomac River and Antietam Creek, it being naturally a strong position.

On Tuesday, the 16th, we changed position, and were under arms all day. The army was all up and massed each side of the Sharpsburg turnpike. The mass of the enemy's infantry was concealed behind the opposite heights.

General Lee's army of invasion comprised about one hun-

---

* General McClellan's Report (p. 374): "The division of General Richardson, following close on the heels of the retreating foe, halted and deployed near Antietam River, on the right of the Sharpsburg road. General Sykes leading on the division of regulars on the old Sharpsburg road, came up and deployed to the left of General Richardson, on the left of the road."

dred and seventy-seven regiments of infantry, besides cavalry and artillery, including General A. P. Hill's division, which was temporarily detached for the purpose of making an attack upon Harper's Ferry. After this post was surrendered to General Hill, he, by a forced march, came up late in the afternoon of the 17th on Lee's right, in time to repel the hitherto successful advance of General Burnside's corps, and which had been delayed too long.*

The regulars were posted near bridge No. 2, and in the center with the reserve artillery. General Burnside's corps (of four divisions), comprising the left, took position on the left of Warren's brigade, their right covering stone bridge No. 3. The day was spent principally in maneuvering for positions, skirmishing, and artillery engagements.

The following day, Wednesday, September 17th, was rendered memorable in our annals by the engagement at Antietam. The action was commenced at daylight by the skirmishers of the Pennsylvania reserves on the right, and the whole of General Hooker's corps soon became engaged, and drove the enemy. Soon afterward the 12th corps engaged, and General Mansfield, its commander, was killed. General Hartsuff, of Hooker's, was badly wounded. General Williams took command of the 12th corps. The battle raged furiously for two hours. General Crawford, commanding the 1st division, 12th corps, was wounded and left the field. General Sedgwick's division of Sumner's corps engaged, and Generals Sedgwick and Dana were wounded.

---

* Colonel Ford, commanding Maryland Heights, an impregnable position, garrisoned by 3,975 men, gave orders to spike and dismount the heavy guns, and to fall back upon Harper's Ferry.

By the cowardly evacuation of this stronghold, which commanded our works at Harper's Ferry, Colonel D. S. Miles, who was in command of the latter post, was attacked on all sides by the Confederates, and was himself mortally wounded. On the 15th, the post with all its guns, stores, and ammunition, and force of 9,000 men, was surrendered to the enemy.

After an examination by a court of inquiry, Colonel Ford was dismissed from the service of the United States.

General Hooker was also wounded and obliged to leave the field. The divisions of Generals French and Richardson, which completed all of Sumner's corps, were engaged. General Meagher was disabled, and General Richardson was mortally wounded. At 1 P.M. a part of General Franklin's corps engaged. General Porter's 5th corps, consisting of Morell's and Sykes' divisions, Humphrey's division not yet having arrived, and all of the reserve artillery, were directly opposite the center of the enemy's line. "It was necessary to watch this part of the line with the utmost vigilance, lest the enemy should take an advantage to assault and pierce the line, which would be fatal."

All the supply trains were in the rear of this corps, and here were the headquarters of General McClellan and staff. In case of a retreat or last resort, Sykes' division would have been obliged to do their best. Toward the middle of the afternoon, two brigades of Morell's were ordered to reinforce the right. Six battalions of Sykes' regulars had been thrown across Antietam bridge on the main road, to attack and drive back the enemy's sharp-shooters, who were annoying Pleasonton's batteries in advance of the bridge. Warren's brigade was detached to hold a position on Burnside's right and rear, so that Porter was left at one time with only a portion of Sykes' division, and one small brigade of Morell's, numbering but a little over three thousand men, to hold the center.

Sykes' division had been in position since the 15th, exposed to the fire of the enemy's artillery and sharp-shooters. The 2d and 10th regulars compelled the cannoneers of one of the enemy's batteries to abandon their guns; but being few in number and unsupported, were not able to bring them off. General Burnside passed by the regiment several times, and the men expected to be ordered to charge the stone bridge No. 3 and get wiped out.

General Burnside attacked at 3 P.M., and fought until

dark, reaching the outskirts of Sharpsburg, where General Rodman was mortally wounded.

After General Burnside's forces advanced across the river, several companies of the Fifth were stationed in turn as look-outs near stone bridge No. 3, which was thickly strewn with the dead of the 51st New York and the 51st Pennsylvania, who first successfully charged across it. Its passage had been defended with great obstinacy by the 2d and 20th Georgia regiments, under the command of General Toombs, who were posted on a wooded height that commanded it, aided by the batteries of General Jones. We obtained a fine view of the engagement, and watched the progress of the 9th New York, Hawkins' Zouaves, with an exciting interest, and were sorry to see that gallant body of men suffer so severely on the field where they played so noble a part. They captured a battery on the outskirts of Sharpsburg, but not being properly supported, were forced to abandon it, after suffering a fearful loss. Late in the afternoon, the brigade was employed in collecting stragglers from the immediate front and forming them into battalions.

Darkness finally put an end to this hard-fought and scientific engagement, in which 140,000 men and 500 pieces of artillery had been employed since daylight, and in which about 25,000 were killed, wounded, and missing. The tired Union troops slept on their arms conquerors.*

About 2,700 of the enemy's dead were, under the direction of Major Davis, Assistant Inspector-General, counted

---

* General McClellan's Report (p. 393): "Night closed the long and desperately contested battle of the 17th. Nearly 200,000 men and 500 pieces of artillery were for fourteen hours engaged in this memorable battle. We had attacked the enemy in a position selected by the experienced engineer, then in person directing their operations. We had driven them from their line on one flank, and securing a footing within it on the other. The Army of the Potomac, notwithstanding the moral effect incident to previous reverses, had achieved a victory over an adversary invested with the prestige of recent success. Our soldiers slept that night conquerors, on a field won by their valor, and covered with the dead and wounded of the enemy."

Battle of Antietam. 317

and buried upon the field of Antietam. A portion of their dead had previously been buried by the enemy. 13 guns, 39 colors, 15,000 stand of small arms, and more than 6,000 prisoners were the trophies of South Mountain, Crampton's Gap, and Antietam. Not a single gun was lost on the Union side.

The Confederate force engaged in this battle comprised 136 regiments, besides the division of D. H. Hill and Rodes' brigade, and the artillery. Their reports show a loss in every regiment of from one to 253.

We remained in position on Thursday, the 18th, the enemy requesting an armistice, under a flag of truce, to look after their wounded and bury their dead, which was granted, and of which they took advantage and retreated by night across the Potomac.

On Friday, the 19th, we marched at 9 A.M., passing through Sharpsburg. Along the route the dead were strewn in every direction and in all conceivable positions. One was caught in the crotch of a tree in falling, and held in an upright position; one young lad, of not more than fifteen years of age, was lying among some others, with his thighs terribly mangled. His long curls fell down over his shoulders, and his face bore a heavenly smile; his lips slightly parted disclosed a set of teeth of remarkable beauty, while his features were the handsomest, and bore the happiest expression, of any corpse that I have ever seen. He was a young Southerner, probably the pride of some aristocratic family, who had sent him willingly to the war.

After marching through the town and nearing the ford on the Potomac, skirmishers were deployed, and a battery with us opened on the enemy across the river. The fire was returned by them, and the shell flew thick and fast. One of the shot killed Colonel Warren's orderly, but the men found partial shelter under a hill. Two brigades of the corps crossed the Potomac about dark and captured four of the enemy's guns. Warren's brigade took position on the high ground near the river, and opened on the enemy on the other side, which obliged them to crawl out of the bushes and run for the cover of a wood further to their rear. We advanced and took position on the tow-path of the canal on the banks of the river, and kept up a scattering fire on the enemy opposite, remaining on picket all night and the next forenoon.

In the afternoon of the 20th, a large force crossed the river on the right, and the 5th Regiment were ordered to ford the river to cover their left flank. Before crossing, the regiment, which numbered less than 400 men, two-thirds of whom were comparatively new men, being drawn up in line on the tow-path of the canal, alongside the river, Colonel Warren said, "Men, we are about to cross the river," and drawing out his revolver, added, that "if any man did not want to cross, let him step out."

We took off our body-belts, slung our cartridge-boxes over our shoulders, and waded into the river. It was difficult and tiresome work to ford a stream 200 yards wide, up to the waist, with a rather strong current, the bottom being covered with slippery stones. Some of the men lost their balance, and had an involuntary bath, and to "get off the line of the ford," meant to go down overhead in the water. After reaching the opposite bank, the men climbed an almost perpendicular bluff, eighty feet high, covered with bushes and trees, and were obliged to employ both hands and feet to accomplish the task. Skirmishers were deployed a short distance, when suddenly the enemy opened in heavy force from the wood beyond the open ground in front. The skirmishers were called in, and the men ordered to keep covered below the bank of the bluff, which they were perfectly willing to do, for the fire was very heavy, and they occupied a critical position, with the river in their rear. But several batteries opened from the high ground on the opposite side of the river, over the heads of the men, which covered their retreat across, which was accomplished in safety. Captain Whitney, in command of Company I, was ordered to remain with his company, and keep up a fire on the enemy to make them think that the bank was still occupied, and to prevent any of their sharp-shooters from creeping to the edge of the bluff and shooting the men as they forded the river on their return. He misunderstood the order, so he said, and did not carry it out, but fortunately the batteries prevented the enemy from advancing. Colonel Warren was much provoked with him, and threatened to shoot him on the spot. The Colonel took command in person, and waded the stream, on foot, with the rest, and on the return stood in the center, and continually warned the men not to get off the line of the ford.

This was the battle of Shepardstown, in which the troops on the right had a severe engagement with Gregg's, Pender's, and Archer's brigades, and lost some 800 in killed, wounded, and prisoners. The enemy's loss was 261. After recrossing the river we took up a position on the canal and remained on picket on the banks of the river, exchanging shots with the enemy during the 21st and 22d. While remaining on this post one afternoon, Colonel Warren gave the regiment a drill on the tow-path of the canal, while the enemy's pickets amused themselves by firing at the men and officers. He also sent a squad of the drummers across the river, for punishment for being timid under fire, under command of Lieutenant Guthrie, to bring over a twelve-pound brass piece left by the enemy in their late retreat. The Lieutenant armed himself with a ramrod to give the boys a gentle reminder once in a while if it was necessary. The boys came back in good order, dragging the cannon after them, and reported that they saw some of the enemy. Subsequently, Sergeant Crowley, of Company E, with a squad of his company, was sent over to a burnt mill, to bring over a caisson, while the regiment in the meantime drew up on the bank to cover them. They had no sooner landed on the other side than some shots were fired at them, and a brisk skirmish ensued around the mill, in which the Sergeant received a bad wound in the leg, but his men succeeded in recrossing, carrying him with them.

On Tuesday, the 23d, we were relieved by the regulars, after three days and nights of not very pleasant duty, during which it rained part of the time. We went into camp, without tents or shelter of any kind, near Sharpsburg, about three-fourths of a mile from the Potomac. General McClellan had his headquarters about a mile from Sharpsburg, and, as usual, Sykes' division lay in the immediate vicinity.

After the battle of Antietam a recruit, one of those who had joined the regiment about a week previous, wandered off to see what he could discover that was new. In his rambles he came to a large house, and seeing an open window, he approached it to gratify his curiosity as to what was inside of it, when, as his head raised above the sill, the gory stump of a man's arm was thrust in his face, with the remark, "Young man, take this away and bury it." That recruit returned to the regiment a sick man. He had ran across one of the hospitals where the wounded were being attended to.

On Wednesday, the 24th, at evening parade, the following list of promotions was read to the regiment :

HEADQUARTERS FIFTH ARMY CORPS,
CAMP NEAR SHARPSBURG, MD.,
September 23, 1862.

[*Special Orders, No.* 130.]

The following-named persons are hereby appointed to fill the vacancies existing in the Fifth Regiment, New York Volunteers, occasioned by losses in battle, resignations, promotions, etc. These appointments are made for gallant and meritorious conduct on the field of battle. These officers will be obeyed and respected accordingly :

Camp near Sharpsburg.

Captain Cleveland Winslow to be Major, *vice* H. D. Hull, promoted.
First Lieutenant James H. Lounsberry to be Captain, *vice* G. Carr, promoted.
First Lieutenant H. G. O. Eichler to be Captain, *vice* Winslow, promoted.
First Lieutenant T. W. Cartwright to be Captain, *vice* Lewis, killed in battle August 30.
First Lieutenant R. E. Prime to be Captain, *vice* Hager, killed in battle August 30.
Second Lieutenant Henry Keyser to be Adjutant, *vice* Sovereign, killed in battle August 30.
Second Lieutenant A. S. Chase to be First Lieutenant, *vice* Lounsberry, promoted.
Second Lieutenant T. R. Martin to be First Lieutenant, *vice* Eichler, promoted.
Second Lieutenant R. M. Gedney to be First Lieutenant, *vice* Cartwright, promoted.
Second Lieutenant Wm. Hoffman to be First Lieutenant, *vice* Prime, promoted.
Sergeant G. W. Wannemacher to be Second Lieutenant, *vice* Dumont, resigned.
Sergeant George Guthrie to be Second Lieutenant, *vice* Keyser, promoted.
Sergeant Wm. H. Chambers to be Second Lieutenant, *vice* Chase, promoted.
Sergeant Philip L. Wilson to be Second Lieutenant, *vice* Martin, promoted.
Private Gordon Winslow, Jr., to be Second Lieutenant, *vice* Gedney, promoted.

By command of
FITZ JOHN PORTER,
FRED. T. LOCKE, *Major-General.*
Assistant Adjutant-General.

On Thursday, September 25th, the 10th New York Regiment was transferred to Max Weber's brigade. During the time they had been in company with the Fifth we had always harmonized and worked well together. We had passed through some pleasant as well as some very hard experiences, and the men heartily wished their late comrades success.*

Colonel Warren left on a flying visit to New York *via*. Washington. Lieutenant-Colonel H. Duryea had just returned from his furlough, having been dangerously ill. We were glad to see him in command again, notwithstanding the strict discipline he always maintained, as we knew it was for the common good; but especially so, as we were relieved from a number of impracticable orders that were issued by the Major. These were: calls every half hour through the day, which made the men feel that they were treated worse than a lot of convicts, and without cause. For instance, in order to wash ourselves, we were obliged to procure an order to pass to the spring, signed by the officer in command of the company, and countersigned by the Adjutant or Major. The consequence was, that it operated as a prohibition to wash at all. Water-calls were sounded several times a day. When those who wished to fill their canteens or the iron pails, holding several gallons, for cooking purposes, they were obliged to fall in line, and march single file, under command of an officer, keeping step down to the spring and back again; to obtain wood, we were obliged to go through the same form, and he was actually driving men to desert every day, to escape this petty and unwarranted tyranny. Discipline should be enforced; but these acts were crushing out all the self-respect and manhood of an intelligent and educated body of men, who felt that they were treated like galley-slaves.

Since leaving Harrison's Landing, August 14th, when the

---

* The Tenth subsequently fought bravely at Fredericksburg, and when they were mustered out after two years' service, six companies were recruited to serve for three years, or during the war, and, under Colonel Hopper, acquired an excellent war record, and served till the collapse of the Rebellion. Colonel Hopper served all through the war, and was the only officer of the old organization who was mustered out with the three years' battalion at the end of the war.

knapsacks were sent away on a vessel, the men had been without a change of clothing. All they possessed was on their backs. They were destitute of soap for about a month, and sometimes had nothing to eat. Only a few had shelter tents, and consequently they passed the nights miserably, as the temperature after the sun went down was chilly, accompanied with heavy dews; and in addition to all these discomforts, they had not received any pay for five months. The men all being in rags, presented a very grotesque appearance. Their own clothing being worn out, they were dressed up in the cast-off clothing of other regiments; some were dressed in dark-blue and others in light-blue pants; some in jackets, some had long-tailed coats and blouses, and others boasted of nothing but a few rags to cover their under-clothes. We mustered, all told, including recruits, 350, of which only 93 were original two years' men. There were several hundreds on the rolls, but they were lying in hospitals, detailed, etc. They belonged to that army, all in good condition, according to General Halleck (who was comfortably seated in Washington, planning campaigns on paper), who were ready and eager to march immediately on a winter's campaign and take Richmond, from the vicinity of which they had been recalled, probably by his advice, some two months previous, when they were in better condition and spirit to fight than they were at this time.

On Friday, the 26th, we were reviewed by the President, ABRAHAM LINCOLN. He looked care-worn. He was in company with General McClellan, who was smoking a cigar. The men had overcoats on, which had been distributed a few days previous, to hide the rags. The President expressed his approbation to the commanding officers at the rapidity with which the different movements were executed. The bayonet drill particularly engrossed his attention.

Our camp at Sharpsburg remained quiet for some time, and the men were in fair spirits. We drilled for five hours a day, for which we had to thank the recruits. About the 5th of October we received a piece of soap, but its size was an aggravation—it was half an inch thick, cut from an ordinary bar, two bars having been allowed to a company. The officers and men anxiously expected the Paymaster, and the sutlers scented him afar off, and were plenty, but still there was no money to buy with, and no credit. Every few hours some one varied the decorum of our situation by raising a false alarm, and shouted, " Here comes the Paymaster!" Forthwith there was a rush out of holes and burrows, only to find it a good-humored joke. Those who used tobacco— which was the case with nearly all the regiment—were suffering for the want of it, and no change of clothing having yet come to our relief, our condition was getting to be more than ever a serious matter.

The "status" of the men under this state of things, from the long-continued use of their garments without change, is more appropriate for the recollection of the sufferer, than for description by the historian. It is enough to say that part of the daily employment of the men, in the retirement of the woods, stripped of their clothing and hunting for vermin, was more picturesque than poetic, and is left to the imagination of the reader.

On Saturday, Oct. 4th, an order came to discharge all who were physically disqualified for effective service; a few of the original men of our regiment were of this class, and some of the latest recruits. An order had also been promulgated from the War Department, directing that all who had not been accounted for during the past sixty days, be dropped from the rolls as deserters. This placed the word "deserter" against the name of many brave men who lost their lives in battle. There may have been a "military necessity" for such an order, but it worked a great injustice to many who died alone and unknown in by-places where they lingered out weary hours, perhaps days, of pain before their eyes were closed in death, beyond the relief that never came —and others who died unrecognized in the hospitals or the prisons of the enemy. It is past now. God grant that no such "necessity" may ever again overshadow the republic. An order to shoot deserters, and cashier absentee officers would have strengthened the army materially, and saved money as well as many valuable lives.

Near our camp was a farm-house, whose occupant was supposed to be a good Union man. The enemy had cleared out all his horses, cattle, wagons, etc., and the Union troops burnt his rail fences for fuel; so that between the two armies, he was a heavy sufferer. Near this house was a spring which supplied the regiment, and one day a dilapidated-looking turn-out, driven by a countryman, made its appearance. Some of the boys were there filling their canteens from the spring, when they asked him what he had in the wagon; for, being a covered one, they could not see into it. He stopped and said that he and the old woman had concluded to go into a bread speculation, and he had his wagon full to sell to the "sojurs." Bread being a great luxury compared with the hard-tack, two or three of the boys got around him and asked the price. "Let's see the size of the loaves? is it fresh?" said one of them, as he bit off a large piece from a loaf. Just then the old man's attention was drawn to the rear of his cart, by seeing about a dozen hands, each clutching a loaf of bread. He skipped around, when the boys in front made a levy, and so it was kept up, until in sheer desperation he sprang into his wagon and drove off down the road at his best speed. One of the boys called out: "Here, mister! aint you going to stop for your money?" But he only went the faster, and one called out: "Well, if you aint got time to wait, just send in your bill to Company J, it's all the same."

The decline of the year was bringing the autumnal change in the season. The weather was becoming colder, and we were visited Sunday, Oct. 12th, by a rain-storm, which added nothing to the comforts of the camp. The regiment was under arms, and the men ordered not to leave their company streets, as Stuart's cavalry were in the rear of the army.

On Thursday, the 16th, we marched at 1 P.M. to Blackburn's Ford, on the Potomac, for picket duty. Detachments from the corps made a reconnoissance on the other side of the river. It rained hard during the night, and the men passed a disagreeable tour of guard duty. The following day we were relieved from picket at 6 P.M., after being on duty for thirty hours, and we returned to camp.

A detail from the regiment went on picket again on Sunday, the 19th. The Lieutenant-Colonel was absent again sick, and Major Winslow was in command. The men were happy, having received a supply of clothing, and confidently went through a general inspection. Captain Burnett, senior Captain, and Lieutenant Agnus, had resigned, the latter to accept a Captaincy in the 165th New York, 2d battalion of Duryée's Zouaves. Adjutant Marvin was on a visit to New York to recruit himself and the regiment.

On Friday, the 24th, we were visited by a severe storm of rain, which lasted for two days, but the men were all in fine spirits notwithstanding, as they had received four months' pay, and could purchase some luxuries (so-called) from the sutlers, who had been patiently waiting to relieve them of their spare cash.

Thirteen men deserted on the capital they had obtained, having money enough to pay their way. Monday, the 27th, was clear and cold, after the storm, blowing hard, and nearly all the men were full of spirits. During the night, the officers were surprised to hear an unusual noise in the usually quiet camp, and the officer of the day, as well as the guard, were astounded. It was very evident that the men had procured whisky somewhere, and in large quantity. The sutlers were not allowed to sell it, and the men had not been out of camp; there had not been any suspicious persons about, and where did they get the whisky? Such a complete demoralization had never happened before, not even in Baltimore, where the facilities of a large city afforded every opportunity for a debauch. Fighting, singing, and general uproar prevailed, even "taps" being almost entirely unheeded. The next morning empty quart bottles were lying about in profusion. The officers never knew the secret of it; but a party, being no other than the well-known "Nicaragua Riley," had been around a little while before with a wagon-load of bread, and a part of the loaves had been cut open and examined, but nothing had been found inside of them. Yet this was the man who had supplied the liquor used the night before. Two barrels containing quart bottles of whisky were sold for two dollars a bottle in that very camp. It had cost him thirty-five cents a gallon, and he had come around to get his money "in a lump," as much as to sell his bread; it was handed to him by an Orderly Sergeant.

The clear and bracing morning of Tuesday, the 28th, found us under marching orders. We had been drilling hard every day under Major Winslow, who followed in the steps of his predecessors. But the exercise kept the men warm, and they liked it on that account.

While staying in this camp one of the regiments in our corps, and, moreover, one of the best fighting regiments in the service, between whom and our own great respect was reciprocated, came over to drill on a field next to that which the Fifth used for the same purpose. They were doing their best. Our Major looked upon the proceeding as a challenge—the men certainly did. Accordingly the drill-call was sounded, and after forming, we were marched out, and were soon going through the movements like clock-work. It was not five minutes before the commanding officer of the other regiment was so much interested in the movements of the Fifth that he ordered his men to a rest, and they remained spectators, and drilled no more. At the guard-mount of the Fifth there was always a concourse of officers from different regiments to witness it.

The benevolent party who sold the bread to the men came around again to sell pies, which, however, were in a greatly demoralized condition, having suffered fearfully by the transportation; the materials were there, but somewhat mixed. It was dealt out at twenty-five cents for a handful of the mush, which consisted of about a dozen different kinds of pastry, and there was great pushing and scrambling to purchase it. He was closely watched, but that did not prevent the necessary arrangements from being made for another smuggle of whisky, under the cover of darkness.

It was clear and pleasant the next day, the 29th. The officers and men were light-headed. We had company drill in the morning, and battalion drill in the afternoon, to straighten up. A great deal of drunkenness was noticed in camp the previous night, the underground railroad having evidently been running its train again. But the engineer made no money by this venture. When he came around for it, having nothing to sell, he was told by the orderly, who had acted on the previous occasion, that the stuff had been seized, and that he was suspected and ordered to be arrested. On hearing this, he left in a very disrespectful and hasty manner, without waiting to hear any further explanations. He had tasted military justice before, on at least one occasion, and wanted no more of it. The orderly quietly pocketed the money, and went into his tent to take a drink.

We left camp on Thursday, the 30th, at 4 P.M., at the close of a warm and cloudy day, marched until 2 A.M. of the 31st, and bivouacked in Pleasant Valley, near Brownsville, after a slow and tedious march of nine miles over the mountains. The night was cold and disagreeable, but the morning was clear and warm. We started again, moving at 6 A.M. about three-quarters of a mile, when we halted four hours on the road. Orders to advance being given, we again fell in, and after marching about eight miles, passing through Brownsville, we bivouacked near Weverton, Md. We had a bayonet drill on dress parade. We were mustered in for two months' pay, and Captain Prime's resignation was announced, to enable him to accept a Lieutenant-Colonelcy in another organization.

Saturday, November 1st, found us in marching order at 7 A.M.; we crossed the Potomac on a pontoon bridge at Harper's Ferry, where we stopped, and were supplied with knapsacks, which we had not seen since leaving Harrison's Landing, two and a half months before; we picked up the genial "Butch" and some others, who had been sent from the former camp to labor on the public works, to pay for a "frolic." We resumed our march and crossed the Shenandoah, and after tramping eight miles through Loudoun Valley, bivouacked on the Leesburg turnpike, near Neversville. We were joined by the 140th New York, Colonel O'Rourke, a regular officer and a graduate of West Point. He was a fine officer, and was subsequently killed at the battle of Gettysburg, in the terrible hand to hand conflict with Hood's Texans on the summit of Little Bald Top. They were a fine body of men generally, but new to the service; they were enlisted from the northern part of the State, and were at this time about 850 strong. Sunday, November 2d, marched at 7 A.M., passing through Hillsborough and Snickersvile, and relieved Sumner's corps at Snicker's Gap, arriving there about 11 P.M., after a tedious stretch of sixteen miles. We bivouacked in line of battle behind stacked arms, on top of the mountain. It was a very cold, windy night. Sykes' division was ordered to hold the pass over the Blue Ridge through the Gap. The roads over which we had marched were rough and stony, water was scarce, and the last two miles being on the ascent all the way, was very tiresome work after a full day's marching. At one time before reaching the foot of the mountain we were deployed in line of battle, expecting a skirmish with the enemy who were in the vicinity. Three men dropped out on the last two miles to make their coffee, after which they kept on. An officer on horseback halted them by a sudden challenge, and asked them where they were going and what regiment they belonged to. It was so dark he could not see their uniform. When they answered him, he told them they would soon be in the hands of the enemy on that road, and gave them proper directions. He had been placing pickets. They lost their way in the darkness, and lay down by a stone wall to rest. While dozing into sleep, one of the pickets close by made a challenge, and receiving no answer, fired his piece. They heard a cry, "I am shot!" and "Corporal of the Guard!" A straggling soldier who failed to answer the challenge had been fatally shot. Our boys found they had made a narrow escape. The 3d was a cold, blustering day, and we were still in line of battle, with strong pickets posted, expecting an attack. The men killed a lot of sheep found running at large about the mountain tops, and had plenty of mutton for the first time in eighteen months. Boxes of crackers were carried three-fourths of a mile by details of men on their backs from the wagons, as they could not ascend any further. One of the companies went down the mountain toward the Shenandoah River, and had a brush with the enemy's pickets who were on the other side of it.

The following morning broke clear and we had a pleasant day. The enemy was in sight in the valley, and heavy firing was heard in the east in the direction of Warrenton. A reconnoissance was made down the mountain, under the command of Colonel Sargent, of General Porter's staff, to Castleman's Ford, Shenandoah River. He had with him a squadron of the 1st Massachusetts cavalry (Captain Pratt), two battalions of the 14th, and battalions of the 6th and 7th U. S. Infantry. When they had proceeded about two miles they were fired on by a masked battery of ten guns posted on the other side of the river. After some preliminary skirmishing, Captain Pratt was shot through the heart, a Lieutenant of the 14th Infantry was wounded, and about forty of the men were killed or wounded; but they advanced to the river. The Fifth were ordered under arms at the first firing, but their services were not required.

The regiment was on picket duty on the 5th, and we could see the enemy, and were obliged to be extremely vigilant. Very heavy firing was heard in the direction of Ashby's Gap, south of us. In the expectation of a night attack, double pickets were posted. The night fell on us cold and cloudy. Notwithstanding the apparent preparations for an attack, everything remained quiet during the night, and at 7 A.M. on Thursday, the 6th, we commenced a march of about eighteen miles, passing through Middleburgh, and bivouacked about one mile distant in the woods. While passing through the town, which was thoroughly secessionist, an old lady stood at her door leaning on a cane, and called out very earnestly, in a cracked voice, and shaking her head, that "it was no use to go that way, you will all come back again."

No males were seen in the town except cripples, paroled and wounded prisoners, in Confederate uniform, awaiting exchange. All the other male inhabitants were in the Confederate army.

We marched the next morning at seven o'clock. It commenced snowing at nine, and continued through the day. We marched about eight miles, and, after the usual inspection of arms, encamped near White Plains. Company A was sent on picket to the rear, to guard against a surprise by Mosby and his men. The night was bitterly cold, from which the men suffered severely, but they kindled large fires, and, with the addition of hay from some stacks near by, made themselves as comfortable as circumstances would permit.

A squad of the new regiment, who had not yet become

accustomed to the grindstone, made a foray on a sutler's wagon which happened to be near General Warren's quarters on the road. He sprang among them and whacked them well with his sword, much to their astonishment. They became well toned down, after a little training, like the rest of us.

On Saturday, the 8th, the reveille woke us at 4.30 A.M. We marched at eight o'clock, advancing nine miles over bad roads through White Plains, and bivouacked near New Baltimore. The next day, Sunday, the 9th, we marched at 8 A.M., about two miles through Thoroughfare Gap, and bivouacked within one mile of Warrenton, and in sight of the spires of that strong secessionist town. The weather was fine, but clear and cold. We were drawn up in line on the beautiful morning of the 10th, but our hearts were sad. We had a farewell review from General McClellan. The men received him with nine hearty cheers, as he always had their entire confidence, and all were sad at parting with him.

At evening parade the farewell address of our beloved Commander-in-Chief was read off, which was as follows :

HEADQUARTERS ARMY OF THE POTOMAC,
CAMP NEAR RECTORTOWN, *November 7, 1862.*

OFFICERS AND SOLDIERS OF THE ARMY OF THE POTOMAC : —An order of the President devolves upon Major-General Burnside the command of this army. In parting from you I can not express the love and gratitude I bear you. As an army, you have grown up in my care. In you I have never found doubt or coldness. The battles you have fought under my command will proudly live in our nation's history. The glory you have achieved, our mutual perils and fatigues, the graves of our comrades fallen in battle and by disease, the broken forms of those whom wounds and sickness have disabled—the strongest associations which can exist among men—unite us still by an indissoluble tie. We shall ever be comrades in supporting the Constitution of our country and the nationality of its people.

G. B. MCCLELLAN,
Major-General U. S. Army.

The regiment did not expect to make a halt so soon, but were not sorry to have a litte rest. A supply of straw had been appropriated by the men, which they were fortunate enough to discover, thereby adding much to their comfort. The wind was blowing a gale from the north, and the sky was overcast with clouds, giving promise of another snow-storm.

The men endured the weather very well, but the horses suffered severely. The 11th was a clear, pleasant day; another review was held, and General Fitz John Porter took leave of his command. He looked pale, and evidently was anxious and ill at ease. The men gave him nine hearty cheers, and the common remark among them was, "Another good General gone."

On Wednesday, November 12th, General Ambrose E. Burnside took command of the army. On the 13th, the 146th Regiment, New York Volunteers, under the command of Colonel Garrard, a regular officer, joined the brigade. It was a fine body of men, enlisted from the Western and Central portion of the State, and about 850 strong. This regiment made for itself, by its active service with the Army of the Potomac, to the close of the war, a splendid war record. Their long list of killed and wounded tells the story of the hard fighting they did at Gettysburg and during Grant's great campaign, which closed with the capture of Richmond.

On Saturday, the 15th, the Fifth was visited about dark by General A. Duryée and aides. As soon as he was recognized by the men, they turned out and gave him a fitting reception, to which he responded by a short and appropriate speech.

On Sunday, the 16th, Colonel Hiram Duryea left us on account of prolonged ill health.

The 17th we left camp in a cold rain-storm, and after a march of twelve miles, passing through Warrenton, went into bivouac about 10 P.M. at Warrenton Junction. The roads were in a very bad condition, which occasioned much delay, but when the wagons and artillery got on clear ground, we were obliged to make up the distance on a half run, which was more fatiguing than a steady, uniform step. At dusk there was no sign of going into camp, and at the halts the men sat down in the mud of the road to rest. Finally we were ordered into a field to camp. The prospect was dreary enough. It was cold and raining hard; wood was at a distance, which we were obliged to feel out in the dark. The men rigged up shelters as best they could, fastening them to the rifles for want of better supports, and slept on the cold, wet ground.

About four o'clock A.M. the men were aroused from their restless slumbers by the blast of the bugle; the sky was cloudy and the sun not visible. We fell in line and marched about eight o'clock across fields, swamps, gulleys, up hill and down, through bushes, woods, and streams, crossing the same stream of water no less than four times, the fording of which did not make one's feet and legs feel any more comfortable, and this march certainly had no attraction. It was raining all the time, and we tramped on in this manner until dark, when the patience of the men was about exhausted, and there was plenty of grumbling, cursing, and groans.

Finally we were turned into a field to rest, after sixteen miles of marching; the ground was rough and uneven, and so thickly ornamented with stones and lumps as to make one feel as if he was lying on a picket fence. This place was Spotted Tavern. One of the men remarked that it ought to be named "Devil's Rest."

On Wednesday, the 19th, marched at daylight through the rain five miles, and bivouacked near Hartwood Church.

The two succeeding days we remained in camp. It rained continually, and the men's clothing was soaking wet day and night; some of them laid with the water running under them, and had a complete, if not satisfactory, experience of that delightful sensation. We started on the march, but encountered an endless train of wagons blockaded in the muddy roads, and were ordered to camp again. The tribulations of the men thus far had not served to increase their joy at the prospect of a " winter campaign."

On Saturday, the 22d, we left camp about 3 A.M., went nearly four miles, and bivouacked near Stafford Court-House. On Sunday, the 23d, marched at 2 P.M. about three miles and encamped near Henry House, in the vicinity of General Hooker's quarters. The night was very cold, and the men were obliged to get up frequently to warm their feet ; the water froze in their canteens.

Thursday, November 27th, Thanksgiving day, the men dined on salt pork and hard-tack. For recreation they had a drill in the afternoon to aid digestion. 28th, the division was reviewed by General Sykes, and had a brigade drill under General Warren. 29th, the corps was reviewed by General Hooker, commander of the center grand division of the army. New uniforms were issued, being the first time since February, 1862. On Sunday, the 30th, we passed for inspection in heavy marching order before General Hooker's quarters, the regiment displaying their new uniforms.

On Monday, December 1st, Colonel Hiram Duryea's resignation was read off on dress parade, the regiment thereby losing a brave and accomplished officer, whose absence was keenly felt during the remainder of their term of service. He was a very strict disciplinarian, and no holiday soldier, and it was greatly owing to this fact that the excellent state of discipline and perfection in drill, to which we had been brought by Colonel Warren, was maintained.

December 3d, a detail from the regiment went on picket with two days' rations. Saturday, December 6th, was a clear, cold day, with snow on the ground five inches deep. The regiment was prepared for a review by General Butterfield, acting in command of the corps. But the order was countermanded.

On Saturday, December 6th, a detail was ordered from the regiment for picket duty, in heavy marching order and two days' rations. After considerable delay in making up the details from the different regiments, they marched over miserable roads and two or three streams about three miles from camp, and about 3 P.M. were in the position assigned them in the rear of the army. The prospect at first was gloomy. The fields and trees were covered with snow, and not a green thing was to be seen; but they were agreeably surprised when they reached their position. A Corporal and six men were assigned to each post, where they found generous fires in front of rude shelters made of rails and boughs of trees, built by the 4th Michigan boys, whom they relieved, and all they had to do was to take their place and keep the fires going. The reserve was posted further to the rear in a hollow of the pine woods, and made themselves comfortable. A man was posted from each squad of six men further to the front in the woods, for two hours at a time. Of course, it was a severe task to stand quietly on duty in the snow, peering around on the watch. But on the other hand, it was a pleasure for the solitary sentinel to occasionally cast a glance to the rear at the gleaming of the picket fires in the woods, and to enjoy in anticipation the comfort that was in store for his chilled body when he should be relieved from his vigil. The weather was very cold, and water froze in the canteens a few feet from the fires. The blankets and overcoats were frozen stiff from previous dampness. Sunday, the 7th, and the succeeding day continued clear and cold, and the snow was still on the ground. The picket was relieved on the evening of the 8th.

Major Winslow was read off on evening parade as Colonel of the Fifth, and Ensign Winslow, his brother, as First Lieutenant; John S. Raymond was promoted to a Captaincy,

On the March to Fredericksburg.

and assigned to Company G; A. S. Chase to Captain of Company D; Sergeant Kitson to Ensign of Company C; Sergeant T. E. Fish to Ensign, and Commissary E. M. Earle, appointed Quartermaster, *vice* A. L. Thomas, promoted to Brigade Quartermaster.

These were the preliminaries and the preparation for the impending struggle, which we were in ardent hope would see the duration of war cease, and that the Union with its benedictions of peace would once more be restored. But our hopes as to the issue of the coming conflict were to be dashed to the ground, and it was destined to form a dark event in the history of the Union cause.

CHAPTER XIV.

BATTLE OF FREDERICKSBURG.

IN SIGHT OF FREDERICKSBURG—THE PONTOON—THE BURNING CITY—THE POSITION—ACROSS THE RIVER—MARYE'S HILL—A DESCRIPTION BY THE PHILADELPHIA *Times*—THE ATTACK—THE ENEMY'S BATTERIES—THE SLAUGHTER PATH—FRENCH'S DIVISION—HOOKER'S CHARGE—HOWARD AT THE FRONT—HUMPHREY'S DIVISION—SYKES' DIVISION—THE DEAD AND WOUNDED—WARREN'S BRIGADE—THE BRIGADE OF DEATH—THE COMPTE DE PARIS—THE FIFTH IN A GARDEN—OUR REGULARS SEVERELY PLACED—THE GLOOM PALL—FORLORN HOPE—STRATEGY—INTRENCHMENTS AT NIGHT—COVERING THE RETREAT—THE LAST MAN CROSSED—THE PONTOON LIFTED—INCIDENTS—HENRY HOUSE—GENERAL SYKES' GENERAL ORDER.

AT half-past 2 o'clock on the morning of Thursday, the 11th day of December, 1862, the regiment was aroused from its slumbers, by the sound of the bugle ringing out the reveille on the clear, cold air. The men immediately turned out and formed in line for roll call. After answering to their names, they commenced their slight preparations for the march. They formed in line and at about six o'clock took the road, already blocked up, as far as the eye could scan, with moving troops, artillery, and ambulances. The sound of a heavy gun in the distance announced that the fiat for battle had gone forth, which, ere it closed, was to send weeping and mourning into many a happy Northern home, and throw a mantle of gloom over every patriot heart throughout the land. Soon other guns sent forth their deep-toned notes, and the roar of artillery became incessant. After many halts, and a march of about three miles, the division was turned into a wood to await further orders. They were finally marched from the wood to a position behind some earthworks on high ground, near the banks of the Rappahannock, from which they could distinctly see the ill-fated

Battle of Fredericksburg.

city of Fredericksburg, lying about two miles to their left, on the other side of the river, and along on their side of the river, and stretching far off in the distance, huge balls of smoke arose from the guns which were playing on the opposite bank.

The men of the 50th New York Regiment, Engineer Corps, were engaged all day in trying to lay the pontoon bridge across the river, but were prevented by the enemy's riflemen, who were posted in the houses along the streets adjacent to the river. This compelled the General commanding to order the guns to be turned upon the city and shell the place. Soon thirty-five batteries, numbering one hundred and seventy-nine guns, were hurling their shell into the city; they continued the bombardment for an hour, each piece discharging about fifty shots; the reverberations of the guns were like long rolls of thunder, and soon the high banks of the river were enveloped in smoke. The city was set on fire by the shell in several places, and continued to burn all day and through the succeeding night. It was a splendid spectacle in the darkness, as the flames burst forth from the burning houses. On Friday, the 12th, detachments of the 7th Michigan, followed by the 19th and 20th Massachusetts, about four hundred men in all, dashed across the river in pontoon boats and routed the enemy's riflemen, lying behind the brick walls of the ruined houses along the river front, but they suffered some loss in their heroic enterprise.

The engineers were now able to lay their bridges without molestation. The enemy's works on the heights to the rear of the city could be plainly seen, as they were built on steep hills ninety and one hundred feet in height; concerning which, wrote the London *Times* correspondent after the battle: "This crest of hills constitutes one of the strongest positions in the world—impregnable to any attack in the front." The Confederates scarcely deigned to reply to the fire of the batteries, and it looked ominous; it seemed as if they were saving their ammunition and biding their time, being sure of their prey when the troops crossed over into the city.

On Saturday, the 13th, by two o'clock in the afternoon, the troops were all across the river, with the exception of Sykes' division, which was held as a reserve, being composed of two brigades of regulars and Warren's brigade, consisting at that time of the Fifth, 140th, and 146th New York, the Fifth being regarded the same in point of steadiness and discipline as the regulars. The two other regiments had not yet been under fire, having been recently recruited.

Since noon the rattle of musketry intermingled with the roar of artillery had been incessant, and told the story of the fierce conflict raging.

We will now halt for a moment and see what is going on in front of Marye's Hill, through the eyes of one who must have been present, or he could not have described the scene so faithfully or so well.

The following was published in the New York *Sunday Sun* of August 5, 1877, credited to the Philadelphia *Times*, and its perusal will bring home to the thoughts of all those who were present on that bloody field, the truthfulness of the scenes described :

"Marye's Hill was the focus of the strife. It rises in the rear of Fredericksburg, a stone's throw beyond the canal which runs along the western border of the city. The ascent is not very abrupt. A brick house stands on the hillside, whence you may overlook Fredericksburg and all the circumjacent country. The Orange plank-road ascends the hill on the right-hand side of the house, the telegraph road on the left. Above Marye's Hill is an elevated plateau which commands it. The hill is part of a long, bold ridge on which the declivity leans, stretching from Falmouth to Massoponax Creek, six miles. Its summit was shaggy and rough with the earthworks of the Confederates, and was crowned by their artillery. The stone wall on Marye's Height was their 'coign of vantage,' held by the brigades of Cobb and Kershaw, of McLaw's division. On the semicircular crest above, and stretching far on either hand, was Longstreet's corps, forming the left of the Confederate line. His advance position was the stone wall and rifle trenches along the telegraph road above the house. The guns of the enemy commanded and swept the streets which led out to the heights. Sometimes you might see a regiment marching down those streets in single file, keeping close to the houses, one file on the right-hand side, another on the left.

"Between a canal and the foot of the ridge was a level plat of flat, even ground, a few hundred yards in width. This restricted space afforded what opportunity there was to form in order of battle. A division massed on this narrow plain was a target for Lee's artillery, which cut fearful swaths in the dense and compact ranks.

"Below and to the right were fences which impeded the advance of the charging lines. Whatever division was assigned the task of carrying Marye's Hill, debouched from the town, crossed the canal, traversed the narrow level and formed under cover of a sharp rise of ground at the foot of the heights.

" At the word, suddenly ascending this bank, they pressed forward up the hill for the stone wall and the crest beyond, *into the jaws of death*.

"From noon to dark Burnside continued to hurl one division after another against that volcano-like eminence, belching forth fire and smoke and iron hail. French's division was the first to rush to the assault. When it emerged from cover and burst out on the open, in full view of the enemy, it was greeted with a frightful fiery reception from all his batteries on the circling summit.

"The ridge concentrated upon it the convergent fire of all its enginery of war. You might see at a mile the lanes made by the cannon balls in the ranks. You might see a bursting shell throw up into the air a cloud of earth and dust, mingled with the limbs of men. The batteries in front of the devoted division thundered against it. To the right, to the left, cannon were answering to each other in a tremendous deafening battle chorus, the burden of which was:

"'Welcome to these madmen about to die.'

"The advancing column was a focus, the point of concentration of an arc—almost a semicircle—of destruction. It was a center of attraction of all deadly missiles. At that moment that single division was going up alone in battle against the Southern Confederacy, and was being pounded to pieces. It continued to go up, nevertheless, toward the stone wall, toward the crest above. With lips more firmly pressed together, the men closed up their ranks and pushed forward. The storm of battle increased its fury upon them; the crash of musketry mingled with the roar of ordnance from the peaks. The stone wall and the rifle-pits added their terrible treble to the deep base of the bellowing ridge. The rapid discharge of small arms poured a continuous rain of bullets in their faces; they fell down by tens, by scores, by hundreds.

"When they had gained a large part of the distance, the storm developed into a hurricane of ruin. The division was blown back as if by a breath of hell's door suddenly opened, shattered, disordered, pell-mell, down the declivities, amid the shouts and yells of the enemy, which made the horrid din demoniac. Until then the division seemed to be contending with the wrath of brute and material forces bent on its annihilation.

"This shout recalled the human agency in all the turbulence and fury of the scene. The division of French fell back; that is to say, one-half of it. It suffered a loss of near half its numbers. Hancock immediately charged with five thousand men, veteran regiments, led by tried commanders. They saw what had happened; they knew what would befall them. They advanced up the hill; the bravest were found dead within twenty-five paces of the stone wall; it was slaughter, havoc, carnage. In fifteen minutes they were thrown back with a loss of two thousand—unprecedented severity of loss. Hancock and French, repulsed from the stone wall, would not quit the hill altogether. Their divisions, lying down on the earth, literally clung to the ground they had won. These valiant men, who could not go forward, would not go back. All the while the batteries on the heights raged and stormed at them.

"Howard's division came to their aid. Two divisions of the 9th corps to their left attacked repeatedly in their support.

"It was then that Burnside rode from the Phillips House, on

the other side of the Rappahannock, and standing on the bluff at the river, staring at those formidable heights, exclaimed: 'That crest must be carried to-night.' Hooker remonstrated, begged, obeyed. In the army to hear is to obey. He prepared to charge with Humphrey's division; he brought up every available battery in the city. 'I proceeded,' he said, 'against their barriers as I would against a fortification, and endeavored to breach a hole sufficiently large for a forlorn hope to enter.' He continued the cannonading on the selected spot until sunset. He made no impression upon their works, 'no more than you could make upon the side of a mountain of rock.'

"Humphrey's division formed under shelter of the rise, in column, for assault. They were directed to make the attack with empty muskets; there was no time then to load and fire. The officers were put in front to lead. At the command they moved forward with great impetuosity; they charged at a run, hurrahing. The foremost of them advanced to within fifteen or twenty yards of the stone wall. Hooker afterward said: 'No campaign in the world ever saw a more gallant advance than Humphrey's men made there. But they were to do a work that no men could do.' In a moment they were hurled back with enormous loss. It was now just dark; the attack was suspended. Three times from noon to dark the cannon on the crest, the musketry at the stone wall, had prostrated division after division on Marye's Hill. And now the sun had set; twilight had stolen out of the west and spread her veil of dusk; the town, the flat, the hill, the ridge, lay under the 'circling canopy of night's extended shade.' Darkness and gloom had settled down upon the Phillips House, over on the Stafford Heights, where Burnside would after a while hold his council of war."

About three o'clock Sykes' division was ordered to move toward the bridge leading direct to the city; it being one of five built of pontoons by the engineers, the other four lying further to the left, three of which led to the open country. As they approached in its vicinity, they met the enemy's shell, who was aiming his guns so as to reach the slope of the hill running down to the foot of the bridge and the plains beyond. They saw numerous sights that reminded them of what was going on in the front; pale-looking men limping to the rear, and long lines of ambulances carrying their burdens of suffering humanity, and here and there a surgeon and assistants, with implements in hand performing their duties, with the wounded and the dying lying about them; terrified-looking stragglers skulking behind trees, where they thought themselves safe from flying shell.

Before crossing the river they met General Burnside, who appeared to look anxious and not well satisfied as to how the battle was progressing. Who could realize the fearful responsibility then resting on him alone? His last troops were going into action; the desperate assaults against an impregnable position had been disastrous failures, and this was the decisive moment. The division crossed the bridge and hurried through a business street, where whole blocks of stores had been destroyed by fire; desolation and destruction were visible on all sides. They turned into Caroline Street, which was lined by the residences of the wealthy, and as they passed up this street on a run, they saw many corpses lying about in the street and on the sidewalks, and met wounded men coming from the battle, reeling like drunken men. Once in a while one of them would fall from weakness occasioned by loss of blood. Two soldiers came out of a drug-store with ashy pale countenances, having been poisoned in their search for whisky.

The din of battle was now terrifying, as nearly all of General Hooker's command, the 3d and 5th corps, were engaged, and for two miles along the front it was one sheet of flame, but the result was *uncertain*. On the outside of the city was a plain about one-third of a mile in width, on the other side of which were the enemy, covered by a stone wall, which was banked with earth, rifle-pits, and batteries on the heights, with another line of earthworks on high ground to the rear of *them;* all these must be overcome at that point, to insure a victory. The division continued up the street on a double-quick, the regulars being in advance; they came to the end of it, which debouched on the outskirts of the city, on the border of the open plain before mentioned, and the "regulars" went into the battle now raging fiercely, relieving Humphrey's division. The Confederates knew who were facing them at the first volley. Warren's brigade formed a second line in their rear. It was now dark, and the heavy firing ceased; occasional volleys from companies or battalions lit up the darkness for a moment, but it soon dropped off to a heavy picket firing.

The assaulting troops, as we have seen, had succeeded in getting near the stone wall, but they were met with such a withering fire from the Confederates, who were repeatedly reinforced, and from the nature of their defenses could mass their men four files deep and fire, that our forces were so decimated they could advance no further, and were obliged to fall back.

The position of the Fifth happened to be in a garden, the soil being wet and muddy, from the heat of the sun during the day, which had melted the frost in the ground. But there they were compelled to wait, being the next in turn for the trying ordeal. The men pulled down a picket fence and portioned what there was of it among themselves to lie on, and keep part of their bodies from the damp, cold earth, each man's share consisting of a space about two and one-half feet long by one and a half broad, and curled themselves up to keep warm. The bullets whizzed over their heads from the firing just in front of them, and some of them were hit; occasionally the shrieking of shell was heard, a little over their heads. Few there were that closed their eyes that long December night, which seemed as if it would never end. As they lay, they thought of the morrow—how many of them would live to come out of the conflict—of home—of eternity.

But worse than all were the cries of the wounded, lying helpless between the lines and on that bloody slope, without any one to help them. They could hear them cry, "Water! water! water! O God! help!" Some of them called out their names and regiment, and sometimes a chorus of shrieks and groans went up on the chill midnight air, telling of human agony beyond the power of endurance. But to quote again from the same writer:

"The dead would not remain unnoticed. The dying cried out in the darkness, and demanded succor of the world. Was there nothing in the universe to save? Tens of thousands within ear-shot, and no footstep of friend or foe drew near during all the hours. Sometimes they drew near and passed by, which was an aggravation of the agony. The subdued sound of wheels rolling slowly along, and ever and anon stopping; the murmur of voices and a cry of pain told of the ambulance on its mission. It went off in another direction. The cries were borne through the haze. Now a single lament; again voices intermingled and as if in chorus; from every direction, in front, behind, to right, to left, some near, some distant and faint. Some, doubtless, were faint and were not distant—the departing breath of one about to expire. They expressed every degree and shade of suffering, of pain, of agony; a sigh, a groan, a piteous appeal, a shriek, a succession of shrieks, a call of despair, a prayer to God, a demand for water, for the ambulance, a death-rattle, a horrid scream, a voice as of the body when the soul tore itself away and abandoned it to the enemy, to the night, and to dissolution. The voices were various. This the tongue of a German; that wail in the Celtic brogue of a poor Irishman. The accent of New England was distinguishable in the cry of that boy. From a different quarter came utterances in the dialect of a far-off Western State. The appeals of the Irish were the most pathetic. They put them into every form—denunciation, remonstrance, a pitiful prayer, a peremptory demand. The German was more patient, less demonstrative, withdrawing into himself. One man raised his body on his left arm, and extending his right arm upward, cried out to the heavens and fell back. Most of them lay moaning, with the fitful movement of unrest and pain.

"It was on the ground over which the successive charges had been made that there appeared to be a thin line of soldiers sleeping on the ground. They seemed to make a sort of row or rank; they were perfectly motionless; their sleep was profound. Not one of them awoke and got up. They were not relieved either. Had the fatigue of the day completely overpowered all of them, officers and privates alike? They were nearest the enemy, within call of him. They were the advance line of the Union army. Was it thus that they kept their watch, on which the safety of the whole army depended, pent up between the ridge and the river? The enemy might come within ten steps of them without being seen. The fog was a veil. No one knew what lay, or moved, or crept, a little distance off. Still they did not waken. If you looked closely at the face of any of them, in the mist and dimness, it was pallid, the eyes closed, the mouth open, the hair was disheveled; besides, the attitude was often painful. There were blood-marks also. These men were all dead."

Thus the night wore through. Toward morning a thick mist hung over the ground, which made the situation more gloomy, if possible, than ever. The men fully expected to face the Confederate hosts in battle array as soon as daylight should appear. Each man felt as if he was passing his last night on earth; but each brave heart had inwardly resolved to obey orders unflinchingly, and preserve the reputation of their regiment in whatever position it might be placed; and if it was the fortune of war that they were to die, they would meet their fate like men.

"In the meantime the troops that had been in the front were withdrawn into the streets of the town, and rested on their arms. Some sat on the curbstones, meditating, looking gloomily at the ground; others lay on the pavement, trying to forget the events of the day in sleep. There was little said; deep dejection burdened the spirits of all. The incidents of the battle were not rehearsed except now and then. Always when any one spoke, it was of a slain comrade—of his virtues or of the manner of his death; or of one missing, with many conjectures respecting him.

Some of them, it was said, had premonitions, and went into the battle not expecting to survive the day. Thus they lay or sat. The conversation was with bowed head, and in a low manner, ending in a sigh.

"It was December, and cold. There was no camp-fire. But no one mentioned the cold; it was not noticed. Steadily the wounded were carried by to the hospitals near the river. The hospitals were a harrowing sight; full, crowded, nevertheless patients were brought in constantly. Down-stairs, up-stairs, every room full. Surgeons, with their coats off and sleeves rolled up above their elbows, sawed off limbs or administered anæsthetics. They took off a leg or an arm in a twinkling, after brief consultation. It seemed to be, in case of doubt—off with his limb. But the sights and scenes in a field-hospital are not to be described."

The Compte de Paris says, in his "History of the Civil War in America" (pp. 596-7):

"This night of December 13th-14th was probably the most painful ever experienced by the Army of the Potomac during its whole existence; its losses amounted to 12,500 killed and wounded, and over 2,000 prisoners, sacrificed uselessly to carry out an idea; 6,300 lay killed or wounded on the slope of Marye's Hill, but there was not a soldier in the ranks who did not believe that their blood had been shed entirely in vain.

"The Confederates, secure in their Gibraltar, had only lost at this point 952 in killed and wounded, and in all parts of the field less than one-half of the Union losses."

At daylight the men were ordered to fall in; they had no sooner done so than the enemy opened on them from their rifle-pits. The bullets flew around them thick, and began to tell; one long line of flashes told where the Confederates were posted, for it was yet quite dark. The regiment was hurried off, and went up the same street they had come down the night before, and closed up *en masse* in a garden partially covered by a dwelling-house and fences, which somewhat screened them from observation; but they were still under easy rifle range. Some of the Fifth were wounded, and a piece of a shell broke the leg of a member of the 146th New York, after crushing the wheel of a caisson. Three men of the 140th New York were also wounded. The regiment had not been long in this spot before some of the wild spirits, whom nothing seemed to tame or overawe, strayed off through the fence toward the enemy, although the bullets were whistling about them. They soon returned with various articles of luxurious diet and clothing. It was a ludicrous profanation of the terrible drama to witness the grotesque appearance of some of the men. But this by-play soon came to an abrupt termination by the interference of the officers.

It was sad to reflect how desolate these happy and comfortable homes were made through the terrible consequences of a war brought about by the treasonable acts of a few ambitious leaders, the majority of whom did not care to hazard their own lives on the battle-field, but were willing that their deluded followers should stand as a bulwark between them and physical danger and hardships. It was surely not strange that it was so difficult to conquer such people, when they were willing to sacrifice everything, the houses and homes in which they were born and brought up, and perchance their parents before them, rather than surrender them willingly and ask protection of a forgiving invader, who had been forced to lay aside the arts of peace, to take up arms to preserve the unity of the States, under one confederation and one flag.

In the afternoon the regiment was marched down the street a short distance toward the river, and turned into a yard in the rear of a large brick mansion, one of several others, with piazzas, gas-fixtures, and water-pipes, the supply to the latter having been cut off by the Confederates. The kitchen, a small brick house, was connected with the main building by a covered way. Behind the kitchen were rows of neat huts for the colored servants. Everything gave evidence of the wealth and rank of the owners. A bell hung out at the rear of the house to waken the "people" in the morning. The officers occupied one of these mansions as their headquarters, from which was heard occasionally some favorite air played on the piano. The men made a fire in the large kitchen stove, and made some unleavened cakes, prepared from flour and water, a barrel of the former having been unearthed. This proved to be a God-send, for the bacon distributed to them the succeeding night, either by accident or design was utterly unfit for consumption. The regiment stayed in this position two days and a night, all of the time under fire of the guns of the enemy, and under great suspense, not knowing at what moment they would receive orders to advance to the front, to battle, and they knew well that such an order meant practical, if not total annihilation.

The regulars were obliged to hold the position assigned to them on the night of the 13th, which was discovered in the morning to be a slight hollow. It was a doleful place. They were obliged to hug the ground, lying on their backs or stomachs; they could not move; when one turned, he was sure to be hit in the shoulder, and the wounded were obliged to lie and suffer. Many who attempted, by permission, to run to the rear, were immediately pierced by minie balls and fell lifeless. In this desperate position they laid all day until it was dark, in the same place they occupied all of the previous weary night, amid the scenes already described. They were completely at the mercy of the Confederates, who were apparently secure in their earthworks. They were out of water, and suffered terribly. At night, when they were able to creep away under the veil of darkness, they left 97 of their number stark and stiff. This is the position that Warren's brigade escaped being placed in, by a mere chance, as the order of march was right in front; Warren's brigade held the left of the division.

Battle of Fredericksburg. 351

On the third day, Monday, the 15th, the condition of affairs looked ominous of evil, as the enemy were advancing their rifle-pits nearer the city every night, and the troops were being hemmed within its limits; the bullets were continually flying up the streets of the city; there was no commanding position for the artillery, and in "the front" death stared them in the face, and the wide Rappahannock flowed in their rear between them and a place of refuge. If the enemy, regardless of the many women and children who remained in the city hiding in the cellars of the houses, should shell the place from the fortified heights commanding it, on which were posted two hundred pieces of artillery, a panic would probably ensue among the troops massed in the city, which included the greater part of Burnside's forces, and the army would be lost, and possibly the cause for which they were fighting.

It is now a matter of history that Stonewall Jackson proposed to General Lee to bombard the city at night, and then in the midst of the confusion that would naturally ensue, to steal down and attack with he bayonet.

General Franklin gained a mile on the left the first day, but was then checked, and could not advance any further. It was rumored that General Burnside proposed to storm the works *en masse* with the 9th army corps in advance, but was overruled by the other officers. It might possibly have resulted in a temporary success at a terrible sacrifice of men, but what would follow? A great many charges had been made the first day, but to no purpose except to sacrifice men. The dead strewed the field; a whole brigade of them in number could be seen lying on the slopes of the hills; it was sure destruction to face the Confederate batteries, and many of the wounded were left to die a lingering death between the lines, the enemy shooting any who ventured to bring them off. No truce was asked or granted.

At this time every man's heart had failed; officers and

men felt alike; they tried to laugh and joke and cheer each other as usual, but it was plain to be seen that they all felt the serious position in which they were placed, and the men looked at one another with compressed lips, but spoke not; the language of the soul was impressive; in their countenances was written "forlorn hope."

It was apparent to the most simple that General Burnside's army had been drawn into a death-trap; they all knew and felt it, and wondered why they were idly kept there without an effort being made to escape or to change the mode of attack. The suspense was worse than death itself; it was lingering torture; and all felt as a man can be imagined to feel the night before his execution. The army had been driven to the sacrifice to satisfy the demands of the Northern press to "do something." It had been robbed of its experienced commanders by political advisers and cliques in Washington, and here was the natural result—disastrous failure. The General should not be blamed, as the command of the army was forced upon him, and he did the best he could with it under the circumstances. That which had been looked upon by the people of the North as so much gasconade in the Richmond papers, was being fulfilled to the letter. This was the sentiment of the soldiers at the time, and it has not been changed by any subsequent developments.

On the night of the 15th the regiment fell in very mysteriously, and was marched toward the front, down a street leading by the outskirts of the city. After some delay they were finally marched into a large grave-yard, with orders to keep very quiet; all the orders were given in an undertone. Here the men laid down for two hours among the graves of the departed; pieces of pork and hard-tack were lying about on the grave-stones, and all those who were hungry had a chance to satisfy their appetites. But no one was very hungry at that time; in fact, quail on toast would have been no inducement whatever, everything looked so mysterious. One of the men came to the conclusion that they were on a hunt for the bones of Washington. It was an aristocratic-looking grave-yard.

They were then marched into another grave-yard nearer *the front*. The men looked at one another and then at the Colonel, tapped their foreheads and nodded at each other knowingly. Finally they were marched directly to the front —all the orders being given in a whisper—and halted near the borders of the canal. A part of the Fifth and the 146th Regiments, aided by the regulars, dug rifle-pits and built barricades across the streets of the city, so that the enemy's artillery could not follow in their final retreat in the morning. They were very near the enemy, worked with a will, and succeeded in throwing up a line of intrenchments along their whole front, which it appears completely deceived the enemy in the morning as to the plans of General Burnside and the movements of the army during the night. General Warren, who had command at the front, worked indefatigably all night, both mentally and physically, as he always did, and it seemed as if he was at all points at the same time; everything, even the slightest details, came under his eye and supervision. Company A, under the command of Captain Whitney, was sent across the canal as an outer picket, and crept out to an old tannery very close to the enemy, who were also digging. They could hear them talking, and some of their pickets were on the other side of the tannery; one of them was heard to say he believed the " Yanks" were near. The wind was blowing quite a gale from the south and west, and therefore the enemy could be heard, but our men were not; and as the night was dark and cloudy, both sides were shielded from observation.

Company I, under the command of Captain Montgomery, was also sent out to the front, further to the left, near the enemy; they dug "fox holes" to cover themselves. The positions of these two companies were very dangerous; they talked in whispers when it was necessary to speak, and their eyes and ears were strained to the closest attention, so that not a footfall should escape detection. They were so close to the enemy that they could hear their conversation. Their orders were not to be taken prisoners or surprised on any account. As soon as the work on the trenches was finished they were occupied by eight companies of the Fifth. An earthwork to cover a battery of artillery was thrown up in the rear of them. Toward morning the men were ordered, in an undertone, by companies, to sling knapsacks; an occasional twang was heard, accompanied by a flash, which was followed by the sound of a rifle-ball hissing near, which told the men that the Confederates were wide awake. The battery in the rear moved off with muffled wheels, and it now flashed upon the minds of the knowing ones for the first time that the army *was retreating across the river*, and that the regiment were to cover the retreat and would be the last to leave.

At this time it commenced to rain in torrents, which filled the rifle-pits; and the men stood in mud and icy water up to their knees; the water ran down their backs and chilled them through and made their teeth chatter. The gray light of the morning was straggling upon them, and before long they would be discovered, and the fire of the enemy's heavy guns and riflemen would be concentrated upon them. Officers and men would have given all they possessed to be out of that position, but there was no escape until further orders, and they knew it. They would have fought to the last man. In times of danger the brief and stern orders were the more impressive.

Their salvation depended on keeping up a bold and steady front. It was much more trying than an active engagement with the enemy. They knew that all the army had fallen back to the other side of the river, and that their small regiment stood alone out on the plain, facing, at close quarters, the whole Confederate host, with the batteries on the heights frowning down upon them, and that if they were attacked they could expect no succor excepting from the 1st brigade of regulars under Colonel Buchanan, who were drawn up near the pontoon bridge, when all would have been obliged to sell their lives as dearly as possible. It was fully expected, from the very nature of the undertaking, that a number were to be sacrificed; and who of the number was it to be?

About an hour and a half before daylight, the companies on picket crept back and joined the regiment. They were moments of terrible suspense. They could now see the Confederate works looming up on the heights in the distance, and a company at a time were ordered to crawl away to the cover of a large store-house, about two hundred yards nearer the city. At this point, almost all the regiment were soon assembled; the enemy's bullets were whizzing about, one of which struck the brick wall, grazing the head of Colonel Winslow. Two companies, A and E, were left behind in the pits to keep up a fire as if they were fully occupied. It was now light, and the enemy were firing at the men in the pits, who returned the fire.

The regiment was drawn up in line behind the wall of a grave-yard, and across the end of a street that led into the city. They were joined by the few men left behind in the pits, at a few minutes past seven A.M. The two other regiments of the brigade had been sent across the river two hours before, and the old 5th New York Volunteers was the last to leave the front. A few battalions of regulars had been drawn up on the edge of the city, further to the right, to make a show of force to the enemy; but they had been ordered to retire and rejoin the 1st brigade near the river.

The officers and men were becoming anxious for General Warren, who was sitting on his horse, perfectly cool and collected, on the right of the regiment to give the signal to move off. The Confederate officers could be plainly seen riding from one fort to another, as if making observations as to the situation of affairs. Lines of troops were beginning to form, and their skirmishers were advancing. The suspense was now very great; but still Warren sat on his horse and gave no sign. At length Adjutant Marvin approached, and in a moment the welcome order was heard—" By the right flank; forward! march!"

Never was order obeyed with more alacrity. Though the danger was not yet over, the spell was broken; the regiment was moving, and the men would soon know their fate, and were ready to meet it. They expected that the enemy would be upon them like wolves after their prey, and they would be obliged to fight their way through the city and across the river, and that most of them would probably be sacrificed.

They were marching briskly along, being saluted by the gibes of some women, from a house, when they met Major Cutting, of General Sykes' staff, who had been sent to see why the regiment did not make its appearance at the bridge. As soon as they crossed over a little hill in the street, which hid them from the sight of the enemy, the order was given, "Double-quick." They passed by the 1st brigade, drawn up in a street, who immediately followed on in the rear, and the head of the column soon reached the only pontoon bridge remaining, which was covered with earth and straw to prevent the tramping of the retreating troops, during the previous night, being heard by the enemy, and crossed over it as quickly as possible. General Sykes sat on his horse at the approach to the bridge, looking as calm as if on parade. The engineer corps were stationed at intervals on the pontoons, ready to cast them loose, which was done as the last man stepped on the other side of the river. This was about half-past seven o'clock on the morn-

Battle of Fredericksburg. 357

ing of Tuesday, the 16th. The enemy had now opened with their artillery, and the shell began to fly; but the Confederates had been outwitted. The men shook hands with a feeling of relief and exhilaration at their safe escape.

Under the circumstances, the retreat, in all its details, was one of the most adroit and successful military events that had occurred during the war, and the credit is due to General Warren. Officers and men were very well satisfied that they had been delivered from the terrible ordeal that threatened the remainder of the army.

The regiment went into bivouac near Falmouth, on the same ground that they had occupied seven days before; and here was this much-abused army again at rest, hav'ng gained nothing and lost about eleven thousand men in killed, wounded, and missing. While, on the other hand, the Confederates, in a late report, stated their loss to be four hundred and fifty-eight in killed, and three thousand seven hundred and forty-three wounded; but among the killed were recorded the names of Generals Howell Cobb and Maxcy Gregg, the latter our opponent at Gaines' Mill.

The last act of the drama remained to be performed—to bury the dead. A detachment was sent over the river for this purpose under a flag of truce. On the battle-field was an immense building, used to store ice; in this structure were placed nine hundred bodies found in the vicinity of the stone wall and sunken road. Over them were packed tons of ice, and they were left to dissolution in one immense tomb. They had died together, and were not separated in their last sleep. The dead found in the other parts of the field were buried where they fell. Only two incidents of the vast number of interesting facts of this remarkable siege are here mentioned.

Charles H. Wilson, a member of Company G, was very badly wounded; a ball went through his mouth, dashing out all his double teeth, and disfiguring him for life; he was conveyed to a hospital, and given up as a hopeless case by the surgeon. He heard him give directions to one of the attendants to lay him aside for dissection, but strange to say he recovered. He was only nineteen years of age; a younger brother enlisted with him in the regiment, and yet another was in the service and badly wounded in the knee at Antietam.

The two wounded brothers, when they were able to be moved, were taken to the home of a widowed mother and kindly cared for. These young patriots had been her main support, and left good situations to serve their country.

A soldier of the regular infantry, whose third term of service (five years each) was about to expire, had permission, as is customary, to remain in the rear with the wagon-train; but when he saw his brigade moving toward the scene of the battle he dashed off and joined them, making the remark to his comrades that he would have another "shy" at them, meaning the enemy. It was his last battle; this true soldier was honorably mustered out of the service by death on the battle-field.

On Wednesday, the 17th, the regiment marched three miles, and encamped near Henry House, on our old camp-ground. The 18th was a clear, cold day, but the weather moderated, and on the 19th was warm and pleasant. In the morning we had a brigade inspection; in the afternoon a drill. At evening parade the general order of our commander was read off. The precise facts as to the covering of the retreat at Fredericksburg have never been published within the knowledge of the writer. The credit was given by one correspondent to Butterfield's brigade, and several regiments that left the city an hour or more before the movement of the regulars and the Fifth have claimed the honor. The official order of General Sykes should remove all doubt on this point. It was as follows:

Battle of Fredericksburg. 359

HEADQUARTERS 2D DIVISION, 5TH ARMY CORPS,
CAMP NEAR HENRY HOUSE, VA.,
December 18, 1862.

GENERAL ORDER, NO. 49.

The General commanding desires to express his thanks to the officers and enlisted men of the division for the cheerfulness, endurance, and valor they have exhibited in the recent operations around the city of Fredericksburg. Though not called on to share in the direct assault upon the enemy's intrenchments, the position assigned them was one of equal peril, and was held under circumstances that tax the best qualities of a soldier—patience, discipline, and courage. The 1st brigade and the 5*th* *New York Volunteers* (3d brigade) had the honor to cover the withdrawal of the troops from Fredericksburg. This manœuvre was accomplished without loss or disaster of any kind, and with skill, celerity, and boldness. The General trusts and believes that the soldiers he has the honor to command will be characterized always by the same devotion to duty, and the same earnest desire to preserve the reputation they have so justly acquired while belonging to the Army of the Potomac.

By command of

Dec. 18, 1862.   BRIGADIER-GENERAL SYKES.
Official: GEORGE RYAN,
A. S. MARVIN, JR.,   *A. A. G.*
A. A. General.

The following magnanimous avowal and noble tribute to the army of the living and the dead is expressed in General Burnside's report:

"To the brave officers and soldiers who accomplished the feat of thus recrossing the river in the face of the enemy, I owe everything.

"For the failure in the attack I am responsible, as the extreme gallantry, courage, and endurance shown by them was never exceeded, and would have carried the points had it been possible.

"To the families and friends of the dead I can only offer my heartfelt sympathies, but for the wounded I can offer my earnest prayers for their comfortable and final recovery."

Thursday, December 25th, Christmas Day, divine service was held in the open air. Six days' rations were distributed, and the men were treated to a dinner of boiled beans and pork; an allowance of whisky was distributed. A brigade provost was established, to have their quarters near General Warren's tent. Lieutenant Meldrum, of the Fifth, was assigned to the command.

On Monday, the 29th, the brigade was formed in line of battle at 10 A.M., and laid under arms for an hour. We heard heavy firing at the front, but the command were not wanted. It was ascertained that Stuart's cavalry had made a dash on our pickets.

CHAPTER XV.

BATTLE OF CHANCELLORSVILLE—OUR LAST STRUGGLE.

THE NEW YEAR—THE SITUATION—DEATH OF CAPTAIN CARTWRIGHT—MORTALITY—DESERTIONS—THE DISLOYAL PRESS OF THE NORTH—THE SOLDIER'S SENTIMENT—AN ARMY OF WATER-CARRIERS—THE MUD MARCH—RESIGNATION OF GENERAL BURNSIDE—GENERAL HOOKER IN COMMAND—PICKETED IN ICE—A DEATH IN HOSPITAL—A SUICIDE—GENERAL WARREN PROMOTED—A DESERTED MANSION—PROVOST GUARD—DEATH OF NICHOLAS HOYT—BETTER SUPPLIES—A SQUARE MEAL—CAVALRY SKIRMISH—ST. PATRICK'S DAY IN THE NINTH MASSACHUSETTS—CAVALRY FIGHT—A SPY—A SMOKY CHIMNEY—A CRIPPLED SHOEMAKER ON JEFF DAVIS—ANNIHILATING THE MEN OF THE SOUTH—A REVIEW—HYBERNATING UNDER GROUND—EASTER—REVIEW BY PRESIDENT LINCOLN—THE TWO YEARS' MEN—GROWLING—REVIEW BY GENS. TOGLIARDI AND MEADE—AN EXPLODED SHELL—THE TIME FIXED—KELLY'S FORD—ELY'S FORD—APPROACHING FREDERICKSBURG—BATTLE OF CHANCELLORSVILLE—EIGHTH PENNSYLVANIA CAVALRY—THE ENEMY REPULSED—JACKSON'S ATTACK ON HOWARD—SICKLES—SLOCUM—FRENCH—CHANCELLOR HOUSE BURNT—WOODS ON FIRE—THE TWO YEARS' MEN RELIEVED—PARTING WITH OLD COMRADES—AQUIA CREEK—HOSPITALITY OF THE 21ST NEW YORK—WASHINGTON—BALTIMORE—PHILADELPHIA—JERSEY CITY—NEW YORK—OUR RECEPTION—NEW YORK *Times*—THE FOURTH REGIMENT—MUSTERED OUT—IN THE BATTLE OF LIFE.

THE year 1862 passed into the shadows, "with the years beyond the flood," with a decimated army waiting for reorganization, and its thousands of invalided and wounded men lying in hospitals, some with shattered constitutions, some mangled or dismembered, some to recover and rejoin their comrades, and many to lie down in a soil rendered "sacred" by the blood of tens of thousands of freemen, poured out in a contest for power by the advocates of the demoniac system of American Slavery. The masses of the Southern people, the industrial and the non-slaveholding whites, who were trained in an atmosphere of political doctrines which for a generation had been antagonistic to the Union, and whose means of information were limited to the local press or the local partisan, were in heart and sympathy attached to the Union. But their feelings had become bitterly aroused against the North by the falsehoods of their leaders, who, with a sublime hypocrisy, professed to be the only true exponents of democratic ideas, governed and owned in fee simple "the Democratic Party," and led the great body of the working classes both North and South in their political opinions.

The commercial and political value of slavery, as a factor in the public and private interests of these men, the " aristocracy" of the slave-whip, and the oligarchs of social and political circles, made these classes supreme, and the majority had no alternative but to submit. Majorities were tolerable to these imperialists so long as they were convertible to their ends. But when majorities differed with them, they scorned " Democracy," revolted against the Union, whose rule they had so long boasted, and sought to crush Union and genuine Democracy in blood.

One of their severest blows had just been struck at the power of free institutions to maintain themselves by the devotion of the volunteers on behalf of freedom, and we were just crossing the bloody ford of another year of war; our pontoon was lifted behind us, and although scarred and mutilated, before us was the future, and we knew that in the blaze of the nineteenth century, our country would not give the lie to the hopes of the world in its aspirations after liberty. It was a contest for the coming centuries and for generations unborn. Let the armor be girded on anew.

The sentiment which, amid all the disasters, underlaid the loyal heart, was well expressed by one of our patriotic writers a short time before in the closing stanza of a poem entitled "The Republic": *

---

* William Oland Bourne, Editor of *The Soldier's Friend*.

Camp near Henry House.

"O toiling millions on the Old World's shore!
  Look up, rejoicing, for she is not dead!
The soul is living as it lived before,
  When sainted heroes spurned the tyrant's tread;
The strife is earnest and the day wears on,
  And ages tremble with the mighty blow—
Beyond the conflict is a glorious dawn,
  A rapturous birth of Freedom out of woe!
·The clouds may gather, and the storm be long,
  And lightnings leap across the darkened sky,
But Freedom lives to triumph over wrong!
  It still will live, for Truth can never die!"

Thus opened the year 1863 with the Army of the Potomac. There was nothing but the calendar to mark the first day of the new year. It was calm, clear, and warm, but the day was dull, uninteresting, and without events. No cooked dinner was provided, and the recruits had a drill as an appetizer for supper.. A day or two before a few of the men had received boxes from their friends at home with some special remembrances of the day, but the loyal thousands who had come out of one of the greatest ordeals of death and slaughter known to history, in defense of their country, submissively took their rations and their rest, and having tendered their friends at home the gift of their lives, wished them all "a Happy New Year," in the hope that the return would find the wish realized in the enjoyment of peace.

Intelligence had just been received of the death of Captain Cartwright, who died in Washington from his wounds received at Gaines' Mill. He had been previously severely wounded at Big Bethel, when serving as a private, but recovered and returned to duty, until he received the double wound from which he died. He was a young man of great promise, and a member of the Methodist Episcopal Church. At the breaking out of the war, he was in the employ of Messrs. Lanman & Kemp, the well-known drug-house, by whom he was highly esteemed. He enlisted as a private, but rose by good conduct and attention to his duties through the different grades to a Captaincy. When he was an Orderly Sergeant, and mustered his company, which at the time numbered over ninety members, he called the roll from memory, taking no notes whatever at the time, but was never known to omit a name or fail to report an absentee. Had he lived he would no doubt have attained an honorable distinction. His father was Adjutant in the Irish Brigade, and several of his immediate kin were officers in different regiments; one was a Colonel of a Massachusetts regiment; another was a member of the Fifth, and was honorably discharged on account of wounds. Captain Thomas W. Cartwright, Jr., of Company G, died for his country's sake in his twenty-second year.

There was more or less mortality in some of the regiments; the 146th New York had a daily average of one hundred on the sick-list. They laid at the side of the Fifth, yet we had not lost one man by sickness in this camp, and but few were sent to the hospital. Captain McConnell, acting Major of the Fifth, resigned his commission on account of ill health, and retired to civil life.

The class of Northern journals known at the time by the political soubriquet of "Copperhead," and their sympathizers, were doing much to demoralize the army and encourage desertion. It was an important, but despicable, element in the political history of the time, and the loyal men at the front were compelled to feel the power of the malign influence thus exerted. The intolerance of the Southern leaders allowed no symptom of disloyalty to their cause to be manifested, and no word to be spoken in opposition, while in the North the most intense antagonism to the loyal cause and to the Union itself was continually outspoken, and went out to the country in millions of sheets of either daily or weekly issue. In one exceptional case the publisher of the most disloyal sheet north of the Ohio or Potomac achieved such fame and popularity that he transferred his chief publishing bureau to the city of New York. These agents of disloyalty were stinging the men who were fighting to protect their property and preserve the Union. They were despised by the soldiers in the army, and more than despised by the Confederates, who looked upon them with utter contempt. A soldier could respect a brave, open enemy; but men who, in the hour of peril, proved themselves so recreant as these, were worthy only of the scorn of all loyal men, and were unworthy of the protection they dishonored and defied.

On Sunday, the 4th, the regiment was inspected by the Division Inspector. The 8th, the 5th army corps was reviewed by General Burnside.

The late defeat had somewhat demoralized the new troops (the old ones were used to them), and there were many desertions. About the 15th of January a circular was issued from headquarters to the commandants of regiments, cautioning them to keep a strict watch on their commands, as the number of desertions had become alarming. General Hooker said that 10,000 had deserted since the battle of Fredericksburg. At the last review of the 5th corps there were probably not more than 12,000 in line, and about as many more in hospitals and in convalescent and paroled camps, or absent without leave.

On Tuesday, the 20th, in obedience to orders, we struck tents at 11 A.M., under threatening weather, with a chilly wind blowing from the east. At 3 P.M. we marched about two miles, and bivouacked in the woods. The road was so blocked with wagons, artillery, and troops, that it was impossible to proceed further. It commenced raining about 5 P.M.; and continued all night, to our great discomfort, for we were not only cold, but wet and dripping. In this condition the reveille roused us at 4 A.M. on Wednesday, the 21st, while the rain was still falling. Our blankets and clothing being soaked, the load on the backs of the men was very burdensome.

The exact amount of avoirdupois we never ascertained, by comparing the weight of a dry and a well-soaked outfit; but if the whole army shared the burdens as *we* felt them, we had the whole Confederacy on our backs in more than the military metaphor. At daylight we again took the road—if such it could be called, for it was a sea of mud, and impassable for wagons or artillery. After marching about five miles we encamped, at 2.30 P.M., on the right of the road, in a cedar wood, near the Rappahannock. The distance traveled was short, but the march was a trying one, and about one-half of the men were straggling behind. Only about two full companies of the 146th New York came to camp in time. During the night four of the three years' men deserted from the Fifth. In the One Hundred and Forty-sixth about thirty were missing. We had rain all the next day (22d), and the roads were in a worse condition than before. Large fires of logs were built, but the wind, which was strong, blew the smoke in all directions, nearly suffocating every one, and as only half a man could be dried at a time, the other side was wet through again during the operation. But the men bore their discomforts cheerfully, and were enlivened by ballads of the sea, sung by Jack Whigam, who had served an apprenticeship in the navy, and was at the bombardment of Vera Cruz; "Butch" and others also contributed their share to the entertainment. Our storm continued through the night, and all of the 23d, the army being imbedded in mud, which, by some means, seemed to cover every object, animate or inanimate, in the army. The artillery and wagons could not move a foot; boxes of hard-tack were, of necessity, carried for a mile or more, on aching shoulders, from the wagons to camp, each box weighing about fifty pounds. Only six crackers were allowed to each man, to last twenty-four hours.

The pontoons were all upset and lying buried in the mud along the roads, while the drivers were absent, trying to make themselves comfortable. Every man that could be spared was sent out to corduroy the roads back to the old camp and help drag the cannon out of the sloughs; they were buried to their muzzles, and ten horses or mules were hitched to each gun and caisson to draw them. The Confederates across the river knew the state of affairs, and their pickets good-naturedly called to the Union pickets, and asked them if they wanted any help. Having had such an ample supply of water, our officers, on the morning of Saturday, the 24th, kindly issued us a ration of whisky, for which we were duly grateful, and at 8 A.M. the command started back for their old camping-ground, arriving there about noon, after a march of seven miles. This move was known as the "mud march." "Man proposes and God disposes." General Burnside could not control the elements.

On Sunday, January 25th, General Burnside resigned the command of the Army of the Potomac.

Wednesday, the 28th, General Hooker took command of the army; General Meade, of the center grand division, composed of the 3d and 5th corps, and General Sykes in command of the 5th corps. The men received two months' pay. The next day we awoke to find the country wearing a dreary aspect, with about a foot of snow on the ground.

On Tuesday, the 3d of February, our regiment, with the brigade, went on picket duty, carrying three days' rations. On Friday, the 6th, they returned at midnight, their clothing covered with ice. They had a rough tour of duty during the four days they were absent from camp. It rained, froze, snowed, and the wind blew a gale nearly the whole time. One of the men was sent back to camp sick, and reported to the surgeon. He had been told that he was "a beat," and playing sick. He went into the hospital tent and laid down. In the morning, it was the old story—he was dead.

The next day a shot was heard just outside of the regimental camp. The provost guard repaired to the spot and found a soldier lying with the side of his head blown off.

They dug a hole a foot deep and buried him forthwith, and took his rifle and belt to their quarters. About an hour afterward a Sergeant of the regulars came to them and said that one of their provost guard was missing, and asked for a description of the man they had buried, which was given ; he proved to be the missing man. It was a case of deliberate suicide. He had fixed a strap so as to discharge his rifle with his foot, after placing it at the side of his head. They opened the grave, lifted the body, and buried their late comrade in the division burying-ground on the hill.

On Tuesday, the 10th, the regiment was thoroughly inspected by Lieutenant-Colonel Webb, Assistant Inspector-General, and pronounced to be in the highest condition. Thursday, the 12th, we learned that General Warren had been appointed Chief of Topographical Engineers, on General Hooker's staff. Colonel Garrard, of the 146th New York, a regular officer, was placed in command of the brigade.

While the provost guard were making a tour on the 14th, they stopped at what had once been an elegant mansion, but at this time was dismantled of almost everything. A Corporal and two men were stationed at the house permanently to preserve it from further destruction, their orders being to prohibit any one from taking away even a brick. Their duties were also to arrest any soldier they found out of camp without leave. Accordingly they were in the habit of hiding and watching for stragglers, and as the land was cleared of trees for many acres in extent around their covert, they seized many a luckless victim. When the Sergeant and his squad came up to the house, he found the Corporal and his two men in an altercation with a Captain from one of the regiments, who had several men and a wagon, which they were loading with bricks. Sergeant Jack Taylor, who was in command of the detail of the provost, and was one of the best duty-men in the regiment, ordered the Captain to stop his work and unload his wagon. The Captain refused with an oath, and the Sergeant was about to arrest him, by force, if necessary, when an officer rode up on horseback, alone and unobserved until quite near. He halted, and it being discovered at a glance that he was Major-General Meade, Taylor had his squad in line in a moment, right dressed, etc., with as much ceremony as if he was in command of a battalion, and presented arms. "What is the trouble here, Sergeant?" inquired the General. The Sergeant informed him, and also explained the orders under which he was acting, when General Meade turned to the Captain with a severe frown and reprimanded him. He asked his name and regiment, and told him that an officer that presumed, by reason of his superior rank, to browbeat those who were not his equal into disobeying their own orders, was not fit to be an officer, informing him that he could return to his regiment and report. The officer left, evidently feeling very much mortified. He then commended Taylor and his squad for doing their duty, and rode on.

At another time Sigel's 11th corps encamped about the house overnight when on a raid. The demolition would have been immediate had not the Corporal of the provost (Powell) gone to General Sigel and told him what his orders were; when he promptly sent an order for a guard to be stationed around the house. In the morning they had disappeared as suddenly as they came; but when Sergeant Taylor arrived there in the afternoon on his rounds, he found a couple of German soldiers sitting comfortably by a fire they had made in one of the fire-places in the lower story of the house, engrossed in a game of cards, with a corpse lying near tied up in a blanket. They were detailed to carry their deceased comrade back to their old camp, as the raid would last only a few days, and they were glad to have the opportunity to do so, and thus avoid a long tramp and perhaps a fight. The Sergeant, on being informed of the facts by the Corporal, notified the intruders that he would be compelled to arrest them, corpse and all, if they did not move. They thereupon collected their traps, grumblingly shouldered their burden, and left. These incidents illustrate the duties of the provost, who were, in fact, the police of the army.

On Monday, the 16th, a heavy detail from the regiment were employed in throwing up earthworks to protect the railroad bridge across Potomac Creek. The 17th it snowed all day, reaching a depth of four inches, and the next day it rained. The working detail returned at night, wet, tired, and miserable. Nicholas Hoyt, a Sergeant of Company C, was buried on the 19th. He was a sailor before he entered the army, and was one of the old Fort Schuyler men, a man of the true stamp. He remained faithful to the last. For months he had been wasting away from a troublesome complaint, which only a change of diet and rest could cure; but he would not yield, doing duty day after day, until he became so weak that he could not stand, and was carried from his own to the hospital tent, where he died a few days afterward. His funeral was attended by Colonel Winslow, Lieutenant-Colonel George Duryea, and the greater part of the officers and men.

The men found the climate at this time as changeable as the people of that section of the country. The condition of the army was improved, for with temporary rest and more liberal supplies they had enough to eat. The cry of the soldier cooks was heard occasionally, "Fall in for your extras," on which summons the men rushed out, each one trying to be first on the line, with tin cup in hand, scrambling and pushing to the infinite diversion of the crowd, some of whom were draining what remained in their cups to make room for the fresh supply. The old hands at one time played tricks on the new ones, when they were not up to the "ways that were so childlike and bland." When there was a stew for dinner, at the given signal every one rushed out as usual with cup in hand. The "old ones," although apparently in a great hurry, took good care to be on the end of the line ; the cook being a two years' man, and consequently sympathizing with the rest of us, would be careful not to dive very deep with his ladle into the kettle when serving the recruits, and the "old ones" coming last, had the substantial part of the stew. The law of gravitation was not suspended in camp-kettles even in Virginia, and the solid parts, consisting of chunks of meat and potatoes, obediently sank to the bottom, and "last come, last served" found us well contented with our share.

A soldier is never supposed to have enough, but an exception was found one day in the case of a man who, after disposing of a couple of quarts of stew and six hard-tack, to make himself, as he said, "a solid man," actually admitted that he had enjoyed "a good square meal."

Sunday, February 22d (Washington's birthday), it stormed without cessation, and by nightfall the snow in some places was two or three feet deep. A number of convalescents from hospitals reported for duty. Salutes were fired in honor of the day.

On Wednesday, the 25th, the cavalry pickets had a skirmish with three brigades of the enemy's cavalry, resulting in some loss on both sides. Reinforcements and artillery were sent out. The fight occurred about two miles to the front of the infantry pickets, and the cavalry came flying in through their lines, some of them without their arms and bareheaded ; the men expected that they would have a brush with the enemy. The reserves were in arms, but the enemy did not approach us. About fifty of our men were taken prisoners. The brigade returned from picket on the evening of the 27th, where they had been doing duty for four days. It stormed nearly all the time, and they passed through many disagreeable hours. The brigade was again on picket duty during the 14th, 15th, and 16th of March, and were relieved on the morning of Tuesday, the 17th, St. Patrick's Day.

The day was celebrated in the 9th Massachusetts (the Irish 9th). They had a greased pole, twenty-four feet high, on top of which was a furlough and a canteen of whisky. They also tried to catch the greased pig. There was a horse-race for quite a large wager, but the horses came into collision, killing both of them, and the drivers were picked up insensible. An amateur prize-fight was also witnessed. Heavy firing was heard all the afternoon, and it was supposed that the cavalry had encountered the enemy. On the 18th the cavalry returned and marched by the camp. They had attacked Fitz Hugh Lee near Culpepper, and after quite a spirited fight had routed him and taken fifty-five prisoners, with their horses in addition, killing and wounding many others. The loss on the Union side was about twenty. One of our men asked a fine-looking prisoner, who had on a good overcoat, how he would swop, when he was answered that his "was not the right color."

The provost guard, on their rounds, arrested a suspicious character, in citizen's dress, prowling about a deserted house. He was questioned, and acknowledged that he came from the South, and was once in the rebel army; he was taken to camp and put under guard, and afterward turned over to the Provost-General, as it was suspected that he was a spy.

One day the guard halted at a log cabin occupied by some poor whites (three women), the husband and brothers being in the Confederate army. They saw the women standing outside of the cabin with arms resting on their hips, gazing at their chimney, from which and the doorway came thick volumes of smoke. The Sergeant thought at first the house was on fire, but soon ascertained from the mother that the chimney only smoked; "it was the ―― chimney she ever seed," and she "wished that the man that built it was lying dead, stiff, stark and naked on the battle-field."

The mother was not very strongly secessionist, and was

only anxious that the war was over, so that her "old man" could come home. The young women, however, were the strongest kind of rebels; one of them was very pretty and smart, and the provost often stopped to stir up her rebel spirit.

Another house the provost occasionally visited, was occupied by a poor cripple and his family. He was a shoemaker by trade, and appeared to be quite an intelligent man, and opposed to Jefferson Davis and the Confederacy. He said that he had escaped conscription so far, on account of his lameness, but he did not doubt when our army moved away from the neighborhood that the Confederates would make him go into their army anyhow, as they were in want of recruits badly. He also said that Jeff Davis would rather have a man die in the army, whether he was of any service or not, than let him remain at home. He said that the poor whites were worse off than negroes, and were not allowed to own any good land, as that was all monopolized by the rich slave-owners, and they were obliged to cultivate some barren patch, from which they could barely raise enough to exist; therefore it was of no advantage for them to fight for the rich man's negroes, but they were compelled to do so. This was an epitome of the whole of the controversy, and of the facts of the war in its most practical form by one of the sufferers. Southern orators, ex-rebel chieftains, and statesmen of the "State Rights" school may protest now that the war on the part of the South was a struggle for "constitutional liberty and the social rights transmitted by our Revolutionary fathers," but the underlying fact will remain on the pages of history that they attempted to destroy the Union in the interests of slavery, and it perished in the attempt. When the bitterness of the disaster to the South shall have passed away, and the authors of the war shall have all laid down in the grave, it is to be hoped that then, if not before, we shall have a moral reunion all the grander and greater, that our land is uncursed by the tread of the slave.

On Friday, March 27th, which was a very pleasant day, one of the few which had favored the army for weeks, the division was reviewed by General Sykes—an occurrence which put the men in good spirits, reviews under fair skies having been for some time quite rare. One of the correspondents for the press reported it as follows:

"*March* 28, 1863.—On our way to the race-ground we encountered the division of Major-General Sykes, out for a review and inspection. Sykes' division looked well, and will evidently give a good account of itself in the coming struggle. The 5th New York Volunteers elicited the admiration of all, and, with due deference to the regulars, it must be admitted that this regiment has a military standing not exceeded in the army. Its present commander is evidently following the excellent example and instruction of its former Colonel (now Brigadier-General), Warren."

General Hooker, at this date, was in command of a fine army, in good condition and discipline; the camps were never cleaner, or the food better; the introduction of soft bread was a beneficial and humane act. Nevertheless, about one hundred men in the division had died since we had encamped on this ground. It was evidence that death by the bullet was not all that the soldier had to contend with.

The month of April opened with a driving gale, cold and fretful. A great mania sprung up among the men for the manufacture of laurel-root pipes, and some of them succeeded in carving and finishing numerous specimens in an elegant and artistic manner. They were wrought out entirely by the penknife; an offer of $25 was refused for one of them.

The weather was almost trying enough to drive an army mad, situated as the men were in shelter-tents, which were of such limited proportions that when taking refuge in them they must either lie down or sit up with their blankets over them all day long in stormy weather, if they wanted to keep from freezing. They were not over four feet high. Some of the men dug pits from four to six feet deep, and covered them over with their shelters; they also built fire-places in them with a chimney leading out to the ground above. Much ingenuity was displayed in making them comfortable, although their materials and tools were very limited.

Whatever they made was from wood, earth, and mud, their tools consisting of one axe to a company, their jackknives, and a borrowed spade. Nevertheless, many a happy hour was spent in these burrows, increased by the certainty that there were neither rent or taxes to pay to the collector.

Sunday, April 5th, the snow was six inches deep in drifts, and the wind blew a hurricane. During the month of March there had been only one really pleasant day, and the men looked forward to April, hoping for a change. The roads were all sloughs, and it was impracticable for the army to move until they dried and hardened. Thus far the change had not come, and having lost their patience, they arrived at the conclusion that the sunny South was a myth. The day being Easter Sunday, and the boys not having any eggs, were obliged to put up with bean soup, and were very thankful to get it, although the cook failed to give us a very good exhibition of his skill in its preparation. The cooking, of course, was done in the open air; and sometimes when the wind blew strong, the kettles would be hanging three or four feet from the heat and flame, although supposed to be hanging directly over where the fire ought to be. Some of the men occasionally stood in a row to keep the wind from the fire as much as possible, being rewarded with, to them, the rich aroma that arose to their gratified nostrils from the boiling bean soup.

On Tuesday, April 7th, President Lincoln, in company

with General Hooker and staff, General Meade and staff, General Humphreys and staff, and a large number of distinguished officers in train, reviewed the different corps of the army. The Zouaves were called out alone, and put through some movements, in ordinary and quick time, before the President and company, after which they closed with the manual of arms and bayonet exercise. The distinguished company seemed to be highly gratified by the very rapid movements, changes of position, and the uniformity and exactness with which all the orders were executed. Through Colonel Winslow, the highest compliments were paid the regiment upon their proficiency and soldierly appearance. One of the provost guard who was on the detail to keep guard near the cavalcade, heard the President make the remark that it was a "gallus" regiment, and General Griffin, who was near by, responded, "Yes! and they can *fight* as well as they can drill."

Colonel Winslow gave the regiment a drill in the afternoon. Their time in the service was drawing so near to its close, that some of them were inclined to be careless; but short as it was, each day seemed a long one to the old members.

On Tuesday, the 14th, the brigade returned to camp after spending three days on picket duty. Eight days' rations and sixty rounds of ammunition were issued to each man; ninety rounds per man were to be carried in the wagons when the army moved, which might occur at any moment. The next day a general muster was held to ascertain the full strength of the regiment. The division was reviewed by the Swiss General, Togliardi, in company with General Meade, on Saturday, the 18th. The Fifth, after returning to their camping-ground, by request gave a drill for the entertainment of the visiting General. The hospital tent and bread ovens were removed on the same day, which was an indication to us of an early movement.

Camp near Henry House. 377

The 19th fell on Sunday, which was a warm, pleasant day, and, withal, there was much excitement in camp. The Sergeants and men reported their time out. The Colonel went over to headquarters to see what was to be done with the regiment. General Hooker went to Washington to consult about the two years' men in the army. On his return Colonel Winslow formed the regiment in a square and made a speech, hoping that for the good name they had earned for themselves, that they would continue to do their duty willingly until they heard from the War Department. The men had all determined to do no duty after the 23d of April.

An accident happened in the forenoon to some of the members of a battery, which was encamped opposite the Fifth, on the other side of the road. It was being inspected by the officers, when a shell in one of the caissons exploded from some carelessness and badly injured and burned three men ; their hair and whiskers were all singed off, and their faces were burned black by the powder. The explosion threw a large piece of the caisson over into the camp of the Fifth, and if all the shell had burst, the loss of life would have been fearful. Some of the Fifth who were playing ball, ran over to see what had occurred, and two of them for some reason became engaged in a fight on the spot just after the injured men had been carried away ; others were pitching their quoits, and did not have curiosity enough to stop even to inquire into the cause of the excitement. It was a curious illustration of the influence of war in making men thoughtless of life or death.

At the morning's inspection the Colonel asked the Orderly of Company I how many days' rations he had on hand. He replied, " Five days'." To the question what the men would do if they marched, he replied, that " they did not expect to march only to Aquia Creek, on their way to New York." Under the expectation of moving at any hour, the order was to have eight days' rations in haversack or knapsack all the time. The officers' tents were removed, the small shelter tents substituted in their place, and their baggage was curtailed. We had been under marching orders for a week. The question which had disturbed the regiment for some days was determined on the 21st. An order from headquarters was read out to the regiment, notifying them that their term of enlistment would expire two years' from the date on which they were sworn into the United States service. The three years' men contended that they were enlisted under false pretenses, as they were promised their discharge with the regiment. Orders Nos. 44 and 85 were read off about re-enlisting.

On Thursday, the 23d, the two years' men were in a great state of excitement. The Colonel arrived from headquarters and assembled the regiment in a square, and read out special orders, that the Government would hold them until the 9th day of May. He made some remarks and hoped that they would do their duty without coercion until that day. They all knew the consequences of insubordination, and that their time would soon be up. The excitement subsided, as the men were too intelligent, and understood their duty too well to make any further resistance, and there was no more trouble. The provost arrested two men for declaring that they would do no more duty. They ran the risk of a trial for mutiny.

The long-expected orders to move came at last, and on Monday, the 27th, the regiment struck tents and marched, about 10 A.M., to Ellis Ford, a distance of about eight miles, the roads being dry and dusty, and we went into bivouac. The men were a little stiff on account of having laid in camp for so long a time. There was much dissatisfaction in the regiment among the three years' men, who expected to be mustered out with the regiment, and some of them dropped out on the road and eluded the guard. Some of these men had cause to feel dissatisfied and aggrieved, as it had been

Battle of Chancellorsville. 379

represented to them when they enlisted that they would certainly be discharged with the regiment. One hundred men were detailed to guard the wagons and trains. The non-commissioned officers, which included the greater part of the two years' men, were kept with the main body. The next afternoon we left at 4 o'clock, and advanced nine miles in the rain over muddy roads, broken by water-runs, and halted at 10 P.M. to bivouac. Twenty rifles were left in this camp in the morning belonging to as many three-year men, who had taken the opportunity of darkness to forsake us rather than be consolidated with the 146th New York, to serve out the remainder of their term. On Wednesday, the 29th, we fell in at 8 A.M., crossed the pontoons at Kelly's Ford, and passed through the flourishing town of Kellysville, consisting of six dwellings and a grist-mill, which was constantly used by the enemy. We pressed on and forded Mountain Run, a wide stream, which soaked our clothing to our waists. After all had crossed we resumed the march, and finally reached Ely's Ford on the Rapidan. The river was wide and very rapid; the water above the waist, and the bottom rocky. It was with great difficulty that the men could keep their feet. Most of the men went in in full uniform; "but some comical scenes were presented by the men taking off their pants, or starting on the voyage as they came into the world, with the exception of their having baggage with them." Cartridge-boxes were hung about the neck or put on top of the knapsacks to keep the "powder dry." We resumed our journey, and after going two miles beyond the river, went into bivouac, having advanced about twenty miles. This march was a very trying one, and the roads were strewn with knapsacks and superfluous clothing accumulated during the winter months, which were thrown away by the men, not being any longer required. Cannonading was heard during the day in the direction of Fredericksburg. Our march, on the morning of the 30th, brought us within half a mile of the United States Ford. The weather was cloudy, with at times a drizzling rain. We rested half an hour and advanced toward the rear of the enemy's position at Fredericksburg, and the division took up a position under arms for the night, it being in the advance. We had marched fifty-six miles in four days.

The following extract from the New York *Daily Times* of May 4, 1863, gives a general account of the movements of Sykes' division on Friday, May 1st:

"The division marched, about 9 A.M., to the left on the turnpike, toward Fredericksburg, to make an attack and compel the enemy to develop his strength at that point. They moved promptly into position, with Weed's former regular battery (but now Watson's). The enemy fired the first gun at 12 o'clock. The 8th Pennsylvania Cavalry skirmished in the very front for some time, and sustained a galling fire from the enemy's infantry, but behaved with great intrepidity. They charged and re-charged upon the infantry, only to be in turn driven back. General Sykes then threw forward two companies of infantry, without knapsacks, on the double-quick, who supported the cavalry and checked the further pursuit of the enemy. The action now became quite general between the two forces, each seeming to be of about equal strength. [The enemy's force thus engaged was Mahone's brigade, supported by McLaw's]. The enemy contested the ground vigorously, giving way only when pressed very hard. Our troops fought for fully an hour with great spirit, and drove the enemy from two successive and strong positions upon ridges of land which run parallel with the Rappahannock. The distance thus gained was nearly one mile nearer Fredericksburg, and some fifty prisoners, mostly belonging to Virginia regiments, were captured.

"About half-past 1 o'clock, just as Colonel Chapman, commanding the 2d brigade of regulars, had expressed a desire to 'take another ridge,' an order was received by General Sykes from General Hooker to suspend the attack and retire nearly to his former position."* "At 2 P.M. General Hooker remarked,

---

* General Warren, at this time Chief of Topographical Engineers, "who bore the order, had vainly urged that it should not be sent." Generals Couch and Han-

'I think I can make them come out and fight me on my own ground.' In two hours the assertion was proven. The enemy mistook our voluntary retirement for a check, and followed us rapidly as we fell back.

"The division had taken their old position, and pickets were thrown out, when the enemy again appeared in force on the ridge, at the foot of which we lay. Our men had stacked arms and were at rest. The whole division, save the Duryée Zouaves, were lying at nearly right-angles with the road. The Zouaves were parallel with the road. Quick as thought General Sykes brought his men into line, the Zouaves on the left half wheeling into line of battle like a machine.

" The enemy paused a moment on the top of the ridge, and, as if to nerve them for the onset, gave one of their proverbial demoniac yells, and came down on the double-quick, shooting, capturing, and literally running over the pickets, who scrambled behind all sorts of obstructions." [Some of the Fifth, who were on picket, came in the next day; one of them, a Sergeant, brought in five rebel prisoners.] "But in an instant more a terrible crash resounded from the Zouave end of the line, and down the column rolled a deafening roar of musketry. It did not last, apparently, two minutes, but its work was effective. The firing at once brought General Hooker into the saddle. This onslaught by the enemy was for the purpose of re-taking the cross-roads; a very important point. The first thing done after this was the massing of artillery near the roads, and in fifteen minutes twenty-two guns were sending shell into the woods, and the roar of artillery became ten times more deafening than that of the musketry had been. The work was soon done. The contest lasted three-quarters of an hour at this point, and the enemy ignominiously retired."

The loss in the division was light, amounting to about one hundred in killed and wounded. Captain Marsh, of the 17th Infantry, was killed. Captain Overton, of General Sykes' staff, was wounded; Lieutenant Wells, 14th Infantry, wounded. In the Fifth only about half a dozen were

cock, advancing on parallel roads to Sykes, on either flank, also protested against it. " Hancock thought that they should advance instead of retreating."

wounded. They being on the left, were able to pour an effective fire into the flank of the enemy, and were shielded somewhat themselves behind an embankment. During the night the men were engaged in digging rifle-pits. The enemy's fires burned unusually bright, and extended along the heights for several miles. A battle was regarded as inevitable.

Fifty men, five from each company, were sent out under the command of Lieutenant Gedney, to act as pickets; they went about half a mile, and took a position in the cut of a road, keeping well covered, and a few of them were sent forward and deployed in the woods as an outpost, so as to keep a sharp lookout. It was a bright moonlight night, and there was not much danger of a surprise, but it was a dangerous post, as the enemy would make their first advance in that direction from Fredericksburg. About midnight their ears detected a slight rustling of the leaves scattered over the ground in the woods front of them, and soon it became more distinct, and the tramp of men was heard. The Lieutenant cautioned his men to keep quiet, and not to fire until he gave the order. They soon saw a long line of the enemy approaching in the woods, being, as well as they could judge, some five or six companies, and the few men on outpost duty fell back to the reserve. The enemy must have discovered them, for they heard an officer say, "Steady, men; they are nothing but pickets, and we will walk right over them." At this moment Gedney gave the order, "*Fire,*" and the flash of fifty rifles told that the order was obeyed. They immediately received a volley in return, most of which went over their heads, as they were lying behind the embankment at the side of the road, but it wounded two of them. A bullet also struck the scabbard of the Lieutenant's sword, bending it. They immediately loaded again and fired, but the enemy retreated in confusion, supposing that they had come into contact with a large force, their object evidently

Battle of Chancellorsville. 383

being only to feel the lines to ascertain the position of the Union troops. From the groaning in the woods during the remainder of the night, they judged that their fire had done good execution. A regular officer with some troops came up on a double-quick in a few moments, and after ascertaining the cause of the firing, told the Lieutenant that he had done well. Toward morning they were again approached, but drove the enemy back. After daylight an officer of the regulars rode up and ordered them to march on a double-quick, and rejoin the command, which they found had moved.

When the morning of the 2d broke, it found both sides well intrenched. The division remained in line of battle during the day, and the enemy spent their time in feeling the lines of the army further to the right. They opened a battery on the ammunition wagons; one of ours promptly responded, and blew up two of their caissons, which obliged them to withdraw.

About 5 P.M. Jackson, with 40,000 men, made a terrific onslaught on the 11th corps, under General Howard, on the right, surprising them completely. General Berry, in command of a division of General Sickles' 3d corps, was sent to the rescue on double-quick after dark, and checked the enemy, aided by General Birney's division of the same corps; and Best's batteries (36 guns), under the command of Lieutenant Franklin B. Crosby, which were ordered there by General Warren. Lieutenant Crosby was killed. The Confederates withdrew to the line of breastworks just vacated by the 11th corps. The regulars were sent after the fugitives who were flying in a panic toward United States Ford. They lost twelve pieces of artillery besides many prisoners, and General Howard was wounded while trying to rally them. Bushbeck's, with Schimmelfennig's brigade, and the 82d Illinois, and 157th New York with Dilger's battery, however, fought until they were overpowered by numbers. The disaster to this corps foiled a maneuver attempted by

Sickles, who pressed the enemy's center, and would have gained a splendid victory by cutting the Confederate army in two.

In the night an attack was made on the right to restore the Union lines. The moon shone bright, and the firing was very heavy; the roar and reverberation of Captain Best's artillery, posted on a ridge, was past all conception. The enemy were driven half a mile, and a portion of the artillery lost was recaptured by General Hobart Ward.

About 6 P.M. the 5th corps (Sykes' division included) was ordered to the right, and remained in line of battle all night, and was also engaged in digging intrenchments to strengthen their position. The 11th corps was reorganized and placed on the extreme left behind the strong intrenchments built by the 5th corps, where it was probable there would be little or no fighting. Thus closed the second day of this memorable contest.

On Sunday, the 3d, the division was placed at the apex of the lines, to the right of the Chancellor House, near the center, where all the reserve artillery was massed, with only room enough between the guns to work them. The lines of the army were in the form of two sides of a triangle, the right longer than the left. The 1st corps, under General Reynolds, held the extreme right of the line ; the 5th corps, Meade's, was on their left. At 5½ A.M. the enemy attacked General Berry's division of the 3d corps, with the design of recovering the plank-road. The rest of the corps, and a part of the Twelfth (Slocum's), were soon engaged in his support. French's division, of the 2d corps, was sent in on the right at 7 A.M., and crushed that portion of the enemy's line. The crashes of musketry were terrific, and the roar of the battle was incessant. Sickles' 3d corps fought parts of five divisions of the enemy at different times, and took 2,000 prisoners ; but being hard pressed, Hancock's division, of the 2d corps, was sent to his relief. General Humphrey's division, of the 5th corps, were also en-

Battle of Chancellorsville. 385

gaged on the left flank of the enemy, and fought valiantly. Most of the fighting was in a thick wood, and the carnage was frightful; the dead and wounded of the enemy lay in heaps, and they fought as if they were utterly regardless of their lives. Many desperate charges were made by the Union troops; Mott's brigade captured seven stand of colors and many prisoners. The engagement lasted, without the slightest intermission, from 5½ A.M. until 8.45 A.M., when a temporary cessation occurred on our side by the troops getting out of ammunition. They were ordered to fall back after holding the position in the woods for an hour at the point of the bayonet, to the vicinity of the Chancellor House. Here the contest was maintained for an hour or more, with great havoc to the enemy and considerable loss to the Union forces. This house was the headquarters of General Hooker, and was now the focus of the fight. It was set on fire by the enemy's shell, and was soon in ruins. The new line, which had been supervised by General Warren, was now established, and the forces withdrawn to it on that front, at half-past eleven the musketry fire ceased. The engagement had lasted six hours, and had been one of the most terrific of the war.

While the battle was raging, General Hooker ordered that the bands should play, to inspirit the men. One of them was blowing away at the "Star Spangled Banner," when a shell made a close flight over their center. This uninvited companion "took the wind" out of some of the players, and they got somewhat mixed. Under the circumstances, the way in which our national air was murdered would have driven a professor of music to suicide.

The enemy were now no longer in the rear, but had been shoved down directly in our front, and between the forces of General Sedgwick that had captured Fredericksburg Heights, ten miles away to the left, and General Hooker's main army. General Sykes' division had been under fire, and there was a considerable loss among the regulars, especially among the artillerists; Captain Temple, Second Infantry, was killed; Captain Morehead, Seventeenth, and Captain Armes, were wounded. The Fourth United States, battery K, lost heavily, forty-eight being killed or wounded, besides many of their horses. The forces of the enemy engaged were the divisions of Anderson, Hood, A. P. Hill, D. H. Hill's old division, and Rhodes.

In the afternoon the enemy made several desperate attempts to force the lines near the Chancellor House, and charged at one time on the massed batteries, being formed in the shape of a wedge, but they were cut down before they could get far, as they were obliged to charge over the only clearing there was on the whole field of battle, which was about a mile in length by half a mile in breadth. Nothing could live in front of the batteries. The position of the Fifth was near these guns. General Hooker rode up at one time and called out, "Is that the Fifth New York?" "Yes!" was the reply. "All right!" he exclaimed, and rode off. The shell from these guns set the brush in the woods on fire, where were lying hundreds of the wounded of the enemy, as well as some of our own. The terrible sufferings of the wounded and dying, under the double horror of being burned to death, made this contest more tragic in this respect than any of its predecessors.

The regiment held the same position that had been assigned to it the day before, when the order came from General Sykes to turn over the three-year men to the 146th New York, Colonel Garrard, who was also acting in command of the brigade, formerly Warren's, and for the two years' men to retire. In fact, they were released from their duties, and their trials in the army were about to cease. They could scarcely realize it, and were utterly bewildered with the intelligence. The reaction from their feelings of intense anxiety and suspense as to whether they were to be

Battle of Chancellorsville. 387

killed, perhaps an hour before the order for their relief should come, and they should never see their loved ones at home again, can not be described. If they had had another year to serve, it would have been a matter of indifference as to where they were; but under the circumstances they could be compared to mariners who had passed through a long and tempestuous voyage, and at last were in sight of their homes, when another storm had reached them and they knew not but that they might be engulfed before they should reach a friendly port.

The regiment, as an organization, terminated its service amid the reverberations of artillery, the crash of arms, the smoke of the battle-field, the funereal pall of the smoke in the burning woods, consuming hundreds of brave men immolated in unrecognizable masses.

"And now four days the sun had seen our woes,
Four nights the moon beheld the incessant fire."

The rest of the story of this engagement belongs to the records of others, to whom we gratefully pay our tribute of praise and honor.

The regiment was drawn up in line, and the following order was read off:

HEADQUARTERS, 2d DIVISION, 5TH CORPS,
CAMP NEAR CHANCELLORSVILLE, VA.,
May 4, 1863.

GENERAL ORDER, No. 99.

The term of service of a portion of the 5th Regiment being about to expire, the Major-General commanding desires the officers and men to know that he parts from them with very great regret, a regret which he is confident is shared with the whole division. The regiment has been distinguished in all the operations of his command, especially at Gaines' Mill and the battle of Manassas Plains. Its ranks, thinned and scarred by battle, are the best and proudest witness of the fact. The

General hopes to see again the brave men who have served under him. Many of their comrades still have to hold in trust the respect of the old regiment, and the General has no fears but that it will be sacredly guarded and preserved. The officers and men who are to leave this army will proceed to New York on the 5th. Colonel Winslow will turn in to the proper department, at Aquia Creek, all ordnance stores, and all supplies or property not needed for the men who remain.

II. The three-year men of the 5th Regiment New York Volunteers are transferred to the 146th New York Volunteers; the proper officers will see the necessary papers are furnished to that effect.

By command of
GENERAL SYKES,
G. RYAN,
Captain, A. A. General.

The question whether the three-year members of the Fifth who were transferred to the 146th New York Volunteers did their duty and upheld the good name of the old 5th Regiment, the following letter received from Brevet Brigadier-General Grindlay, Colonel of the 146th New York Volunteers, will sufficiently answer:

BOONEVILLE, N. Y., *Feb.* 14, 1878.

ALFRED DAVENPORT, ESQ.:

Dear Sir:—In answer to your inquiry, I would say that at the battle of Chancellorsville, some 237 enlisted men of the old 5th New York Volunteers were transferred to the 146th New York Volunteers to serve out the unexpired term of their enlistment.

I considered the " Duryée Zouaves " the best drilled and disciplined regiment in the corps, if not in the army. They reached that great state of proficiency by having, as you well know, among their corps of instructors, such soldiers as Major-General G. K. Warren, afterward our beloved corps commander, than whom no abler or better man served in the Union army. The men transferred to us were worthy representatives of their regiment, and while cherishing a strong love for their old command, they became, ere they left, as strongly attached to their new regiment. We shortly afterward adopted the "Zouave Uniform" in our brigade, and their pride in the "Zouave Brigade" equaled that for their first love. Several were promoted for gallantry in battle and soldierly conduct. Among the number I remember Peter Froeligh to be First Lieutenant, afterward killed at the Wilderness; Hugh Chalmers to be Second Lieutenant, afterward killed at Cold Harbor, both gallant soldiers. The witty and adventurous Lawrence Fitzpatrick to Captain. He served through the war, was captured and escaped several times, always spoke proudly of the Old Fifth, and ever did his duty. Henry G. Taylor and John McGeehan to be First Lieutenants, and several others whom I do not now recall. They were all good soldiers, and by their bearing and conduct set an example to their new comrades worthy of all emulation. The members of the 5th New York Volunteers have every reason to be proud of their gallant regiment.

I am, my dear sir,
Very respectfully yours,
JAS. G. GRINDLAY,
Brevet Brig.-Gen. and Colonel 146th N. Y. Vol. Infantry.

Now came a sad as well as a joyous scene. The three years' men felt that they were parting with their old comrades with whom they had lived and fought, to be thrown into companionship with comparative strangers, and had the ground been about to open and swallow them, they could scarcely have felt more deeply. The two years' men, on the other hand, were about to turn their faces homeward, many of them for the first time since they had enlisted, two years before, and their feelings were exuberant and beyond expression. They were elated to the highest degree, but nevertheless the parting was a sad one even to them. The tie becomes very strong between those who have suffered hardships and dangers in common, and as the men wrung each other by the hand, many a tear was brushed away; hastily written notes were taken in charge, and hurried messages were delivered to carry to mothers, fathers, brothers, and sisters at home, and to the loving fair one waiting the return of her soldier pride. But the scene was soon over, and comrades grasped each other's hands for the last time; alas! in many instances forever.

Among the men who remained, there were many who subsequently fell in the battle of Gettysburg, or in Grant's great campaign against Richmond. The departing company marched toward United States Ford, and after crossing the pontoon bridge, the remainder of the two years' men who were guarding the wagons were taken up, and all marched briskly for Stoneman's Switch. The full regiment numbered about *two hundred men*. This large increase in numbers was caused by a number of convalescents and detailed men, who had rejoined the command during the previous few months. After marching nearly all night, the atmosphere being intolerably close, the men were halted and went into bivouac; the firing on Fredericksburg Heights was plainly distinguishable, and the men were harassed with doubts as to whether they would not be again ordered to the front. A little before daylight the regiment was suddenly aroused and fell into line, a report being brought that a body of the enemy's cavalry were in the vicinity. We again marched, and halted near a clear stream of water, when the men immediately stripped and gave themselves a good scouring, and put on clean under-clothing, which they had been saving for their home trip, with as much care as does the bride her wedding trousseau. After their bath, the men felt much refreshed.

On Tuesday, the 5th, we entered the freight cars at Stoneman's Switch, and soon arrived at Aquia Creek. The 21st New York Volunteers, lying there guarding the army stores, entertained the men with great hospitality, and gave them coffee, fresh bread, and bacon, which were heartily relished. The regiment was lying on the side of a steep hill in the afternoon, chatting and smoking their pipes, when a very violent thunder-storm, which had been threatening for some time, burst upon them, accompanied with hail, some of which was of the size of a walnut. The men stood it for some time, some of them jokingly calling it Bull Run No. 3, when they were ordered to take refuge in some barracks near the landing, but their clothing had been completely soaked through. In the barracks they were much crowded for want of room, but did well enough under the circumstances. The rain continued all night, accompanied with a cold northeast wind.

The morning of Wednesday, the 6th, broke cold and rainy. We embarked on board the transport *John A. Warner*, and sailed for Washington, where we arrived in the afternoon, and were marched up Pennsylvania Avenue, past the Capitol, through a heavy rain, and halted at the Soldiers' Retreat, near the depot. Supper was served, and the men found ways and means to fill their canteens with something stronger than coffee, notwithstanding the guard that was placed on the doorways. Finally, we were ordered into some iron baggage cars, without seats of any kind, penned up in them like any other live stock, but all was joy and hilarity from one end of the train to the other. The men sung and shouted, but among their songs it was noticed that they did not sing anything about "hanging Jeff Davis on a sour apple tree." That was omitted. They had been trying to catch him for two years, and had seen a number of sour apple trees suitable for the purpose, but never had caught sight of "Jeff." The regiment arrived in Baltimore about midnight, and while marching through the city to the Philadelphia depot, awoke the good citizens with their songs. A large number of the convalescent wounded belonging to the regiment were taken from the hospitals; and finally all were put into baggage cars, with planks for seats, and the train started for Philadelphia. It seemed to the men that never did a train move so slow. Jack Whigam, who could run a locomotive, went forward to take charge himself, but of course the engineers had their time-tables, and would not deviate from them. We arrived in Philadelphia about 11 A.M. on the the 7th, and had a plain, but to us luxurious lunch at the hospitable retreat conducted by the patriotic ladies of that city, and known as the Cooper Retreat. After spending an hour very agreeably among the visitors who came to see us, and becoming more impressed with the atmosphere of home, we crossed the ferry to Camden and took the cars for Jersey City, where we arrived in the afternoon, and were dismissed to report in the morning.

Friday, the 8th, we assembled at Jersey City and crossed the river, landing at Cortland Street, and made a grand parade through the city. The regiment was the first to come home with their arms, in accordance with the new order of the War Department.

It was noticed that some men who had done little or no fighting or service in the regiment were very anxious to show themselves in the front rank; but perhaps they had lost their cunning, and were not aware that their bright uniforms and store-made shoes betrayed them. They were like the "Jackass in the Lion's skin." This comparison, of course, is not intended to apply to any member of the regiment who had been compelled to be absent from duty on account of sickness or wounds.

The men who had lived through the *hard work* of the camp and field, who had pressed to the front in the hour of danger, cared little where they were placed in the procession; they were worn and scarred; they carried with them the consciousness that would remain with them as they journeyed through life—that they *had earned* the honorable discharge to which they had looked forward as their star of hope, through many an hour of hardship or of the severest duty and danger. Among the number forming the regiment that marched up Broadway, only about eighty had served the whole term for which they had enlisted, and had not

Our Reception. 393

been absent at any time by furlough, or from wounds or sickness.

The following report of the reception, published by the New York *Daily Times*, gives a faithful narrative of this event, not less interesting to the men who had done the hard work of the camp and field so long, than to those who so kindly tendered the expression of their regard and approbation :

"THE RETURN OF THE GALLANT FIFTH.

"*Reception of the Regiment—Triumphal March up Broadway —Banquet at the City Assembly Rooms.*

"The gallant Fifth Regiment met yesterday with such a reception as they had a right to look for. The regiment has been an especial favorite here ever since its organization. Its achievements have been regarded with especial interest and pride by the people of this city and State, and, as might have been expected, its return was signalized by a demonstration, the like of which has been accorded to no other regiment. . . . .

"The streets through which the Fifth had to pass were thronged by enthusiastic crowds all through the afternoon, and a fleeting ray of the spontaneous excitement, which anything connected with the war was wont to produce, once more shone forth in more than pristine brilliancy.

"About half-past three o'clock the Fifth left. Jersey City on board the ferry-boat *New Jersey*, landing on the New York side within five minutes. Marching thence into Broadway, they were received by the Tenth Volunteers (Bendix's Zouaves), who had generously turned out for the occasion, and by the Thirty-seventh and the Seventy-first Regiments of State National Guard. As the war-worn and battle-stained heroes filed along the line they were vociferously cheered. Never was a more hearty meed of admiration and respect paid to brave, devoted soldiers since first the world learned to worship military glory. Presently the line of procession was formed. In the front came the Tenth, led by their intrepid Colonel (Acting Brigadier-General Bendix); following came the Thirty-seventh and the Seventy-first, and then the "red-legged devils," marching in close Zouave order,

17*

and giving those who saw them a better idea of the effect of two years' service than could ever be learned from the perusal of the most glowing newspaper correspondence that ever was written. The men were brown and rugged; their colors were weather-stained and bullet-torn; their uniforms were tattered and stained with Virginia mud and the smoke of hard-fought conflicts. They looked magnificent. Officers and men were the speaking types of rough, hard service. They bore no holiday aspect, but seemed what they were—the veterans of this terrible war, who had toiled and suffered in the cause of their beloved country. They had won the reward prepared for them.

" For once a Republic was not ungrateful. To descend to details. The order of the line was thus arranged :

" The 10th New York Volunteers, Lieutenant-Colonel W. Marshall, 250 men.

" The 37th New York S. M., Colonel Roome, 300 men.

" The 71st New York S. M., Colonel Trafford, 275 men.

" Hook and Ladder Company, No. 9, and Hose Company, No. 61.

"Interspersed were the Seventh Regiment Band, Helmsmuller's Band, Dodworth's Band, and several others of musical popularity. Bringing up the rear were the ex-members of the Fifth who had been discharged, wounded and diseased, but who were now recovered, and, in carriages, the wounded who were too much hurt to walk. It was a prodigiously effective procession, and drew forth acclamations of applause as genuine as ever greeted those who deserve well of their compatriots for sacrifices made in a common cause and for the common weal.

" The procession marched in review through the Park before the Mayor and Common Council, and then up-town to Union Square and round by Fifth Avenue, down-town again to the City Assembly Rooms. There, at eight o'clock, the men and officers of the Fifth, the officers of the escort, and many invited guests sat down to a plentiful, if not a very elaborate, banquet.

" Toasts were given and speeches made, and cheers were plentiful and vociferous. General Duryée, Hiram Walbridge, and Colonel Winslow were the principal speakers. The occasion was one long to be remembered by all who participated in the celebration."

In the Battle of Life.

But there is a time to rejoice, and a time to mourn; and it is the lot of many to mourn while others have their rejoicings. Among the thousands who greeted the Fifth on their march up Broadway, what a multitude must there have been scattered through the gay and thoughtless throng, who scanned with silent grief the faces in the ranks, as if they expected to see a husband, son, or brother—a dear friend or relative, who they already knew could not be there; and as they gazed with tearful eyes, endeavored to picture the lost one as he appeared when he so proudly waved a last farewell, two years before, when he marched away to battle to save his country. All honor to our dead! Let their names be engraved on the tablet of our memories, and may those to whom they were near by the ties of relationship, find consolation in the thought that their sufferings and death were a part of that inestimable price which was paid to secure the national life for the present and for the future.

On Monday, the 11th, the members of the regiment paraded in uniform and with arms, to receive the 4th Regiment, New York Volunteers, Scott Life Guard, and were glad to welcome their comrades home again. They were reviewed by General WINFIELD SCOTT, at the Fifth Avenue Hotel.

Thursday, May 14, 1863, the men were mustered out by companies and paid off, all who were entitled receiving an honorable discharge, which they had endured so much to obtain. Many of the officers and men again re-enlisted in the Fifth Veterans, under their last Colonel, Winslow, and in other organizations, and rose to various grades as officers. Many of them were either killed or wounded in their subsequent service. Others went into the regular army as officers or privates, where those who survive still remain. The rest returned to their various callings in civil life, some to the profession of the law; some are in the ministry, others are engaged in mercantile and industrial pursuits, or hold positions of honor and trust, while some others are afloat under the flag on the trackless sea. Several members of the regiment have represented their constituents in the State Legislature. One is United States Consul to La Rochelle, France, another the second in command of the Franklin Search Expedition. Some have made fortunes, others have risen to distinction in their professions, and there are many others who still suffer from their wounds, or move about under the disadvantage that a loss of limb occasions. Some are shattered by diseases engendered in the swamps of the Chickahominy. Some are "floating on a waveless tide." But among them all, be they rich or poor, be they humble or mighty, there are none but are proud to say that they served in the 5th New York Zouaves.

Whatever may be the fortune of each in the vicissitudes of their life-battle, may the final struggle with "the last enemy" bring to them the crown of the conqueror in the blissful fields of immortality.

APPENDIX.

CASUALTIES.

COMPANY A.

Name.	Rank.	Killed, Wounded, and Died.
TIEBOUT, GEORGE H.	Private	Killed at Big Bethel June 10, 1861.
VINCENNES, ADOLPH	"	Died of wounds received at Big Bethel June 10, 1861.
BARNES, ALFRED	"	Killed at Gaines' Mill June 27, 1862.
TIERNEY, MATHEW W.	"	"
TURNER, CHARLES W.	"	"
HUNTSMAN, GEORGE	Corporal	Died of wounds September 4th, received at Second Bull Run Aug. 30, 1862.
SEELEY, HENRY	Private	Killed at Second Bull Run August 30, 1862.
STANTON, HENRY	"	"
STEVENS, HENRY W.	"	"
THELEMUS, JOSEPH O.	"	"
FULLER, HENRY	"	Died of typhoid fever at Yorktown May 30, 1862.
HUNTER, DAVID D.	"	Died of consumption at Camp near New Bridge, Va., June 24, 1862.
NEIDHEIMER, LEONARD	"	Died of typhoid fever at Washington May 18, 1862.
PIKE, CHRISTOPHER C.	Sergeant	Wounded (twice) at Gaines' Mill June 27, 1862.
HOFFMAN, EDWARD	"	"
DELANEY, THOMAS	Private	"
DURYEA, ALBERT P.	"	"
PEROCHEAN, JOHN A.	"	"
SHANE, IRVIN A.	"	"
TUTHILL, DANIEL	"	"
BOYD, CARLISLE	Captain	Wounded at Second Bull Run August 30, 1862.
KEYSER, HENRY	Second Lieut.	"
GILLIGAN, PATRICK	First Sergeant	"
VAIL, JOSEPH A.	"	"
HART, THEODORE M.	Corporal	"

COMPANY A.—(Continued.)

Name.	Rank.	Killed, Wounded, and Died.
VETHAKE, WM. J.	Corporal	Wounded at Second Bull Run, August 30, 1862.
BLAIR, ANDREW	Private	"
BONESTELL, CHARLES A.	"	"
BAILEY, WILLIAM R.	"	"
COMSTOCK, AUGUSTUS	"	"
FOX, THOMAS H.	"	"
MCPYKE, JOHN	"	"
MCQUADE, JOHN	"	"
NIEBUHR, GEORGE A.	"	"
PETERS, GUSTAVUS	"	"
RYER, THOMAS	"	"
TITUS, SAM'EL D.	"	"
THOMAS, ISAAC C.	"	"
WICKER, THOMAS M.	"	"

COMPANY B.

Name.	Rank.	Killed, Wounded, and Died.
TAYLOR, JAMES L.	Private.	Killed at Big Bethel June 10, 1861.
DE O'LAVEA, LEON	Color Corporal	Killed at Gaines' Mill June 27, 1862 (of French army, expert in bay't ex'e).
CUNNINGHAM, PATRICK or THOMAS	Private.	"
MURPHY, LUKE	"	"
MCGEAR, JOHN	"	"
WESTLAKE, FREDERICK S.	"	"
BOYD, J. C.	Corporal	Killed at Second Bull Run August 30, 1862.
ELLSWORTH, E. CLARENCE	"	"
HARRISON, WILLIAM B.	Private.	"
AMISLER, CHARLES	"	"
COLLINS, CHARLES	"	"
GEE, HENRY C.	"	"
LONGSTAFF, CANNIN	"	"
LEWIS, EDWARD W.	"	"
MCKENNA, PATRICK	"	"

COMPANY B.—(Continued.)

Name.	Rank.	Killed, Wounded, and Died.
MESSENGER, ROBERT or W. F.	Private	Killed at Second Bull Run August 30, 1862.
POWELL, BARTON W., JR.	"	"
SUTHERLAND, JOHN	"	"
SOBY (Attorney at Law, Philadelphia)	"	"
WOOD, ——	"	"
WHITE, JOHN	"	"
WARREN, NATHANIEL C.	"	"
HOPKINS, CHARLES S.	"	Died of typhoid fever at Chesapeake Hospital, Hampton, Va.
ARMSTRONG, MARTIN	"	Died.
McLEAN, WILLIAM S.	"	Died.
WILLOCK, WILLIAM C.	"	Ruptured on march from Harrison's Landing to Newport News; died at Philadelphia from its effects.
DUNHAM, JOHN E.	Orderly Sergeant.	Shot through head at Camp Hamilton, Virginia, June 7, 1861 (recovered).
BELL, EDWARD G.	Ord. S. & Act. Lt.	Wounded at Big Bethel (knee) June 10, 1861.
DUMONT, THEO. S.	Second Lieut.	"
ARMSTRONG, JOHN	Private	Fort Federal Hill, Baltimore, and discharged.
McCARTHY, EUGENE	Sergeant	Gaines' Mill June 27, 1862, and transferred to 146th New York May 4, 1863; taken prisoner at battle of Wilderness May 5, 1864, and died from disease engenderd in Andersonville.
McGEEHAN, JOHN	"	Wounded at Gaines' Mill June 27, 1862.
BEDELL, WILLIAM A.	Private	"
CORNELL, LUDLOW	"	" (twice)
LEWIS, FREDERICK	"	"
MOREAU, E.	"	" (head) (and killed at Second Bull Run).
WARREN, NATHANIEL C.	"	"
CREIGHTON, FREDERICK	Sergeant	Wounded at Sec. Bull Run Aug. 30, 1862.
PECK, HERBERT C.	"	"
COLWELL, GEORGE F.	Corporal	" (left leg amputated, ball through right thigh, left forefinger amp.)
RODGERS, OLIVER J.	"	"
SAXTON, WILLIAM W.	"	" (arm)
FARRELL, JOHN	Private	"
FELT, RICHARD K.	"	" (6 wounds) "

COMPANY B.—(Continued.)

Name.	Rank.	Killed, Wounded, and Died.
Fowler, Frederick	Private	Wounded at Sec. Bull Aug. 30, 1862.
Flynn, William	"	"
Greenwood, Henry	"	" th'gh head "
Harris, William	"	"
Johnson, Jesse C.	"	" and trans'd to 146th N.Y. May 4, 1863; k'd in bat. of Wild'ness May 5, 1864.
Munnie, Robert	"	"
Robinson, Joseph	"	" (leg) " and trans'd to 146th N.Y.; wounded and cripp'd for life bat. Gettysburg.
Sands, C. V.	"	"
Smart, Frederick G.	"	"
Slater, Alfred	"	" (groin) "
Stevenson, John	"	"
Williams, James	"	"
Dixon, Robert	"	Wounded at Chancellorsville May 3, 1863.
Wilson, Charles	"	"

COMPANY C.

Name.	Rank.	Killed, Wounded, and Died.
Hopper, Benjamin F.	Sergeant	Killed at Big Bethel June 10, 1861.
Wooster, Franklin	Corporal	" Gaines' Mill June 27, 1862.
Potts, William	Private	"
Roan, Patrick J.	"	"
McCauley, Dennis G.	Sergeant	Killed at Second Bull Run August 30, 1862.
Humphreys, Charles P.	Corporal	"
Bryant, Jonas A.	Private	"
Chatterton, William	"	"
Gibbs, John	"	"
Geer, Eugene P.	"	"
Lespinesse, Henry	"	Died of two wounds received at Second Bull Run August 30, 1862.
Loderhouse, Henry	"	Killed at Second Bull Run August 30, 1862.
O'Brien, Dennis	"	"

COMPANY C.—(Continued.)

Name.	Rank.	Killed, Wounded, and Died.
Ronalds, Thomas B.	Private	Killed at Second Bull Run August 30, 1862.
Sturgess, Reuben P.	"	Died of wounds received at Second Bull Run August 30, 1862.
Sofield, George W.	Corporal	Killed at Second Bull Run, August 30, 1862.
Gross, James G.	"	Died.
Hoyt, Nicholas H.	"	" in camp near Henry House, Virginia.
Lorton, Charles B.	Private	
Pickens, Nicholas B.	"	
Reeves, Francis.	"	
Brinkerhoff, Daniel.	Corporal	Wounded at Big Bethel June 10, 1861.
Duryea, George.	Captain	Wounded (severely) at Gaines' Mill June 27, 1862.
Prime, Ralph E.	Lieutenant	" "
Hermany, Elihu W.	Sergeant	" (twice) "
Atkins, Alfred.	Color Corporal	" (three times) "
Chatterton, William.	Private	" (knee) "
Engart, Martin.	"	" (head) "
Charles, Frank.	"	" (leg) "
Finnan, James.	"	" (leg) "
Grogan, John.	"	" (twice) "
Kretzler, Arthur C.	"	" (thigh, severely) "
O'Leary, Cornelius.	"	" (foot) "
Odell, John H.	"	" (thigh) "
Reubish, James.	"	" (elbow) "
Donohue,	Sergeant	Wounded at Second Bull Run August 30, 1862.
Wannemacker, George W.	"	" "
Reddington, Lawrence.	Corporal	" "
Kretzler, H. B. (or Reitzer)	"	" "
Brennan, John.	Private	" "
Chalrott, Henry.	"	" "
Callagan, George.	"	" "
Demarest, Daniel.	"	" (stomach) "
Grogan, John.	"	" " and missing.
Labagh, J. G.	"	" "
McAnespie, John.	"	" "

COMPANY C.—(Continued.)

Name.	Rank.	Killed, Wounded, and Died
TOBIN, JAMES H.	Private	Wounded at Second Bull Run August 30, 1862. (arm amputated).
WHYTAL, JAMES	"	"
SMITH, EBENEZER	Corporal	Missing in action, Second Bull Run August 30, 1862.
MATOS, LEWIS	Private	"
O'DONOGHUE, ———	"	Wounded at siege of Yorktown, Va., May 3, 1862.
(And others, unknown).		

COMPANY D.

Name.	Rank.	Killed, Wounded, and Died
MATHEWS, JOHN E.	Corporal	Killed at Gaines' Mill June 27, 1862.
STONE, ARNOLD G.	"	Died of wounds received at Gaines' Mill June 27, 1862.
BERRIAN, ABRAHAM	Private	Killed at Gaines' Mill June 27, 1862.
DENTON, JAMES	"	"
DEMAREST, WILLIAM	"	Died of wounds received at Gaines' Mill June 27, 1862.
HILBERT, BARNEY	"	Killed at Gaines' Mill June 27, 1862.
HOAGLAND, ABRAHAM	"	"
MCDONALD, ARCHIBALD	"	"
PRICE, JOHN B.	"	"
SNIFFEN, GEORGE H.	"	"
SMITH, JESSE	"	"
LEWIS, WILBUR F.	Captain	Killed at Second Bull Run August 30, 1862.
WRIGHT, EDWARD O.	Second Lieut.	Died of wounds received at Second Bull Run August 30, 1862.
PIERCE, JOSEPH H.	Sergeant	Killed at Second Bull Run August 30, 1862.
BERRIAN, BENJAMIN	Corporal	"
BLUNT, JAMES S.	Private	"
COLLUM, HENNESSEY	"	"
HAGADORN, CYRUS	"	Died of wounds received at Second Bull Run August 30, 1862.
JOHNSON, JOHN	"	"
MCCARTY, JAMES	"	Killed at Second Bull Run August 30, 1862.
MAHON, JOHN T.	"	"
CARR, CHARLES H.	Sergeant	Died of disease July 10, 1862.
BROSCHER, JOHN D.	Private	Wounded at Big Bethel June 10, 1861.

COMPANY D.—(Continued.)

Name.	Rank.	Killed, Wounded, and Died.
MOORE, EDWARD D.	Private	Wounded at Big Bethel June 10, 1861.
REISLAND, GUNTHER	"	Wounded at Cold Harbor June 1, 1872.
SHURTER, JAMES W.	First Sergeant	Wounded at Gaines' Mill June 27, 1862.
SCREEDER, WILLIAM S.	Corporal	" " " " (leg amputated).
WUST, JOHN	"	" " " "
CARR, FLAVELL W.	Color Corporal	" " " "
BANCKER, ABRAHAM	Private	Wounded (knee) at Gaines' Mill June 27, 1862.
BLYTHE, ISAAC	"	" (ankle, severely) " "
DISBROW, WILLIAM H.	"	" " " "
HALLORAN, THOMAS	"	" (arm, severely) " "
MURNIN, JAMES	"	" " " "
REILLY, JOHN	"	" (leg, severely) " "
REILLY, JOHN H.	Sergeant	Wounded at Second Bull Run August 30, 1862.
HILLS, JAMES L.	Corporal	" " " "
MELDOWNY, GEORGE M.	"	" " " " (shot through body).
BICKEL, FRANCIS B.	Private	" " " "
BROSCHER, JOHN D.	"	" " " "
BANCKER, ABRAHAM	"	" " " "
BENHAM, JAMES P.	"	" " " "
BIRD, EDWARD J.	"	" " " "
DALY, GEORGE	"	" " " "
FENNER, JOHN R.	"	" " " "
HOLTHEYSER, JACOB	"	" " " " and missing, Gen. Or. No. 92.
NEWMAN, JOHN E.	"	" " " " (lost right arm).
PEASE, BENJAMIN F.	"	" " " " and missing, Gen. Or. No. 92.
SHAW, DAVID A.	"	" " " " " " "
WILDEY, WILLIAM R.	"	" " " "
MURNIN, JAMES	"	" " " "
BOSHART, WILLIAM	"	" " " "
SCHOONMAKER, GARRETT J.	"	Compound fracture of ankle.

COMPANY E.

Name.	Rank.	Killed, Wounded, and Died.
ALLEN, CHARLES M.	Private	Killed at Gaines' Mill June 27, 1862.
EDMONDS, JAMES S.	"	Died (July 3, 1862) of two wounds received at Gaines' Mill, June 27, 1862.
GALBRAITH, WILLIAM.	"	Killed at Gaines' Mill June 27, 1862.
GILLIGAN, LUKE.	Corporal.	Killed at Gaines' Mill June 27, 1862.
SODEN, OWEN.	Private.	Died of wounds received at Gaines' Mill June 27, 1862.
ALLAIRE, JAMES M.	Corporal.	Died of wounds received at Second Bull Run August 30, 1862.
BILLETER, CHARLES E.	Private.	Killed at Second Bull Run August 30, 1862.
BLAKE, RICHARD.	"	"
BRADY, JAMES.	"	"
CLARK, ALFRED B.	Color Corporal.	"
CRAFT, JOHN.	Private.	"
KERR, JOHN.	"	Died of wounds received at Second Bull Run August 30, 1862.
KIMBALL, FLETCHER.	"	"
MCGEEHAN, GEORGE.	"	"
MORRISON, GEORGE.	"	Killed at Second Bull Run August 30, 1862.
MOREAU, LEON.	"	"
SPENCER, GEORGE T.	"	"
ROSS, CHARLES H.	"	Died of wounds received at Second Bull Run August 30, 1862.
ROY, THEOPHILUS E.	"	Sept. 4th of wounds received at Second Bull Run, August 30, 1862.
BAZELEY, WILLIAM T.	"	Died of typhoid fever, Dec. 3, 1862.
DE WAR, ALEXANDER.	"	disease April 18, 1862.
SCHULLENBURG, JACOB.	"	congestion of lungs, in camp, near Henry House, Va., Feb. 5, 1863.
KNOWLES, JOSEPH.	First Lieutenant.	Wounded at Big Bethel June 10, 1861 (lost right arm).
COLLINS, JOHN.	First Sergeant.	Wounded at Gaines' Mill June 27, 1862, and ———.
QUAY, WILLIAM.	Corporal.	"
SCHOLLAND, VALENTINE.	"	"
GLANCY, JACOB.	"	"
BONE, JOHN F.	Private.	"
COVENTRY, JOHN C.	"	"
DE GROOT, WILLIAM H.	"	"
FORFAR, ROBERT.	"	"
FRANK, EMILE.	Bugler.	" (3 times)
GILLIGAN, JAMES S.	Private.	"

COMPANY E.—(Continued.)

Name.	Rank.	Killed, Wounded, and Died.
HORAN, GEORGE	Private.	Wounded at Gaines' Mill June 27, 1862.
JOHNES, ARTHUR	Corporal.	" (twice) (foot amputated).
JONES, WILLIAM	Private.	"
KERCHNER, PHILIP	"	"
RAY, ALFRED	"	" (twice)
WOOLSEY, CHARLES L.	Corporal.	" and missing, Gen'l Order, No. 92.
WINSLOW, MIRON	"	"
BURLOW, GEORGE P.	Private.	Second Bull Run August 30, 1862.
BRENNAN, JOHN	"	"
BRADY, CHARLES	"	"
CRUGER, EDWARD	"	"
CASSIN, JOHN	"	" (through both thighs and head).
COCHRAN, JAMES	"	"
CONNOLLY, JOHN	Corporal.	"
COATES, ANDREW	Private.	"
DE GROOT, WILLIAM H.	"	"
DOLSON, HENRY J.	Sergeant.	"
GATES, JOSEPH	Private.	"
LEAHY, JOSEPH	"	" (thigh)
MENGES, JACOB	"	"
RICHTON, THOMAS	Corporal.	"
ROGERS, JOHN	"	"
SINCLAIR, GEORGE M.	Private.	Missing June 27, 1862.
VAN GEN DEREN, PETER	"	" August 30, 1862 (reported dead).
LEACH, WILLIAM R.	"	Wounded and _____
SYLVESTER, AUSTIN	"	
LUFF, NICHOLAS	"	
PORTER, WILLIAM B.	"	
CROWLEY, JEREMIAH	Sergeant.	" (severely) in skirmish on Potomac September 21, 1862.

COMPANY F.

Name.	Rank.	Killed, Wounded, and Died.
PHILLIPS, EDGAR	Sergeant	Killed at Gaines' Mill June 27, 1862.
RYER, WILLIAM C.	Corporal	" " " " "
MANDERVILLE, WILLIAM H.	Private	" " " " " (two balls through the chest).
SWEENEY, WILLIAM	"	Died of wounds August 11, 1862, received at Gaines' Mill June 27, 1862.
O'NEIL, CHARLES	"	Killed at Gaines' Mill June 27, 1862.
DEALY, SIMON	"	" " " " "
HAGER, GEORGE O.	Captain	Killed at Second Bull Run August 30, 1862.
SOVEREIGN, FREDERICK W.	Adjutant	" " " " "
LEAVITT, GEORGE W.	Corporal	" " " " "
MORGAN, FRANCIS A.	"	" " " " "
COWLES, CLINTON S.	Private	" " " " "
DAVIDSON, WILLIAM F.	"	Died of wounds September 3d, received at Second Bull Run Aug. 30, 1862.
FLYNN, WILLIAM H.	"	Killed at Second Bull Run August 30, 1862.
MCGIBB, EDWARD	"	" " " " "
SIMMONDS, EDWARD	"	" " " " "
VELOUX, LOUIS	"	" " " " "
WELLS, JOHN (or DAVID)	"	" " " " "
WANNAMAKER, DREW	Sergeant	Died Sept. 5th of wounds received at Second Bull Run Aug. 30, 1862.
MITCHELL, GEORGE A.	Corporal	Wounded at Gaines' Mill June 27, 1862 (left forearm).
BROWN, JAMES W.	"	1
LEAVITT, GEORGE W.	Private	"
MAHONEY, J: MES	"	"
NEALE, JOHN W.	"	"
PLETSCH, JACOB	"	"
RUSSELL, TIMOTHY	First Sergeant	Wounded at Second Bull Run August 30, 1862 (hip).
MITCHELL, GEORGE A.	"	" " " " " (twice).
POTTER, CHARLES B.	"	" " " " "
MARSH, EFFINGHAM W.	Corporal	" " " " "
FRANKLIN, JAMES H.	"	" " " " "
WHEAT, WILLIAM A.	Private	" " " " "
BREHM, CHARLES E.	"	" " " " "
FARRELL, JOHN F.	"	" " " " " (four times).
HITCHCOCK, GEORGE A.	"	" " " " "

COMPANY F.—(Continued.)

Name.	Rank.	Killed, Wounded, and Died.
HEALY, THOMAS	Private	Wounded at Second Bull Run August 30, 1862.
HAUSMAN, NICHOLAS V.	"	"
KIEMILE, BRUNO	"	"
MORRISSEY, JAMES	"	"
MCGUFFIN, WILLIAM H.	"	"
PARKINSON, SAMUEL	"	"
PAUL, NATHANIEL S.	Corporal	"
POST, GEORGE	Private	"
RILEY, CHARLES F.	"	"
RILEY, JAMES H.	"	"
SADLER, ROBERT	"	"
SULLIVAN, BENJAMIN A.	"	"
SHERRIDAN, JAMES	"	"
WEBB, JAMES W.	"	"
DILLON, ROBERT	Sergeant	Leg amputated at Fort Federal Hill, Baltimore.

COMPANY G.

Name.	Rank.	Killed, Wounded, and Died.
CARTWRIGHT, THOMAS W., Jr.	Captain	Died of wounds received at Gaines' Mill June 27, 1862.
AMICI, AUGUSTO	Corporal	"
COLBY, WALTER S.	Private	" (fought under Garibaldi.)
HASSELL, JOHN	"	"
WILLIAMS, ANDREW	"	"
MURRAY, FRANK	First Sergeant	Killed at Gaines' Mill June 27, 1862.
MCDOWELL, WILLIAM	Color Sergeant	Killed at Second Bull Run August 30, 1862 (hit twice).
SPELLMAN, FRANCIS	Corporal	Died about Sept. 3d of wounds received at Second Bull Run Aug. 30, 1862.
NOBLE, JOHN A.	Private	" of wounds received at Second Bull Run August 30, 1862.
BRADY, PATRICK H.	"	Killed at Second Bull Run August 30, 1862 (hit twice).
BALDWIN, CHARLES W.	"	"
CATHEY, JAMES	"	"
ENTRES, IGNATZ	"	
HOFFMAN, EDWARD	"	

COMPANY G.—(Continued.)

Name.	Rank.	Killed, Wounded, and Died.
REED, CHARLES	Private	Killed at Second Bull Run August 30, 1862.
ROONEY, THOMAS	"	"
TAYLOR, GEORGE W.	"	" (hit seven times).
VAN BENSCHOTEN, GEORGE	"	"
WHIGHAM, ROBERT R.	"	"
WILSON, WILLIAM	"	Died of wounds received at Second Bull Run August 30, 1862.
CARTWRIGHT, THOMAS W.	Captain	Wounded at Big Bethel June 10, 1861.
BRADLEY, JOSEPH A.	Private	Wounded at Gaines' Mill June 27, 1862.
CARTNEY, THOMAS H.	"	"
CARTWRIGHT, GEORGE	"	" (both arms).
FINCH, JOHN K.	Corporal	"
HART, JAMES	Private	"
SNYDER, CHARLES	"	"
ALBRECHT, CHRISTIAN P.	Second Lieut.	Wounded at Second Bull Run August 30, 1862.
MARTIN THOMAS R.	Private	"
AMOS, ROBERT	"	"
BOYLE, JOHN	"	" (b'th thighs)
BYRNES, DAVID	"	"
BRISCOE, THOMAS J.	"	"
BROWN, LEANDER	"	"
COLE, WILLIAM	"	"
GILLEN, JOHN	Corporal	" (twice, lame)
GITTERE, PETER	Private	"
GUINAN, DENNIS	"	"
LAWSON, ENICK	"	" (lame)
MCMAHON, MACHAEL	"	"
PATTERSON, JAMES	"	" (3 times)
ROGERS, NICHOLAS D.	"	"
REILEY, JAMES J.	"	"
ROGERS, ALONZO J.	Corporal	" (5 times)
SHEPARD, WILLIAM F.	Private	" (3 times)
SMITH, GEORGE W.	"	" (arm)
TAYLOR, CHARLES H.	"	" (twice)

COMPANY G.—(Continued.)

Name.	Rank.	Killed, Wounded, and Died.
WILSON, PHILIP L.	Sergeant	Wounded (3 times, lame) at Second Bull Run August 30, 1862.
FIELDS, JOSEPH	Corporal	Wounded at Fredericksburg, Va., Dec. 14, 1862.
WILSON, CHARLES H.	Private	" (severely)
CALLAHAN, JAMES	"	Wounded at Snicker's Gap, Va. (discharged).
DILL, JAMES E.	"	Injured by a mortar, Yorktown, Va.
ROUSE, LEVI	"	Wounded on picket.
TAYLOR, CHARLES H.	"	Shot through leg at Baltimore.
(Five injured by accidents).		

COMPANY H.

Name.	Rank.	Killed, Wounded, and Died.
GRIGGS, JAMES J.	Private	Killed at Big Bethel June 10, 1861.
ALLISON, ANDREW B.	Color Sergeant	Killed at Second Bull Run August 30, 1862.
AMES, WILLIAM H.	Private	"
HEFFERMAN, JOHN	"	"
KENT, JAMES	"	Died of wounds received at Second Bull Run August 30, 1862.
MARSH, WILLIAM H.	"	Killed at Second Bull Run, August 30, 1862.
McLAREN, JAMES	"	Died of wounds received at Second Bull Run August 30, 1862.
REYNOLDS, JAMES	"	"
USSHER, JAMES	"	Killed at Second Bull Run August 30, 1862.
WILLIAMS, HORACE E.	"	"
STEVENS, PETER C.	"	Died of disease December 2, 1862.
KILPATRICK, JUDSON	Captain	Wounded at Big Bethel June 10, 1861.
COHEN, HENRY E.	Sergeant	"
COCHRANE, JAMES A.	Private	"
DUNN, JOHN	"	" (lost right arm).
LYONS, ALFRED	"	November 8, 1861 (hand amputated).
AGNUS, FELIX	Second Lieut.	at Gaines' Mill June 27, 1862 (left arm useless).
COHEN, HENRY E.	Sergeant	" (severely).
FAY, JOHN	"	"
GREEN, CHARLES	Corporal	" (wrist).

COMPANY H.—(Continued.)

Name.	Rank.	Killed, Wounded, and Died.
KEENEY, JOHN H.	Corporal	Wounded at Gaines' Mill June 27, 1862 (severely).
BUTLER, WILLIAM H.	Private	" " " " " (abdomen).
PYNNER, WILLIAM H.	"	" " " " " (shoulder).
COCHRANE, JAMES, JR.	"	" " " " " (severely).
CHALMERS, HUGH	"	Wounded at Gaines' Mill June 27, 1862 (arm), subsequently promoted First Sergeant, transferred to 146th N. Y. Vol. as Second Lieut, and killed at Cold Harbor near the scene of his first wound.
DIPPLE, GEORGE W.	"	Wounded at Gaines' Mill June 27, 1862 (severely).
HIGGINS, FRANCIS	"	" " " " "
HODGKINSON, FRANCIS S.	"	" " " " "
LEWIS, CHARLES S.	"	" " " " " (neck).
MILLER, CHARLES C.	"	" " " " "
MYERS, ALFRED	"	" " " " "
REED, JAMES O.	"	" " " " " (head, severely).
RICHARDS, JOHN B.	"	" " " " "
ROBINSON, MICHAEL	"	" " " " " (shoulder).
STRUBLE, JULIUS J.	"	" " " " " (head).
TRAVERS, ALVIN M.	"	" " " " " (leg).
TUCKER, ROBERT C.	"	" " " " " (severely).
WOODFULL, HENRY	Second Lieut	Pamunkey Bridge May 26, 1862.
RAYMOND, JOHN S.	Private	Second Bull Run August 30, 1862.
ALEXANDER, WILLIAM	Corporal	" " " " (severely).
BOYD, JAMES S.	Private	" " " " (lost arm).
BOLLET, FREDERICK	"	" " " " (four times).
COCHRANE, JAMES A.	"	" " " "
ENGEL, EDWARD	"	" " " " (severely).
FINLEY, GEORGE F.	Corporal	" " " " (thigh).
GLEASON, PATRICK	Private	" " " " (severely).
KILILEA, FRANCIS	"	" " " " "
LIVINGSTON, WILLIAM	"	" " " " "
LUNNEY, CHARLES	"	" " " " "
MADDEN, THOMAS J.	"	" " " " (severely).
RILEY, JAMES	"	" " " " "

Casualties—Company I.

COMPANY H.—(Continued.)

Name.	Rank.	Killed, Wounded, and Died.
ROGGENSTEIN, WILLIAM	Private	Wounded at Second Bull Run August 30, 1862. (severely).
SCHERER, LOUIS	"	"
WALKER, WILLIAM	"	"
ZINK, WILLIAM	"	"

COMPANY I.

Name.	Rank.	Killed, Wounded, and Died.
THEFORTH, DAVID	Private	Killed at Big Bethel June 10, 1861.
WHITE, PATRICK	"	"
PARTRIDGE, WILLIAM T.	Captain	Killed at Gaines' Mill June 27, 1862.
RAILTON, JOHN E.	Private	"
SOUTHERN, GEORGE W.	"	"
VAN SICKLIN, GEORGE D.	"	"
VAN KEUREN, THEORON	"	"
VAN WAGNER, JAMES	"	"
LYONS, ELI H.	Sergeant	Killed at Second Bull Run August 30, 1862.
ALLMACK, JOHN W.	Private	"
BRADLEY, JOHN (or LERON S.)	"	"
DILLON, EDWARD	"	"
HANNON, JOHN C.	"	"
MILLIGAN, JOHN	"	"
SINCLAIR, GEORGE W.	"	"
SAULT, HENRY S.	Color Corporal	Died of wounds received at Second Bull Run August 30, 1862.
ROBINSON, JAMES B.	Private	Killed at Second Bull Run August 30, 1862.
BLAKE, SAMUEL H.	Sergeant	"
UPTON, ——	Corporal	Died at Harrison's Landing.
STEVENS, ——	Private	Wounded on picket, Camp Hamilton.
KETCHAM, BENJAMIN	First Lieutenant	Wounded at Big Bethel June 10, 1861.
YORK, JOSEPH S.	Private	" (both shoulder-blades).
YEAGER, JOSEPH	"	"
MAJOR, THOMAS R.	Sergeant	Wounded at Gaines' Mill June 27, 1862 (head).

COMPANY I.—(Continued.)

Name.	Rank.	Killed, Wounded, and Died.
MELDRUM, ALBERT R.	Sergeant	Wounded at Gaines' Mill June 27, 1862 (leg).
WALKER, CHARLES A.	Corporal	" " " " (head).
BROGAN, JOHN C.	"	" " " " (head).
DAWSON, CHARLES H.	Private	" " " " (leg).
FARLEY, JOHN	"	" " " " (arm).
PINE, THOMAS	"	" " " " (neck).
ROONEY, EDWARD T.	"	" " " " (missing).
WOOD, GEORGE A.	"	
CRAWFORD, JAMES P.	"	
HOFFMANN, WILLIAM	Lieutenant	Wounded at Second Bull Run August 30, 1862 (3 times).
BOYD, JAMES	Corporal	"
RANKIN, ALFONSO	Color Corporal	" (missing).
CABE, JOHN	Private	"
HEARNE, JAMES H.	"	" (leg).
HENDRY, WILLIAM H.	"	" (twice).
PINE, THOMAS	"	"
JONES, MOSES G.	"	"
SLOAT, WILLIAM B.	"	"
SIMON, HENRY	"	"
WILSON, ALLEN	"	"
MADDEN, HENRY	"	Wounded at Fredericksburg Dec. 14, 1862.
(Others, names not ascertained).		

COMPANY K.

Name.	Rank.	Killed, Wounded, and Died.
MCCANN, JAMES C.	Sergeant	Killed at Gaines' Mill June 27, 1862.
POPE, THOMAS T.	Corporal	" " " "
BEEBE, JOHN K.	Private	" " " "
LEWIS, GEORGE	"	" " " "
NEIL, ROBERT	"	Died of wounds received at Gaines' Mill June 27, 1862.
OLIVER, PERCY E. J.	"	Killed at Gaines' Mill June 27, 1862.
SANGLE, FREDERICK	"	

COMPANY K.—(Continued.)

Name.	Rank.	Killed, Wounded, and Died.
SMITH, JOSEPH A.	Private	Killed at Gaines' Mill June 27, 1862.
STAKEM, JAMES P.	"	Died of wounds July 26th, received at Gaines' Mill June 27, 1862.
WEEKS, JOSEPH A.	"	Aug. 24th, "
WEBB, JOHN	"	Killed at Gaines' Mill June 27, 1862.
HOGEBOOM, WILLIAM B.	Sergeant	Died of wounds Sept. 10th, received at Second Bull Run Aug. 30, 1862.
BUXTON, HENRY H.	"	Oct. 21st, "
SHANNON, WILLIAM G.	Corporal	Oct. 30th, "
KEYES, JOHN C.	"	Killed at Second Bull Run August 30, 1862.
ACKERMAN, RICHARD	Private.	Died of wounds March, 1863, received at Second Bull Run Aug. 30, 1862.
COPPERS, JAMES	"	Killed at Second Bull Run August 30, 1862.
DAVIS, DAVID	"	"
HERRICK, THOMAS	"	"
JONES, ROWLAND	"	"
PLUMB, FRANCIS M.	"	"
SILLECK, ALBERT	"	"
REYNOLDS, WILLIAM T.	Color Sergeant	Died of typhoid fever June 24, 1861.
BEACH, MICHAEL	Private.	" 10, " (sick fourteen days).
GILDER, FRANCIS	"	Sept. 12, " (in an ambulance, and buried under a large pine tree).
MINOR, LAFAYETTE	"	June 27, "
CONWAY, JOHN	Private.	Wounded at Big Bethel June 10, 1861.
WINSLOW, CLEVELAND	Captain	Federal Hill (foot).
PARKER, SIMEON B.	Sergeant	Gaines' Mill June 27, 1862.
BUXTON, HENRY H.	"	"
SHEFFREY, JOHN J. L.	Corporal.	" (in breast, and arm amputated).
KIMBER, HERBERT P.	"	"
DECKER, JAMES W.	Private.	"
HAUGHWOUT, SIMON	"	"
O'KEEFE, DANIEL	"	"
WINZER, JULIUS E.	"	"
CADY, JOHN N.	Corporal.	at Second Bull Run August 30, 1862.
CLAYTON, JOHN H.	"	"
PATTERSON, GARDNER	"	"

COMPANY K.—(Continued.)

Name.	Rank.	Killed, Wounded, and Died.
*Swain, Lucien B.	Corporal	Wounded at Second Bull Run August 30, 1862.
Baldwin, Lemuel	Private	"
Carter, James W.	"	"
Cary, Pierce	"	"
Davidson, George	"	"
Egan, Edward	"	"
Finn, John	"	"
Fraleigh, David M.	"	"
Haughwout, John H.	"	"
Horgan, John	"	"
Kerrigan, John	"	"
Lesne, Henry	"	"
Martin, John H.	"	"
Mills, Henry	"	"
Newberry, Francis D.	"	"
Pond, Levi T.	"	"
Stuyvesant, Charles	"	"
Sturgis, Oscar C.	"	"

* His being wounded certified to by Thomas Antisell, M.D., Surgeon of Harewood Hospital, Washington, D. C.

COMPANIES UNKNOWN.

Name.	Rank.	Killed, Wounded, and Died.
Frank W. Doolittle	Surgeon	Wounded at Gaines' Mill June 27, 1862 (ankle).
Smith, _____	"	Died of fever at Yorktown, Va., May 5, 1862.
Name unknown	"	Drowned at Baltimore, Md.
Reed, Thomas	"	Shot and killed at No. 101 Mercer Street, New York City, Feb. 6, 1863, by Michael Brady, who, in company with Clark W. Beach, both Special Detectives in the service of the U. S., were attempting his arrest for desertion from the regiment.
Name unknown	"	Wounded at Big Bethel June 10, 1861.

COMPANIES UNKNOWN.—(Continued.)

Name.	Rank.	Killed, Wounded, and Died.
GREGG, JAMES		Wounded at Gaines' Mill June 27, 1862.
MURPHY, THOMAS (supposed E Co.)		" " " (shoulder).
GRAY, JOHN (supposed C Co.)		" " "
ASHEIDER, CHRISTOPHER		Wounded at Second Bull Run August 30, 1862.
CRAGEN, JOHN		" " "
GILLMAN, G.		" " " (knee and thigh).
GARSTENACKER, JOHN		" " "
TAYLOR, ——		" " "
MORGAN, ANDREW G.		Missing from June 27, 1862.
HANTON, JACOB		Wounded and missing from August 30, 1862.
PERRIN, WILLIAM		Missing from August 30, 1862.
Names unknown of three		Wounded at Fredericksburg, Va.
" " eight		Wounded at Chancellorsville, Va.

(Besides some missing.)

RECAPITULATION.

KILLED	177
DIED OF DISEASE	25
MISSING IN ACTION	7
WOUNDED IN ACTION	340
INJURED	6
	555

STATISTICS.

In round numbers, the total number of officers and men in the regiment who were sworn into the United States service, was:

For two years, about............................	900
" three " "	600
	1,500

Of the above there were—

Killed in action, died of wounds or disease.....	202
Missing in action............................	7
Discharged on account of wounds, disease engendered in the service, commissioned in other regiments, dishonorably discharged, deserted or unaccounted for and dropped from the rolls, under Gen. Order, No. 92...................	754
Loss in two years' service....................	963
Three years' men transferred to 146th New York, May 4th, 1863, to serve the balance of their unexpired term............................	237
Two years' men mustered out May 14, 1863, 273	
" officers................... 27	
	300
	1,500

Of the two years' men who came home with the regiment, about 100 bore the scars of wounds, and had been in hospital on account thereof, for periods of from four to ten months. There were only about 80 men out of the 900 who were in every engagement, and had not been absent from the regiment on account of sickness or wounds during the two years' service. All of these, with very few exceptions, had received from one to seven balls through their clothing, or had received shaves, not, however, serious enough to be classed as wounds.

Statistics. 419

A number of the two years' men re-enlisted, or served as officers in the 5th Veterans, or in other organizations, many of whom were killed, died, or were disabled from wounds or sickness.

There were three regiments organized by the officers of the old Fifth, besides the parent organization, viz.: The 5th Veterans; the 165th New York; and the 2d New York, Harris' Light Cavalry. Of the 237 men transferred to the 146th New York, a large proportion of them were killed or wounded in their after service, in various campaigns of the Army of the Potomac—Gettysburg, the Wilderness, Spottsylvania, or front of Petersburg.

On the 6th day of July, 1861, twenty-six men enlisted in the Fifth for three years. When the regiment left the front, those who remained of these men, were transferred, with others, to the 146th Regiment; to serve out the remainder of their time. On the 6th day of July, 1864, only one of the 26 remained in the service to be mustered out. His name was James W. Webb, formerly of Company F, 5th New York. His companion who remained of the twenty-six, Christian Neuber, was wounded the day before, in front of Petersburg.

The average age of the men enlisted in the Fifth was not quite twenty-three years; of the officers, about twenty-seven.

List of Members of the Fifth Regiment who lost their lives during the War after the muster out of the original regiment. The list is not complete, owing to the impossibility of ascertaining the various organizations in which many of our Members re-enlisted.

Name.	Rank.	Killed, Wounded, and Died.
Cleveland Winslow	Colonel 5th Vets	Died July 7, 1864, of wounds received in action of Bethesda Church, Va.
Rev. Dr. Gordon Winslow, D.D.	Chaplain	Drowned in the Potomac.
Henry A. Swartwout	Capt. & Bvt. Maj. 17th In. U. S. A.	Inspector-General of the Depar't of Texas, died at Galveston Oct. 8, 1867.
Oliver Wetmore, Jr	Maj. and Bvt. Lieut-Col.	Died in Washington, D. C.
Joseph S. York	Captain U. S. A.	Died, or was killed in the West.
Charles S. Montgomery	Capt. & Bvt. Maj. U.S.V.	Killed at Hatcher's Run, Va., Feb. 6, 1865—5th veterans.
Peter D. Froeligh	First Lieut. 146th N.Y.V.	Killed in the Wilderness May 5, 1864.
Robert P. Warren	First Lieut. 14th U. S. In.	Died at Camp Douglass, Utah Territory, Jan. 24, 1876.
Hugh Chalmers	Second Lt. 146th N.Y.V.	Died June 9, 1864, at Richmond, Va., of wounds rec'd at Tolopotomoy, Va.
Thomas J. Taylor	Adjutant 5th N.Y.V.	Died in the Regular service.
James H. Everitt	Sergeant 146th N.Y.V	
—— Berrian	Sergeant	Killed.
Eugene McCarthy		Died from disease engendered while prisoner in Andersonville, Ga.
Henry Boody	Corporal	Killed in the Wilderness, Va., May 5, 1864.
James Duff	"	"
Samuel Hart	"	"
George T. Wing	"	"
James Lynch	"	Died of wounds received in action June 10, 1864.
Aaron P. Muckridge	Private	Killed at Laurel Hill, Va., May 10, 1864.
Frank M. Dennis	"	Killed at Gettysburg July 3, 1863.
Frederick Miller	"	Died at Gettysburg Oct. 30, 1863, of wounds received July 3d.
Sherwood C. Hines	"	
Samuel Schilling	"	Killed in the Wilderness, Va., May 5, 1864.
John N. Longworth	"	"

LIST OF MEMBERS, Etc.—(Continued.)

Name.	Rank.	Killed, Wounded, and Died.
Henry B. Curtiss	Private	Killed in the Wilderness, Va., May 5, 1864.
William Curtiss	"	"
James McCluskey	"	Died from wounds received in the Wilderness, Va., May 5, 1864.
George M. Baker	"	Died in U. S. General Hospital, Alexandria, Va.
William Kniffin	"	Died of wounds June 17, 1864, receiv'd in the Wilderness, Va., May 5, 1864.
Thomas Cody	"	received in action May 25, 1864.
Louis Polex	"	Killed in action near Petersburg, Va., June 18, 1864.
Jacob H. Stark	"	Killed at Hatchers' Run, Va., February 6, 1865.
Cornelius Lane	"	Died of disease Sept., 1864, in Andersonville, Ga., while prisoner of war.
Jessie C. Johnson	"	" Oct. 24, " "
David T. Newcomb	"	" Aug. 10, " "
James Rodman	"	" " "
John P. Forsman	"	" " "
S. W. Ford	"	Died of fever at Fort Warren, Boston Harbor.
Frederick A. Price	"	in Hospital at Washington, D. C.
John B. Swift	"	City Point, Va., September 1, 1864.
Nathaniel Dickson	"	December 9, 1863, in Camp near Bealton Station, Va.
Henry C. Van Voorhies	"	November 23, 1864, at Galesburgh, N. C., while prisoner of war.
David Coon	"	at Wilmington, N. C., February 25, 1865.
Edward Holland	"	Killed by the explosion of a cannon at West Point, N. Y., July 4, ——
Charles Fleet	"	"
Lenox Millard	"	
John Clark	"	

The number of members of the Fifth Regiment who were killed, wounded, or died in the service during the war was over 700, or about 50 per cent. of their total number. Of whom, one served as an officer in the English army, another in Turkey, Several went abroad and served in foreign armies. two in Mexico, and one was killed under the French flag during the late war with Germany. In the city our number is small, and, though many efforts have been made to perfect an organization, we have failed for want of numbers. Though we still have Generals Duryée, Warren, Davies, Kilpatrick, and Colonel Hiram Duryea, we have lost since the war many brave hearts, who have gone to join their comrades who died in uniform."

PERSONAL SKETCHES.

COLONEL ABRAM DURYÉE.

COLONEL ABRAM DURYÉE, late commander of the Seventh Regiment, National Guard, was born in the city of New York in 1815. He descended from a French Huguenot family, who came to America on the revocation of the Edict of Nantes by Louis XIV. of France, in 1685.

He engaged in mercantile business in New York, in which pursuit he met with honorable success and realized a fortune.

He commenced his military career, at the early age of eighteen years, as a private in the One Hundred and Forty-second Militia, and subsequently served in the ranks of one of the companies of the National Guard—then Twenty-seventh Regiment—September, 1838; and after passing through all the different grades of the non-commissioned officers with distinction, he obtained a Second Lieutenant's commission on the 21st of February, 1840, and was promoted on the 4th of October, 1841, to the First Lieutenancy, and on January 16, 1844, he was elected to the post of Captain. On the 22d of September, 1845, he was elected a field officer, with the rank of Major. On November 24th of the same year he was promoted to the rank of Lieutenant-Colonel, and on January 29, 1849, he succeeded to the command of the regiment, with the rank of Colonel.

Like many eminent men, he has achieved distinction by his skill, perseverance, untiring energy, and strict attention to his duties, until he ascended from the lowest to a high rank as a military commander, and the acknowledged chief of the first volunteer regiment in the country.

The present enviable reputation of the National Guard is owing, in a great degree, to his ability and exertion as an officer.

He determined to place the regiment in the front rank from the moment he was placed in command. While stern and exacting as a disciplinarian, he was affable, modest, and kind-hearted in his social intercourse. At the head of his regiment, he was always the *soldier*, but never forgetting the relative position and standing of the men under his command. The possession of these traits of character secured the attachment of the members of his regiment. The proof of his decision of character, and to what extent he possessed the affection of the men, was illustrated in that unfortunate and ever-to-be-remembered bloody riot at the Astor Place Opera House, on the occasion of Mr. Macready's appearance. When the turmoil was at its height, missiles were thrown at his command, and his men fell wounded in all directions around him. A shout was raised by the law-and-order party for them to fire, as it would be impossible for the military to retain their position longer unless something of a determined and defensive character was done. But the authorities held back, in the hope of being able to restore peace and quiet without bloodshed. The Colonel, knowing that he had no authority to act in the premises without orders from his superiors in command (Generals Sandford and Hall), was observed walking up and down in front of his regiment, encouraging his men; and while doing so, he was struck twice in quick succession, by stones thrown from the crowd. His men, observing the imminent danger he was in, shouted to him to fall in the rear of his regiment; but, instead of this, he renewed his efforts of encouraging his command to be patient, until he was compelled to fall in the rear by the order given by the sheriff to fire. This forbearance on the part of himself and his men was very praiseworthy, and will never be forgotten by those who witnessed the exciting scene on that remarkable night. He had been on duty in all the riots for the twenty years last preceding the great civil war, and was particularly instrumental in subduing the police and "Dead Rabbit" riots of July, 1857. He also commanded his regiment on two expeditions to Boston, and drilled on the Common of that city with great success, in presence of a large number of distinguished persons, and thousands of its inhabitants. He was also the commanding officer at Camp Trumbull, New Haven; Camp Worth,

Kingston, besides quartering his regiment one week at Newport, R. I., to which is to be added the escort expedition to Richmond, Washington, Mount Vernon, and Baltimore.

The Seventh Regiment bears the name, and deservedly too, of being a pattern to its associates in arms; and they have exemplified the truth, that the best *citizens are the best soldiers*, and that it is no mark of courage, or indication of prowess, to cast aside the courtesies or amenities of life.

To Colonel Duryée we may not invidiously ascribe the maintenance of that high discipline and gallant bearing which so distinguishes the Seventh Regiment above its compeers; and this may be said without detracting, in the slightest degree, from the merits of any officer and soldier of his command. The superior in all cases gives the general tone to his subordinates.

He is the author of Rules and Regulations for the government of the regiment in the field or in quarters; also, several treatises on street-fighting. The latter was adopted by the New York State Legislature in the fall of 1857, after a committee of army and militia officers witnessed the admirable performance of the Seventh Regiment on the Fifth Avenue, in the summer of that year.

Colonel Duryée adopted Colonel Hardee's beautiful light infantry tactics in the year 1855, and his was the first military body that went through any of the exercises contained in that work; but the laws for the government of the army and militia of the United States then in force, prevented his adopting it until it was recognized and approved by the War Department.

In the autumn of 1857 he adopted the system in full, and, after a thorough course of drill throughout the winter, he invited the author to witness its performance by the 7th Regiment at a battalion drill at the City Arsenal, Friday evening, March 19, 1858. The room was crowded with a large number of ladies and gentlemen, among whom were seen the beautiful uniforms of our army and navy officers, and the familiar faces of some of our most distinguished citizens. After the marching was over, the Colonel ordered his regiment to prepare for review. Colonel Hardee, accompanied by other officers and staff of the regiment, made a thorough inspection, after which Colonel Hardee took up his position at the side of Colonel Duryée, and the latter went through the manual.

The precision with which the regiment made the different movements of loading and firing, and the steadiness of the men, drew forth tremendous applause from the spectators present. Colonel Hardee was much surprised, and expressed astonishment at the result. He said that never had he witnessed a performance by any military body, in or out of the army, which surpassed it. At the conclusion, the regiment was greeted with a storm of plaudits.

After being connected with the Seventh for a period of twenty-one years, Colonel Duryée resigned his command, in the latter part of the year 1859; being succeeded by the late lamented Colonel Marshall Lefferts.

On the breaking out of the civil war, Colonel Duryée immediately responded to the call for troops by Governor Morgan, and tendered his services to the country. His offer was gladly accepted, and he was granted authority to raise a regiment of infantry, and received a commission as Colonel of Volunteers.

As the result of his efforts, the 5th Regiment New York Volunteers, otherwise known as Duryée's Zouaves, was organized. This regiment he brought up to a thorough state of discipline, and in drill it was excelled by none. It was destined to continue the hard drills after the command devolved on Colonel Warren and other officers, and, as it became older in the service, arrived at a still greater state of proficiency, especially in field tactics and bayonet exercise; so that when it became a part of the Army of the Potomac, it was generally acknowledged to be the most perfect volunteer regiment in general drill in the 5th corps, and probably in the whole army; but in bayonet exercise it was without a *rival*.

On May 27, 1861, Colonel Duryée was placed by General Butler in command of Camp Hamilton, as acting Brigadier-General—his brigade consisting of the 1st, 2d, 3d, 5th, and 10th Regiments New York Volunteers. General Pierce, of Massachusetts, having arrived at Fortress Monroe, Colonel Duryée was superseded by that officer, June 4th, when he again assumed command of his regiment.

On the 10th of June he took part with his regiment in the attack on Big Bethel, where he exposed himself, without flinching, to the enemy's fire.

General Pierce having been relieved, Colonel Duryée again assumed command of the brigade, with the addition of Colonel Baker's California regiment and the 20th New York. On the 31st of August, Colonel Duryée was commissioned a Brigadier-General of Volunteers by the President, and ordered to report to General Dix; and he was assigned to the command of the 17th and 21st Massachusetts, 7th and 10th Maine, 21st Indiana, 87th and 111th Pennsylvania, 2d, 3d, and 5th Maryland, and the 5th New York—the latter being assigned to the right of the brigade.

When General McClellan made his advance on Richmond *via* the Peninsula, General Duryée, with part of the troops under his command in Baltimore, was ordered to Washington, where he arrived and reported to General McDowell, and his command was assigned to General Ricketts' division of the 1st corps.

General Duryée served under General Pope in his campaign of 1862, and was engaged in the battles of Cedar Mountain, Rappahannock Station, Thoroughfare Gap, Groveton, Second Bull Run, and Chantilly.

The following are extracts from the official report of General Pope's Virginia campaign.

General Pope says: "General Duryée commanded his brigade, in the various operations of this campaign, with ability and zeal."

General McDowell, in his report, says: "General Ricketts, who, at Cedar Mountain and at Rappahannock Station, was under my immediate command, and rendered valuable service with the division, speaks in high terms of the gallantry of Generals Duryée and Tower, both at Thoroughfare Gap and the battle of the 30th, in which the former was slightly and the latter severely wounded."—*Exec. Doc. No.* 81, *3d Sess. 37th Congress.*

In General Ricketts' report of the second battle of Bull Run, we find the following:

"At sunrise on the 30th, ordered by you to send two brigades to report to General Kearney, and conducted the 1st brigade, General Duryée; 4th brigade, Colonel Thorburn; which relieved a portion of General Kearney's division. General Duryée's brigade advanced into the woods, driving the enemy along the old railroad excavation until directly under their guns. While occupying this ground General Duryée was subjected to a heavy fire of artillery and infantry, in which he received a slight wound and a severe contusion by a shell, but remained at his post animating his men, who behaved admirably. On recapitulating the services of brigade commanders, I would make particular mention of Brigadier-General Duryée for his noble conduct at Thoroughfare Gap, and his indomitable courage displayed at Bull Run while holding a trying position."—(Gen. RICKETTS' *Report*, p. 70).

"General McClellan again assuming command of the army, General Duryée served under him in the campaign in Maryland. He reinforced General Meade and fought under that officer at South Mountain, driving the enemy to the sanguinary field on Antietam, where he fought in the famous corn-field, where he was wounded and his horse shot under him; a portion of the time he commanded the division, owing to the wounding of General Hooker, who was compelled to retire from the field."— (SWINTON).

General Meade's report of the battle of South Mountain speaks highly of the promptness of General Duryée in ascending the mountain in support of the Penn Reserves, which resulted in the defeat of the enemy.

General Ricketts says in his report of the battle of Antietam :

"I commend the general good conduct of the division, and would mention particularly Brigadier-General Duryée, Colonels Coulter and Lyle, and Captains Matthews and Thompson of the artillery; indeed, both officers and men displayed courage under a severe fire."

General Duryée resigned his commission in the early part of 1863, and again retired to private life. He was breveted Major-General of Volunteers by the President, March 13, 1865. Governor Fenton, in forwarding the commission, says: "Conferred by the President, in recognition of your faithful and distinguished services in the late war." And added: "In behalf of the State, allow me to thank you for the gallantry and devotion which induced this conspicuous mention by the General Government."

From the New York *Times*, 1866:

Personal Sketches. 429

"At a meeting of the field officers of the seven regiments composing the 4th brigade, 1st division, N. G. S. N. Y., held pursuant to orders from General Headquarters, State of New York, at the armory of the 22d Regiment, N. G. S. N. Y., General Abram Duryée was unanimously elected Brigadier-General of the brigade, *vice* General John Ewen, resigned.

"The General's many years experience as Colonel of the 7th Regiment, National Guard, afterward Colonel of the famous 5th Regiment, New York Volunteers (Duryée's Zouaves), which has given a Warren, Kilpatrick, and Winslow to the army, and finally as Brigadier-General of Volunteers, eminently qualify him for the command."

In 1873 General Duryée was appointed Police Commissioner by the Hon. W. F. Havemeyer, and during his term of service devoted himself to the discipline and efficiency of the department. On the 13th of January, 1874, the formidable assemblage of Communists at Tompkins Square took place. General Duryée, with a small body of police, attacked the vast crowd with impetuosity, capturing their blood-red flags, destroying their inflammatory banners, and drove them in utter confusion from the park.

LIEUTENANT-COLONEL GOUVERNEUR KEMBLE WARREN.

GOUVERNEUR K. WARREN was born in Cold Spring, State of New York, January 8, 1830. He graduated second in a class of forty-five at the early age of twenty, from the United States Military Academy at West Point. Breveted Second Lieutenant in the Engineer Corps, he was employed in the survey of the Mississippi Delta, under the present General Humphreys. He remained here for three years, and then took the place of Robert E. Lee, subsequently the military chief of the Rebellion, who had charge of the rapids of the Mississippi at Rock Island and Des Moines ; and Joseph E. Johnston, whose fame is linked with the history of the attempt to destroy the Union, succeeded him. In 1854 he was employed under Jefferson Davis in the Mississippi railroad office. "In 1855 he served under Harney in an expedition against the Sioux Indians, and had two engagements with them, in which many were killed. In 1856 and '57 he explored Nebraska Territory. The Smithsonian Institute published his report of Geological Explorations."

"Afterward he was transferred to West Point, and in 1859 and '60 he was Assistant Professor of Mathematics. In 1854 he was promoted to the rank of a full Second Lieutenant, and First Lieutenant in July, 1856."

When the war broke out, he asked leave of absence to serve in the Volunteer Army, and in April, 1861, was appointed Lieutenant-Colonel of the 5th New York Regiment. He was promoted Colonel, September 11, 1861, and to the grade of Captain in the regular army. On September 27, 1862, he was commissioned Brigadier-General, and breveted Lieutenant-Colonel of the regular army.

When Hooker took command of the army, February, 1863, General Warren was made Chief Topographical Engineer, and rendered efficient service at the battle of Chancellorsville, and was appointed Topographical Engineer-in-Chief. During the battle of Gettysburg, while under a heavy fire, a bullet cut his chin underneath, inflicting a slight wound. In speaking of that battle, Swinton* says: "Sickles' line of battle was drawn up on the low ground front of Round Top, his left covering that point. Little Round Top was a commanding spur of Round Top Mountain, a rugged and wild spot, covered with huge boulders. Warren, while moving about in the performance of his duties as Engineer, on the morning of the second day visited this spur, on which some of the signal corps were stationed, and found that they were gathering their flags together preparatory to vacate. He discovered a body of the enemy, who were Hood's Texans, that had got around Sickles' left flank, and were advancing to occupy this important point. He immediately saw the strategic position with the eye of an engineer, and ordering the men to continue waving their flags boldly, to deceive the enemy into the belief that it was occupied by a force of troops, dashed off to bring troops to occupy it. He met Barnes' division of Sykes'

---

* "Army of Potomac," p. 346.

corps, which was marching to the relief of Sickles, who was hard pressed, and on his own responsibility detached Colonel Vincent's brigade, composed of the 16th Michigan, Lieutenant-Colonel Welsh; 44th New York, Colonel Rice; 83d Pennsylvania, Captain Woodward; 20th Maine, Colonel Chamberlain, and Hazlitt's battery; the 140th New York, Colonel O'Rourke, accompanied the latter, which by great labor was dragged and lifted up the hill. As the troops rushed up the height, Hood's Texans were coming up on the opposite side without skirmishers; they met face to face, and a terrible conflict ensued; they fought hand to hand with the bayonet, officers grasped rifles from the hands of the fallen, and after half an hour's desperate struggle, the Union forces secured the position, until reinforced by Weed's brigade of Ayres' division. Later at night, three regiments occupied Round Top proper. The loss was a fearful one; among the ledges of the rocks lay many hundred of the Union soldiers. General Weed, a regular officer, was killed, and Hazlitt fell dead over his body, while trying to catch his last words; Colonels Vincent and O'Rourke, the latter a regular officer, were killed. This was the key of the position, as it enfiladed Cemetery Hill, and if Warren had not acted as promptly as he did, Gettysburg might have been one of those fields that decide the issues of war."

Warren was made Major-General of Volunteers August 8, 1863, and received the brevet of Colonel in the Regular Army to date from Gettysburg, and given the command of the Second corps.

"When in the following October, Meade lay along the Rapidan, Warren was accustomed to put on a private's uniform, and reconnoiter the enemy's position. In this garb he could approach very near the enemy's lines, and gained much valuable information.

"When Lee suddenly outflanked Meade, compelling him to retreat in great haste, Warren commanded the rear guard. Near Bristoe Station the enemy made a sudden and heavy onset upon him, and at first, having all their batteries planted, possessed greatly the advantage. But Warren, who now for the first time had an opportunity to display his great abilities as a strategist, soon reversed this state of things; and the manner in which he chose his position, handled his troops, and planted his batteries, and for five hours repelled every effort of the enemy to advance, and finally drove him to cover, showed him to be perfect master of the art of war, and called forth a congratulatory order from General Meade. He captured in this engagement five guns, two colors, and four hundred and fifty prisoners. The precision, promptitude, and sagacity he exhibited on this his first field, on which he commanded separately, made him at once a conspicuous man in the army. Dash and daring do not go so far with military men as with the public, and a battle so completely planned and perfectly fought as this, could not escape the observation of such men as Meade and Grant."*

Swinton,† in his sketch of the Mine Run move, says that Warren, who was in command of the Second corps, and two divisions of French's, was to attack the enemy on their right.

"Looking at the position with the critical eye of an engineer, but not without those lofty inspirations of courage that overleap the cold dictates of mathematical calculation, Warren saw that the task was hopeless; and so seeing, he resolved to sacrifice himself rather than his command. He assumed the responsibility of suspending the attack.

"His verdict was that of his soldiers—a verdict pronounced not in spoken words, but in a circumstance more potent than words, and full of a touching pathos.

" The time has not been seen when the Army of the Potomac shrank from any call of duty. Recognizing that the task now before them was of the character of a forlorn hope; knowing well that no man could here count on escaping death, the soldiers, without sign of shrinking from the sacrifice, were seen pinning on the breasts of their blouses of blue, slips of paper on which each had written his *name*."

"That this judgment of General Warren, and of his troops, was correct, General Meade himself became convinced, on riding over to the left and viewing the position." "It was, in fact, even

---

* " Grant and Sherman, their Campaigns and Generals."—J. T. HEADLEY.

† " Army of Potomac," pp. 396–'7.

more formidable than the line of the Rapidan, which it had been considered impracticable to assail by a front attack."

When the army began its great campaign against Richmond the next spring, Warren, at the head of the Fifth Corps, held the center, one of the three grand divisions of the army as reorganized under Grant.

Swinton says: "Warren, young in the command of a corps, owed his promotion to the signal ability, proofs of which he had given, first, as a Brigadier, then as Chief Engineer of the Army, and, latterly, as the temporary commander of the Second Corps. Of a subtle, analytic intellect, endowed with an eminent talent for details, the clearest military *coup d'œil*, and a fiery, concentrated energy, he promised to take the first rank as a commander."

"In the terrible battle of the Wilderness,* his command acted a conspicuous part. The second day, in reinforcing the hard pressed wings, he reduced his corps to two divisions, yet with these he firmly maintained his position. At Spottsylvania, Robinson's division of the Fifth Corps was terribly cut up, and their leader having fallen, were breaking in disorder; when this intelligence reached Warren, he put spurs to his horse, and dashing forward, seized the colors and planted them amid the rebel fire, and by his voice and gallant bearing, rallied the division, but in the daring act had his horse shot under him. In the flank movement at the North Anna, and in the severe fight that followed, he handled his troops with such skill and success, and punished the enemy so severely, that Meade complimented him publicly. All through that terrible advance, until the army sat down before Petersburg, he exhibited a tactical skill and fighting power unsurpassed by the oldest General in the field, and equaled by few.

"In the fore part of December, with his own corps and a part of the Second, he moved out of his camps and destroyed twenty miles of the Weldon Railroad, besides station-houses and bridges. On his return he burned Sussex Court-house, in retaliation for brutal treatment and murder of some of our stragglers; and was back in his old quarters before the enemy had fairly waked up to see what a terrible blow had been struck them.

---

* "Grant and Sherman, their Campaigns and Generals."—J. T. HEADLEY.

"In the final movement of the campaign of Grant, when General Sheridan took the advance on the extreme left of Dinwiddie Court-house, he came upon the enemy a few miles beyond, at 'Five Forks,' and was defeated and compelled to fall back to Dinwiddie.* Warren's corps was at once sent to his relief. It had been fighting all day (one division, Griffin's, had been engaged also the day before, and the corps had suffered a loss of eighteen hundred in killed and wounded), yet he sent a portion of it forward immediately, which marched all night, reaching Sheridan next morning. The rest of his corps rapidly followed, and Warren, as ordered, reported to Sheridan on his arrival, who assumed entire command. Sheridan now being strong, advanced against the enemy, and at 'Five Forks' found them at bay, strongly intrenched. Warren was now directed to move with his whole corps on the enemy's left flank while the cavalry attacked in front. With his usual skill and promptitude, he advanced on the strong position in three lines of battle, and sweeping steadily down, carried everything before him, capturing the rebel artillery, which was attempting to move north, and many prisoners. Finding the Confederate front still holding its ground against Sheridan's cavalry, he, without waiting to re-form, swept down on the hostile line, breaking it to fragments, and giving the cavalry a chance to dash in and finish the work. Warren in this last movement rode with his staff in the front, and was still there just at dusk, his men shouting the victory, when he received Sheridan's order relieving him of command, and directing him to report to General Grant. Before doing so, he sought a personal interview, and asked the reason of his being relieved. With strange discourtesy and injustice, the latter refused to give him any."

How Grant viewed this proceeding may be inferred from the fact that he immediately placed Warren in command of the defenses of City Point and Bermuda Hundred.

In May he was assigned to the command of the Mississippi Department, but he did not retain it long, and offered his resig-

---

* Extract from dispatch—General Sheridan to General Grant, March 31, 1865: "This force is too strong for us. I will hold out at Dinwiddie Court-house until I am compelled to leave."

nation as Major-General of Volunteers, but retaining his rank in the Engineer Corps.

He asked for an investigation, but Grant replied that it was impossible, in the disturbed state of affairs, to assemble a court of inquiry at the time, and so the matter dropped.

"Although this was unjust to Warren, perhaps it was quite as well it should rest so. The war was over, the country jubilant and filled with praises of Sheridan, who had fought nobly, and contributed largely to the capture of Lee. A court of inquiry would, of course, have been compelled to censure him—an ungracious task just then; while his condemnation would have changed the opinion of scarcely any one in or out of the army. The people felt that it was an act of injustice, born of sudden impatience and excitement, such as he has often committed, and were sorry that he had been guilty of it, but preferred to forget it in consideration of his gallant services; while among military men, if it had any effect at all, it only raised Warren higher in their estimation. A court of inquiry, therefore, would have had no effect on his reputation, though, as an act of justice, it was demanded. He could much better afford to let it pass than Sheridan can. A sudden act of injustice may be pardoned; persisting in it constitutes its chief criminality."

"Warren at this time was about thirty-five years of age. By those most qualified to judge, he was considered one of the best, if not the best, tacticians in the army. With a nervous, quick temperament, balanced by strong reflective powers, and perfect knowledge of his profession, he combines all the qualities of a great General."

The author is indebted to Headley's work for many of the facts above given, with which he has incorporated his own notes and the statements of other writers. For a detailed account of the "Battle of Five Forks," and all the movements of General Warren with the Fifth Corps, with maps and copies of his orders, see "Warren's Defense," published by D. Van Nostrand (1866).

General Warren was breveted Major-General in the Regular Army, March 13, 1865.

In speaking of Warren's attack, Swinton says in his History: "After the first success, the men halted. Seeing this hesitation,

Warren dashed forward, calling to those near him to follow. Inspired by his example, the color-bearers and officers all along the front sprang out, and, without more firing, the men charged at the *pas de course*, capturing all that remained of the enemy. The history of the war presents no equally splendid illustration of personal magnetism. Warren led the van of the rushing lines; his horse was fatally shot within a few feet of the breastworks, an orderly was killed by his side, and he himself was in imminent peril, when a gallant officer, Colonel Richardson, of the Seventh Wisconsin, sprang between him and the enemy, receiving a severe wound, but shielding from hurt the person of his loved commander."

" A charge of cavalry completed the rout ; there were captured many colors and guns and about 5,000 prisoners ; the Fifth Corps capturing of these, 3,244 men, with their arms, eleven regimental colors, and one four-gun battery, with its caissons. The cavalry loss was a few hundred, that of the *Fifth Corps*, 634 killed and wounded."

General Warren says in his " Defense "—" General Sheridan says : ' I therefore relieved him from the command of the Fifth Corps, authority for this action having been sent to me before the battle, unsolicited.'

" From the time that authority reached him, he, apparently, sought occasion to use it. I say this with regret ; but the tone of the report toward me, and his hasty action, indicate that it was so. If a victory won by my command, under my direction, could not gain me credit, where the plans made were, as he says, ' *successfully executed*,' and where my efforts and directions were known to almost every one, then nothing could."

An incident that occurred at the re-union of several of the Army Corps will indicate the opinion of the soldiers, as well as of the highest officers in the land, in their estimate of Warren's services, even in the presence of Sheridan himself. The Associated Press gave the following report of the occurrences :

THE VETERANS' RE-UNION.

" HARRISBURG, PENN., May 12, 1874.—This morning, the 2d, 5th, and 6th corps met respectively in the House of Representatives, State Library, and Senate Chamber. The 5th corps convened in the State Library, General Sweitzer in the chair. General Warren, the gallant commander of the old 5th corps, was called upon to address the meeting, which he did.

"The 6th corps meeting was held in the Senate Chamber—General Taylor in the chair. The attendance was fair. At 11 o'clock a grand procession was formed in front of the Capitol, with Generals Sherman, Sheridan, Hancock, Doubleday, Schofield, and McDowel, Governor Hartranft, Senator Cameron, Auditor-General Allen, Supervisor-General Heath, and other distinguished soldiers and civilians in carriages. Amid the thunder of cannon the line was formed, and the march to the Grand Opera-House commenced. The Masonic building was gayly decorated with the national colors and the army flags and devices of the different corps of the Army of the Potomac. Upon the spacious stage were Generals Sherman, Sheridan, Hancock, Schofield, Doubleday, Burnside, and a host of others.

"As the presence of General Warren was announced from the platform, loud cries for the veteran commander of the old 5th corps went up from hundreds of throats. As nothing else could restore order, the General, who was in the audience, arose and came forward, amid deafening applause. There were two thousand persons in the house, and at least three times that number surging outside."

This episode shows conclusively that the great military ability and services of General Warren, from the first battle of the war to the last, were acknowledged, in a conspicuous manner, by those most competent to judge; and that the imputations of one man, though a successful and great General, were wiped out by the verdict of thousands.

General Warren says, in a communication to the New York *Herald,* dated at Newport, R. I., July 26, 1878: "At the battle of Five Forks I was not relieved till after the battle had ceased. Thousands of soldiers in the 5th army corps, and many in the ranks of our foes, can testify that I led the final attack that completed that victory. There was no cause to take me away from any misconduct, and General Grant would never allow me a court of inquiry, because thereby I could have shown there was no cause. I claim the honors of that day are mine."

During the time that General Warren was connected with the 5th New York, which covered its full term of service, with the exception of about four months, he was either in command or had it under his eye in his brigade, where it held the post of honor. The men placed implicit confidence in him as a leader, and were always ready to obey his orders unflinchingly. They were sure that he would never shrink from any duty, and always set an example by leading the way. In action, it seemed to the men that he was everywhere at the same moment, and he always appeared to be perfectly indifferent to bullets or shell, and must have borne a charmed life, from the manner in which he exposed himself. He attended to the slightest details personally, and many a time has he seized a spade or pick out of the hands of a lazy soldier to show him how to dig. From the first day General Warren made his appearance in the regiment, to the last, the effect of his superior practical knowledge, in all matters appertaining to the school of the soldier, was apparent in the discipline, drill, and efficiency of the regiment. The men often wondered whether he passed any time in sleep. General Warren disliked bombast, and was not in the habit of speaking of his own deeds, but preferred to let the results of his actions show for themselves.

The army and the nation have a common interest in the record and the life of such a soldier.

MAJOR—J. MANSFIELD DAVIES.

J. MANSFIELD DAVIES was a son of Professor Davies, formerly instructor of mathematics at the West Point Military Academy, and received his education at Kinsley's Military School, West Point. He resigned from the 5th Regiment August 17, 1861, having been commissioned Colonel of the 2d New York, Harris Light Cavalry; from which regiment he received an honorable discharge December 6, 1862, on account of ill-health, engendered from exposure in the field. Through his exertions he aided greatly in the organization of the 5th Regiment New York Volunteers, and was much respected by the whole command.

CHAPLAIN—REV. GORDON WINSLOW, D.D.

The Rev. GORDON WINSLOW, the Chaplain of the 5th Regiment, was a man somewhat advanced in years when the war broke out, his age being about sixty. At that time he was settled over a parish at Staten Island, as an Episcopalian minister. He was a type of the old Revolutionary stock, possessing an iron constitution, capable of enduring any amount of hardship, with an active, untiring, energetic disposition, and having a strong love for his country, he was among the first to volunteer his services when the authority of the Government was set at defiance. He was a man that knew no fear, and always was to be found on the advance line, sometimes even ahead of the skirmishers, and he never thought of danger or spared himself when he could be of any benefit to the wounded. He obtained the appointment of Chaplain to the 5th New York Volunteers, but the performance of the duties that rightfully belonged to the position was only a small part of the responsibilities that he assumed. He served all through with the regiment, and was mustered out with it, May 14, 1863. One of his sons was a Lieutenant in the Fifth; another, Cleveland Winslow, Col. of the Fifth, organized a new regiment of Zouaves, called the 5th Veterans, and on his being ordered to the front with his command, his father accompanied it as Chaplain, but he was soon after made Sanitary Inspector of the Army of the Potomac, and in this position his services were invaluable. There are thousands of the sick and wounded, who, if living to-day, can testify to his kindness and untiring zeal in their behalf night and day. Hundreds of soldiers, could they wake from the dead, would tell how he ministered unto them in their dying hours, and received their last message or memento for the friends at home. The fate of many a fallen hero would never have been known to surviving relatives had it not been for his fidelity and sympathy. The perusal of his daily journal awakens surprise that a man of his advanced years could perform all the duties which he undertook. He visited camps and inspected the sick of the various regiments day after day and night after night, traveling with his favorite horse, "Captive," over the most difficult roads, in storm or calm, often under fire, and partaking of such hospitality as a camp affords. A few hours were spent in sleep here and there on the ground, and then his tireless rounds were resumed, looking after ambulances and the sick and wounded, who were always demanding his attention; he inspected the medical stores, examined and weighed blankets to see that they came up to the standard, and performed a thousand other duties of the long detail of a sanitary officer.

On May 3, 1864, when General Grant's great army commenced their move on Richmond, he was on General Warren's staff. From his journal, the author quotes, under date of May 3d, Tuesday:

"Left at night for Culpepper to join General Warren; moved at 12½ A.M." "Fourth, Wednesday, A.M., moved the entire army to Germania Ford; General Warren and myself arrived at the Ford at 6¼ A.M., before the pontoons were completed; went over and saw them completed," etc. Thus he continued from day to day, leading a most active and useful life. Occasionally on his rounds, he visited his son, the Colonel. Finally, Wednesday, June 1st, after describing the movements of the troops, and an engagement then taking place, he says:

"General Ayres, of the regulars, received the old 5th New York Veteran Volunteers, who were at once put into the fight, and acquitted themselves well." On the 2d, after giving a detailed account of more fighting, and his own movements, he closes his account for the day with "*Cleve was wounded.*" Friday, June 3d: "Went over to find 'Cleve;' found him in a cellar of a house, which was being shelled, on our right." And then continues with a general description of a heavy engagement, and—"Rode all day to the several hospitals;" "brought Cleve to the 6th corps hospital and stayed with him overnight." "Wound in the left shoulder, minie ball, making exit from the back," etc. "The wound was much inflamed by his return to the field, after being dressed. He passed the night comfortably. I slept on the ground under the same fly."

Two brave hearts, father and son! The wounded Colonel, a month after was laid in his grave. The father who watched over him, in three days after his son's wound, was drowned in the Potomac.

The last entry in the journal, June 5th, White House, appears to be a copy of a note sent:

"SUNDAY EVG.

" DEAR GEN. :—I have hardly time to say we arrived on Saturday, and expect to go out to-morrow at 3 o'clock." " June 6th." (A loving hand has written, as if the dead Divine was continuing his journal). *June 7th, Tuesday morning.* " AT HOME IN THE PARADISE OF GOD." Also, " Dr. Winslow was spared the agony of knowing the extent of his son's wound—a gun-shot · fracture of the left shoulder—which resulted in the death of the Colonel on the 7th of July, 1864, at the Mansion House Hospital, Alexandria, Va."

PRESS CORRESPONDENCE.

"Our boats were being filled with special cases of wounded ones ; among whom was Colonel Winslow, a son of the lamented Dr. Winslow, so long and so favorably known in connection with the United States Sanitary Commission. He was brought from the front to the boat by his father, whose tenderness for his child equaled that of a mother," etc., etc.

Dr. Winslow was drowned from this boat, while in the act of drawing a bucket of water from the side of the vessel while sailing up the Potomac, being in the sixty-fifth year of his age. (His body was never recovered).

The following extracts from some of the letters written by Dr. Winslow during the earlier part of the war, will be read with interest by all members of the Fifth, not only as mementoes of our much respected Chaplain, but as a part of the history of the regiment. It is to be very much regretted that the journal which he kept during the two years' service of the Fifth, was lost from one of the wagons, at Aquia Creek, during our homeward march :

" CAMP BUTLER, *May* 27, 1861.

" We are well settled at our camp life—the staff occupying quarters with the Colonel in an old mansion, on a plantation of great beauty directly upon the bay. This carries us quite out beyond all the others, and gives us the right to our title of the ' Advance Guard.' The Secession arms glistening in our sight.

But they begin to realize the dangerous proximity of our Zouaves. Every day we push out somewhat, and every night a scout or an attacking party is on the move, and thus far without bloodshed. Last night a company was detailed on a secret expedition to attack a large building, called a college, declared to be dangerous, being well stored with Secessionists. I was detailed to accompany the expedition, which opportunity I was glad to improve. We started at eleven o'clock, with muskets, and ten rounds of ball cartridge, revolvers, etc. Our passage lay up the banks of a stream for some two miles, then crossing over and passing down upon the other bank some two and a half miles, much of the time upon our knees or in a stooping position quite to the ground, listening at every few steps till within a few hundred yards, when we divided into separate parts and surrounded the college and several villas, and closed in gradually till near the spot of attack, when the Captain, with two or three, went forward and demanded a surrender unconditionally. The thing was done without resistance, and we took possession, and passed the night in guarding the grounds about from outward or inward attack. Several shots were fired from across the stream and arm of the bay, on either side, during the night, but nobody was hurt."

After giving an account of an encounter with a patrol from camp, who were mistaken for an enemy, as they did not have the countersign, and in which he fired his first shot, he says:

"At sunrise we raised the flag of our Union on top of the dome, and gave the whole into the hands of a relief guard and returned to camp. It was considered a successful enterprise. Last night Captain Winslow was detailed on a similar enterprise with his company. He reported a complete success, having taken the place occupied by some Secession spies. Captain Winslow returned with his prisoners at about three o'clock A.M. The prisoners have just been called before a court of inquiry, and turned over to General Butler for judgment."

Extract of a letter dated Washington, July 29, 1861:

"I am getting to be quite a business man, which agrees with me much. I should like to be General for about one month, to try my hand at it."—"I have no wish to leave the Chaplaincy, but I am determined to stick to the war to the last, and do it like a man; and if they cut me off in one direction, I shall turn their flank in another, and carry the day."

Doctor Winslow had a former slave as his servant, who was brought on with him from Camp Hamilton, but not without some trouble, as the following goes to show:

"CAMP FEDERAL HILL, BALTIMORE,
August 9, 1861.

"Jim is with me. He is a regular specimen of an old aristocratic slave. The Dutch soldiers at Hampton were about to hang him as a spy when I arrived from Washington. When I demanded his release, he was brought to Colonel Webber's quarters, and on seeing me, nearly fainted. When revived, he cried: 'Lord God Almighty! I'd rather see ole massa than my fader and modder raisin' out ob der graves—Oh, golly! whew?' If he continues faithful, I shall be sorry to part with him."

In speaking of his horse, which was captured by some of the Zouaves, back of Hampton, while on a scout, he says:

"Captive is well, and quite the admiration of all. I had quite a time in getting him from the Provost Marshal. The Regulars called it storming Gibraltar, and thought it could not be taken. But they lived to see it was taken, and by a regular process, and so effectually that no question can hereafter be raised on the subject of rightful ownership."

CAMP FEDERAL HILL, *August* 11, 1861.
Sunday, 10 P.M.

It is almost impossible to keep up with time when anything extra is expected. Every hour has its allotted work. A thousand visitors at least have been in camp to-day. At 7 A.M. we had a battalion inspection and review on the street in the city; then came inspection of hospital; then inspection of camp and quarters, which brought us near to 11 o'clock; then divine service, which held till dinner at 1 P.M; then general lounging and repose from two to three; then mustering of delinquents and squads for evening parade, which calls for special inspection from the officers of the several companies. In the meantime I look after the sick in hospitals and the ailing in camp, which brings us to time for dress parade and general drill; after which the general orders are published, which this evening were very lengthy, and among which I am personally interested, viz.: the one which confirms my commission and rank as that of cavalry Captain in the army, defining the duties, responsibilities, etc. ("I have a call from two officers"). It is now eleven as I resume. The subject of conversation with the officers was peculiar. It related to the possibility of our being blown up. The fact is, the hill on which our camp is situated is completely undermined. For many years it has been the resort for white sand for making glass, etc., until immense caves running in all directions and nearly through the whole extent have been excavated, and probably owing to this fact, it has been suggested that a few barrels of powder placed beneath our camp would, if ignited, give us an uncomfortable ascent to unexplored parts. We have come to the wise conclusion that this must be looked after. I have not yet been out into the city to any extent except to give "Captive" a little airing on two occasions. We generally are hailed with "cheers for Jeff Davis and the Southern Confederacy," which is indicative that the cat is only scotched, not killed, in these parts. We never retort, and probably in time they will find that it don't pay to cheer us. We had the long roll last night, or rather this morning, about 2 o'clock. The camp was all alive and every man under arms in about five minutes. It was a false alarm, but it shows the discipline of the regiment. It is raining and very dark, with prospect of a wet time, etc. I have been so accustomed to sleep on a board that a bed would now appear strange, etc.

The poor fellows on guard to-night will have a moist time of it. One man yesterday fell off the bank and injured his back—and one man was sun-struck to-day on guard while we were at service, etc. My eyes begin to ask for sleep, so I will add a line in the morning.

Morning.—It rains and has done so nearly all night, yet the gun fires and the reveille beats as regularly as under clear skies, etc. G. W.

CAMP FEDERAL HILL, BALTIMORE.

Since I last wrote I have been like a shuttle-cock, to and from Washington and Fortress Monroe, with dispatches, which has brought me in contact with all the heads of departments and with the different Generals. I found General McDowell at Arlington Heights, in sadness at his discomfiture. He said, the victory was ours at Bull Run up to the opening of a masked battery on the flank, near where an array of spectators, editors, Congressmen, women, etc., were assembled to see the battle, and who at once took to flight; this alarmed the teamsters, and finally the retreat, or rather stampede, was irresistible. At this moment large reserves of the enemy came up and changed the whole fate of the day. It was a bad affair, but I have no doubt it will do good by bringing up our officers and men to the true idea that we are warring with men of prowess and determination, with the best materials of warfare, in positions of strength and where strategic movements are greatly facilitated by a familiar acquaintance with the topography of the country. We have much more to do than has been imagined, and I think that General Scott was decidedly right in his judgment and plans, which unfortunately were overruled by the host of politicians, Congressmen, editors, President, and all. The fact is, they wished to see a battle, supposing of course we must whip the Southerners. I hope hereafter all civilians found on the battle-field from curiosity *will be shot*, by order of court-martial; and all women found there will be obliged to carry a pack and arms. It is no place for idle spectators or curiosity-mongers, etc. We have had a grand review by Major-General Dix, who seems much pleased with the regiment. Our desire was to be placed on the advance of the army, but Scott and Dix regard this as the most important position at this moment to be occupied. There is, it is believed, a deep plot to cross from Harper's Ferry and join the secret enemies in this city. This requires the utmost discretion, forbearance, and soldierly bearing, to know all that transpires without provoking resistance, and yet be able to quell them at a moment's notice, etc. We have a great number of applicants for officers from our regiment. I think no less than ten Captains and twice as many Lieutenants have been taken from us. But still we can stand it. Half of our men are capable of making officers better than we often find.

Major-General Dix also desired me as military secretary, which would rank me as Major, but it would be too inactive. I would rather be a *soldier* on constant drill than be idle. You will believe this from what you know of my habit, etc.   G. W.

The correspondent of a New York journal, in speaking of the wounded at Gettysburg, reported as follows:

" The Sanitary Commission are still supplying the wounded at Gettysburg with delicacies. The patients are reported to be improving slowly. The good work is in charge of the Rev. Mr. Gordon Winslow, chaplain of Duryée's Zouaves, 5th New York Regiment, who is unremitting in his attention to the sufferers under his care," etc.

After the battle of Big Bethel, Dr. Winslow remained in the rear of the retreating troops, looking after and caring for the wounded. He was at one time cut off from the main body by a party of mounted Confederates, and remained hid in the brush for several hours. He saw the enemy pass by his hiding-place several times, and a Confederate sentinel was posted within eighty feet of him. At camp he was thought to have been surely taken prisoner by the enemy, but he eluded them and made his way back, arriving at camp about midnight.

ADJUTANT—JOSEPH E. HAMBLIN.

JOSEPH E. HAMBLIN was a man of giant proportions, standing six feet four inches in height, and was a universal favorite with the officers and men. He had been through some military experience before the breaking out of the war of the Rebellion. He was conspicuous in the Kansas border troubles, and was in the expedition to Montgomery, and on General Frost's staff. At the breaking out of the war he was a member of the 7th Regt.

Personal Sketches. 447

N. G. S. New York, and received a commission as Second Lieutenant in the 5th New York Volunteers.

The following is from the New York *Times* of March, 1867 :

"In General Order No. 3, under date of March 7, Major-General Alexander Shaler announces, among other officers appointed to his staff, the name of Joseph E. Hamblin, Division Inspector, with the rank of Colonel.

"Colonel and Brevet Major-General Joseph E. Hamblin was for several years a member of the 7th Regiment, having served as Orderly Sergeant in one of the companies of that command.

"When the Rebellion broke out in 1861, Hamblin was appointed by Colonel (afterward Brigadier-General) Abram Duryée, as Adjutant of the Zouave Regiment (5th New York Volunteers), which was organi 1 g for two years or the war. In this capacity he served in the summer of 1861, at Old Point Comfort, under General Benjamin F. Butler, and was present at Big Bethel, the first battle of the war.

"The Fifth was transferred to Baltimore in July, 1861, and Hamblin was commissioned a Captain August 27th. He was subsequently commissioned Major in the 65th New York Volunteers (United States Chasseurs), dated from November 3, 1861. After the Peninsula campaign, Hamblin, with rank from July 20, 1862, became Lieutenant-Colonel of his regiment."

"This promotion he had won by hard service before Yorktown, at Williamsburgh, Fair Oaks, Glendale, and Malvern Hill."

As Lieutenant-Colonel, he participated in the battles of Antietam, Fredericksburg, first and second; in the storming of Marye's Heights in the morning, and the defense of Salem Heights in the afternoon—both on the left of that line of engagements known as Chancellorsville. Colonel Shaler having received his Brigadier's commission for gallant conduct at the capture of Marye's Heights, Hamblin became Colonel of the Chasseurs, with rank from May 26, 1863, and as such (in the 6th Corps), was at Rappahannock Station, Gettysburg, and Mine Run under Meade; in the Wilderness, Spottsylvania, and Cold Harbor, under Grant; and at Winchester, Fisher's Hill, and Cedar Creek, under Sheridan, when he was made Brevet Brigadier-General " for gallant and meritorious conduct at the battle of Cedar Creek," at which battle he was desperately wounded in the thigh. On his return to the Army of the Potomac in front of Petersburg, General Hamblin assumed command of a brigade in Wheaton's (1st division) of the Sixth Corps, where he participated in the second battle of Hatcher's Run, Va., and finally at Sailor's Creek, commissioned as Brigadier-General of Volunteers, with rank from May 19, 1865. Hamblin was made Brevet Major-General, with rank from April 5, 1865, for "conspicuous gallantry in Sheridan's great victory of Sailor's Creek," and with that rank was mustered out of the United States service.

The following obituary tribute to General Hamblin appeared in the New York *Times*, July 5, 1870:

"Major-General Joseph E. Hamblin, a brief announcement of whose death appeared in these columns yesterday, was one of the most gallant soldiers that fought for the Union in the late war, and a gentleman whose character was without a blemish. He was born in Massachusetts, in 1828. In April, 1861, he was appointed Adjutant in the famous 5th New York Volunteers— better known as Duryée's Zouaves. [The sketch of his military career is omitted]. He sheathed his sword at the end of the war, when his country had no further need of his services, and has since resided in this city; and, at the time of his death, which occurred in the forty-third year of his age, he held the responsible position of Superintendent of Agencies for the Commonwealth Fire Insurance Company. General Hamblin's genial and generous qualities endeared him to a host of friends."

> HEADQUARTERS 7TH REGIMENT,
> NATIONAL GUARD S. N. Y.,
> NEW YORK, *July* 4, 1870.

The Commandant with regret announces to this command the death of Brevet Major-General Joseph E. Hamblin.

General Hamblin was for many years a prominent member of this regiment, and served with great distinction in the army during the recent Rebellion. As a token of respect to his memory, the members of this regiment are requested to act as mourners, and will assemble in full uniform (gray pants), at the Armory, on Tuesday, 5th inst., at 1 o'clock P.M.

By order of
COLONEL EMMONS CLARK.
LOUIS FITZGERALD,
Brevet Lieutenant-Colonel and Adjutant.

HEADQUARTERS 1ST DIVISION,
NATIONAL GUARD S. N. Y.,
NEW YORK, *July* 4, 1870.

GENERAL ORDERS, NO. 5.

I. It is with the deepest regret that the General commanding announces to the division that Brevet Major-General Joseph E. Hamblin, late Assistant Adjutant-General and Chief of Staff of the 1st division, who served with such well-known distinction in the late war for the Union, died at his residence yesterday, the 3d inst.

II. The following detail is ordered as an escort to his remains: The 9th Regiment Infantry; the troop of Washington Grays, Cavalry; and the Separate Troop Cavalry, Captain Klein commanding; two sections of Battery K, Artillery.

III. The escort will be commanded by Brigadier-General Postley, and will report to him in Madison Avenue, between Twenty-fifth and Twenty-sixth Streets, at 1.30 o'clock P.M. on the 5th inst.

IV. The General commanding feels that this information will be received with the profoundest sorrow by the officers and men of the division, and is assured that all who have known the late General Hamblin, either in his military or social character, will readily accord the last respects due one who has been so well known and so well-beloved. The officers of the division who desire to take part in the ceremonies are invited to attend his funeral, at his late residence, No. 136 Lexington Avenue, in uniform, and will assemble at the Apollo Rooms, corner of Twenty-eighth Street and Broadway, at 1.30 P.M.

V. The following officers have been requested by the friends of the family to act as pall-bearers, and will meet, in uniform, mounted, at the residence of the General commanding, No. 346 West Twenty-eighth Street, at 1.30 o'clock P.M.:

 Major-Gen. Alex. Shaler,   Brig.-Gen. J. H. Libeneau,
 "   C. K. Graham,   "   G. W. Palmer,
 "   M. T. McMahon,   "   L. Burger,
 "   A. Duryée,   Colonel John Fowler, Jr.,
Brig.-Gen. Thomas H. Neill,   "   Wm. H. Chesebrough.
 "   H. E. Tremain,   Lieut.-Colonel Geo. T. Haws.

   By order of
     MAJOR-GENERAL ALEX. SHALER.
WM. H. CHESEBROUGH,
 Colonel and Assistant Adjutant-General and Chief of Staff.

   HEADQUARTERS 9TH REGIMENT INFANTRY,
    NATIONAL GUARD S. N. Y.,
     NEW YORK, *July* 4, 1870.
GENERAL ORDERS, NO. 13.

This regiment having been detailed as funeral escort to the late Brevet Major-General Joseph E. Hamblin, late A. A. G. and Chief of Staff, 1st division N. G. S. N. Y., the several companies of this command will assemble at the Armory on Tuesday, July 5, at 12 o'clock M., in full-dress uniform, white cross and body belts (white gloves). Officers will wear the usual badge of mourning.
   By command of
     COLONEL JAMES FISK, JR.
EDGAR S. ALLIEN, *Adjutant.*

The members of Kane Lodge, No. 454, F. and A. M., and the Veterans of the 7th Regiment N. G., under the command of Colonel Marshall Lefferts, were also in attendance at the funeral.

QUARTERMASTER—JOHN HOWARD WELLS.

JOHN HOWARD WELLS was a member of the 7th Regiment N. G. S. N. Y. He was an executive and competent officer, possessed of superior business qualifications. He resigned his commission February 25, 1862, to accept the appointment of Commissary, with the rank of Captain in the United States army. He served to the end of the war, and resigned his commission May 19, 1865.

SURGEON—DR. RUFUS H. GILBERT.

DR. GILBERT was promoted to the rank of Major August 3, 1861, and transferred to the regular service, where he continued to the end of the war, the regiment thereby losing the services of a skillful surgeon and an accomplished gentleman. Dr. Gilbert is the well-known projector of the Gilbert Elevated Railroad.

SURGEON'S MATE—B. ELLIS MARTIN.

DR. MARTIN rendered efficient aid in the care of the wounded on the field at Big Bethel, June 10, 1861, and was mentioned in general orders. He resigned his commission February 11, 1862.

CAPTAIN OF COMPANY A—HARMON D. HULL.

HARMON D. HULL was an officer of the 7th Regiment N. G. S. N. Y., commissioned Captain May 9, 1861, in the 5th Regiment, New York Volunteers; Major, September 7th of the same year; Lieutenant-Colonel, October 29, 1862. He was a dashing officer, and distinguished himself at the battle of Gaines' Mill, June 27, 1862. He resigned his commission in October, 1862, and subsequently organized the 165th Regiment, New York Volunteers, of which corps he was commissioned Colonel, and was ordered with his command to the Department of the Mississippi, where he did much active service, but was obliged on account of ill-health to resign the command January 22, 1863, and retire to private life.

CAPTAIN COMPANY B—ROBERT S. DUMONT.

CAPTAIN DUMONT was a member of the 7th Regiment N. G. S. N. Y., raised the first company for the 5th Regiment, New York Volunteers, and after seeing some active service during the earlier months of the war, was obliged to resign October 1, 1861, on account of ill-health, the effect of a sun-stroke. Subsequently he was appointed Secretary to Rear-Admiral Bell, commanding Pacific Squadron, December 11, 1861, with the rank of Lieutenant in the Navy. Was appointed Judge Advocate General of Squadron May 9, 1863. Resigned his commission on account of continual ill-health, March 1, 1864, and died a few years afterward.

CAPTAIN OF COMPANY C—HENRY E. DAVIES, JR.

HENRY E. DAVIES, JR., son of Judge Davies, for many years Chief-Justice of the Court of Appeals, and a nephew of Professor Davies, Instructor of Mathematics at the United States Military Academy, West Point. He was a strict disciplinarian and a brave and dashing officer. He was mustered into the service April 23, 1861, as a Captain in the 5th Regiment, and went with it to Fortress Monroe; took an active part in several scouting expeditions, and in the battle of Big Bethel, where he greatly distinguished himself by his coolness and bravery under fire. Two days after the battle he visited Yorktown under a flag of truce, to look after the wounded, and to obtain the body of Major Winthrop, aide to General Butler, who was killed in the engagement. When the regiment was ordered to Baltimore, Captain Davies went with it, and shared in the arduous duties of building Fort Federal Hill, which work was performed during the hot summer months. He was commissioned Major of the 2d New York Cavalry (Harris' Light) August 27, 1861, and went to Washington, where the Regiment was being concentrated. Took command of the 1st battalion there in camp, and from that time until the close of the war, remained with the *Army of the Potomac*. Was commissioned Lieutenant-Colonel 2d New York Cavalry, December 30, 1862; Colonel, January 24, 1863; appointed and afterward commissioned as Brigadier-General, United States Volunteers, September 16, 1863, and assigned to command of the 1st brigade, 3d division, cavalry corps, Army of Potomac; April 25, 1864, was assigned to the command of the 1st brigade, 2d division, cavalry corps; received Brevet of Major-General United States Volunteers October 1, 1864, for gallant and meritorious conduct, and was commissioned Major-General United States Volunteers June 9, 1865, with rank from April 6, 1865, which appointment was confirmed by the Senate. At the close of the war General Davies was assigned to duty in the middle district of the Department of Alabama, where he remained until December, 1865, when he resigned his position in the army and returned to civil life. General Davies was engaged in nearly all of the battles and raids of the cavalry corps of the Army of the Potomac, in which he was especially distinguished, and was always found at the post of danger, serving in company with such distinguished officers as Custer, Kilpatrick, Buford, Gregg, Merritt, Devin, and others, and was considered to be one of the most able and effective leaders of cavalry in the service. He was particularly distinguished in the severe engagement at Br ndy Station, one of the hardest fought cavalry fights of the war. In one of these engagements, he and a few others were entirely surrounded, and they literally hewed their way through the ranks of the enemy, and escaped capture. He also served under General Sheridan, by whom he was highly prized. He always promptly and successfully executed the orders of that distinguished soldier, and was with him in the final movements at Five Forks. To enumerate all the b ittles, raids, and skirmishes in which he was engaged would be equivalent to summarizing the history of the Army of the Potomac, but whoever reads the history of that army, will notice that the name of Major-General Henry E. Davies, Jr., occupies a prominent place.

The following sketch from the New York *Evening Post*, November 15, 1866, narrates in a condensed form the services of General Davies:

"In making arrangements preparatory to the new army organization, General Grant recently applied to General Sheridan for the names of the twelve most distinguished officers who had served under him in the cavalry during the war, it being General Grant's wish to appoint them as field officers in the new organization. General Sheridan immediately wrote to General Davies, saying that he had selected him as one of the twelve, and requested him, if willing to accept such appointment, to signify his purpose by letter to General Grant. General Davies, however, had already resigned his commission, and resolved to devote himself to the practice of law, which he abandoned on the breaking out of the war; and he therefore wrote to General Sheridan gratefully declining the proposed honor.

"The young gentleman to whom this high compliment was paid has a remarkable record. He entered the army in April, 1861, as a Captain in the Duryée Zouaves. His first battle was at Big Bethel, in which he was actively engaged. He was soon after transferred to the Harris Light Cavalry, by order of President Lincoln, with the commission of Major. He was thence successively promoted to the office of Lieutenant-Colonel and Colonel, and in the autumn of 1863 he was appointed Brigadier-General. He was subsequently breveted Major-General for his gallantry in the fight at Hatcher's Run, in October, 1864. His greatest single exploit was his attack on a body of 1,500 Confederate troops intrenched at Sailor's Creek. He literally led this attack, in having been the first man to leap the intrenchments, and although his numbers were inferior to the enemy, he captured the entire force, with four pieces of artillery and twelve stand of colors. For this victory he received a Major-General's commission."

General Davies was engaged in more than forty battles, and had no less than fifteen horses shot under him, but by marvelous good fortune he was not once wounded to the extent of drawing blood, a few bruises being the sum total of injuries that he received.

CAPTAIN OF COMPANY D—JAMES L. WAUGH.

JAMES L. WAUGH was a Captain in the 7th Regiment N. G. S. N. Y., and Drill Officer to the Metropolitan Police. He brought his company up to an efficient state of discipline and drill in the manual of arms and field tactics. He took an active part in the first campaign of the regiment at Old Point Comfort. Receiving a commission in another regiment as Major, he resigned from the Fifth August 9, 1861.

CAPTAIN. OF COMPANY E—HIRAM DURYEA.

HIRAM DURYEA had received a thorough military education before the war, and was also for eight years Adjutant of the 48th Regiment N. G. S. N. Y. (the Oswego regiment). He was commissioned Captain in the Fifth May 9, 1861; Lieutenant-Colonel September 7th; Colonel October 29, 1862, being the third Colonel of the Fifth. He was acting in command of the regiment during the greater part of the Peninsular campaign, Colonel Warren being in command of the brigade. He was a very strict disciplinarian, and in the line of duty was impartial alike to both officers and men, requiring of all in their different spheres a strict attention to their duties. In personal intercourse he was always to be met as the accomplished gentleman. He greatly distinguished himself during the seven days' retreat, although he was ill and suffering from a malarial disease, contracted by constant exposure at the siege of Yorktown, where he was obliged to be on duty night and day, parts of the regiment being detailed at widely separated points, in different batteries and on working details, incidental to the siege. At the desperate engagement at Gaines' Mill June 27, 1862, he disdained to dismount from his horse during the hottest part of the fight, and stood the fire unflinchingly, keeping close to his men in the several charges that were made, and animating them by his voice and example. His health continuing to fail, and becoming conscious that he could not continue in command of the regiment during a winter campaign and do it justice, as well as to prolong his own life, he reluctantly resigned November 12, 1862, after eighteen months' arduous service. The regiment thus lost the services of a skillful, brave, and courageous officer, who, had he been able to remain in the service, would undoubtedly have risen to a high rank.

He received the brevet of Brigadier-General for his distinguished services in the field.

RESIGNATION OF COLONEL HIRAM DURYEA.

HEADQUARTERS 5TH REGIMENT, N. Y. V.,
CAMP NEAR FALMOUTH, VA.,
December 5, 1862.

At a meeting of the officers of the 5th Regiment, New York Volunteer Infantry, held at their camp near Falmouth, Virginia, the following preamble and resolutions were adopted:

WHEREAS, It became necessary for Colonel Hiram Duryea to tender his resignation owing to a protracted sickness, contracted during the arduous campaigns on the Peninsula and in Maryland, be it

Resolved, That while regretting the loss of so valuable an officer we feel that, knowing his inability from physical prostration to do his duty longer to his regiment and country, and his high sense of honor as an officer and a gentleman, have led him to take this step.

Resolved, That in the loss of Colonel Hiram Duryea the country loses the services of a brave, but not rash, a prudent, but fearless officer; the regiment a true friend and soldier. May his future be as honorable as his past, and may he soon be restored to health to finish the career of his soldier life so creditably begun.

G. K. Warren, Brigadier-General Volunteers, formerly Colonel 5th New York Volunteers.
A. S. Marvin, Jr., Captain and Assistant Adjutant-General.
Gordon Winslow, Chaplain 5th N. Y. V.
A. L. Thomas, Captain, A. Q. M.
Cleveland Winslow, Major Commanding 5th N. Y. V.
George Duryea, Captain 5th N. Y. V.
A. Sidney Chase, Lieutenant and Acting Adjutant.
Charles S. Montgomery, Captain Company C.
James McConnell, Captain Company H.
James H. Lounsberry, Captain Company K.

Personal Sketches. 457

J. Henry Whitney, Captain Company A.
Stephen W. Wheeler, Captain Company F.
John S. Raymond, 1st Lieutenant Company E.
Thomas R. Martin, 1st Lieutenant Company G.
Roderick M. Gedney, 1st Lieutenant Company K.
William Hoffman, 1st Lieutenant Company B.
George L. Guthrie, 1st Lieutenant Company A.
William H. Chambers, 1st Lieutenant Company D.
George W. Wannemacher, 1st Lieutenant Company B.
Gordon Winslow, Jr., 2d Lieutenant Company F.
William H. Uckele, 2d Lieutenant Company H.
Albert R. Meldrum, 2d Lieutenant Company I.

CAPTAIN OF CO. F—HENRY A. SWARTWOUT.

HENRY A. SWARTWOUT received his education at a Military Academy in Maryland, where he was for three years commandant of battalion. He was an able, cool, and reliable officer. Receiving a commission as First Lieutenant in the 17th Infantry, U. S. A., he resigned from the Fifth, August 12, 1861. He subsequently rose to the rank of Captain and Brevet Major, August 1st, 1864, and was assigned to the Department of Texas, as Acting Assistant Inspector-General. He died at his post of duty, at Galveston, Texas, October 8, 1867. He was born in Louisiana, in the year 1834.

CAPTAIN OF COMPANY G—ABRAHAM DENIKE.

ABRAHAM DENIKE was a member of the 27th and subsequently of the 7th Regiment N. G. for thirty years, and was a Captain in the latter. At the time of the breaking out of hostilities between the North and South, he had retired from active business, being possessed of a fortune, accumulated by years spent in industry. He immediately offered his services to his country from purely patriotic motives.

Mrs. Denike was much opposed to his going to the war, and

20

intimated to him that his first duty was to his family. He replied that his first duty was to his God; secondly, to his country; and last, to his family. He received a commission April 20, 1861, as Captain, thus making him the senior line officer in rank, and his Company was assigned to the right of the line. He was a brave and spirited officer, and was respected and beloved by his command, who looked up to him as their father. He was a true soldier under fire, and never faltered on the long marches. Having been outranked in the Majorship by a younger officer, he resigned his commission, September 6, 1861. The men of his Company presented him with a sword that cost $100, as a token of their esteem. He was subsequently commissioned as Lieutenant-Colonel, and raised the 153d Regiment New York Volunteers. Colonel Denike is at present a member of the 7th Regiment Veterans.

CAPTAIN OF COMPANY H—JUDSON KILPATRICK.

JUDSON KILPATRICK was born in the Valley of the Clove, Northern New Jersey, in 1838. At the age of seventeen he took such an interest in politics that he was chosen a delegate to the State Convention. He entered the West Point Military Academy June 20, 1856. While there, he whipped a cadet much larger than himself, who, for some trivial cause, had attacked him. The battle lasted three-quarters of an hour, and he suffered severely; but the event made Kilpatrick very popular. He was chosen to deliver the valedictory of his class, in which he graduated fifteenth. He immediately received a commission as Captain of Volunteers, and was assigned to the command of Company H, 5th New York Volunteers. He took a very active part in the battle of Big Bethel, in which affair he greatly distinguished himself. He was severely wounded, and did not recover sufficiently to take the field again until September. He was now made Lieutenant-Colonel of the Harris Light Cavalry, and promoted to First Lieutenant of the First Artillery, regular army. He was made a member of the Examining Board for examining cavalry officers of the volunteer service, and Inspector-General of McDowell's division.

In March, 1862, when the army moved on Manassas, his regiment led the advance. When Pope assumed command of the army, Kilpatrick broke up the railroad running from Gordonsville to Richmond, thus severing Lee's communications. He marched eighty miles in thirty hours, spreading ruin and consternation along his path. He was continually making dashes against the enemy, and fighting them at every opportunity. At one time he rode seventy-four miles in twenty-four hours, besides having several fights with the Confederates, in which he had several hair-breadth escapes. On another occasion, he found a paper in the enemy's camp, stating that General Stuart was building a bridge over the North Anna ; so he left a note for him, telling him he need not trouble himself farther about the bridge, as he would give him all he could attend to on the other side. In the disastrous campaign of Pope he did efficient service, under Bayard, who commanded the whole cavalry force, and was employed chiefly in protecting the Rapidan and covering the retreat of the army.

When Hooker, in command of the army, commenced his move on Chancellorsville, Kilpatrick commanded a brigade of cavalry, and General Stoneman sent him, with about four hundred and fifty men, to burn the railroad and bridges over the Chickahominy, five miles from Richmond. He rode rapidly forward, avoiding the large bodies of the enemy, and attacking those whom he was able to cope with, until he had come within two miles of the rebel capital. Here he captured Lieutenant Brown, aide to General Winder, and eleven men, within the fortifications. Then he passed down to Meadow Bridge, on the Chickahominy, which he burned, and ran a train of cars into the river, checked a party of cavalry sent in pursuit of him, burned a train of thirty wagons loaded with bacon, and captured some prisoners. He resumed his march down the Peninsula at one o'clock the next morning, and surprised a force of three hundred of the enemy, capturing two officers and thirty-three men, burned fifty-six wagons and the depot, containing 20 000 barrels of corn and wheat, quantities of clothing and stores, and crossed the Mattapony, destroying the ferry just in time to escape the Confederate cavalry in pursuit. He destroyed a third wagon-train and depot, and made a forced march of twenty miles, followed by the enemy. He kept on his way, and finally found safety within the Union lines, at Gloucester Point. He had made a march around the Confederate army of nearly two hundred miles in less than five days, having captured and paroled upwards of eight hundred prisoners, with a loss of only one officer and thirty-seven men.

When Lee, following up Hooker's defeat at Chancellorsville, commenced his great movement around Washington into Maryland, the cavalry was again brought into active service. The enemy's cavalry being massed near Beverly Ford, Pleasonton, in command of the Federal cavalry, moved out to make a reconnoissance, and came upon the enemy at Brandy Station, where the severest cavalry fight of the war, thus far, took place. Determined charges were made on both sides, hour after hour. Gregg came very near being overborne, when Kilpatrick made one of his gallant charges. He flung out his battle-flag, and with the Harris Light, 10th New York, and 1st Maine, came thundering down—the 10th New York in advance. It fell with a shout against the enemy's squadrons, but rebounded from the blow and swung off. The Harris Light repeated the charge, but was also borne back. Stung into madness at the sight of his own regiment repulsed and shattered, he flung himself at the head of the 1st Maine, still further in the rear, and, moving forward on a walk, shouted: "Men of Maine, you must save the day! Follow me."

Closing up, the regiment marched off behind its leader, who circled to the right till he got on the flank of the enemy, when he ordered the bugles to sound the charge, and, coming down on a wild gallop, struck the enemy, forcing back his hitherto steady line. As they swept past the other two shattered regiments, Kilpatrick shouted out over the tumult, in his clear, ringing tones: "Back, the Harris Light! Back, the 10th New York! Re-form your squadrons, and charge!"

The field was won; but a heavy body of infantry coming up, Pleasonton withdrew across the Rappahannock.

Kilpatrick was now made Brigadier, and in the fight at Aldie,

Personal Sketches. 461

again met Lee. Securing a strong position, he resisted every attempt of the enemy to dislodge him, although charge after charge was made.

Later in the day, when his squadrons were borne back, he again put himself at the head of the 1st Maine, as at Brandy Station, and leading it in person, charged with such desperation that the enemy broke and fled. His horse was killed under him in the onset; but mounting another, he ordered the whole line to advance, and drove Lee in flight, until night put an end to the pursuit. The next morning he made a sabre charge into the town of Upperville, driving the enemy out.

When Meade was put in command of the army, Kilpatrick was placed in command of a division of cavalry, numbering 5,000 men. He was in constant and active service. He captured Ewell's long train of wagons, and the guard, consisting of four regiments, and up to the end of the campaign, after the battle of Gettysburg, his division had captured some 4,500 prisoners, nine guns, and eleven battle flags.

On the last day of February, 1864, Kilpatrick, in command of 4,000 men, started on his daring raid on Richmond for the purpose of releasing the Union prisoners confined there, and which created such consternation and dismay in the Confederate stronghold. In this expedition the lamented Dahlgren was killed.

General Kilpatrick was now transferred to the West to cooperate with General Sherman in his campaign against Atlanta. At Resaca he had a severe battle, but held this important point until the infantry came up, but he was severely wounded by a rifle ball, which barely escaped a vital point, and passed out at his hip. Before he was again able to take the saddle, he ascertained that Sherman was in front of Atlanta, and that the place must fall in a few days. Determined not to lose the glory of partaking in the final movements for its overthrow, he took the next train and rode night and day till he reached his command at Cartersville. Still unable to sit on his horse he rode forward in a carriage fitted up for him, and joined Sherman before Atlanta.

During Sherman's great march to the sea, having received a commission as Major-General of Volunteers, he commanded the cavalry corps, and performed all the duties of the advance, skirmishing, etc., and in covering the flanks of the infantry in that great march, fighting, burning, and laying waste the country when the opposition of the enemy made it necessary. He also performed the same duties on a subsequent march through the Carolinas. Near Averysboro he had a severe battle with the Confederate infantry, and held a vital point until the infantry of General Slocum's column came up.

This was the last battle in which Kilpatrick's cavalry took an active part, and here he rested on his laurels. He issued an address to his troops, closing with the following words: "Soldiers, be proud! of all the brave men of this great army, you have a right to be. You have won the admiration of our infantry, fighting on foot and mounted, and you will receive the outspoken words of praise from the great Sherman himself. He appreciates and will reward your patient endurance of hardships, gallant deeds, and valuable services. With the old laurels of Georgia entwine those won in the Carolinas, and proudly wear them. *General Sherman is satisfied with his cavalry.*" J. T. Headley,* from whom the author chiefly compiles the foregoing sketch, remarks: "Though but a youth, still Kilpatrick has won a world-wide reputation. He is in every respect fitted for a cavalry commander, for he has all the dash necessary to success, and that chivalrous daring which wins the admiration and love of the common soldier."

CAPTAIN COMPANY I—CHARLES G. BARTLETT.

CHARLES G. BARTLETT is a son of Professor Bartlett, of the West Point Military Academy, and had received a military education. At the commencement of hostilities he was a member of the Seventh Regiment, National Guard, and was commissioned as Captain in the 5th New York Volunteers. Courteous and kind, he endeared himself to both officers and men. He was conspicuous at Big Bethel for the part he took with his company in skirmishing in the advance with the enemy, and for his coolness and nonchalance while under fire. He remained by the side of

---

* "Grant and Sherman, their Campaigns and Generals."

the lamented Lieutenant Greble for a long time during the action while the latter officer was sighting his guns in the most exposed part of the field of battle. He continued with the regiment until he received a commission in the United States Army, when he resigned from the Fifth, September 11, 1861. He was subsequently Brigadier-General of Volunteers, and is now (1878) Major and Brevet Lieutenant-Colonel 11th United States Infantry.

CAPTAIN OF CO. K—CLEVELAND WINSLOW.

CLEVELAND WINSLOW was born May 26, 1836, in Medford, Mass. He received a collegiate education, and in 1861 was a member of the 71st Regt. National Guard, in which organization he had served seven years. He was possessed of a robust constitution, and was not troubled with any serious sickness during all his arduous campaigning services, up to the time he received the wound which caused his death. He entered the 5th Regiment as one of its original Captains, the eighth in rank; commanded Company K as skirmishers at Big Bethel, and was mentioned in orders on file in the War Department; commanded as Captain, four companies of infantry, one light battery and a squadron of lancers at Hanover Court-house. He was on the reserve with his regiment at Mechanicsville; acting Major at the battle of Gaines' Mill, where he distinguished himself in all the qualities that make a good soldier; at Charles City Cross-roads, and Malvern Hill, where he was in command of the brigade skirmishers, and a section of light twelves; two days and nights in command of the regiment as Captain, at the battle of Manassas Plains, where his horse was killed by seven gun-shot wounds; commanded the regiment as Major at the battle of Antietam; commanded as the fourth and last Colonel of the Fifth at Fredericksburg, and had command of the trenches on the night of the re-crossing of the river. At Chancellorsville he commanded the skirmishers of Sykes' division of regulars, engaged four times with the enemy, was surrounded, and cut his way through and rejoined the command. He was several times mentioned in General Orders for bravery, etc., all on file with regimental papers. Commanded at different times, the 3d brigade, 2d division, 5th army corps; and also at times, the 2d division (Sykes') in the absence of the General.

Colonel Winslow served during the Draft Riots in New York. The daily press published full reports of those riots, in the suppression of which Colonel Winslow took a very active and prominent part. Colonel Winslow was engaged with the rioters at the corner of 19th Street and 1st Avenue.

His command consisted entirely of citizens, although the majority of them had seen service in the army. They enrolled themselves for the purpose of aiding in preserving the peace of the city.

They did not exceed one hundred in number, and were commanded by ex-officers of the 5th New York. The men had been enrolled only a short time, and had little or no drill. They were accompanied by two howitzers. The resistance, he said, was very severe, and the rebellious citizens fought with great determination. Four citizen soldiers were killed, and a number of officers and citizens wounded, among whom was Captain Uckele, formerly a 1st Lieutenant of the old 5th New York. The injured citizens were carried into a house between 19th and 20th Streets. Colonel Jardine, formerly of the Hawkins Zouaves, was very badly wounded in the thigh; Dr. White, the surgeon of the Hawkins Zouaves, volunteered his services to remain with him.

After this, Colonel Winslow went to Colonel Brown and obtained a reinforcement of 150 regulars and one rifled gun, under command of Captains Shelby and Putnam, and proceeded to the scene of action and brought off all their wounded to the 7th Regiment Armory.

During the action, nine rounds of canister were fired into the crowd. Colonel Winslow gives great credit to the officers who were on the ground, for the steadiness with which they stood to their guns under the galling fire with which they were assailed on all sides.

About eight o'clock a crowd of four or five thousand assembled in the neighborhood of 8th Avenue and 32d Street. They beat and kicked one colored man almost to death and hung him to a lamp-post, and then commenced an indiscriminate onslaught on all the negroes they could find, and were about to burn the block of houses chiefly occupied by the colored people, when Colonel Winslow made his appearance on the scene with a strong detachment of infantry and one twelve-pound howitzer. The howitzer was unlimbered and poured a deadly charge of canister into the crowd. Signs of resistance were evinced, and an evident determination to wrest the gun from the hands of the artillerists.

The infantry received the order to fire, and again a shower of bullets thinned the crowd. No symptoms were evinced of their retiring, and the howitzer again thundered forth a deadly discharge of canister. The fire was by this time too hot to withstand, and with shrieks and yells they commenced to scatter in all directions. During the whole time, the military had been under a strong fire of stones, missiles, pistols, and gun-shots, not only from the crowd in their front, but from the house-tops. The crowd dispersing, orders were given to return. After cutting down the body of the negro, the military commenced to fall slowly back.

The crowd at once reassembled, and closed up in their rear. Four separate times, before the crowd would desist from the pursuit, was the order given to fire. After considerable difficulty, Colonel Winslow and his command returned to the Arsenal, having successfully carried out the orders they had received. It was impossible to ascertain anything like a definite or reliable account of the casualties among the people, as those shot were hastily removed by their friends. A number of the military were badly hurt.

GENERAL WOOL'S ACKNOWLEDGMENT TO COLONEL WINSLOW.

"TROY, N. Y., *July* 29, 1863.

"SIR:—For your communication of the 25th inst., received the 27th, containing a detailed account of your services, as well as of other officers and citizens, in quelling the recent riot in the City of New York, I tender you my thanks.

"For your gallant conduct, and all who took part with you in their efforts to quell the riot, you are entitled to the thanks and gratitude of your fellow-citizens, and especially the wounded, among whom was Colonel Jardine, who was seriously injured.

"Being all citizens, who in a few hours were organized, under your command, at the Arsenal, Seventh Avenue, where they were stationed three days and nights, patrolling the avenue and dispersing the mob at such places as they had collected, your services will no less be remembered than appreciated by a grateful people.

"I am, very respectfully, your obedient servant,

"JOHN E. WOOL, *Major-General.*

"To CLEVELAND WINSLOW, *Colonel 5th N. Y. Volunteers.*"

The following is a letter from General A. A. Humphreys, U. S. A., who commanded a division of volunteers, subsequently General Grant's Chief of Staff, and, after the resignation of General Hancock, succeeded the latter in command of the 2d army corps. He was promoted to the rank of Brigadier-General, U. S. A., and Chief of the Corps of Engineers—the post occupied by him at the present time (1878):

"CAMP NEAR FALMOUTH, VA.,
"*June* 10, 1863.

"DEAR COLONEL:—I learn that you are endeavoring or desire to raise a brigade of infantry, the skeleton of which is to be formed of the remnants of the splendid regiment you recently commanded—the 5th New York. I trust you may be successful in your efforts; for, having had the opportunity of knowing you and your regiment for more than a year, during the latter half from almost daily observation of it, in the severe service the Army of the Potomac has passed through, I know what fine, well-prepared material you will have out of which to give form and instruction to a brigade; and I know well, too, how admirably qualified you are to command such a brigade. Under such auspices, I should expect to find the reputation of the brigade emulating that of the regiment, which was equaled by few in the service—certainly surpassed by none. I do not know how I

Personal Sketches. 467

can aid you in carrying out your wishes. I would gladly do anything in my power in that way.

"Wishing you every possible success,
"I am, very truly, yours,
"A. A. HUMPHREYS,
"*Brigadier-General Vols.*"

Colonel Winslow organized a regiment called the 5th Veterans, composed of men who had been mustered out with the disbanded two years' regiments, and as a number of the old Fifth re-enlisted in this new organization, either as privates or served as officers, the following notes from the New York *Daily Times* are deemed worthy of preservation:

"DEPARTURE OF THE 5TH REGIMENT N. Y. VOLS.—VETS.

"One battalion of this well-known regiment is again ready for the field, and will leave to-day, the 23d inst., under its old commander, Colonel Cleveland Winslow. All the officers are gentlemen who have had two years' experience in the field; consequently, the same discipline and efficiency will continue, and the good reputation enjoyed by the old regiment will be perpetuated in its successor. The ranks have been filled by the consolidation of the 31st, 37th, and part of the 38th and 9th Regiments New York Volunteers, and the men are, with few exceptions, re-enlisted men. On arriving in the field, the battalion will be attached to the 2d corps, Major-General G. K. Warren, under whom the regiment has long been commanded. The former duty done by this regiment is too well known to require recapitulation; and there is every reason to believe that, under Colonel Winslow and his officers, many brave deeds will be added to the record this regiment has already placed in the history of the war."

HEADQUARTERS 5TH ARMY CORPS,
BETHESDA CHURCH, VA.,
June 2, 1864, 9 A.M.

THE DURYÉE ZOUAVES.

The 5th New York Zouaves, Colonel Winslow, deserve special mention for the part they took in yesterday's engagements. With other reinforcements they had just arrived from Port Royal, Va. Travel-weary and begrimed with dust from their long day's march, General Ayres' regulars, to whose brigade they had been assigned, proposed to let them rest.

"We came here to fight, not to rest," said the Colonel.

"If your boys want to fight I sha'n't hinder them," replied the General.

"Do you want to go into the fight or not?" the Colonel asked his men, after explaining his interview with General Ayres. They chose fighting, and they fought as this regiment used to fight— heads cool, arms steady, aim sure. *The Old Fifth New York Zouaves* have a reputation as lasting as the Army of the Potomac. The new regiment shows a purpose to maintain the brilliant reputation of the founders of its name and imperishable glory. Colonel Winslow was wounded in the first assault; but after the wound was dressed, resumed his place at the head of his regiment. He is that sort of man who will stick to his regiment and to fighting as long as he holds a sword and can sit upon a horse.

"Colonel Winslow, wounded during the recent campaign (at Chapin's Ford), is reported from Washington to be much worse, with but little hope of his final recovery. The ball passed through his shoulder-blade, causing a very serious injury."— *New York Times*, L. A. HENDRICKS' *Dispatch*.

Colonel Winslow died from the effects of his wound July 7, 1864, and his country thus lost the services of a very valuable officer.

FIRST LIEUTENANT OF COMPANY A—WILLIAM T. PARTRIDGE.

WILLIAM T. PARTRIDGE rose to be Captain of Company I, and was killed in action at the battle of Gaines' Mill, June 27, 1862. He was brave to rashness, and a strict disciplinarian. Captain Partridge had a presentiment that he would lose his life in battle, and gave directions as to the disposition to be made of his body if he should fall. He was a very strong abolitionist, and made the remark to a gentleman in New York during the organization of the regiment, that "he could see the image of John Brown with outstretched arms ready to receive him."

FIRST LIEUTENANT OF COMPANY B—GOUVERNEUR CARR.

GOUVERNEUR CARR rose to the rank of Captain in the regiment, but resigned September 24, 1862, having been commissioned as Major of the 2d battalion, 165th Regiment, New York Volunteers, which he subsequently commanded as Lieutenant-Colonel, until it was mustered out, September, 1865. He was wounded severely at the siege of Port Hudson on the Mississippi, May 27, 1863, and also wounded at Sabine Cross-Roads, La., and was breveted Colonel for meritorious services.

FIRST LIEUTENANT OF COMPANY C—J. FRANCIS EVANS.

LIEUTENANT EVANS was a member of the 7th Regiment N. G. S. N. Y. He was a quiet, steady, and brave officer. He rose to a Captaincy in the regiment, but resigned his commission April 26, 1862, on account of ill-health contracted in the service,

FIRST LIEUTENANT OF COMPANY D—WILBUR F. LEWIS.

LIEUTENANT LEWIS became acting Major in the regiment, and was killed in the action of Second Bull Run, August 30, 1862. He was a brave and efficient officer; he refused to dismount from his horse at the engagement in which he lost his life, notwithstanding the earnest entreaties of the men. He had two brothers in the regiment, one of whom was killed in action, and the other badly wounded.

FIRST LIEUTENANT OF COMPANY E—GEORGE DURYEA.

LIEUTENANT DURYEA was a member of the 48th Regiment N. G. S. N. Y. He served actively with the 5th Regiment until receiving a very severe wound at the battle of Gaines' Mill, June 27, 1862, while in command of a company as Captain. Upon his recovery he returned to duty again with the regiment, and was promoted successively Major and Lieutenant-Colonel, and was mustered out with the regiment on its expiration of term of service, May 14, 1863, as Brevet Colonel, being one of the five original officers, including the Chaplain, that returned with the regiment.

FIRST LIEUTENANT CO. F—OLIVER WETMORE, JR.

LIEUTENANT WETMORE was a gentleman of education, having graduated with high honors from Columbia College, and was a Professor in the College of the City of New York. He was a member of the 7th Regt. N. G. S. N. Y. He served with the regiment until June, 1862, when his health yielded to the exposure in the Peninsula campaign, and he applied for a discharge, which was granted June 30, 1862. He was subsequently commissioned as Major in the 13th Regt. New York Heavy Artillery. He died in Washington after the close of the war.

FIRST LIEUTENANT OF CO. G—JACOB E. DURYÉE.

LIEUTENANT DURYÉE, son of General Abram Duryée, was a member of the 7th Regt. N. G. S. N. Y. He greatly distinguished himself at the battle of Big Bethel, June 10, 1861, where he led a charge with a handful of men against the enemy's works. He was made a Captain in the Fifth, and in September, 1862, was commissioned Lieutenant-Colonel of the 2d Maryland, in which he served under General Burnside in North Carolina,

Personal Sketches. 471

and under General Pope in Virginia; was under General McClellan during his Maryland campaign, at South Mountain, and Antietam, where he commanded the regiment. He was subsequently breveted Brigadier-General of Volunteers.

FIRST LIEUTENANT OF CO. H—CHURCHILL J. CAMBRELLING.

LIEUTENANT CAMBRELLING, son of Judge Cambrelling, was a member of the 7th Regt. N. G. He was in the engagements at Big Bethel, Hanover Court-house, and Gaines' Mill, etc., where he was distinguished for his bravery. He was promoted to a Captaincy in the regiment September 3, 1861. Owing to the hardships of the Peninsula campaign, his health became impaired, and he was obliged to apply for a discharge, which was granted July 23, 1862. He was a fine officer, and much esteemed by both officers and privates for his personal qualities and character. He was subsequently commissioned as Major in the 10th Senatorial District Regiment.

FIRST LIEUTENANT OF CO. I—JOSEPH S. YORK.

LIEUTENANT YORK had received a military training, and was promoted to a Captaincy in the Fifth. He took a leading part in the charge on the enemy's works at Big Bethel, in which he was wounded. He served with the regiment until August 29, 1861, when having received a commission as Captain in the 15th U. S. Infantry, he resigned his command. Subsequently he died in the performance of his duties in the regular service, after the war.

FIRST LIEUTENANT OF CO. K—WILLIAM H. HOYT.

LIEUTENANT HOYT was a gentlemanly officer, and a great favorite with the men. He behaved well under fire, and was as self-possessed as he was brave. He resigned his commission in 1862.

SECOND LIEUTENANT OF CO. B—THEODORE S. DUMONT.

THEODORE S. DUMONT was a member of the 7th Regt. N. G. He was in the engagement at Big Bethel, and served in the Peninsula campaign, during which he was transferred to the Signal corps; he rendered efficient service in the corps during the battle of Malvern Hill, where he retained his position under fire and signaled the gun-boats to direct their aim. He was complimented for this service in General Orders. He resigned his commission, having been promoted to 1st Lieutenant August 13, 1862.

SECOND LIEUT. OF CO. C—CHARLES H. SEAMAN.

LIEUTENANT SEAMAN received his education in a military school. He resigned his commission June 2, 1861.

SECOND LIEUT. OF CO. D—JOHN A. COCHRANE.

LIEUTENANT COCHRANE was a member of the 71st Regiment, National Guard. He was a good soldier and strict disciplinarian, and passed through considerable service with the regiment. He was promoted to First Lieutenant, and resigned his commission on account of ill-health December 29, 1862.

SECOND LIEUT. OF CO. E—HENRY H. BURNETT.

LIEUTENANT BURNETT was an admirable officer, and well liked by the members of the regiment, particularly by the en-

Personal Sketches. 473

listed men, to whom he was a faithful friend. He was promoted to a Captaincy, and served actively with the regiment up to the time of his resignation, October 16, 1862; which event was much regretted by the men.

SECOND LIEUT. OF CO. F—CARLISLE BOYD.

CARLISLE BOYD rose to a Captaincy, and commanded a company at the Second Bull Run engagement, where he was wounded and taken prisoner. He served the full term with the regiment, was promoted Major, and mustered out as such with the regiment, May 14, 1863. He was subsequently commissioned as Lieutenant-Colonel, and served in the Invalid Corps until he received a commission in the regular army, July 28, 1866, where he is serving at present (1878) as Captain of the 17th Infantry. He was breveted Lieutenant-Colonel U. S. Army March 2, 1867.

SECOND LIEUT. OF CO. G—JOSEPH H. BRADLEY.

LIEUTENANT BRADLEY was educated at a military academy. He was advanced to the Captaincy, was slightly wounded at Gaines' Mill July 30, 1862, and went into another regiment as Chaplain.

SECOND LIEUT. OF CO. H—JAMES MILLER.

LIEUTENANT MILLER was a member of the 7th Regiment, National Guard, and enlisted as a private in the Fifth, April 20, 1861. Promoted Second Lieutenant May 9, 1861. Was detailed by General Butler as Drill-Master to the Union Coast-Guard July 15th, relieved August 13th, and rejoined the regiment at Baltimore. He was promoted First Lieutenant, and resigned his commission September 6, 1861, on account of disease contracted in the line of his duty.

SECOND LIEUT. OF CO. I—J. HENRY WHITNEY.

SECOND LIEUT. OF CO. K—WILLIAM FERGUSON.

LIEUTENANT FERGUSON was a gentlemanly officer, and was much esteemed by the men. He was mentioned in Colonel Duryée's report of the battle of Big Bethel, and was subsequently promoted to a First Lieutenancy. On account of ill-health he resigned his commission October 12, 1862. He afterward received a new commission, and recruited a company for the 5th Veterans.

ORIGINAL OFFICERS OF THE FIFTH REGT. N.Y.V., DURYEE'S ZOUAVES.

FIELD AND STAFF, MAY 14, 1861.

Name.	Rank.	Remarks.
ABRAM DURYEE	Colonel	Age 46; formerly Col. of the 7th Regt. N. G. S. N. Y.; commis. Brig.-Gen. Sept. 10, 1861; res'd Jan., 1863; Bvt. Maj.-Gen., 1865.
GOUVERNEUR K. WARREN	Lieut.-Col.	Age 31; U. S. A.; commis. Col. Sept. 7, 1861; Brig.-Gen. Vols. Sept. 26, 1862; subsequently Chief of Top. Eng. Army of Potomac, and Maj.-Gen. Vols. Aug. 1863; res'd May 27, 1865; Bvt. Mar. 13, 1865, Maj.-Gen. U. S. A.; at present of Eng. Corps U. S. A.
J. MANSFIELD DAVIES	Major	Age 32; received a military education; res'd Aug. 17, 1861; commis. Col. Harris Light Cavalry.
JOSEPH E. HAMBLIN	Adjutant	Age 33; from 7th Regt. N. G. S. N. Y.; commis. Capt.; res'd Nov., 1861; subsequently Bvt. Maj.-Gen Vols.
JOHN HOWARD WELLS	Quartermaster	Age 31; from 7th Regt. N. G. S. N. Y.; commis. Capt. U. S. A. Feb. 25, 1862.
RUFUS H. GILBERT	Surgeon	Age 29; commis. Maj. U. S. A. Aug. 3, 1861.
B. ELLIS MARTIN	Assist. Surgeon	Age 22; res'd Feb. 11, 1861.
JOHN COLLINS	Sergeant Major	Age 30; served 10 years in U. S. A.; commis. 1st Lieut.; wounded slightly at Gaines' Mill, and ―――― July 30, 1862.
PETER G. GORMLY	Drum Major	Age 24; discharged at Fort Schuyler. Succeeded Gormly, and served with regiment until discharged Aug. 1862, for disease contracted during the Peninsular campaign; at present Drum Major 7th Regt. and 13th of Brooklyn.
JOHN M. SMITH	"	
CHARLES L. ISAACS	Fife Major	Promoted Ord. Sergt., and on detached service; commis. 2d Lieut.
REV. GORDON WINSLOW	Chaplain	Age 60; served all through with the regiment, and subsequently in the Sanitary Commission, etc., up to the time of his death; drowned in the Potomac June 7, 1864.

LINE OFFICERS, MAY 9, 1861.

Name.	Rank.	Remarks.
HARMON D. HULL	Captain Co. A	From 7th Regt. N. G. S. N. Y.; promoted Maj. Sept. 7, 1861; Lieut.-Col. Oct. 29, 1862; res'd Dec. 30, 1862; Col. 165th N. Y. Vols.; res'd Jan. 22, 1863.
ROBERT S. DUMONT	" " B	From 7th Regt. N. G. S. N. Y.; raised the first company; res'd on account of ill-health from sun-stroke Oct. 1, 1861.

LINE OFFICERS.—(Continued.)

Name.	Rank.	Remarks.
HENRY E. DAVIES, JR.	Captain Co. C	Res'd Aug. 15, 1861; commis. Maj. Harris Light Cavalry; Brig.-Gen. Sept. 16, 1863; subsequently Maj.-Gen. Cavalry.
JAMES L. WAUGH	" D	Capt. 7th Regt. N. G. S. N. Y., and Drillmaster of Metropolitan Police; res'd Aug. 9, 1861; commis. Major in another regiment.
HIRAM DURYEA	" E	A military education; 1st Lieut. 48th Regt. N. G. S. N. Y. (Oswego); promoted 3d Col. of the 5th; res'd Nov. 12, 1862, on account of disease engendered during Peninsula campaign; Bvt. Brig.-Gen.
HENRY A. SWARTWOUT	" F	A military education, res'd Aug. 12, 1861, to accept commis. of 1st Lieut. U. S. A.; subsequently Inspec.-Gen. Dept. of Texas; died as Bvt. Maj. U. S. A. Oct. 8, 1867.
ABRAHAM DENIKE	" G	Capt. 7th Regt. N. G. S. N. Y.; res'd Sept. 6, 1861, as Senior Capt; commis. Lieut.-Col. 153d N. Y. Vol.
JUDSON KILPATRICK	" H	From U. S. A.; wounded at Big Bethel, June 10, 1861; res'd Aug. 14, 1861; commis. Lieut.-Col. Harris Light Cavalry; subsequently Maj.-Gen. Vol.
CHARLES G. BARTLETT	" I	A military education; from 7th Regt. N. G. S. N. Y.; res'd Sept. 11, 1861; commis. U. S. A., and Bvt. Brig.-Gen. Vol.; at present Maj. and Bvt. Lieut.-Col. 11th Infantry U. S. A.
CLEVELAND WINSLOW	" K	From 71st Regt. N. G. S. N. Y.; rose to be 4th Col. of the 5th from the 8th Capt. in rank; served all through with the Regt. Col. 5th Veterans; died July 7, 1864, from wounds rec'd in action of Bethesda Church, Va.
WILLIAM T. PARTRIDGE	First Lt. Co. A	Promoted Capt., and killed in command of Co. I, at Gaines' Mill, June 27, 1862.
GOUVERNEUR CARR	" B	Res'd as Capt. Sept. 24, 1862; subsequently Lieut.-Col. in command 2d Battalion 165th N. Y. V., and Bvt.-Col.; wounded at Port Hudson, Miss., May 27, 1863; also wounded at Sabine Cross Roads, La.
J. FRANCIS EVANS	" C	From the 7th Regt. N. G. S. N. Y.; res'd as Capt. April 26, 1862.
WILBUR F. LEWIS	" D	From the 71st Regt. N. G. S. N. Y.; promoted Capt., and killed as Acting Major at Second Bull Run Aug. 30, 1862.
GEORGE DURYEA	" E	From 48th Regt. N. G. S. N. Y.; promoted Bvt. Col. of the 5th; badly wounded at Gaines' Mill June 27, 1862.
OLIVER WETMORE, JR	" F	From 7th Regt. N. G. S. N. Y.; promoted Capt.; res'd on account of ill-health June 20, 1862; commis. Major and Bvt. Lieut.-Col. 13th N. Y. Heavy Artillery.
JACOB DURYEE	" G	From 7th Regt. N. G. S. N. Y.; promoted Capt.; res'd Sept., 1862; commis. Lieut.-Col. 2d Maryland; Bvt. Brig.-Gen.

Line Officers. 477

LINE OFFICERS.—(Continued.)

Name.	Rank.	Remarks.
CHURCHILL J. CAMBRELING..	1st Lieut. Co. H...	From 7th Regt. N. G. S. N. Y.; promoted Capt. Sept. 3, 1861; discharged on account of ill-health Aug., 1862; commis. Maj. 10th Senatorial District Reg.
JOSEPH S. YORK..........	" I....	A military education; promoted Capt.; wounded at Big Bethel June 10, 1861; res'd on account of receiving a commis. as Capt. 15th U. S. Infantry, and died in the service as Major.
WILLIAM H. HOYT..........	" K...	Res'd Aug. 1, 1861.
THEODORE S. DUMONT	2d Lieut. Co. A...	From 7th Regt. N. G. S. N. Y.; wounded June 10, 1861; transferred to Signal Corps; promoted 1st Lieut.; res'd Aug. 13, 1862.
CHARLES H. SEAMAN	" C..	Res'd June 2, 1861.
JOHN A. COCHRANE..........	" D..	From 71st Regt. N. G. S. N. Y.; promoted 1st Lieut.; res'd on account of ill-health Dec. 29, 1862.
HENRY H. BURNETT..........	" E..	Promoted Capt.; res'd Senior Capt. Oct. 16, 1862.
CARLISLE BOYD	" F..	Promoted Maj.; served all through with regiment; wounded and taken prisoner Aug. 30, 1862; Lieut.-Col. in Invalid Corps; at present (1878) Capt. and Bvt. Lieut.-Col. 17th Infantry U. S. A.
JOSEPH H. BRADLEY.........	" G..	A military education; from 7th Regt, N. G. S. N. Y.; promoted Capt.; wounded slightly at Gaines' Mill, and _____ July 30, 1862; Chaplain in another regiment.
JAMES MILLER	" H..	From 7th Regt. N. G. S. N. Y.; promoted 1st Lieut.; res'd April 25, 1862, and a Capt.
J. HENRY WHITNEY..........	" I..	Foreman 61 Hose Vol. Fire Dept.; promoted Capt.
WILLIAM FERGUSON	" K..	Promoted 1st Lieut.; res'd Oct. 12, 1862; Capt. in 5th Vets.

OFFICERS WHO SERVED IN THE FIFTH REGIMENT AT VARIOUS TIMES, AND NOT NOTED IN THE OTHER LISTS.

Name.	Rank.	Remarks.
Duryea, William	Lieut.-Colonel	Not mustered.
Brouner, Richard R.	Adjutant	From 2d Co. 7th Regt. N. G.; promoted from 1st Serg't May, 1861, to 2d Lieut.; 1st Lieut. Aug. 16, 1861; disch'd for physical disability June 13, 1862.
Sovereign, Frederick W.	"	Rose through the various grades from private; killed at Sec. Bull Run Aug. 30, 1862.
Thomas, Augustus L.	Quartermaster	from Serg't; served to the end of the War; Chief Quartermaster of the 5th Corps, with the rank of Col.
Van Ingen, James L.	Surgeon	Disch'd Feb. 14, 1862.
May, Henry C.	"	Res'd Aug. 12, 1862.
Munson, Owen	"	Disch'd Aug. 2, 1862.
Freeman, John N.	Mate.	
Mitchel, ——	"	
Thompson, ——	"	
McConnell, James	Captain	Rose from Corp. to Act. Maj.; disch'd for physical disability Jan. 11, 1863.
Prime, Ralph E.	"	private; wounded June 27, 1862; disch'd for phys. dis. Oct. 31, 1862; Lieut.-Col. 6th N.Y. Artillery; was nominated on March 4, 1863, by Pres. Lincoln, Brig.-Gen., the first person so nominated who entered the service as a private.
Sergent, Charles	"	Rose from private; disch'd for phys. dis. March 7, 1863.
Hager, George O.	"	" killed at Sec. Bull Run Aug. 30, 1862.
Cartwright, Thomas W., Jr.	"	Rose from private; wounded at Big Bethel June 10, 1861; also at Gaines' Mill June 27, 1862; died of latter wound.
Eichler, Herman G. O.	"	Rose from private; performed active duty until his constitution was completely undermined past all recovery; disch'd Oct. 4, 1862, and died soon afterward.
Churchill, J. K.	First Lieutenant	Not mustered.
Shunway, Robert	"	" (from 7th Regt. N. G.)
Parker, Simeon B.	"	Rose from private; severely wounded at Gaines' Mill June 27, 1862; returned to duty twice, and sent away by surgeon; disch'd for phys. dis. April 22, 1863.
Tracy, Prescott	"	Res'd Aug. 1, 1861.
Wright, Charles W.	"	Was in the Mexican War; rose from private; disch'd for phys. dis. Nov. 15, 1861.
Fowler, Erwin G.	"	Rose from Serg't.; discharged for physical disability July 5, 1862.
Wilson, Philip L.	"	Rose from private; crippled for physical disability April 15, 1863, and served as an officer in In'd Corps.
Wannemacher, George W.	"	Rose from private; w'ded at 2d Bull Run Aug. 30, 1862; disc. for ph. dis. Dec. 30, 1862.

Miscellaneous. 479

MISCELLANEOUS OFFICERS.—(Continued.)

Name.	Rank.	Remarks.
Smith, James	First Lieut.	Not mustered.
Agnus, Felix	"	Rose from private; wounded at Gaines' Mill June 27, 1862; discharged for physical disability, right arm being useless; subsequently Maj. and Bvt. Lieut.-Col. of 165th N. Y. Vols.
Keyser, Henry M.	"	Rose from Sergt.; wounded at Second Bull Run Aug. 30, 1862; res'd Feb. 16, 1863.
Catlin, George L., Jr.	Captain	Rose from Sergt.; detached as A. D. C. to Gen. Birney; discharged for physical disability Nov., 1862; at present (1878) U. S. Consul, Rochelle, France.
Dunham, John E.	Second Lieut.	From 71st Regt. N. G.; promoted from 1st Sergt.; wounded at Camp Hamilton June 7, 1861; discharged for physical disability Feb. 10, 1862.
McGeehan, John	"	Rose from private; wounded at Second Bull Run Aug. 30, 1862; discharged for physical disability Feb. 3, 1863; Bvt. Capt. of 146th N. Y. V. Dec. 1, 1864.
Wright, Edward O.	"	Rose from private; died from wounds received at Second Bull Run Aug. 30, 1862.
Whitmore, S. Hayward	"	Not mustered.
Patten, J. W.	"	"
Reany, Joseph	"	Rose from private; discharged for physical disability Oct. 7, 1862.
Mayer, Moritz	"	Not mustered.
Bell, Edward G.	"	Promoted from 1st Sergt.; wounded at Big Bethel June 10, 1861; res'd Feb. 20, 1862.
Allen, William H.	"	Promoted from Sergt.; res'd Nov. 8, 1861.
Van Tine, F. E.	"	July 28, 1862; Capt. 165th N. Y. V. (wounded).
Cregier, George W.	"	Rose from private; discharged for physical disability Aug. 6, 1862.
Torry, Charles W.	"	Res'd May 11, 1861.
Davies, Charles F.	"	Not mustered.
Berrian, John H.	"	Rose from private; Color Sergt.; promoted for bravery July 5, 1862; discharged for physical disability Oct. 3, 1862.
James, Julian	"	A. D. C. to Gen. Warren.
Potter, James N.	"	Not mustered.
Barnett, Henry W.	"	"
Horton, Nathaniel T.	Drum Major	Drum Major 71st Regt. N. G. S. N. Y.; rose from drummer boy.
Jenks, Abraham	"	" " " " "
McKeever, Jacob	"	37th Regt. N. G. S. N. Y. "
Mulhearn, Andrew	"	22d " " " "
Strube, Gardner A.	"	" " " "
Cahill, Thomas	"	Yonkers Brass Band.

A partial list of Members of the Fifth Regiment N. Y. V. who were enlisted as privates, and received commissions in other regiments. The rank to which the majority attained in the service, or whether killed or wounded, not ascertained.

Name.	Rank.	Remarks.
RUSSELL, THEODORE	Company A	Commis. in another reg't Oct. 21, 1861.
SIDELL, WILLIAM H.	"	" " " March 24, 1862.
PIKE, CHRISTOPHER C.	"	Wounded at Gaines' Mill June 27, 1862; disch'd; Capt. 14th Cav.; Col. of a colored Regt., and act. in com'd of a Brigade.
HOFFMAN, EDWARD G.	"	Wounded at Gaines' Mill June 27, 1862; disch'd; Capt. in 165th N. Y. V., and A. D. C.; subsequently Chief of Military Police, Charleston, S. C.
FITZPATICK, LAWRENCE	Company B	Transf. to 146th N. Y. V. May 4, 1865; taken prisoner, and escaped several times; rose to be a Capt. and Bvt'd. Maj. Feb. 1, 1865; served to the close of the War, and then entered the regular service.
MULLER, CHARLES	"	Re-enlisted in Heavy Art.; rose to be 2d Lieut.
CREIGHTON, FREDERICK	"	Wounded at 2d Bull Run Aug. 30, 1862; taken prisoner twice, and paroled within one week; commis. 2d Lieut. 170th N. Y. V.
BLACKWELL, HENRY T.	"	Commis. Capt. of Vols.
SKELDING, THOMAS	"	A. D. C. to a Gen. of Div.
MOREY, BENJAMIN F.	"	Commis. in a Mass. Regt.
TAYLOR, A. STEWART	"	A. D. C. to Gen. Taylor, of New Jersey Brigade.
GILDER, WILLIAM	"	Private, Color Corp., Sergt.; promoted 2d Lieut. 40th N. Y. V.; wounded at Fredericksburg 20 yards in front of the Regt., while urging them to follow him in a charge; made 1st Lieut. and Adjt.; app'd Capt. and A. A. Gen. on the Staff of Maj.-Gen. T. W. Egan, and served with him in the Army of Potomac and in the Shenandoah until the close of the War; Capt. G. was brev'd Maj., Lieut.-Col., and Col.; at present (1878) second in command of the Franklin Search Expedition fitting out by the Geographical Society.
CLARK, GEORGE	" D.	Commis. in the 3d Maryland Regt. Jan. 31, 1862.
MOLTKE, MAGNUS	" E.	" in another reg't. Nov. 5, 1861.
FRELEIGH, PETER D.	" "	Transf. to 146th N. Y. V. May 4, 1863; rose to be 1st Lieut.; killed in the Wilderness May 5, 1864.

MISCELLANEOUS OFFICERS.—(Continued.)

Name.	Rank.	Remarks.
Marsh, Effingham W.	Company F.	Wounded Aug. 30, 1862; commis. in the 145th N. Y. Vols. Nov. 11, 1862.
Swift, Charles W.	" F.	Transf. to 146th N. Y. V. May 4, 1863; commis. Capt. of colored troops.
Haggerty, Mark.	" G.	" " " " 1st Lieut. 19th N. Y. V.
Chalmers, Hugh.	" H.	Wounded at Gaines' Mill June 27, 1862; transf. to 146th N. Y. V. May 4, 1863; commis. 2d Lieut.; killed at Cold Harbor, Va.
Onderdonk, Benjamin F.	" "	Commis. in another regt. July 18, 1861: rose to be Col. 1st Mounted Rifles May 18, 1863.
Seymour, Allan M.	" "	" Capt. 2d N. Y. Cavalry July 18, 1861.
McBeath, James E.	" "	" in another regt. Mar. 26, 1863.
Morgan, Alphonse C.	" I.	
Meinell, Henry C.	" K.	" " " Nov. 4, 1861.
Moore, William A.	" "	" " " Sept. 22, "
Moore, Thomas B.	" "	" " " ?, "
Inwood, Henry.	" "	Capt. 165th N. Y. V. Oct. 3, 1862.
Griffin, George H.	" "	Adjt. 5th Cav.; Quart. 12th Cav. Sept. 20, 1861.
Addison, Joseph T.	" "	in another regt. Dec. 3, 1861.
Shane, John H.	" "	" " " Nov. 28, "
Taylor, Henry G.	" "	Transf. to 146th N. Y. V. May 4, 1863; Bvt. Capt. Feb. 1, 1865.
Warren, Robert P.	" "	Capt. 146th N. Y. V.; Bvt. Maj. Feb. 1, 1865; assigned to Gen. Warren's Staff; commis. 2d Lieut. 24th U. S. Inf.; died in reg. serv. Jan. 24, 1876, as 1st Lieut. 14th Inf.
Burns, Thomas.		2d Lieut. 5th Vets.
Reddington, Lawrence.		" 5th Art.
Williams, George A.		Col. Sergt. and Sergt. Maj. 146th N. Y. V.; wounded, taken prisoner, and recaptured; Bvt. Capt., etc.
Roberts, Samuel.	" F.	Commis. 2d Lieut. in another regt.
Berrian, Richard.	" D.	" " " 5th Vets.
Linguist, Gustav F.	" A.	Bvt. Capt. 165th N. Y. V.
*Jones, P. Owen.		Maj. 2d N. Y. Cav.
*Decker, Nelson J.		1st Lt. " " " killed in action near Falmouth, Va., April 17, 1862.
Broome, ———.		Capt. (deceased).
McKeon, James.		" d° and Bvt. Maj. and Lieut.-Col. 5th Vets.
Walker, Charles A.		" " 165th N. Y. V.
Palmieri, Casseli A.		1st Lieut. 165th N. Y. V., and Capt. U. S. C. T.

21

List of Officers who were mustered out with the Regiment May 14, 1863. Those marked with an Asterisk—five in number—were of the original Officers; the remainder do not appear in the other lists.

Name.	Rank.	Remarks.
*Winslow, Cleveland	Fourth Colonel.	
*Duryea, George	Fifth Lieut.-Col.	
*Boyd, Carlisle	Major.	
*Winslow, G., Rev. D.D.	Chaplain	
Marvin, Azor S., Jr.	A. A. Gen. Brig.	Rose from private ; Capt. Dec. 1, 1862.
Taylor, Thomas J.	Adjutant	" " Col's Orderly etc. ; served nearly all his life in the English Army ; died in the U. S. service.
Earle, Edward M.	Quartermaster.	" "
Doolittle, Frank W., M.D.	Brig. Surg.-Maj.	Wounded at Gaines' Mill Jan. 27, 1862.
Grimes, Frank S	Surgeon	Rose from private.
Hyatt, Frank W.	Sergeant-Major.	" " drummer.
Horton, Abraham	Drum-Major.	" " 2d Lieut.
*Whitney, J. Henry	Captain Co. A	Rose from private ; wounded three times at 2d Bull Run Aug. 30, 1862, as Lieut ; Capt. of 13th N. Y. Art. ; must'd out Aug. 24, 1865 ; at present (1878) 1st Lieut. 11th U.S. Infantry.
Hoffman, William	" " B	
Chase, A. Sidney	Captain Co. C	wounded as 2d Lieut., Comd'g. Co. G. at 2d Bull Run Aug. 30, 1862.
Martin, Thomas R.	" " D	Rose from private ; slightly wounded at 2d Bull Run Aug. 30, 1862 ; Bvtd. Maj.
Chambers, William H	" " E	Rose from private ; re-enlisted as a private in 5th Vets., and must'd out with Regt. Capt. and Bvt. Maj.
Wheeler, Stephen W.	" " F	Rose from private ; Capt. in 5th Vets.
Raymond, John S.	" " G	Rose from private ; wounded and taken prisoner at 2d Bull Run Aug. 30, 1862, as 2d Lieut. ; Quartermaster of 5th Vets.
Montgomery, Charles	" " I	Rose from private ; taken prisoner at 2d Bull Run Aug. 30, 1862, as Capt. ; Bvtd. Maj. ; killed as Maj. 5th Vets. at Hatcher's Run, Va., Feb. 6, 1865.
Lounsberry, James H	" " K	From the 7th Regt. N. G. ; promoted Capt. from 1st Sergt. ; died in 1876.
Uckele, William H	First Lt. Co. H	Rose from private ; in command of company ; wounded in the N. Y. Riots as Capt. in 5th Vets.

MISCELLANEOUS OFFICERS.—(Continued.)

Name.	Rank.	Remarks.
Guthrie, George L.	First Lieut.	Rose from private to Capt., but not mustered as Capt.; Lieut.-Col. 5th Vets.
Meldrum, Albert R.	" Co. E.	" wounded at Gaines' Mill June 27, 1862.
Frie, John	"	"
Winslow, Gordon, Jr.	"	Rose from private; Capt. in 5th Vets.; Bvtd. Maj. on Gen. Warren's Staff; 1st Lieut. 8th U. S. Infantry (1868).
Fish, Thomas E.	"	Rose from private; died in Rochester, N. Y., 1868.
Vail, Joseph A.	" Co. G.	" severely wounded at 2d Bull Run Aug. 30, 1862, as a Sergt.; promoted 2d Lieut. Sept. 25, 1862; 1st Lieut. Jan. 23, 1863; died in New York, 1876.
Gedney, Roderick M.	" " K.	Rose from private; promoted 2d Lieut. June 30, 1862; 1st Lieut. Oct. 29, 1862.
Tiebout, Samuel	2d Lieut. Co. F.	" " Dec. 26, 1862.
Burns, John T.	" " G.	" " Oct. 11, "
Walsh, Matthew M.	"	" " Dec. 4, "
Gilligan, Patrick	"	" wounded at Sec. Bull Run Aug. 30, 1862; prom. 2d Lt. Dec. 7, 1862.
Carr, Flavile W.	"	" " as Col. Cor. at Gaines' Mill June 27, 1862; promoted 2d Lieut. Dec. 4, 1862.
Kiltson, William H.	" Co. E.	" promoted 2d Lieut. Oct. 16, 1862.
McIlvaine, William	" " H.	" " Dec. 29, 1862.

RECAPITULATION.

OFFICERS FROM THE FIFTH REGIMENT NEW YORK VOLUNTEERS.

Major-Generals	3
Brevet Major-Generals	2
Brigadier-General	1
Brevet Brigadier-Generals	3
Colonels	6
Brevet Colonels	3
Lieutenant-Colonels	5
Brevet Lieutenant-Colonels	2
Majors	6
Brevet Majors	8
Captains	35
Brevet Captains	5
First Lieutenants	33
Second "	44
Total	156

COLONEL ROBERT C. BUCHANAN, formerly in command of the 1st brigade, Sykes' division, 5th army corps, died in Washington, D. C., November 29, 1878, of apoplexy. He graduated from the West Point Military Academy in 1830, and served in the "Black Hawk War," and in the war against the Seminoles in 1841–2. Served actively in the field all through the war with Mexico, and during the great Rebellion. He was breveted Major-General U. S. A. March 13, 1865, and retired from active service December 31, 1870.

LIEUTENANT-COLONEL WILLIAM CHAPMAN, formerly in command of the 2d brigade, Sykes' division, graduated from West Point July 31, 1831, and served in the Mexican war, and in various campaigns against the Indians. He was breveted Colonel U. S. A. August 30, 1862, and placed on the retired list August 26, 1863.

www.ingramcontent.com/pod-product-compliance
Lightning Source LLC
Chambersburg PA
CBHW051233300426
44114CB00011B/719